BIBLE KEY WORDS

VOLUME II

Previously Published:

BIBLE KEY WORDS—Volume I

four books in one:

i

BIBLE KEY WORDS

Volume II

from **GERHARD KITTLE'S**

THEOLOGISCHES WÖRTERBUCH
ZUM NEUEN TESTAMENT

TRANSLATED AND EDITED BY

J. R. COATES and H. P. KINGDON

A ONE-VOLUME EDITION CONTAINING
FOUR BOOKS:

I. LORD

by Werner Foerster *and* Gottfried Quell

II. GNOSIS

by Rudolf Bultmann

III. BASILEIA

by K. L. Schmidt, H. Kleinknecht. K. G. Kuhn,
and Gerhard von Rad

IV. APOSTLESHIP

by Karl Heinrich Rengstorf

Harper & Brothers, Publishers, New York

Library of Congress catalog card number: 58-11930

I

LORD

BY
WERNER FOERSTER
AND
GOTTFRIED QUELL

Translated from the German
first edition, Stuttgart, 1933,
and with additional notes,
by H. P. Kingdon

TRANSLATOR'S PREFACE

THIS volume is a translation of the article in Kittel's New Testament *Wörterbuch* entitled *Kurios*—the Greek word used in the Septuagint for the Hebrew *Yahweh* as well as the periphrase for the name of God, *'ādhôn*, "lord". Thus the article is concerned not only with the root meanings of the word *kurios* in classical Greek, but just as much with the Old Testament *Yahweh* or Jehovah, and also with similar terms used of God in Syria and Egypt which came to be rendered as *kurios* in Greek. In fact it is maintained that the basic meaning of *kurios*—a lord who commands willing service—owes much to this oriental background.

Many more quotations have been left in the original Greek than in the companion volume on *Basileia*, as the contentions here advanced demanded a greater wealth of detailed evidence in their support. But here too a few of the key Greek words have been transliterated, as well as all the Hebrew terms, in order to help non-specialists pick up the main thread of the argument. It should be obvious that, e.g. *rhabbi* is a transliteration of the Greek, *rabbî* of the Hebrew form of the word meaning "teacher", which the German text prints in Greek or Hebrew letters respectively.

The expression "op. cit." refers to books listed in the Bibliography as well as to earlier references in the text or footnotes. Less than one-tenth of the detailed citations in the German text have been omitted, the most important of these omissions being indicated, usually by printing dots in the translation. All the other few additions I have made are printed in square brackets. In the transliteration of the Hebrew in this volume, invaluable help has been given by the Rev. Islwyn Blythin, tutor at Didsbury College and

Recognised Teacher in Hebrew and Religious Knowledge at Bristol University.

Of the two authors of the original German, Professor Quell of Rostock is mentioned in the prefaces to the volumes in this series entitled *Love* and *Sin*. It may be added that in 1952 he published a monograph on *Wahre und falsche Propheten*. Professor Foerster was born in 1897 and has spent most of his life teaching in Münster. Besides the book mentioned in the Bibliography, and the articles he has contributed to the *Wörterbuch* (for which he is also working on the subject *christos*), he is the author of works on Gnosticism and of two volumes on *Neutestamentliche Zeitgeschichte* (1940 and 1956), and he brought out a *Kurzgefasste Bibelkunde des N.T.* in 1952. He has kindly contributed several of my additions to the original Bibliography. My thanks are due to him and also to Professor G. Friedrich of Erlangen, Kittel's successor as Editor of the *Wörterbuch*.

H. P. KINGDON

CONTENTS

vii

SELECT BIBLIOGRAPHY

W. Bousset : *Kyrios Christos*, 2nd edn. (1921).
A. Deissmann : *Licht vom Osten*, 4th edn. (1923).
H. Lietzmann : *Kommentar zum Römerbrief*, 3rd edn. (1928).
H. Cremer : *Bibl.-theol. Wörterbuch. d.N.T. Gr.*, 11th edn., revised by J. Kögel (1923), pp. 644-55.
E. Rohde in *Z.N.W.*, xxii (1923), pp. 43 ff.
K. Prümm : *Herrscherkult und N.T.*, in *Biblica*, ix (1928), pp. 1 ff.
W. W. Graf Baudissin : *Kyrios als Gottesname* . . . (1929).
I. A. Smith in *J.T.S.*, xxxi (1930), pp. 155-60.
A. D. Nock in *Essays on the Trinity and Incarnation*, ed. A. E. J. Rawlinson (1928), pp. 51 ff.
C. H. Dodd : *The Bible and the Greeks* (1935), pp. 8-11.
[K. Prümm : *Der christliche Glaube und die heidnische Welt*, i, (1935), 214-25.]
Further literature in W. Foerster, *Herr ist Jesus* (1924), pp. 11-56.

Chapter I

K. Stegmann von Pritzwald : *Zur Geschichte der Herrscherbezeichnungen von Homeros bis Platon* (1930), §§86, 110, 155.
[K. Prümm : *Religionsgeschichtliches Handbuch für den Raum der altchristlichen Welt*, 2nd edn. (1954), s.v. 'Herrscherkult'.]

Chapter II

W. Drexler, in Roscher's *Lexikon der griechischen und römischen Mythologie*, s.v.
O. Eissfeldt : *Götternamen und Gottesvorstellung bei den Semiten*, in *Zeitschrift der Deutschen Morgenländischen Gesellschaft* (1929), pp. 21-36.

Chapter III

A. Alt : *Jahwe*, in *Reallexikon der Vorgeschichte*, vi (1926), 147 ff.
W. R. Arnold : "The Divine Name" in *Journal of Biblical Literature*, xxiv (1905), 107 ff.
M. Buber : *Königtum Gottes*, 2nd edn. (1936).
M. Buber-F. Rosenzweig : *Die Schrift und ihre Verdeutschung* (1936), pp. 184 ff., 332 ff.
O. Grether : *Name und Wort Gottes im A.T.* (1934).
C. Toussaint : *Les Origines de la religion d'Israel*, vol. i, *L'ancien Jahvisme* (1931).
[G. R. Driver : "The Original Form of the name Yahweh : Evidence and Conclusion" in *Z.A.W.* (1928).]

Chapter IV

G. Dalman : *Worte Jesu*, 2nd edn. (1930), pp. 266-80.

G. F. Moore : *Judaism*, i (1927), 423 ff.

Strack-Billerbeck : Kommentar zum N.T. aus Talmud und Midrasch, vol. iii, p. 672, on Heb. 1, 2.

A. Marmorstein : *The Old Rabbinic Doctrine of God*, vol. i (1927), *The Names and Attributes of God*.

Chapter V

H. Weinel : *N.T. Theologie* (1928).

P. Feine : *N.T. Theologie* (1934), pp. 104 f., 175; [8th edn. (1951). pp. 30-3, 165 f.]

E. von Dobschütz : *Z.N.W.*, xxx (1931), 97-123.

E. Lohmeyer in *Z.N.W.*, xxvi (1927), 164-9.

F. H. Stead : "The chief Pauline names for Christ", The Expositor, III, Series 7 (1888), pp. 386-95.

E. W. Burton : *Galatians* (I.C.C.), pp. 393, 399-404.

K. Holl : *Gesammelte Aufsätze*, ii (1928), 115-22.

W. Schmauch : *In Christus* (1935).

[R. Bultmann : *N.T. Theologie*, pp. 52 f., 123-27.

M. Meinertz : *N.T. Theologie*, vol. i, p. 216 f., vol. ii, pp. 70-2.

O. Cullman : "Kyrios as a designation for the oral tradition concerning Jesus", in the *Scottish Journal of Theology*, 1950, pp. 180-97.

L. Cerfaux : "Kyrios dans les citations Pauliniennes de l'Ancient Testament" in *Ephemerides Lovanienses*, xx (1943), 5-17.

F. C. Grant : *An Introduction to New Testament Thought* (1950), pp. 130-7.

A. E. J. Rawlinson : *The New Testament Doctrine of the Christ* (1926), pp. 231-7.

E. Schweitzer : *Erniedrigung und Erhöhung bei Jesus und seinen Nachfolgern* (1955), esp. pp. 93 ff.]

ABBREVIATIONS

B.G.U.	Aegyptische Urkunden aus den kgl Museen zu Berlin.
C.I.G.	Corpus Inscriptionum Graecarum.
Ditt.Or.	W. Dittenberger, Orientis Graecae Inscriptiones.
Ditt. Syll.	W. Dittenberger, Sylloge Inscriptionum Graecarum.
I.G.	Inscriptiones Graecae.
J.H.S.	Journal of Hellenic Studies.
J.T.S.	Journal of Theological Studies.
L.	Material found only in St. Luke's Gospel.
LXX	The Septuagint.
Oxyr. Pap.	The Oxyrhyncus Papyri.
par.	" and parallel passages "
R.G.G.	Religion in Geschichte und Gegenwarth[2] (1927 ff.)
Str-B.	H. L. Strack und P. Billerbeck, Kommentar zum N.T. aus Talmud und Midrasch (1922-28).
v.l.	varia lectio.
Z.A.W.	Zeitschrift für die alttestamentliche Wissenschaft.
Z.N.W.	Zeitschrift für die neutestamentliche Wissenschaft.

INTRODUCTION

In German the word " Herr " (lord) is the most common expression of a situation confined to the personal sphere of human life, and indeed of a situation which constitutes an important part of personality, the circumstance that there is such a thing as the exercise of personal power over men and things. Moreover man, whether in the human sphere he is himself the subject of this exercise of power (as lord), or its object (as slave) is, in relation to God, its object. In the concept of lordship two things are brought together into an organic unity : the exercise of power as such, and the *personal* quality of its exercise, which passes beyond mere external compulsion into the legal and moral sphere. The exercise of power as such occurs also in non-human experience as the expression of the ordering of what is most expedient (the strongest animal as the leader). The decisive difference about the exercise of power amongst men is that it is legitimated not only by the inescapable presence of expediency but by an element of law which goes beyond what is merely natural and expedient, which turns merely temporal possession into the moral category of ownership, changes the momentary superiority of the stronger into the authority of the ruler, and turns the superiority of parents over children (which naturally demands their subjection), or the power of the slave-owner over his slaves, into something which calls for subservience and imposes responsibility. It seems that in the course of human history, from the earliest stages to be inferred from the history of language, the realisation of a unique unity of the two elements in lordship was a matter of gradual development;

and very varied attempts to comprehend it rightly
confront us in the general spiritual and religious
history of men.   But in none of these is achieved the
full understanding that the two elements in their
complete form are destined to be organically inter-
woven.   This understanding is only arrived at where
man sees God as the Creator over against him, who
" places " him in the exercise of His absolute power,
i.e. creates him, and, as Creator, is at the same time
his supreme authority, to serve whom connotes not
slavery but freedom—in the sphere of the biblical
revelation.   There a humanity which has flung off
all mere subordination to its creator confronts Him
who with the authority of the serving and forgiving
love of God woos its willing subservience, and makes
all lordship-relations new.

I. THE MEANING OF THE WORD ΚΥΡΙΟΣ

Ὁ κύριος, substantivised adj. κύριος, itself derived from the noun τὸ κῦρος, comes from an indo-germanic root keu(ā), kū, meaning " to swell " (cf. κνέω, ἔγκυος, ἐγκύμων, κῦμα), hence also " to be strong "; κύριος is connected with the old Indian śūra (strong, brave, hero). τὸ κῦρος (since Aeschylus) means " strength ", " power ", " might ", cf. Aeschylus Suppl. 391: οὐκ ἔχουσιν κῦρος οὐδὲν ἀμφὶ σοῦ, also " cause ": Soph. El. 918 f.: ἡ δὲ νῦν ἴσως πολλῶν ὑπάρξει κῦρος ἡμέρα καλῶν.

(1) *The adjective κύριος*

Hence the adjective κύριος means " possessing might ", or " having the power of law ", " legal ", " valid ", " justified ", " appropriate ", " plenipotentiary "; also " important ", " decisive ", " paramount ". As adjective, κύριος occurs from the classical to the N.T. period, but not in the N.T. nor in late-Jewish literature. This is bound up with the fact that the Hebrew and Aramaic equivalent to the noun ὁ κύριος has no corresponding adjective.

(a) " possessing might " (strength, power): Pindar, *Olymp.* 1. 104, δύναμιν κυριώτερον " higher in power ": cf. fr. 260 (ed. W. Christ, 1896) of Palamedes: ὄντα μὲν αὐτὸν κυριώτερον τοῦ Ὀδυσσέως εἰς σοφίας λόγον. See also *Isthm.* 5, 53: Ζεὺς ὁ πάντων κύριος; cf. Plutarch, *Def. Orac.* 29 (II, 426a): " if there are several worlds, does it follow that there are also several Zeuses, and not one, οἷος ὁ παρ' ἡμῖν κύριος ἁπάντων καὶ πατὴρ ἐπονομαζόμενος? [1] The

---

[1] In the Pindar quotation κύριος must be an adjective, in that from Plutarch it is more of a noun.

I

possession of physical strength is, by and large, not indicated by κύριος: the nearest passage to this is Plutarch, *Aristides* 6 (I, 322b): three emotions possess mankind vis-à-vis the divine, ζῆλος, φόβος, τιμή. . . . ἐκπλήττεσθαι δὲ καὶ δεδιέναι κατὰ τὸ κύριον καὶ δυνατόν. It is far more a question of *power of disposing or enacting*: cf. Demosthenes, *Or.* 50, 60 of the dying mother—οὐκέτι τῶν ὄντων κυρία οὖσα, 8, 69—a constitution, in which πλειόνων ἡ τύχη κυρία γίνεται ἢ οἱ λογισμοί: 18, 194: οὐ . . . τῆς τύχης κύριος ἦν, ἀλλ' ἐκείνη τῶν πάντων, ibid. 321: τούτου γὰρ ἡ φύσις κυρία τοῦ δύνασθαι δὲ καὶ ἰσχυειν ἕτερα.

The expression κύριος γενόμενος (Plutarch, *Quaest. Conv.* VI, 8, 2 (II, 694c) often occurs in connexion with the military overpowering of a town. κύριος also connotes possession, e.g. of money, Demosthenes, *Or.* 21, 98; 27, 55 ff., etc., especially man's possession of control over himself: Plato, *Ep.* 7, 324b—εἰ θᾶττον ἐμαυτοῦ γενοίμην κύριος. So Aristotle, *Eth. Nic.* III 6, p. 1113b, 32—κύριος τοῦ μὴ μεθυσθῆναι, Plutarch, *Quaest. Conv.* VIII, 9, 2 (II, 731c)—αὐτοκρατὲς δὲ ἡ ψυχὴ καὶ κύριον, also *Apopth. Praef.* (II, 172d)—τῶν μὲν λόγων ἔφη κύριος αὐτὸς εἶναι, τῶν δὲ πράξεων τὴν τύχην. More generally it often means, " providing the decisive factor ": Plato, *Republic* IV, 429b—whether a city is brave or cowardly is decided by its soldiers, the others in the city οὐ . . . κύριοι ἂν εἶεν ἢ τοίαν αὐτὴν εἶναι ἢ τοίαν, " they have not got it in their hands ". Thus the δαίμων of a man in Dio Chrysostom, *Or.* 25, 1 is described as τὸ κρατοῦν ἑκαστοῦ, and the question whether it is something inside man or something ἔξωθεν ὂν ἄρχον τε καὶ κύριον τοῦ ἀνθρώπου is answered in the affirmative, and this then explains that kings, leaders and generals have been good or evil spirits (δαίμονες) for their subjects; thus to be κύριος means to exercise a powerful influence.

He who is *kurios* exercises a power which is not immediate, brutal or external, his power can take effect
as unintelligibly and yet ineluctably as that of faith.
It follows that *kurios* is also the right word to express
" valid ", i.e. " having the force of law ". The transition may be seen in Andocides I, 87 ; ψήφισμα δὲ
μηδὲν μήτε βουλῆς μήτε δήμου νόμου κυριώτερον εἶναι. In
the case of laws which are operative, it means " of
legal force ", " valid " : cf. Demosthenes, *Or.* 24, of
the law, κύριος εἰ γενήσεται. So often in papyri of
treaties, agreements, signatures, e.g. *Oxyr. Pap.* II, 261,
17 f. : κυρία ἡ συγγραφῆι (a slip for συγγραφή)—A.D. 55.
Of persons (with infinitive or participle), it means
" plenipotentiary ", " entitled ", " commissioned " ;
Demosthenes, *Or.* 59, 4, Eur, *Supplices* 1189 f. : οὗτος
κύριος, τύραννος ὤν, πάσης ὑπὲρ γῆς Δαναϊδῶς ὁρκωμοτεῖν
(to take an oath) ; with the participle, *Elephantine
Papyri* I, 15 f. (a marriage settlement 311-310 B.C.)—
κύριοι δὲ ἔστωσαν Ἡρακλείδης καὶ Δημητρία . . . τὰς
συγγραφὰς αὐταὶ τὰς αὐτων φυλάσσοντες, Polybius, 6, 37,
8, κύριος δ᾽ ἐστι καὶ ζημιῶν ὁ χιλίαρχος καὶ ἐνεχυράζων
(to take a pledge) ; with the infinitive, Andoc. 4, 9 :
τοὺς δικαστὰς ἀπολέσαι μὲν κυρίους εἶναι. With the genitive, it denotes " with full powers concerning ",
Antiphon, *Or.* III, 1, 1 (ed. L. Gernet, 1923)—
ὑπὸ . . . τῶν ψηφισαμένων, οἳ κύριοι πάσης τῆς πολιτείας
εἰσίν, Isocrates, 19, 34— τὴν μητέρα καὶ τὴν ἀδελφὴν τῶν
αὐτοῦ κυρίας . . . κατέστησε, Plato, *Laws*, XI, 929d—if
the sick or demented father οἰκοφθορῇ . . . ὡς ὢν τῶν
αὐτοῦ κύριος, the law empowers him to do what he will
with his own. The *nomos* is *kurios basileūs*, Plato, *Ep.* 8,
354c : the opposite is *turannos*. *Elephantine Papyri* 2, 4 f. (a
will of 285-284 B.C.)—ἐὰν δέ τι πάσχῃ Καλλίστα Διονυσίου
ζῶντος, κύριον εἶναι Διονύσιον τῶν ὑπαρχόντων. Hence *ta
kuria* means "the legal power" in the state, Demosthenes,
Or. 19, 259—τὰ κύρι᾽ ἄττα ποτ᾽ ἐστὶν ἐν ἑκάστῃ τῶν πόλεων.

(b) " Decisive ",   " important ",   " chief ".   Cf.
Pindar, *Olymp.* 6, 32—κυρίῳ δ' ἐν μηνί. Cf. Aeschylus,
Ag. 766, Euripides, *Or,* 48 f., *Iph. Aul.* 318—οὑμὸς οὐχ ὁ
τοῦδε μῦθος κυριώτερος λέγειν ; Aristotle, *Eth. Nic.*
VI, 13, p. 1143b, 34—(ἡ φρόνησις) τῆς σοφίας κυριωτέρα;
Plato, *Laws,* I, 638d—λέγειν τι κύριον, " to say something
correct ", *Philebus,* 67b—κύριοι μάρτυρες, " completely
adequate witnesses " ; also *Symp.* 218d : οἶμαί μοι
συλλήπτορα οὐδένα κυριώτερον εἶναι σοῦ—" suitable support ".   Hence κυριώτατος is often tacked on to μέγιστος,
e.g. Plato, *Sophist.* 230d, *Politicus* VIII, 565a (next to
πλεῖστος), *Tim.* 84c, 87c ; for Aristotle see the Index.
Kurios is similarly used as an adjective by Epictetus: in
his *Diss.* I, 20, 8, Epicurus is asked " τί κυριώτερον ἔχεις "
than the body, while Epictetus himself says (*Diss.* II, 10,
1) that man has nothing κυριώτερον προαιρέσεως. Of the
three *topoi* for the προκόψων the κυριώτατος is ὁ περὶ
τὰ πάθη (*Diss.* III, 2, 3)—" the most important " or
" chief ".   He and Plutarch also use κυριώτατος alongside μέγιστος.[1]

(2) *The substantive* κύριος

The noun ὁ κύριος occurs occasionally, and hardly
as yet differentiated from a substantised adjective,
in the Attic tragedians—Aeschylus, *Cheoph.* 658, 688 f.,
Sophocles, *Ajax,* 734 ; in *Oed. Col.* 1643 f. the γῆς ἄναξ
(l. 1630), Theseus is called ὁ κύριος Θησεύς ; in lines
288 f. Oedipus says to the Chorus : " ὅ ταν δ' ὁ κύριος
παρῇ τις, ὑμῶν ὅστις ἐστὶν ἡγεμών ".   In Euripides, *kurios*
once means the father giving his child in marriage
(*Iph. Aul.* 703) and in *Andromache* 558 Neoptolemus is

---

[1] [The German text gives references.]   For further uses of the
adjective, such as κυρία ἐκκλήσια, κύριος τόνος, κύριον ὄνομα,
etc., see Liddell and Scott, and e.g. the word-index to Aristotle,
s.v.

kurios of the captured Andromache.[1] The only pre-Socratic reference to call for mention is Democritus' mot[2] τόλμα πρήξιος ἀρχή, τύχη δὲ τέλεος κυρίη—" is decisive with regard to the end ".

As a noun with a definite significance *kurios* first occurs in the first half of the fourth century B.C. and begins to be fixed in two meanings—the " lord " as the person with rights of disposing over a slave, Demosthenes, *Or.* 36, 28, 43 f.; 37, 51; 47, 14 f. (but *despotēs* is used some sixteen times of a master of slaves), Xenophon, *Oec.*, 9, 16, Aristotle, *Pol.* II, 9 (1269b, 9 f.) —lord of subject peoples, who τῶν ἴσων ἀξιοῦσιν ἑαυτοὺς τοῖς κυρίοις, lord of the house—Demosthenes, *Or.* 47, 60 (cf. n. 1 supra. In the sense of one who " is there for a purpose " who is put in charge of certain things and has them " under him ", probably also Antiphon, *Or.* II, 4, 7 (ed. L. Gernet, 1923)—of a slave who was not tortured—οὐδὲν θαυμαστὸν ἔπαθεν ὑπὸ τῶν κυρίων, cf. Plato, *Crito*, 44a—φασί γέ τοι δὴ οἱ τούτων κύριοι. The second meaning in which *kurios* begins to crystallise is the legal " spokesman " of a wife or a girl—Isaeus, 6, 32, Demosthenes, *Or.* 46, 15, etc. . . . Both usages of the noun link on to the adjective in the sense of " plenipotentiary ". The idea of " legitimate " included in this is clear in the *Hibeh Papyri* (243-242 B.C.) 34, 3—a claim ἢ τὸ ὑποζύγιον ἀποδοῦναι τῷ κυρίῳ (the legal possessor), or to pay the price. How strong was the sense of legality in the word in Athens about 400 B.C. is shown in Aristophanes, *Plutus*, 6 f., where the lot of a slave is gloomily depicted : fate does not allow the legal *kurios*, namely the slave himself, to dispose of his

---

[1] *Kurios* is also the head of the family, *Oxyr. Pap.* II, 288, 36 (first century A.D.). But Plutarch calls the householder as such, *despotēs*, *Septem Sapientium Convivium*, 12 (II, 155d). This word occurs 106 times in Euripides, 17 in Aeschylus.

[2] Fr. 269 (II 115, 8 f., Diels).

body, but him who bought him—who has been called
despotēs in line 2. . . . In Attic Greek *kurios* keeps the
adjective's limitation to legal power of disposition
(which it also never quite loses in Hellenistic Greek) :
Dio Chrysostom in his speeches *De Servitute* (*Or.* 14
and 15) always uses *despotes* for the slave's lord.
Typical of him and of Attic usage, is *Or.* 14, 22 :
Odysseus as beggar οὐδὲν ἧττον βασιλεὺς ἦν καὶ τῆς
οἰκίας κύριος. Lucian also uses *despotēs* as *kurios* is
used in the *Koinē:* in *Dialogi Marini*, 7, 2, Zephyrus
says of Io, ἡμῶν ἔσται δέσποινα, ὄντινα ἂν ἡμῶν ἐθέλῃ
ἐκπέμψαι. Antiatticistes (*Anecd. Graec.* I, p. 102, 20)
κύριαν οὔ φασι δεῖν λέγειν, ἀλλὰ κεκτημένην· τὸν δ
κεκτημένον μὴ λέγεσθαι ἀντὶ τοῦ δεσπότου . . . In the frag-
ments of the Attic comic poets *despotēs* occurs fifty-six
times, *despoina*, 11 ; where *kurios* occurs as a noun, that
is mostly in contexts where *despotēs* does not fit or where
the distinction between noun and adjective disappears ;
cf. *Philemon* [1]—ἐμοῦ γάρ ἐστι κύριος μὲν εἷς ἀνήρ (the slave
is speaking) τούτων δὲ καὶ σοῦ μυρίων τ' ἄλλων νόμος:
here *kurios* means " has to speak "—*despotēs* would not
express this so directly ; *Alexis*,[2] fr. 262 : if thou
marriest, οὐδὲ σαυτοῦ κύριον ἔξεστιν εἶναι (cf. supra,
p. 2, line 18) ; idem, fr. 149 : οὐχ ἀρχιτέκτων κύριος τῆς
ἡδονῆς μόνος καθέστηκ'—enjoyment of art does not
depend solely on the artist. *Kurios* means " the
possessor " only in *Crito*,[3] μεγάλου κύριον βαλλαντίου
. . . ποιήσας. In Menander, *kurios* occurs as a
noun, meaning a child's spokesman (*Epitrepontes*,
89), a slave's lord (*Pericles*, 186), and in *Samia* 287 it is
used of Ἔρως as ὁ τῆς ἐμῆς νῦν κύριος γνώμης. W.
Schmid, in *Der Atticismus in seinen Hauptvertretern*
(1887-1897) speaks of *kurios* only as an adjective in his

[1] *Comicorum, Atticorum Fragmenta* (ed. Kock) II, 486, fr. 31.
[2] Op. cit., II, 393.
[3] Op. cit., III, 354, fr. 3.

Register, Eustathius Thessalonicensis (*Opuscula*) has ὅπου
γε ἡ εὐγενὴς ἀττικὴ γλῶσσα τὸν κύριον ἐπὶ ἀνδρὸς
τίθησιν, ᾧ γυναῖκα ὁ νόμος συνέζευξε. Dionysius of
Halicarnassus, *Antiquitates Romanae*, II, 27, 2, has
τὴν ἐλευθερίαν εὐράμενος (sc. ὁ θεράπων) αὐτοῦ τὸ λοιπὸν
ἤδη κύριός ἐστιν—which shows the same usage as is
described above. The later relationship between
kurios and *despotēs* is shown by Manuel Moschopulos
(*c.* A.D. 1300) in his *Sylloge Vocum Atticarum*, s.v. *despotēs*: δεσπότης λέγεται πρὸς δοῦλον, κύριος δὲ πρὸς
ἐλεύθερον, and s.v. *despoina*: δέσποινα λέγεται οὐ μόνον ἡ
βασιλίς, ἀλλὰ καὶ ἡ τοῦ οἴκου δεσπότις, ἣν ἰδιωτικῶς κυρίαν
φαμέν. Thus in Attic Greek *kurios* has a closely limited
use. The broadening of the term seen in the N.T.
belongs to the *Koinē*—especially the extended use of
the noun.[1]

In the *Koinē despotēs* and *kurios* are widely used side
by side. *Kurios* is the possessor of slaves and property.
In the treaty between Miletus and Heraclea,[2] the legal
proprietors of runaway slaves are called *kurioi*. But a
distinction between the two words is still discernible.
Epictetus uses both, often alternately, for the slave's
master (e.g. *Diss.* IV, 1, 116). But he prefers *kurios*
for the exposition of his concept of freedom, since this
word is capable of a further application : in *Diss.* IV,
1, 59, πᾶς ὃς ἂν ἐξουσίαν ἔχῃ τῶν ὑπ' αὐτοῦ τινος θελομένων
πρὸς τὸ περιποιῆσαι ταῦτα ἢ ἀφελέσθαι is *kurios*, the rich are

[1] It must be specially stressed that Demosthenes does not *call*
Philip *kurios*, but that *kurios* when used of him (always with a
genitive) says that he is the one person given the full powers
which Greek law gives to the people (*Or.* 18, 235 f., cf. 19, 64 ;
6, 6 ; 18, 201 ; 1, 4, etc. The noun which Demosthenes uses
for the position of the king over his subjects is *despotēs* (*Or.* 5, 17 ;
6, 25 ; 15, 27 ; 18, 296 ; 19, 69 ; 20, 16). To be *kurios* means
to have supreme sovereignty in one's hands, G. Busolt, *Griechische
Staatskunde*, i. p. 304, and n. 4.
[2] Ditt. Syll³ 633, 95.

οἱ τὸν κύριον τὸν μέγαν ἔχοντες καὶ πρὸς τὸ ἐκείνου νεῦμα καὶ κίνημα ζῶντες, IV, 1, 145. The difference between the two words is clear from the changes in their use, *Diss.*, IV, 1, 12 f. : the senator asks who could compel him εἰ μὴ ὁ πάντων κύριος Καῖσαρ, to which Epictetus replies: οὐκοῦν ἕνα μὲν δεσπότην σαυτοῦ καὶ σὺ αὐτὸς ὡμολόγησας. The senator names the emperor *kurios*, as the one who has the power and right of disposing over everything, but from the point of view of Epictetus' concept of freedom he is thereby a slave who has his *despotēs* over him. Thus there easily enters into *despotēs* an element of hardness, as is also shown by Plutarch, *Lucullus*, 18 (I, 503a) a lady taken prisoner-of-war bewails her beauty as having secured her a *despotēs* instead of a husband. Of Philip, the father of Alexander, it was reported that he said μᾶλλον πολὺν χρόνον ἐθέλειν χρηστὸς ἢ δεσπότης ὀλίγον καλεῖσθαι (Plutarch, *Apophthegmata, Philippus*, 4 (II, 177d). . . . But *kurios* is he who has *exousia*. The element of legality which is also inherent in this word, is occasionally more clearly apparent : Plutarch, *Aratus*, 9 (I, 1031b), says of those who have been exiled : κατελθόντες δὲ οἱ πλεῖστοι πένητες ὧν κύριοι πρότερον ἦσαν ἐπελαμβάνοντο. Again, κύριοι τῆς ὁλκάδος are those who give the word on board ship (Plutarch, *De Mario* 37 (I, 427a) ; Aratus says to Philip of Macedon, *Aratus* 50 (I, 1050e) : " If you approach them with trust and friendliness τῶν μὲν (of the Cretans) ἡγεμών, τῶν δὲ (the Peloponnesians) κύριος ἤδη καθέστηκας." The explanation of both terms is given shortly beforehand. " Although you Philip, have not won any fixed position, πάντες ἑκουσίως σοι ποιοῦσι τὸ προστασσόμενον " ; *Kurios* is he whose authority wins obedience. Cf. Plutarch, *Apophthegamata Laconica, Pausanias Plistonactis*, 1 (II, 230 f.) : τοὺς νόμους . . . τῶν ἀνδρῶν, οὐ τοὺς ἄνδρας τῶν νόμων κυρίους εἶναι δεῖ. *Kurios* denotes the lord of a slave in

Plutarch, *Apophthegmata*, *Agathocles*, 2 (II, 176e). Finally, the gods are called *Kurioi* as those who dispose over some sphere of life : *An recte dictum sit latenter esse vivendum* 6 (II, 1130a)—τὸν δὲ τῆς ἐναντίας (set over against the sun) κυρίον μοίρας . . . Ἀίδην ὀνομάζουσιν, *Def. Orac.* 29 (II, 426a—cf. *supra*, p. 1, *ad fin.*), *Quaest. Conv.* V, 3, 1, 4 (II, 675 f.)—Poseidon and Dionysius τῆς ὑγρᾶς καὶ γονίμου κύριοι δοκοῦσιν ἀρχῆς εἶναι. *Kurios* is the word which the inferior is glad to use of the superior, since it emphasises the authority and legality of his position. Thus Cassius was greeted in Rhodes as βασιλεὺς καὶ κύριος, and the answer cuts like a knife : οὔτε βασιλεὺς οὔτε κύριος, τοῦ δὲ κυρίου καὶ βασιλέως φονεὺς καὶ κολαστής (Plutarch, *Brutus* 30 (I, 998b), while Brutus himself says (op. cit. 22—I, 994c) : οἱ δὲ πρόγονοι . . . ἡμῶν οὐδὲ πρᾴους δεσπότας ὑπέμεινον.

Kurios is he who can dispose of things or persons, *despotēs* he who possesses a thing or person. That shows how far the two words touch one another, .and how far they are separate. The more popular the speech and the nearer to the time of the N.T. the more does *kurios* oust *despotēs* ; the closer the contact with the written word and the nearer the beginning of the Hellenistic era, the greater is the authoritative and legal element in *kurios*. We may end with the interesting passage from Lucan, *Nigrinus*, 26 : the philosopher despises earthly goods, as he maintains ὅτι τούτων μὲν φύσει οὐδενός ἐσμεν κύριοι, νόμῳ δὲ καὶ διαδοχῇ τὴν χρῆσιν αὐτῶν εἰς ἀόριστον παραλαμβάνοντες ὀλιγοχρόνιοι δεσπόται νομιζόμεθα. *Kurios* and *despotēs* cannot be confused here.

Not everyone who can dispose over a thing or person is therefore called *kurios* without qualification. In general the (legal) owner (also of slaves) receives the title *kurios*. But gradually the usage established itself of addressing members of a higher class as *kurie* (or

kuria) and speaking about them as *ho kurios*, in the case
of officials often adding the title of the office. The
letters of the general Apollonius of the beginning of the
second century A.D. show that not only his employees
and slaves but, e.g. the villagers address him as *kurie*,
Giessen Papyri, 61, 17 (A.D. 119), whereas a wealthy
ναύκληρος calls him alternately φίλτατε and κύριε.
(*Giessen Papyri*, 11, 12, and 20—A.D. 118) and his
family (with one exception, *vide infra*) does not so
address him. Appollonius for his part addresses his
superiors as ἡγεμὼν κύριε (*Giessen Papyri*, 41, I, 4, 9,
and 13). This usage can be traced back to the first
century A.D. : Epictetus has high officials (*Diss.* IV,
1, 57), philosophers being feted (III, 23, 11 and 19)
the doctor (II, 15, 15, and III, 10, 15) and the μάντις
(II, 7, 9) addressed as *kurie*, the cynic even as κύριε ἄγγελε
καὶ κατάσκοπε (III, 22, 38) : in his *Encheiridion*, 40,
he says generally that wives of fourteen years standing
were addressed as *kuriai* by their husbands. According
to Dio Chrysostom LXI, 20, 1, Nero as lute-player
addressed the spectators as *kurioi mou*, while *kurios
hēgemōn* occurs as early as A.D. 45 in *Oxyr. Pap.* II, 283,
18 : similarly in *Oxyr. Pap.* I, 37, II, 8 (A.D. 49) τὰ ὑπὸ
τοῦ κυρίου ἡγεμόνος κριθέντα, and in the year A.D. 71-72
(*Tebtunis Papyri* 302, 11 and 20) we find attached
to *hēgemōn* the phrase σοῦ τε τοῦ κυρίου γράψαντος.
An apparently unique example dates back to the first
century B.C.—τῷ κυρίῳ στρατηγῷ—*Aegyptische Urkunden
zu Berlin*, 1819, 2 (60-59 B.C.). When, as early as the
first century A.D. (op. cit. 665, II, 18) a son addresses
his father as *kurie mou*, when that is probably used by
Hermaios to his brother, the general Apollonius
(*Giessen Papyri* 85, 16—early second century A.D.),
that may still be the expression of a certain subordination : but finally even a father addresses his son as *kurie*,
Oxyr. Pap. I, 123, 1—κυρίῳ μου υἱῷ Διονυσοθέωνι ὁ πατὴρ

χαίρειν ; and line 24—κύριε υἱέ (third and fourth century A.D.). See further F. J. Dölger, *Antike und Christentum* V (1936), pp. 211-17.

Even before the beginning of the Constantine epoch, *despotēs* begins to oust *kurios* in every sphere. In *Oxyr. Pap.* I, 67, 10 (A.D. 338) *despotia* is used to designate legal ownership, but the address *despota hēgemōn* is used as early as A.D. 266 (*Tebtunis Papyri*, 326, 3) and in the letter from a father to his son mentioned above (*Oxyr. Pap.* I, 123) the former calls the addressee in line 7 *despota mou* and speaks of *despoina mou mētēr humōn* (l. 22). In the emperor's titles, too, *kurios* was more and more replaced by *despotēs*.

The whole development can thus be summarised by saying that *kurios*, originally the plenipotentiary, the person entitled to dispose, discarded the element of arbitrariness which was easily associated with *despotēs*, and for that very reason was used in the first instance by slaves to their masters in a kind of delicate flattery [1] and so gradually ousted *despotēs* in everyday speech. For the same reasons, however, since *despotēs* more strongly stressed the immediacy and unlimitedness of possession, the latter term was once again preferred in the age of dawning Byzantinism.

Thus at the beginning of the Hellenistic era, *kurios* was still relatively seldom used as a noun and in the relatively limited sense of legal lord and possessor and of plenipotentiary. The later practice of calling gods and rulers *kurios* must have developed in the Hellenistic epoch. There is no proof that Philip of Macedon or Alexander the Great or any of the first of the Diadochoi were called *kurioi* any more than that any gods were in this period. For the well-known passage in the paean

---

[1] In two letters, recorded in Josephus, *Ant.* XVII, 137 and 139, the slave calls her mistress her *kuria*, whereas Josephus (loc. cit. § 138) calls her *despoina*.

which the Athenians sang in honour of Demetrius
Poliorketes [1]—πρῶτον μὲν εἰρήνην ποιήσον, φίλατε, κύριος
γὰρ εἰ σύ—is to be translated " for thou canst do it,
thou hast it in thy hand " (vide supra, p. 2, ad init.).
The earliest instance of kurios being used of a god is in
the LXX, which has already been shown [2] to be most
unlikely to be linking on to some already established
usage. The earliest instance of the developing Hellenistic usage is the treaty between Philip VI of
Macedonia and Hannibal reported by Polybius
(VII, 9 5) : ἐφ᾽ ὧτ᾽ εἶναι σωζομένους . . . κυρίους
καρχηδονίους καὶ Ἀννίβαν τὸν στρατηγόν. Next follows the
Greek translation of the Egyptian Pharoah-title in the
form kurios basileiōn [3] and kurios triakontaetēridōn.[4]

[1] Athenaeus, VI, 63 (p. 253e). See Foerster, op. cit. p. 110.
But the passage is differently interpreted : see Baudissin, op.
cit. II, p. 288 : but to interpret it as an adjective (as does W.
Schubert, Die Religiöse Haltung des frühen Hellenismus (1937), p. 19)
seems to me to fit the context.

[2] An argumentum e silentio from the silence of the sources is not
entirely convincing (though vide infra, p. 19, ad init.), but it
gains weight in the context of the philological evidence.

[3] Deissmann, Licht vom Osten, p. 300, n. 2 (Ptolemy Philopator,
221-205 B.C.), C.I.G., 4697 (196 B.C.).

[4] Ditt. Or. 90, line 2. With these two notes cf. Baudissin, op.
cit. II, p. 288, nn. 2 and 3.

II. GODS AND RULERS AS *KURIOI*

AN indispensable constituent of every religion is the
element of legitimate power, i.e. the power in which
man must acknowledge authority and bow before its
superiority. If this element of legitimacy is lacking,
religio is replaced by the fear of spirits against which
man tries to defend himself in every way, against
which he fights. If the element of power is absent,
then the divinity is only an idea. The two together,
power and right, as an unified conception, are bound
up with the personality of their bearer. For right and
its counterpart, responsibility, are categories only to
be used between persons. In Greek religion, too, the
conception of God does not altogether lack the element
of personal, legitimate power. Its expression is the
term " Lord ". Now *despotēs* (*despoina*) is applied to
the Gods in classical Greek and occasionally also later,
and denotes the relationship of the Gods to nature and
to men. But the dividing line between Greeks and
" Barbarians " in the whole human sphere, political as
well as religious, is precisely that the Greeks are fundamentally averse from regarding their gods as lords and
themselves as slaves (*douloi*). This is bound up with
the fact that in Greek religion the basic personal act,
the creativity of God, is almost entirely lacking.

(1) Κύριος *for gods and rulers in classical Greek*

The word *kurios*, it is true, was also applied to the
Greek gods from the classical era up to the imperial
epoch, first as adjective then more as substantive, and
applied when the intention was to predicate that they
can dispose over distinctive spheres of life.

13

Pindar, *Isthm.* V, 53 has Ζεύς ὁ πάντων κύριος ;
Plato, *Laws*, XII, 13 (966c) says the φύλακες must know
of the gods ὡς εἰσίν τε καὶ ὅσης φαίνονται κύριοι δυνάμεως,
(cf. *Republic*, VII, 517c) ;[1] Xenophon, *Memorabilia*,
I, 4, 9, says that against the proof of God from the
nous of man the objection is raised : " οὐ γὰρ ὁρῶ τοὺς
κυρίους ". In his *Oeconomicus* VI, 1, he says that
" with the gods one must begin ὡς τῶν θεῶν κυρίων
ὄντων οὐδὲν ἧττον τῶν εἰρηνικῶν ἢ τῶν πολεμικῶν ἔργων.
Demosthenes, *Or.* 60, 21, has ὁ πάντων κύριος δαίμων.
In his *Ep.* 4, 6, he says of the gods : ἁπάντων τῶν
ἀγαθῶν ἐγκρατεῖς ὄντας κυρίους εἶναι καὶ αὐτοὺς ἔχειν
καὶ δοῦναι τοῖς ἄλλοις. Sosiphanes, fr. 3, has

> ἢν δ᾿ εὐτυχῆτε, μηδὲν ὄντες εὐθέως
> ἴσ᾿ οὐρανῷ φρονεῖτε, τὸν δὲ κύριον
> Ἅιδην παρεστῶτ᾿ οὐχ ὁρᾶτε πλησίον.

Dio Chrysostom (*Or.* 37, 11) calls Poseidon and Helios
kurios respectively of water and fire ; Plutarch (*Isis
and Osiris*, 35—II, 365a) says that the Greeks consider
Dionysus *kurios kai archēgos* not only of wine, but
also πάσης ὑγρᾶς φύσεως ; also that Poseidon and
Dionysus τῆς ὑγρᾶς καὶ γονίμου κύριοι δοκοῦσιν ἀρχῆς εἶναι
(*Quaest. Conviv.* V, 3, 1). Aelius Aristides (*Or.* 37, 17)
says that *Nikē* (victory) is not *kuria* of Athene, but
Athene is *kuria* of *Nikē*. In Plutarch, *Isis and Osiris*,
40 (II, 367a), Isis is called ἡ κυρία τῆς γῆς θεός, Osiris
is greeted as ἁπάντων κύριος (ibid. 12—II, 355e) and as
ὁ τῶν ἀρίστων πάντων ἡγεμὼν καὶ κύριος (ibid. 49—II,
371a). Philo of Byblos says of Beelsamen ὅ ἐστι παρὰ
Φοίνιξι κύριος οὐρανοῦ, Ζεὺς δὲ παρ᾿ Ἕλλησι. In similar

---

[1] Plato, *Ep.* 6, 323d has : τὸν τῶν πάντων θεὸν ἡγεμόνα τῶν τε
ὄντων καὶ τῶν μελλόντων, τοῦ τε ἡγεμόνος καὶ αἰτίου πατέρα
κύριον ἐπομνύντας. Here θεὸς ἡγεμών corresponds to πατὴρ κύριος.
Possibly *kurios* stresses the position of the " Father " as head of
the family. Cf. n. 1, p. 5.

strain Epictetus (*Diss.* IV, 1, 12) speaks of ὁ πάντων κύριος Καῖσαρ (*vide infra*, p. 27, *ad fin.* and p. 24, note 2).

It is to be observed, however, that in contrast to the oriental and Egyptian divine names, the gods are not actually here named as *kurios* of their own sphere, and that thus the being lord is not their vital characteristic, whereas in Babylon and Egypt they are named precisely in virtue of what they are lords of : " May the deeds of Marduk, the lord of the Gods, be seen by all the gods and goddesses, Anu, Enlil, the lord of the ocean, the sovereign Ea." [1]   This situation is connected with the fundamental structure of Greek theology, namely that for the Greeks the gods are in principle only the " basic forms of reality ", and so do not personally confront the world and mankind as creators or designers and are also not lords of the reality which holds together all realities, namely fate.   The latter is rather, and often, an independent entity alongside the gods.   Since gods and men " breath from one mother " and are organically connected limbs of one reality, their mutual relationship cannot be described by *kurios-doulos* terminology.[2]   Man has no basic personal responsibility to these gods, nor do they confront mankind with punishment.   A prayer to them is

[1] A. Ungnad, *Die Religion der Babylonier und Assyrer* (1921), p. 174, etc.   In Egypt the gods become not only " lords " of a town (e.g. G. Roeder, *Urkunden zur Religion des alten Aegyptien*, p. 5, on Amon-Re as lord of Karnak) but also lord of eternity, of existence (Roeder, op. cit. p. 5) lord of justice, lord of corn, (loc. cit. p. 7), Aton is also called lord of heaven, lord of earth, (p. 69).   A transferred use of " lord " is also found frequently (as with *ba'al* in the O.T.), e.g. lord of worship (p. 5, *ad fin.*). Further information in A. Erman and H. Grapow, *Wörterbuch der ägyptischen Sprache*, vol. ii (1928), s.v. *nb*.

[2] Conceivably the reason why *despotēs* (*despoina*) could be applied in the classical era to gods is because it suggests the " paterfamilias ", i.e. the organic link between the human and divine?

fundamentally illogical—as is the fact that Zeus turns
up again as lord of fate. But that only shows that a
further *motif* is appearing—that a theology in which
the gods are only the basic forms of reality is bound to
disintegrate.

Each passing conception of the lordship of the gods
is indissolubly connected with the contemporary ideas
of lordship-relations in the whole of life. If the gods
are the epitome of reality, it is a question of finding
this epitome of reality in other spheres. The political
consequence of this is democracy, in which each individual contributes towards comprehending the depths
of reality. In so far as the Greek " serves " the laws,
he freely submits to what binds him, which he has
himself, by his powers of reason, recognised as such,
and to the formation and ratification of which he has
himself contributed. Yet Law is not simply what the
citizens resolve, but stands above them : that is shown
by the passage of Andocides quoted on page 3, line 6.

However distant the Hellenistic monarchies may
appear to be from Greek democracy, however much the
Greeks later repeatedly hailed the proclamation of
their " freedom ", it must nevertheless be stressed that
the Hellenistic worship of the ruler had roots in the
classical Greek spirit. For in the ruler was crystallised,
to a special degree, the divine, of which the world is
full ; he did not need the ratification of the people,
since the latter's decisions would of course agree with
those of the ruler who shares in " virtue " to an unparalleled degree. He is *theos*, *theos epiphanēs*, *neos
Dionysos*, etc., but not *kurios*, he is not contrasted with
the people, he is only inspired to a special degree by
the divine which lives in all Greeks. The Hellenistic
ruler is *nomos empsuchos*.[1]

[1] E. R. Goodenough, *The Political Philosophy of Hellenistic
Kingship*, in Yale Classical Studies, i (1928), pp. 55-102.

(2) *Gods and rulers as lords in the Orient and in Egypt*

For orientals the gods are lords of reality, they have
fate in their hands. To the gods who have created
him the individual man owes personal responsibility,
just as they intervene in his life with punishments.[1]
From these two standpoints it is essential that the gods
should there be called " lords ", lords over the world
and its components, lords over fate, lords over men.
There is nothing here of what is essential among the
Greeks—that reality shows itself to men to be divine,
and that man as a free agent takes up an attitude
towards it. As the gods ordain what is right, so the
ruler proclaims it to the subjects, and these have no
other course open to them but to subject themselves to
it in silence. This is what the Greeks felt to be servile.
But in the East there was a strong feeling that the
operation of justice demanded a personal authorisation.
That leads to the oriental worship of the ruler. There
the king is not conceived as a new manifestation of the
divine, but the power which he has and the justice
which he administers sets him above the level of mankind, and near to that of the gods to whom he owes his
position. As king, as dispenser of justice, the ruler
stands above men and can therefore, since the administration of justice has been handed over to him by the
gods, give unconditional orders to men, who must
obey him as unconditionally as they obey the gods.
Everything here depends upon the personal contrast
between God and man.

(3) *The Hellenistic Κύριος*

The consideration of the use of the Hellenistic title
of *kurios* for gods and rulers demands a bird's-eye view
of the evidence.

---

[1] Cf. The Babylonian penitential psalms, e.g. Ungnad, op. cit.
p. 220. " I suffer as though I did not fear my God, or my goddess.
Sorrow, sickness, destruction and decay are fallen to my lot ! "

(a) *The dates of its use.* No instance of *kurios* applied to gods or rulers (except for *kurios* with the genitive, *supra*, p. 3, *ad fin.* and p. 7, note 1) is earlier than the first century B.C.[1] The earliest instance is *kurios* used of Isis, in Egypt : C.I.G. 4897a (99-90 B.C.) ; Cf. C.I.G. 4898, 4899, 4904, 4917, 4930b, 4931, Ditt. Or. 186, 8 f., all first century B.C. As early as 81 B.C. we find the formula προσκυνήσας τὴν κυρίαν θεὰν Ἴσιν (C.I.G. 4936d addenda)—all from Philae. Similarly it is used of the god Soknopaios (Seknebtynis) in the first century B.C. : ὡς θέλει ὁ Σεκνεβτῦνις ὁ κύριος θεός (*Tebtunis Papyri*, 284, 5 f.). From Gizeh comes the dedication of a building τῷ θεῷ καὶ κυρίῳ Σοκνοπαίῳ (Ditt. Or. 655, 24 B.C.). In the time of Augustus or Tiberius we have the Syrian inscription with the formula θεὸς κρόνος κύριος (Ditt. Or. 606).

Of rulers, *kurios basileus* is found often in Egypt between 64 and 50 B.C. (B.G.U. 1767, 1 ; 1768, 9 ; 1816, 3 ; Ditt. Or. 186, 8): in 52 B.C. there is mention of festivals τοῖς κυρίοις θεοῖς μεγίστοις—referring to Ptolemy XIII and his co-rulers (*Berlin Akad.* (1902) 1096 : similarly C.I.G. 4717, l.25 and 29). . . . Similarly Augustus is named θεὸς καὶ κύριος Καῖσαρ Αὐτοκράτωρ 12 B.C. in Egypt (B.G.U. 1197, I, 15—in part restored) ; cf. B.G.U. 1200, 10 ff., and *Oxyr. Pap.* VIII, 1143, 4 : θυσίας καὶ σπονδὰς ὑπὲρ τοῦ θεοῦ καὶ κυρίου Αὐτοκράτορος (first century A.D.) ; Herod the Great was called βασιλεὺς Ἡρώδης κύριος (Ditt. Or. 415) ; similarly Agrippa I and II (ibid. 418, 423, 425, 426) : in Upper Egypt Queen Candace was called, in

[1] J. J. E. Hondius, *Supplementum Epigraphicum Graecum*, iii (1929), nos, 510-11, says that two Thracian inscriptions, one with (κυρ)ίῳ Διί, the other with (κυ)ρίῳ Ἀσκληπιῷ, date from the third century B.C. But the *Revue des études anciennes* XXVI (1924), 32, and notes 1 and 2, shows that this is an error or misprint—they are from the third century A.D.

13 B.C., ἡ κυρία βασίλισσα (Mitteis-Wilcken, I, 2, 4). A ptolemaic general is called, in 51 B.C., ὁ θεότατος καὶ κύριος στρατηγός (B.G.U. 1838, 1—cf. 1819, 2).

Thus in Egypt *kurios* occurs within a life-span, used of gods, rulers and high officials. Since we have a considerable number of Greek documents of every kind from the preceding centuries in Egypt, in which *kurios* does not occur in this usage, it is not to be supposed that gaps in our material give us an essentially false picture of the time when *kurios* first appears in these connections, nor that new discoveries will make any essential difference to this picture.

In Syria, although the situation could conceivably be different, since we have no sacred Greek inscriptions from there from the second and third centuries B.C. (Baudissin, op. cit. II, 258), it may well be the case that there, too, the Greek *kurios* was not applied to gods and rulers before the first century B.C. The oldest Syrian evidence for *kurios* in the sense discussed is the inscription already mentioned (Ditt. Or. 606) in which besides Kronos, the imperial house is also named: ὑπὲρ τῆς τῶν κυρίων Σεβαστῶν σωτηρίας, lines 1 and 2. This situation is to be explained from the fact that it was not till the first century before Christ that the counter-stream from the East began, which poured the oriental ideas of lordship into Greek moulds.

It is noticeable that *kurios* almost immediately occurs in close connexion with the substantives *theos, basileūs, stratēgos* (without any intervening *kai*). This usage cannot possibly mark the beginning, but it denotes an end. But since it is no ending of any Greek development, then it must be a translation of a long-existing Egyptian and Syrian usage. There the word corresponding to *kurios* was tacked on to terms such as god or king, without any conjunction (*vide infra*, p. 1052, 31).

(b) *The area of its use.* So far as concerns the geographical dissemination of the use of *kurios* for gods,
we do best to begin with Egypt. It is used predicatively once each of Ammon, Anubis, Apoll, Asclepius,
the Dioscuri, Horogebthios, Priotos, Rhodosternos,
Sruptichis, twice of Soknopaeus, three times of Pan,
four times of Bes, nine of Mandulis, sixteen of Hermes,
thirty-eight times each of Sarapis and Isis.[1] Outside
Egypt we find Egyptian gods called *kurios*, e.g. Sarapis
in Asia Minor, Crete and Italy, Helios in Spain, Isis
in Asia Minor and Rome. Moreover, according to
Oxyr. Pap. XI, 1380, κυρεία is the official name for Isis
in Heraclia Pelagos (ll. 61-2), and she was also addressed
as κυρία ῏Ισι (l. 142) and often called *kuria* with the
genitive of the sphere ruled over ; so with Horus and
Hermes (ll. 210-11 and 265-6). Plutarch speaks
similarly of Osiris (1046, 20 ff.) and in a hymn to Isis,
from Cyrene,[2] Isis is four times called *kuria* with a
noun in the genitive. Of the 119 times I have counted
kurios in Egypt, in ninety-five it occurs in the phrase
τὸ προσκύνημά τινος ποιεῖν παρὰ τῷ κυρίῳ (τῇ κυρίᾳ)
with the name of the god following, or similar phrases
connected with a προσκύνημα.

In Syria it occurs of various gods, especially Athene
and Zeus, less often in Arabia ; once each of Athene
(Allat) and Helios—certainly Syrian gods—in Spain.

In Asia Minor *kurios* occurs once each of Asclepius,
Hermes, Sarapis, Tiamos, Zeus, twice each of Helios,
Isis, Sabazios and Apoll, thrice of Nemesis, four times
of Πατρίς, thirteen of Artemis. The Ephesian

[1] The figures given here and below make no claim to complete-
ness : but the material from which they are drawn is so comprehensive that the conclusions drawn from them are most
unlikely to be disproved. They are drawn from Drexler's list in
Roscher's Lexicon, supplemented by the Papyri.

[2] W. Peek, *Der Isishymnus von Andros und verwandte Texte* (1930)
pp. 122 ff.

Artemis is once called *kuria* in Italy, and is probably referred to in two further inscriptions in Italy which speak of κυρία Ἄρτεμις (without Ἐφεσία).

Besides these, *kurios* (*kuria*) occurs without names of gods four times in Syria, and once there in the phrase θεῷ οὐρανίῳ πατρῴῳ τῷ κυρίῳ ;[1] and often in the phrase ὁ κύριος θεός in Egypt.

On the other hand it is to be observed that Jupiter Heliopolitanus is only called *kurios* once, and Jupiter Dolichenus, never.

The result of all this is that *kurios* as a divine predicate was common only where it corresponded to some native, non-Greek usage and scarcely at all moved away from these regions. When used of gods, it is fundamentally a translation of foreign usage and no more. To corresponding with the very common use of ʾādhōn in Semitic inscriptions, the number of cases to be expected of κύριος in Syrian Greek inscriptions should be considerably larger. The Greek κύριος is relatively less frequently used in Syria than its Semitic equivalent, thus the writers of Greek inscriptions in Syria have often shunned it.[2]

---

[1] *Kurios* is also used of various gods in Thrace, but only once on the Greek mainland of πατρίς, in Sparta. For the Gnostic examples see Baudissin, op. cit. ii, p. 270, n. 2 : they are not here cited, nor are the Magical texts, which contain much that is old but many very different influences as well. Κύριος in astrological texts, despite E. Peterson's contention in *Byzantinisch-Neugriechirche Jahrbücher*, V (1926-7), p. 224, does not help us, as becomes clear from the course of the enquiry.

[2] As a random test, in the section of P. le Bas' and W. H. Waddington's great work *Inscriptions Grecques et latines recueillés en Grèce et en Asie Mineure*, III (1870) concerned with Syrian inscriptions (nos. 1826-2677) Zeus is called *kurios* 6 times, but 5 times only Zeus, once θέος Ζεύς, once Ζεὺς κεραύνιος, once Ζεὺς ὕψιστος, 5 times Ζεὺς ὕψιστος καὶ ἐπήκοος, 5 times he has various other predicates. . . . Altogether 20 κύριος-passages stand over against 106 other names for a god.

(c) *Its meaning when used of gods.* It follows that the significance and content of *kurios* applied to gods, must be extracted in essentials from indigenous linguistic usage. But the Greek evidence also clearly shows a definite trend.

First, the predicate *kurios* is not intended to distinguish great or dominating gods from lesser, subordinate divinites.[1] In Syria there is no place for any such distinction, and in Egypt local divinites of small importance are also called *kurios*.[2] Nor is it a circle of divinites specially worshipped that are so named. Our observations point rather to the conclusion that *kurios* gives expression to the personal relationship of an individual to a god. For Egypt the noticeable frequency of *kurios* in *proskunēmata*, which represent a prayer or petition, may be mentioned first. Next, *kurios* is especially common in inscriptions conveying thanks : in the case of the Ephesian Artemis *kuria* only occurs in connexion with the phrase εὐχαριστῶ σοι, κυρία Ἄρτεμι,[3] and the same is true of Egyptian gods . . . Sarapis[4] and Mandulis (C.I.G. 5070), Hermes[5] and Nemesis,[6] and, slightly differently, the Dioscuri.[7] In petitionary prayer Sarapis is addressed as *kurie*[8] and the same address is found in consultations of the oracle[9] and the invocation to Helios to exact vengeance.[10] A personal relationship to an

[1] Baudissin, op. cit. ii, pp. 271 ff.
[2] Cf. the list given above (p. 20).
[3] *British Museum Greek Inscriptions*, 578c, 580, 582a, 586a, 587b, 588, 588b, 590 ; Hondius, op. cit. iv (1930), 535, 9 f.
[4] B.G.U. 423, 6 ff. (second century A.D.).
[5] *Giessen Papyri* 85, 6 f.
[6] Hondius, op. cit. vii (1934), 804.
[7] . . . Drexler (in Roscher), 1760.
[8] . . . Ibid. 1763, and C.I.G. 4710 (Lycopolis) . . . and 4712b.
[9] *Oxyr. Pap.* VIII, 1148, 1 (first century A.D.) . . .
[10] J.H.S. v (1884), p. 253, no. 4 ; Hondius, op. cit. vi (1932), 803.

unnamed god appears in the inscription καθαρμοῖς κὲ
θυσίαις ἐ[τίμησα τὸν κ]ύριον ἵνα μυ(—μοι) το ἐμὸν cῶ[μα
σῴζ]ει (= σῴζοι),[1] and presumably also in that well-
known invitation to the κλείνη τοῦ κυρίου Σαράπιδος [2] as in
the ἐγκατοχήσας τῷ κυρίῳ Σαράπιδι.[3] In Syria *kurios*
occurs as a name for god very often in the dedication
of consecrated memorials, in which the author of the
monument expresses his personal relationship to this
god. On the other hand, in contexts in which a
personal relation to the divinity is not expressly implied, *kurios* is used but seldom.[4] There remains
(besides texts of which the context is not clear) a
group of inscriptions containing *kurios*, in which the
author designates himself as standing under the
command of the divinity he calls *kurios:* Λούκιος . . .
πεμφθεὶς ὑπὸ τῆς κυρίας Ἀταργάτης ;[5] κατ'ἐπι-αγὴν
τῆς κυρίας Ἀρτέμιδος ;[6] cf. *Tebtunis Papyri*, 284, 2 ff.
(first century B.C.).

Thus *kurios* is especially used as the expression of a
personal relationship of men to god, expressing itself
in prayer, thanksgiving and devotion, and as correlative to *doulos*, whereby the person concerned addresses
the god whom he calls *kurios* as his master. But we
must now distinguish this range of thought from the
power of gods over nature, or parts thereof. It can be
no mere chance that in the case of Isis and Sarapis, the
two who are most often called *kurios* (*kuria*), the idea of

[1] *J.H.S.* viii (1887), p. 388, no. 17.
[2] *Oxyr. Pap.* I, 110, III, 523, XII, 1484, XIV, 1755 (first to
third centuries A.D.).
[3] C.I.G. 3163 (Smyrna).
[4] Examples of this are in Le Bas-Waddington, op. cit.
1879. . . . Hondius, op. cit. ii (1925), 830, 3 ff. . . . and 832.
I have found thirteen such texts where a personal relationship of
the speaker to the god named *Kurios* is not discernible.
[5] Le Bas-Waddington, 1890.
[6] Hondius, op. cit. iii (1929), 691 (Mytilene).

dominion over nature and fate most clearly confronts us. For Isis the best sources are *Oxyr. Pap.* XI, 1380, 121 ff., the Hymn of Cyrene (p. 20, n. 2 *supra*) and Apuleius, *Metamorphoses* XI, 5 ; for Sarapis, the *Sarapis-Aretologies*.[1] The *motif* of power in *kurios* reaches its zenith in the Hermetic writings.[2]

Thus the Greek evidence leads to a result similar to the analysis of the meaning of the corresponding Semitic word arrived at by Baudissin in his detailed discussion. *Kurios* corresponds not to the Semitic *ba'al*, but to the Phoenicean Canaanite *'ādhôn*, Fem. *rabbath* and Aramaic *mârē'*. These words were frequently tacked on as epithets before a god's name, as was also the Hellenistic *kurios*, and they were generally linked with a personal suffix, relating to the worshipper of the god, and occasionally also added as the genitive of a personal pronoun to the Greek *kurios* as a divine name.[3] The personal relationship expressed in this personal suffix or personal pronoun is not found among the Greeks and Romans.[4] This is connected with the

[1] O. Weinreich, *Neue Urkunden zur Sarapis-Religion* (1919).

[2] The content of *Kurios* in the *Corpus Hermeticum* (I, 6, V, 2, XIII, 17, 21) is not so clear as in the rest of the Hermetic literature, in which it is linked with expressions of universality : ὁ τῶν ὅλων κύριος, Κόρη Κόσμου, 25 ; πάντων κύριος, fr. 12, 23, 24, 29, 33 : Lord and creator of all : Ascl. I, 8 : fr. 32 ; . . . Ascl. III, 29b : " summa vero gubernationis summo illi domino paret ", Ascl. III, 19c ; especially Ascl. III, 20a—" deus etenim vel pater vel dominus omnium quocumque [alio] nomine . . . nuncupatur. . . . Non enim spero totius maiestatis effectorem omniumque rerum patrem vel dominum uno posse quamvis e multis conposito nuncupari nomine ". " Deus " and " Pater " are also linked in Ascl. III, 22b, 23b, 26a . . . (Quotations from *Corp. Herm.* ed. W. Scott, 1924.)

[3] ἐκ τῶν τοῦ κυρίου αὐτῶν θεοῦ Ἀμέρου, Hondius, op. cit. vii (1934), 1069, 7 (Arabia). . . . *Louvre Papyri*, 19, 5.

[4] Baudissin, op. cit. iii, p. 556 and n. 1.

general difference between Oriental and Greek religion discussed above. That the correlative to this concept of lord is " slave ", in Greek *doulos*, is shown by some inscriptions (*vide supra*, p. 23, lines 11 ff.) and, for the Semitic sphere, by the frequent use of *'ebhedh* in personal names linked with a god. Now it is not possible to see, in the use of " lord " linked with the god's name, only the *motif* of personal belonging to, and not also the *motif* of personal authority which the worshipper ascribes to his god, and which on his side expresses subjection of the will. Nor is it possible to separate the element of power from that of greatness, as Baudissin once contended.[1] If all Semitic personal names linked with a god which are based upon some other word than " slave " express something of what the god has done, or will do, for the salvation of his worshippers, or else name some characteristic on which is based the certainty or the hope of intervention of the god on behalf of his worshipper,[2] then it is implied that the god has the power to act thus on behalf of his slave. Whether his sphere of power perhaps extends only to what is dependent upon the development of the corporation, or of individual members of it,[3] is here immaterial, though it is also important for N.T. times that the power of the god was always extending and in Palmyra the divine names *mârē' 'âlmā'* and *mâre' khol* are found.[4] And if for orientals too the power of the ruler in earliest times expressed itself not in ruling but in judging,[5] the administration of justice presupposes an authority which will be obeyed, i.e. in

---

[1] Op. cit. p. 631. " The designation of the god as lord expresses man's bowing before a greatness which only permits of humble adoration rather than a power before which he stands helpless."

[2] Op. cit. p. 527. [3] Op. cit. p. 625.
[4] Op. cit. pp. 684 f. [5] Op. cit. pp. 613 ff.

fact some "power". . . .[1] But the linking of a personal suffix with the designation "lord" also indicates that "even in primitive conditions, his (the slave's) relationship to his lord as his property provides also the guarantee of protection against dangers from other people".[2]

In Hebrew *ba'al* denotes more the owner, *'ādhôn* rather the lord as "he who has power".[3] Baethgen formulates it : "the lord in relation to his slave is called *ba'al* in so far as he is the possessor of the slave : he is called *'ādhôn* in so far as he can do what he likes with this possession".[4] Thus the distinction between the words is related to that between δεσπότης and κύριος, and the latter is the counterpart of *'ādhôn*.

Perhaps there is even more evidence in Egyptian for the link between the lordship of the deity over nature, or parts of it, and the spoken expression for it in the concept of the lord. It seems to be the case that the transference of *kurios* to gods because of an indigenous, non-Greek, usage took place independently in Egypt and Syria ; Baudissin's supposition that this use of *kurios* as a divine epithet came from Syria to Egypt, is very improbable.[5] In this he was led astray by the erroneous belief that in Egypt "lord" is "never used for an epithet standing alone or linked with a pronominal suffix",[6] which he bases upon an obviously misunderstood statement of Erman's.[7] In fact the link of *nb* (lord) and (less frequently) *nb.t* ("lady")

[1] Op. cit. p. 620.

[2] Op. cit. p. 526.

[3] Gesenius-Buhl, s.v. *'ādhôn*. G. Dalman, *Der Gottesname Adonaj und seine Geschichte* (1889), pp. 10 f.

[4] F. Baethgen, *Beiträge zur semitischen Religionsgeschichte* (1888), p. 41.

[5] Baudissin, op. cit. ii, pp. 266-9.

[6] Op. cit. p. 266.

[7] Op. cit. p. 267, n. 1.

not only with a genitive, but also with a personal
suffix, is " the normal and continuous usage ". " The
use, with a suffix of the first person, ' my lord ' as a
mode of address, ' o my lord Re ', ' O King, my Lord ',
etc. is naturally of specially frequent occurrence, but
nb (*nb.t*) is also linked with all other suffixes—' thy
lord ', ' his lords ', ' our lord ', ' your lady ', etc." [1]
Thus the use of *kurios*, found in Egypt from the first
century B.C. (*vide supra*, p. 18, line 4 ff.), corresponds
to an old indigenous usage, by the transference of which
into Greek, in accordance with Greek style, the personal suffix came to be omitted.[2]

Thus *kurios* [3] linked with a genitive of the sphere of
lordship and *kurios* added as an epithet to a divine name,
where the personal suffix mostly disappeared in the
transference into Greek, are not, in spite of the obvious
distinction, to be completely separated.

(*d*) *Its meaning when used of rulers.* We have already
seen the earliest examples of *kurios* applied to rulers. We
must leave on one side the phrases κύριος βασιλειῶν and
κύριος τριακονταετηρίδων (see p. 12, *ad fin.*), taken from
Egyptian titles. This is a mode of expression in con-
formity with foreign usage, alien to Greek sensibilities.
The examples cited on pages 18-19 *supra*, for phrases
such as *kurios theos, kurios basileūs, kurios Kaisar* and
theos kai kurios basileūs, etc., ceased at the latest during
the reign of Tiberius (Ditt. Or. 606—ὑπὲρ [τ]η[ς]

[1] Information from H. Grapow.

[2] The use of " lord " without genitive or suffix is indeed " relatively infrequent compared with the huge number of instances at
all times of the use with genitive or suffix ". It is limited to
(*a*) the superior officer, especially in writing letters (where it was
replaced by " my lord " since the Middle Kingdom), (*b*) to the
King (since the Middle Kingdom), (*c*) the gods, quite often,
especially Osiris, since *c.* 500 B.C. On all this see Erman-
Grapow, op. cit.

[3] Especially often of Isis (cf. 1049, l. 19 ff.).

τῶν κυρίων Σε[βαστῶν] σωτηρίας—comes from the time of Augustus or Tiberius). These phrases found in the Orient are translations of indigenous usage, and are paralleled by the fact that the *stratēgos* is similarly named (p. 1048, 36 f.) and *ho theos kai kurios* is also used of priestly superiors.[1] In the Semitic sphere we can instance the formula *'ᵃdhôn mᵉlākhîm* of the Ptolemies.[2]

In the imperial epoch, on the other hand, *kurios* occurs not in solemn and detailed formulations but as a brief summary of the emperor's position in unstressed phrases, especially those giving dates.

The oldest example is *Oxyr. Pap.* I, 37, 5 f. : ζ (ἔτους) Τιβερίου Κλαυδίου Κάισαρος τοῦ κυρίου, also a contemporary *ostrakon*.[3] For Nero, *Oxyr. Pap.* II, 246, provides an interesting example—the smallholder dates his appearance by the year Νέρωνος Κλαυδίου Καίσαρος Σεβαστοῦ Γερμανικοῦ Αὐτοκράτορος and uses the same formula in the attestation of his evidence (ll. 11 f., 24 f.) ; but the three certifying officials date according to the year Νέρωνος τοῦ κυρίου, or Νέρωνος Καίσαρος τοῦ κυρίου (ll. 30, 33, 36). This style of dating begins on *ostraka* with Nero, and grew increasingly predominant.[4] In the longer, official, designations of the emperor, *kurios* by itself appears from the time of

---

[1] B.G.U. 1197, I, 1 (5-4 B.C.) ; 1201, 1, (A.D. 2).

[2] Baethgen, op. cit. p. 41.

[3] Deissmann, *Licht vom Osten*, p. 301.

[4] Deissman, loc. cit. and P. Viereck, *Grieschische . . . Ostraka zu Strassburg*, i (1923), registers, for Nero, 8 times the longer formula, 15 times Νέρων ὁ κύριος ; for Vespasian 3 times only the name, once the longer formula, 8 times Οὐεσπασιανὸς (Καῖσαρ) ὁ κύριος; for Domitian 8 times only the name, 4-5 times Δομιτιανὸς ὁ κύριος ; 3 times Δομιτιανὸς Καῖσαρ ὁ κύριος ; for Nerva, 3 times Νέρουας (ὁ) κύριος; for Trajan, once each Τραιανὸς and Τραιονὸς Ἄριστος, 17 times each Τραιανὸς Καῖσαρ ὁ κύριος and Τραιανὸς ὁ κύριος, once Τραιανος Ἄριστος Καῖσαρ ὁ κύριος.

Nero. (*London Papyri*, 280, 6 . . . cf. Ditt. Syll³ 814, 55.) . . . But the addition of *kurios* to the emperor's full name is more common since the time of Trajan. Then ἡμῶν is increasingly added to κύριος (Ditt. Or. 677, 1 ff., *Giessen Papyri*, 7, 10 ff., 21 f.). This gradual infiltration of *kurios* into the imperial names is independent of the increasing degree to which the emperors assigned, or allowed to be assigned, divine honours to themselves ; after the reigns of Nero and Domitian, which marked a zenith in this connexion, this use of *kurios* does not disappear, nor become less frequent. Although Domitian's " dominus ac deus noster " was eschewed after his death, the short formula with *kurios* and the use of *kurios* as part of the full name do not disappear from the *ostraka*. Thus a steady increase of this use of *kurios* is noticeable from the time of Nero.

Beside this use of the word with the emperor's name, *kurios* is also used absolutely, the earliest example being Acts xxv. 26. . . .[1] The adjective *kuriakos*, meaning imperial, which is common in bureaucratic usage, must also be mentioned.[2]

From the beginning of the imperial epoch, however, the word " dominus " (*kurios*) plays a yet further part. If we are to believe the formulation of Plutarch, Cassius was greeted in Rhodes as βασιλεὺς καὶ κύριος but declined it with the words : οὔτε βασιλεὺς οὔτε κύριος, τοῦ δὲ κυρίου καὶ βασιλέως φονεὺς καὶ κολαστής (cf. *supra*, p. 9, line 13 f.) and Brutus mocks similarly at Caesar, in saying : οἱ δὲ πρόγονοι ἡμῶν οὐδὲ πρᾴους δεσπότας ὑπέμεινον (cf. *supra*, p. 9, line 15 f.). Here an oriental-style monarchy is refused under the name of *kurios* and *despotēs*. Thus Caesar's heir Augustus refused

---

[1] Examples . . . especially from Ditt. Syll³ 880, 8 (Pizos, A.D. 202), *Giessen Papyri*, 3, 12 (Hadrian), 7, 21 f., etc.

[2] Examples in Foerster, op. cit. p. 115, n. 3.

to be called "dominus". Suetonius says :[1] "Domini
appellationem ut maledictum et opprobrium semper
exhorruit. Cum spectante eo ludos pronuntiatum
esset in mino : O dominum aequum et bonum!
et universi quasi de ipso dictum exultantes com-
probassent, et statim manu vultuque indecoras
adulationes repressit et insquenti die gravissimo
corripuit edicto ; dominumque se posthac appellari
ne a liberis quidem aut nepotibus suis vel serio vel
ioco passus est, atque eius modi blanditias etiam inter
ipsos prohibuit." Similar is the attitude of Tiberius,
of whom Dio Cassius (57, 8, 2) has passed down the
saying : δεσπότης μὲν τῶν δούλων, αὐτοκράτωρ δὲ τῶν
στρατιωτῶν, τῶν δὲ δὴ λοιπῶν πρόκριτός εἰμι. In these passages "lord" is a very definite concept of an absolute
position of a monarch, which also has a legally intelligible aspect.

The special factor in the Roman imperial epoch,
however, is that, under a concealing constitutional
mantle, what resulted was an absolute monarchy, for
the protagonists of which the Orient has always
used the expression "lord". The scene reported by
Suetonius under Augustus has already shown how
strongly the word for this was already in the air at
Rome. The exposition given above of the emergence of the word *kurios* as a brief expression for the
emperor shows how, despite the official repulse of it
on the part of most emperors, the word "lord"
nevertheless established itself slowly but surely, but
shows at the same time that in these phrases it was not
spoken in "high tones". With emperor-worship the
noun *kurios*, like the adjective *kuriakos*, has, in the
first instance, nothing in common. There is no text
in which *kurios* applied to a Roman emperor denotes
by itself that the emperor is god. The imperial priest

[1] *Augustus*, 53.

is practically never called *hiereūs tou kuriou*.[1] So too
with the formula for the oath to the emperor,[2] with
coin inscriptions and acclamations.[3] On the private
house-altars of Hadrian in Miletus, which apparently
stood once " in every citizen's-house in Miletus ",
kurios is not found.[4] *Kurios* applied to the emperor
has nothing to do with the divine predicate discussed
above.

The difficulty lies in another sphere. Though the
emperor is not *kurios* as god, he can yet, as *kurios*, be
god. In the epigram to Augustus—

Καίσαρι ποντομέδοντι καὶ ἀπείρων κρατέοντι
Ζανί, τῷ ἐκ Ζανὸς πατρός, Ἐλευθερίῳ
δεσπότᾳ Εὐρώπας τε καὶ Ἀσίδος, ἄστρῳ ἁπάσας
Ἐλλάδος, [ὃς] σωτ[ὴ]ρ Ζεὺς ἀν[έ]τ[ει]λ[ε] μέγας

(C.I.G. 4923) all the predicates are equally steeped in
a kind of religious air : as Zeus rules over all, so is
Augustus ποντομέδων and ἀπείρων κρατέων ; and as
Helios shines over all parts of the earth, so is Augustus

---

[1] Foerster, op. cit. p. 103. To the exception named there in
n. 1, Le Bas and Waddington, op. cit. no. 2606 is relevant
(Palmyra A.D. 263).

[2] Foerster, 114 f.

[3] *Kurios* occurs seldom on coins, and apparently not before the
second century A.D. Instances have been collected by B. Pick in
the *Journal International d'Archéologie Numismatique*, i (1898), pp. 451-
63. W. Wruck, *Die syrische Provinzialprägung von Augustus bis Trajan*
(1931), gives no instance of *Kurios*, nor does P. L. Strack, *Untersuchungen zur römischen Reichsprägung des II Jahrhunderts*, vol. i (1931),
vol. ii (1933), gives one for " dominus ".   In Hadrian's second
year appears in Alexandria the coin inscription ΤΡΑΙΑΝΟΣ
ΣΕΒΑΣΤΟΣ ΠΑΤ ΚΥ and in Gallienus' tenth another with,
ΔΕΚΑΕΤΗΡΙΣ ΚΥΡΙΟΥ (J. Vogt, *Die alexandrinischen Münzen*, ii,
pp. 40, 155. Most coins show *kurios* in acclamations, in which
it also occurs in Suetonius' *Domitian*, 13, Dio Cassius 72, 20, 2
(of Commodus), *Oxyr. Pap.* I, 41, 3, 11, 20, 30 (third to fourth
century A.D.).

[4] T. Wiegand, *Milet*, I, 7 (1924), pp. 350 ff., nos. 290-7.

lord over the then known world. Still clearer an
expression of divinity, which is given with the universality of the sphere of lordship, is the inscription of
honour for Nero—ὁ τοῦ παντὸς κόσμου κύριος Νέρων [1]
... and of Antoninus Pius we have : ἐγὼ μὲν τοῦ κόσμου
κύριος, ὁ δὲ νόμος θαλάσσης.[2] The mental atmos-
phere behind this is shown in the homage paid by
Tiridates to Nero : in Naples he greets him as *despotēs*
and expresses *proskunēsis* towards him, in Rome he
solemnly declares : ἐγώ, δέσποτα, Ἀρσάκου μὲν ἔκγονος,
Οὐολογαίσου δὲ καὶ Πακόρου τῶν βασιλέων ἀδελφός, σὸς δὲ
δοῦλός εἰμι. καὶ ἦλθόν τε πρὸς σὲ τὸν ἐμὸν θεόν, προσκυνή-
σων σε ὡς καὶ τὸν Μίθραν, καὶ ἔσομαι τοῦτο ὅ τι ἂν σὺ
ἐπικλώσῃς (decree)· σὺ γάρ μοι καὶ Μοῖρα καὶ Τύχη.[3]
Although *kurios* is not used here, he who is *Moira* and
Tuchē for another man, is his lord.   Tacitus, *Annals* II,
87, clearly shows a link between " dominus " and
divinity in saying of Tiberius : " acerbeque increpuit
eos, qui divinas occupationes ipsumque dominum
dixerant ".   But in one place a " dominus " spoken in
high tone is applied to the emperor, and indeed at his
own instigation : Domitian not only expressed pleasure
at the acclamation in the theatre " domino et dominae
feliciter ",[4] but he let official letters begin with
" dominus et deus noster hoc fieri iubet ".[5]

It may be that Caligula had already anticipated
him in this formula ; [6] about Aurelian we have coins
bearing the inscription " dominus et deus (natus) "—
though from a provincial site.[7]   It is doubtful whether

[1] Ditt. Syll³ 814, 31.

[2] Justinian, *Digest*, 14, 2, 9, Caracalla is ὁ γῆς καὶ θαλάσσης
δεσπότης, I.G. XII, 3, 100.

[3] Dio Cassius 63, 1, 2 ff., especially 63, 2, 4, and 63, 5, 2.

[4] Suetonius, *Domitian*, 13, 1.

[5] Ibid. 13, 2.   [6] . . . Foerster, op. cit. p. 104.

[7] W. Kubitschek in *Numismatische Zeitschrift*, xlviii (New Series
VIII) (1915), pp. 167-78.

in the case of Domitian's formula the Greeks wrote
kurios for " dominus ", and not rather *despotēs*.[1] Statius
and Martial give many instances of " dominus " and
" dominus et deus ".[2] We have a poem of Martial's
in which he disassociates himself from his earlier custom
of calling Domitian " dominus et deus ".[3] The two
titles are not an hendiadys [4] but hang most closely together. It is precisely because " dominus " here
denotes the position of the ruler *vis-à-vis* his subjects [5]
that the bearer of this title also styles himself " deus ".
Neither of the two titles may here be omitted. The
thought which they convey may be evidenced by
Domitian's great predecessor, Caesar, who answered a
soothsayer who announced an unfavourable omen :
" futura laetiora, cum vellet ".[6] It is the same outlook
that is expressed by Tiridates before Nero : " dominus "
pronounced thus binds a man as God binds him, and
if he allows himself to be so bound he must give up his
being bound to God, while he who so binds him must
take the place of divinity or fate.

It is doubtful, however, whether *kurios*, applied to
the emperor, normally had this heightened meaning.
The steady increase of the use of *kurios* described above
can only be explained if it was in general not used
in this sense. Thus Tertullian appropriately distinguishes between " dominus " and " dominus " :
" dicam plane imperatorem dominum, sed more

---

[1] Dio Cassius 67, 4, 7.

[2] F. Sauter, *Der Römische Kaiserkult bei Martial und Statius*,
pp. 31-40.

[3] X. 72—p. 31 in Sauter.

[4] Lietzmann, *Römerbrief*, on X, 9.

[5] Martial X, 72 : " non est hic dominus, sed imperator ",
shows the legal meaning of " dominus " even here, where Martial
disassociates himself from the formula " dominus et deus noster ".
Cf. Sauter, p. 39, *ad fin.*

[6] Suetonius, *Julius Caesar*, 77.

communi, sed quando non cogor, ut dominum dei vice dicam." [1]

It is not surprising that in the *Acta* of Christian martyrs the opposition to the absolutist claims by the Roman state which sweep away the claims of God also appears in the form that the "dominus noster imperator" is contrasted with the "dominus meus, rex regum et imperator omnium gentium ",[2] but the use of "rex" and "imperator" beside "dominus" shows that it was not a question of the title of "lord" but of the religious claim of the state, in rejecting which the Christians had to show their loyalty to God and the State. In contrast to this stood the *sicarii*, who rejected the emperor as such as their overlord, and therefore refused to call him *despotēs*.[3] With the Christian martyrs religion came up against religion, with the *sicarii*—in the light of Matt. xxii. 21—politics against politics. Since they were excused from the duty of joining in emperor-worship, it was not a question of "lord" pronounced in high tones. The content of *kurios* applied to the emperor could vary greatly, according to the context or the inner disposition of the user of the word : in one of the pagan *Acta Martyrum, Oxyr. Pap.* I, 33, the condemned Appian, who calls the Emperor *turannos*, addresses him with a further request as *kurie Kaisar* (III, 1) ; on the other hand, on the lips of Tiridates (*supra*, p. 32, line 8 ff.) the address *despota* expresses the full religious veneration which he then showed and expressed, to Nero. Moreover, the Jews, who rejected the imperial cult, none-the-less consecrated a synagogue ὑπὲρ σωτηρίας τῶν κυρίων ἡμῶν Καισάρων Αὐτοκρατόρων Λ. Σεπτιμίου Σεουήρου Εὐσεβοῦς

---

[1] *Apologeticus*, 34.
[2] *Akten der scilitanischen Märtyrer*, ed. R. Knopf, *Ausgewählte Märtyrerakten* (1913), p. 33.
[3] Josephus, B.J. II, 188 : VII, 418.

Περτίνακος Σεβαστοῦ κτλ.[1] This shows incidentally, how empty the word Σεβαστός, which originally expressed the religious worth of the emperor, had become even by A.D. 197, but it shows especially that the Jews did not hesitate to address their rulers as οἱ κύριοι ἡμῶν.

[1] R. Cagnat, *Inscriptiones graecae ad res Romanas pertinentes III* (1906), 1106.

III. THE OLD TESTAMENT NAME FOR GOD

1. *The name for God in the LXX*

In the LXX the word κύριος, meaning God, is only an actual translation where it reproduces 'ādhôn or (in the K^ethîbh) '^adhônāi. As a rule it occurs as a clear periphrasis for the divine name Yahweh, roughly expressing what in the basic passage means the name or the use of the name. That this cannot be completely carried through is obvious from the changing over from the name to the general concept, and from the fact that in the Bible itself, as in ordinary conversation, κύριος is by no means confined to being a designation for God. It corresponds rather to the Hebrew 'ādhôn, used just as much of men, e.g. in the respectful term of address '^adhônî (in the plural '^adhônāi—Gen. xix. 2) which occurs 192 times, as of God. It is also used regularly (15 times) to translate ba'al when it occurs in its non-religious meaning of " owner ".[1] The same is true of g^ebhîr " master " (Gen. xxvii. 29, 37) and of the Aramaic mârē' (used also of God) in Dan. ii. 47, iv. 16, 21, v. 23, and shallît " ruler " (Dan. iv. 14). On the other hand, where ba'al means a heathen divinity, the LXX treats the word either as a proper name (ὁ or ἡ) βάαλ, or interprets it by εἴδωλον (Jer. ix. 13 ; II Chron. xvii. 3, xxviii. 2) or αἰσχύνη (I Kings xviii. 19, 25). Thus in the sphere of religion the designation κύριος or ὁ κύριος is confined to the true God and so corresponds (except for unimportant periphrases in metaphorical language) almost

[1] Cf. Gen. xlix. 23 ; Exod. xxi and xxii (11 times), Judges xix. 22 f. ; Isa. i. 3 ; Job. xxxi. 39.

regularly—to be precise, 6,156 times—to the divine name *YHWH* in all its punctuations, and when followed by *ṣᵉbhā'ôth*, or shortened to *yāh*. Only by way of exception are the Hebrew terms for God translated as κύριος —'*ēl* 60 times, '*ᵉlôah* 23 times, '*ᵉlôhîm* 193 times, '*ᵉlôhê ṣᵉbhā'ôth* 3 times. The phrases κύριος θεός, κύριος ὁ θεός and ὁ κύριος θεός mostly indicate a masoretic *YHWH* with or without the apposition '*ᵉlôhîm*. Only in Jer. xv. 11 (in the vocative) is *YHWH* translated by δεσπότης ; otherwise δέσποτα κύριε occasionally reproduces '*ᵃdhônāi YHWH* (Gen. xv. 2 (Swete) and 8 ; Jer. i. 6, iv, 10), which is otherwise usually translated by κύριος κύριος.

The presence or absence of the article before κύριος seems not to be without significance for the understanding of the meaning of the Greek, however arbitrary the scribes must be admitted to have been. For, being a free periphrasis for *YHWH*, κύριος ought in some sense to be a pointer to the basic word, and the use of the article should be a good means of telling whether or not it denotes the singular nature of the name. Unfortunately the tradition gives us no clear picture in this respect, but as the use of the article with θεός in the LXX betrays a certain amount of method,[1] it may be supposed that the same is true of κύριος, at least in the case of some of the translators. At any rate κύριος without the article preserves the character of the Hebrew basic word as a proper name more clearly than the form ὁ κύριος which, like εὐεργέτης or σωτήρ, merely denotes a title.

The consensus of the translators in using this title

---

[1] Baudissin, op. cit. i, p. 441 f. As a general rule κύριος without the article is only used as a designation for God, and occurs more often in the nominative than in the other cases, where the article may be thought of as being due to a Hebrew *lᵉ* or '*ēth*. Cf. Baudissin, op. cit. i, pp. 17 ff.

" lord " or " the lord " for *YHWH* is not completely
explained by the supposition that they used some
uniform prototype. Especially is this so if one supposes that this prototype in the *Qᵉrê* was *'ᵃdhônāi*,
which is common in the final masoretic edition of the
Bible text. One would then have to suppose that
there was an early form of this tradition spread abroad
long before the Christian era in the transcriptions
written in Greek—ἀντιγραφαί as Origen probably
called them—in which ἀδωναι was substituted for
the divine name.[1] But the uncertainty of this hypothesis leaves scope for the other no less uncertain
supposition that the Greek translators, from the
knowledge of the being of the Old Testament God
which was common in Hellenistic Judaism, in free
creativeness and making use of the existing usage of
κύριος as a divine epithet, used κύριος as a periphrasis for the name of God. In any case there is
good reason to suppose that *'ᵃdhônāi* as *Qᵉrê* first came
into use as a result of the Greek text, and even as
Kᵉthîbh seems to have infiltrated relatively late into
the Bible text, so that it can only be regarded with
reserve, especially in the prophetic books, as being the
actual expression of the writers.[2]

Thus the rights and wrongs of the use of κύριος as
the Old Testament name for God will not so much be
made clear from the use of *'ādhôn* or *'ᵃdhônāi* as from an
examination of the reason for and essence of the use of
the name *YHWH* in the basic text.

[1] So F. Wutz, *Die transkriptionen von der LXX bis zu Hieronymus*,
pp. 145 f.
[2] This is the result of the extensive researches of Baudissin,
Kyrios, especially vol. ii, p. 305. He infers from the form δέσποτα
κύριε for the masoretic *'ᵃdhônāi YHWH* that the translator
knew neither the masoretic pronunciation *'ᵃdhônai 'ᵉlôhîm* nor
'ᵃdhônāi for the simple *YHWH* (vol. i, p. 523).

2. " Lord " as a designation for Yahweh

The periphrasis " Lord " has undeniably been of as great significance in the history of the Bible and the effect of its message as has the use of the sacred name in the basic passage. Its function has not been completely identical with that, but has overlapped to such an extent that the content of the texts, equally directed towards the fundamental aim of the recognition of divine power, can speak with a telling effect.

'ᵃdhônāi and 'ādhôn differ in that the former (distinguished by the afformative) is reserved for sacred use whereas the simpler 'ādhôn can also be used of human leadership. 'ādhôn is used in the O.T. as the commonest expression for the possessor of power over men (Ps. xii. 5 : of the King, Jeremiah xxii. 18, xxxiv. 5,[1] less frequently over things (Gen. xlv. 8 ; Ps. cv. 21 bayith—which includes men). It is closely linked to ba'al, " possessor ", the stress being significantly less on the legal than on the emotional aspects, as may be inferred from the mode of address 'ᵃdhônî—" my lord "—which is also preferred to ba'al in legally defined relationships of allegiance.[2] It is the term used by the slave to his owner (e.g. Gen. xxiv. 12 ; Exod. xxi. 5) or by the wife to her lord (e.g. Gen. xviii. 12). But it is also usual in the language of the court ('ᵃdhônî hammelekh, e.g. I Sam. xxvi. 17) of adoration (e.g. Num. xi. 28 ; Gen. xxxi. 35) and of common politeness as enjoined by custom (Gen. xxiii. 6 ; Judges iv. 18).

A peculiarity occurs in the secular use of the word in that it often assumes plural forms and suffixes where

---

[1] The cry Hôy 'ādhôn has a formal analogy in the Phoenician Adonis-lament αἴαι Ἄδωνιν, cf. W. W. Count Baudissin, Adonis and Esmun (1911), p. 91.

[2] Ba'ᵃlî occurs only in Hos. ii. 18.

it is not referring to a plurality of persons.[1]   Since the
same happens with *ba'al* (e.g. Joshua i. 3) one might
look for the solution in the need for the raising of the
expression to the all embracing level of the conception.[2]
The only difficulty here is the lengthening of the " a "
in *'ᵃdhônāi*, which shows itself to be not due to the pause
and can therefore only be a specially chosen characteristic of the word in its function of giving a name, and
epithet, to God.   The conjecture that this is not an
afformative, as the Masoretic text describes it, but a
part of the root, and that the word is borrowed from
some non-semitic language,[3] considerably exaggerates
the philological value of the Masoretic text, while
Punic texts show clearly the pronominal nature of the
suffix.[4]   On the other hand, *'ᵃdhônāi* also occurs in
we-texts (e.g. Ps. xliv. 24) so that the interpretation of
it as possessive—" my Lord "—in the Bible texts is
not always tenable without presupposing a formal
petrification of an originally intended vocative to a
nominative.[5]   Granted this presupposition, it may be
assumed, without denying the philological possibility
mentioned above, that *'ᵃdhônāi* as a designation for
God is derived from a private prayer-form, as is in fact

[1] Typical is *'ᵃdhônîm qāsheh*—" an austere master ", Isa.
xix, 4.

[2] Gesenius-Kautsch, *Hebräische Grammatik* (1909), § 124, i.

[3] H. Bauer and P. Leander, *Historische Grammatik der Hebr.
Sprache*, i (1922), § 2, h, 29, t.   *'ādhôn* would then be a " secondary
singular ", § 61, i, a (p. 469).   The word is not in all semitic
languages, but only found among Israelites and Phoenicians—
that too suggests borrowing.

[4] Cf. e.g. *'ᵃdhônî Ba'alshāmēm* (Umm-el-'Awâmîd, *Corpus
Inscriptionum Semiticarum*, ed. E. Renan I, 1 (1881), 7, l. 7 ;
M. Lidzbarski, *Altsemitische Texte*, i (1907), p. 22).   Further
material in Baudissin, *Adonis and Esmun*, p. 66.

[5] For the transition of the vocative into other cases, Baudissin
in *Kyrios*, ii, pp. 35 ff. compares *rabbî* as title, the Syriac *mârî*,
also the Accadian *belti*.

often to be found in the Masoretic text.[1] The lengthening of the " a " must be due to the Masoretes' desire
to mark the word as sacred by this small change.
The fact that they were probably also keen on the
circumstance that *'adhônāi* has four Hebrew letters
corresponding to the tetragram,[2] perhaps explains why
the " my-form " established itself instead of the " our-
form " *'adhônênû* found in Ps. viii. 2, 10, cxlvii. 5,
cxxxv. 5, etc.[3]

When used of Yahweh, *'ādhôn*, like *melekh*, connotes
His sovereign power. It is a title which corresponds
to His being, only seldom does it point to His position
as Lord of a district—as probably in the appositional
linking of the words " The Lord Yahweh " in Exod.
xxiii. 17, xxxiv. 23,[4] where the theme is harvest festivals. As *'abhîr Yiśrā'ēl*, " the strength of Israel " (cf.
Gen. xlix. 24) he is called *'ādhôn* in Isa. i. 24. From
this it may be inferred that Isaiah in other passages
too [5] may only use the word in this sense, if it really
does belong to his own vocabulary at all.[6] But in
general the O.T. texts about Yahweh as *'ādhôn* have
already passed beyond the conception of Yahweh as
Lord of the land and people, and more or less clearly
presuppose the prophetic faith in Yahweh as lord of
all. The form " Lord of the whole earth " (Mic. iv.

---

[1] The list in Baudissin, *Kyrios*, p. 60, shows 55 cases, with 31
'adhônāi yahweh.

[2] Cf. A. Geiger, *Urschrift und Übersetzungen der Bibel* (2nd edn.
1928), p. 262.

[3] Baudissin, op. cit. ii, p. 27, considers *'adhônênû* as derived from
'adhônāi.

[4] Cf. Buber, op. cit. p. 124.

[5] The full-sounding phrase *Hā 'ādhôn Yahweh ṣ ebhā'ôth* is confined to the Book of Isaiah, occurring twice in the audition-
formula (i. 24, xix. 4) 3 times in free introductions of woes.

[6] The tradition is not clear ; cf. *Biblia Hebraica*, ed. R. Kittel
(3rd edn. 1929) on the passages cited in the previous note.

13 ; Zech. iv. 14, vi. 5 ; Ps. xcvii. 5 ; Joshua iii. 11 and 13) shows most clearly how the meaning has risen to be comprehensive. Thus this will also be the meaning when 'ādhôn stands in isolation (only Ps. cxiv. 7),[1] and there can be no question about the " total " meaning for the lengthened form 'adhônāi as well.

The questionability of the Kᵉthîbh 'adhônāi has already been recalled, page 38 above. But the fact is that this Kᵉthîbh, even where it can be considered the foundation of the text, as in Isa. vi, in the main does its best, like the Qᵉrê derived from it, to avoid mentioning the name of God. In Isa. vi. 11, the prophet uses the vocative 'ᵃdhônāi spontaneously under the undiminished impression of the nearness of God's majesty, and one might ask whether 'ᵃdhônî was not used there. But the desire to avoid mentioning the name, since man is confronted by the majesty that " fills the whole earth " is as clear in that passage as almost anywhere. On the other hand, the use of 'ᵃdhônāi at the beginning of Isa. vi. 1 and 8,[2] suggests that here there is an exemplary desire to instil into the reader the thoughts expressed in the seraphim-hymn by a choice of words to match the prophet's reverence. That is also probably the significance of the phrase so frequent in Ezekiel, 'ᵃdhônāi Yahweh or Yahweh 'ᵃdhônāi (212 times according to Baudissin) : it serves to some extent as an elucidation of the name as an expression for the divine majesty, and the transition of the stress from name to title is undeniable. Thus the Kᵉthîbh's use of 'adhônāi seems to have inaugurated a development of the technique of the tradition which finally resulted in the Qᵉrê's complete exclusion of the divine

[1] Hā 'ādhôn in Mal. III, 1 can also, despite Baudissin's hesitations (Kyrios, vol. ii, p. 305) be interpreted thus.

[2] The Biblia Hebraica note on this passage says that c. 100 MSS. read Yahweh!

name from the text. Such desires were probably strongly fostered by the use of the courtesy title " my lords " in the story of Sodom (Gen. xviii-xix), so significantly valued by the Masoretes,[1] for the visitors to Abraham and Lot, among whom (as the reader gathers from the context) was " the judge of the whole earth " (xviii. 25) who had " come down " (xviii. 21).

The substitution of '^{a}dhônāi, cautiously adopted by the K^{e}thibh, and carried through by the Q^{e}rê to the complete exclusion of the pronunciation of the divine name, gives us nothing less than a summary exegesis of the entire Holy Scripture of Israel. Together with the LXX's use of κύριος it betokens an act of unlimited significance in the history of religion. The considerations which prepared the way for it and led to its adoption cannot be reconstructed with a high degree of certainty (vide infra, p. 59, line 5 ff.). Not even does the question touched upon above (vide infra, p. 72, ad fin.), whether the LXX or its precursors gave the first impulse, admit of a satisfactory answer. A definite missionary impulse is unlikely to be the reason, at any rate the chief one, since the active missionary epoch of Judaism had not yet dawned when the LXX was finished, and was already over when the last Masoretes set their seal to the Q^{e}rê. But the missionary activity has left many traces in the text of the LXX.

An enormous missionary power lies in the last verses of Ps. cxxxiv (Heb. and Eng. cxxxv), when, after the House of Israel, Aaron and Levi, the φοβούμενοι τὸν κύριον, are also called upon to praise the Lord of all. It stands beyond all doubt that this expansion

---

[1] The words addressed to the three (xviii. 3) are pointed as a designation of God, because God must be one of them. The two other men are greeted by Lot in secular style (xix. 2). In the end the mythical motif of the three men fades away, and it is a question of Yahweh alone (xix. 18).

of the terminology used for expressing God, theologically due to the prophets, played a most important
part in the spreading of the O.T. message.   If it signified a relaxation of its historical ties, it was no
severance of them.   If it diminished its numinous
power over Israel, it surrendered to a decisive point
the national character of the canon, and thereby interpreted its deepest meaning.   The God to whom the
canon bears witness is called " Lord " because He is
there shown to be the sole exerciser of power over the
universe and all mankind, as the creator of the world
and disposer of life and death.   Thus the term
" Lord " conveys a summary of the faith of the O.T.
It is the completely successful attempt to express what
God is, what is the practical significance for mankind
of the holy, i.e. the advent of a personal will, and to
express this with almost the same pregnancy and
inevitability as is demanded by the special characteristics of the term *Yahweh*.

3. *The name Yahweh as a concept of experience*

The O.T. faith in God is grounded in historical
experience and developed in continuous contact with
history.   The clearest expression of this fact is the use
of the name Yahweh in speaking of, and calling upon,
God.   This name, like every name for God, is a
concept of experience and as such, through its concrete
and individual content, differs in degree from general
concepts verging upon the abstract such as '*ēl*, '*elôah*,
and '*elôhîm*, and from the designation of honour '*ādhôn*.
It denotes not just any divinity, but a definite, unambiguous, divine person.   It fills the terms " God "
and " Lord " with so strongly numinous a content,
that the final result is that it completely overshadows
their general meaning, so that " God " is no longer an
appellation of multifarious application and " Lord "

comes to mean " the Lord of all ". It follows that the
general concepts, although infrequent in the canon,
can often be used as synonyms for Yahweh, and
'ᵃdhônāi itself replaces them. They have absorbed the
significance of the personal name, they have become
experimental concepts of unambiguous form. Thus
the understanding of the translators must orientate
upon such sentences as " the Lord is God " (I Kings
xviii. 39 ; cf. Joshua xxiv. 15) or " the Lord is His
name " (Exod. xv. 3) if the clear direction of the Bible
terminology towards the person of Yahweh is to be
faithfully retained. For the basic text does not say
that " God " or " Lord " is a name, but in the naming
any other word than Yahweh is expressly excluded.
" Yahweh is His name ", or " Yahweh of hosts
(Yahweh ṣᵉbhā'ôth) is His name "—these are phrases
common in hymnody.[1] They ensure first and foremost that the personal designation of God, with a vivid
consciousness of its extent, has been directed to a very
definite experience of the divine. God thus named is
for His confessors as for others a figure strongly defined,
the numen praesens in person. " To call Yahweh by
name " (qārā' bᵉshēm Yahweh, e.g. Isa. lxv 1) means to
owe allegiance to, and hold oneself ready to encounter,
this figure.[2] Only he who " knows Him not ", as the
heathen, (Ps. lxxix. 6 ; Jer. x. 25) can achieve nothing
with the name of Yahweh, which is the addressible
" Thou " of the man of prayer,[3] symbol of all the

[1] Cf. the complete indication of the passages concerned in Grether,
op. cit. p. 55. On their meaning see Buber-Rosenzweig, op. cit. p. 335.
[2] For the " de-magicing " of the phrase, cf. Grether, op. cit.
pp. 21-2.
[3] This may be the meaning of the almost untranslatable word
wᵉ'attāh-hû' in Ps. cii. 28, a stammer of " Thou art He " with the
accent entirely on " Thou ". hû' only fills up the tone as in
'ᵃnî-hû', Isa. xli. 4, etc., cf. Job iii. 19. It follows that all these
passages are of no relevance to the derivation of the word Yahweh.

power and will of God. In the language of doctrine this may also be expressed by saying "*shēm* is always the name of God as He is revealed ".[1]

Thus wherever this proper name for God occurs in the texts, it creates quite independently of its meaning, but as a result solely of its nature as a concept of experience, an indissoluble link between religion and history, the history in which the use of this name originated and developed in the fashion indicated above. The name Yahweh, no matter if and when it was used before (*vide infra*, p. 50) was the framework of revelation in the religious foundation of Moses and points back implicitly to this historical confrontation of God and man and all that resulted therefrom. It is as unspiritual as the one designation for God well can be, and it provides practically no opportunities for speculation about the divine, but it recalls [2] silently and permanently a vitalising proclamation of God which was known to have happened in the early age of the people of Israel, and reminds us of encounters in the lives of prophetic men who were called to declare, as Yahweh's mouthpieces, in full authority, " Thus has Yahweh spoken ". The use of the name makes visible the essential and ineradicable features of the picture of God which is painted by the biblical tradition in the portrayal of the inner history of the people of God and the spiritual moulding of its religious leaders up to the inevitable showing forth of divine reality. The deeply-felt pathos, the searing honesty of O.T. piety, is rooted in the message about Yahweh, in whose clearly defined divine personality, in whose insistent will man finds a norm and criterion for life and the

[1] Grether, op. cit. p. 18 ; cf. pp. 159 ff.
[2] Cf. the synonym *zēkher* for *shēm*, e.g. Exod. iii. 15 and the cultic phrase " to bring the name into remembrance " (Exod. xxiii. 13).

world, now cowering in a feeling of creaturely dependence before the Holy, now satiated with rapt gazing at
the figure (Ps. xvii. 15) in whom all salvation lies guaranteed. " The fact that in Yahweh the features of
the personality are so incomparably great is of the
essence of his value and his superiority over all the
gods of the peoples." [1]

4. *The Foundation of Moses*

The religion of the O.T. as the cult of Yahweh is a
founded religion. Moses' proclamation of the divine
name did not mean only " a yahwistic reform of
Canaanite animism " [2] but a new beginning of religious
life to which no theories of evolution or balancing out
can do justice. True, both ancient and modern
traditions include full reports of a history of faith in
Yahweh in the pre-Mosaic generations of the patriarch.
The migration of Abraham from Mesopotamia to
Canaan was undertaken out of obedience to Yahweh,
and the rejection of the service of other gods (Joshua
xxiv. 2 f. ; Gen. xii. 8, xxxv. 2 ; Judith v. 5-7). The
kernel of these traditions—the significance of which
for salvation appears with especial impressiveness in
Gen. xii. 1 ff.—must be confined to the message that
religious movements played a certain, though perhaps
not decisive part in the obscure incidents in the pre-
history of the tribes of Israel. [3] The account of the J
source, which, unlike E and P, assumes that in the
very earliest age of man the name of Yahweh was used

[1] R. Otto, *Das Gefühl des Überweltlichen* (1932), p. 269.
[2] G. Van der Leeuw, *Phänomenologie der Religion* (1933), p. 581.
For the concept " founder ", *vide* pp. 618 ff. The functions of
witness, prophet, teacher, even theologian, are comprised in the
biblical tradition about Moses, of which the legendary extent
vouches for his position as acknowledged founder.
[3] Cf. R. Kittel, *Geschichte des Volkes Israel*, i (1923), pp. 289 f.

(as a result of some primitive revelation) for calling
upon God (Gen. iv. 26) cannot, in view of the lack of
precise statements such as Hos. xii. 10 (" I am Yahweh,
thy God from the land of Egypt "; cf. xiii. 4) or Exod.
vi. 3 (" By my name Yahweh, am I not known to
them ", P), seriously question the historical value of
the tradition of the founding of the worship of Yahweh
by Moses.   The attempt to fit the name of Yahweh,
and especially the observation taught in Gen. iv. 26,
into pre-history as evidence of an innate conception of
the creator and Lord of the world is, from an historical
standpoint, no more than a faint echo of the scarcely
comprehensible fact that the divine name already
existed, and had some prehistoric location somewhere
before Moses introduced it to the children of Israel
(*vide infra*, pp. 50, *ad fin.* ff.).

It was in the age of Moses that the worship of
Yahweh enters the sphere of history—if it was not then
that it first came to life itself.   Then first, at any rate,
it begins to have visible effects as the religion of a
nationally conscious federation of the tribes of Israel,[1]
as the cause of political actions and the sovereign norm
of the pattern of life.   The history of the foundation,
it is true, is itself shrouded in a saga, not completely
free of legendary elements, about a theophany vouch-
safed to Moses.   As a result of the revelation received,
Moses became the founder of the loyalty, sworn in the
Covenant, of a league of Israelite clans, to the commanding and protecting God Yahweh.   The religious
inheritance of these tribes—which previously seems to
have embraced a manifold variety of divine beings,[2]

---

[1] The name Israel, which occurs as early as 1223 B.C. on a
stēlē of Merneptah, does not presuppose the worship of Yahweh,
but aptly indicates its basic impulse if the most likely derivation,
" God fights, or strives ", is correct.   Cf. W. Caspari, *Zeitschrift
für Semitistik*, iii (1924), pp. 194 ff.

[2] Cf. A. Alt, *Der Gott der Väter* (1929), pp. 3 ff.

each with his own *hieros logos*—was from now on strongly directed towards the concretely-formed reality perceived by Moses. As a result, a previously unknown outlook now dominated all the utterances of the " people of Yahweh " (Judges v. 11) the trust in the guiding will and power of the God who was subject to no natural limitations, who in the most critical moment of the exodus of Moses' troop out of Egypt had revealed His transcendent majesty as He hurled horse and rider into the sea (Exod. xv. 21).[1] It is from the time of Moses that the tradition of a common worship of Yahweh can be dated.[2] The tribes leave Egypt, to honour Him in a festival in the wilderness (Exod. iii. 12 (E), iv. 23 (J), etc.). To this epoch, moreover, belongs the first appearance of God-linked personal names which indicate allegiance to Yahweh : *Yᵉhôshûaʿ* [Joshua] is probably the earliest—if one regards *Yôkhebhedh* [Jochebed], the name of Moses' mother (Exod. vi. 20 (P)) as not derived from Yahweh or as not authentic.[3] Now, too, the " Wars of

---

[1] O. Eissfeldt, *Baal Zephon* . . . (1932), pp. 66 ff. cautiously discusses the possibility that the help experienced was ascribed at first to the " God of this district ", later to Yahweh. This hypothesis is only possible under gross misunderstanding of the circumstances of Exod. xv. The hymn about the sea centres on what was a decisive turning point for the whole future of Israel and was reckoned as the rock bottom of her hymnody ; cf. A. Weiser, *Glaube und Geschichte im A.T.* (1931), pp. 3 f. A transposed legend could not attain such significance. It presupposes, moreover, that the revelation of Yahweh came after the Exodus for which there is no evidence.

[2] This has given rise to the thesis that the community-form of the Yahweh-tribes is analogous to the Amphictyonic League in ancient Greece. Cf. A. Alt., R.G.G.², III, 438 f.

[3] The name is missing in Exod. ii. 1, where it ought to occur. Probably it was taken from some other context by P and given to Moses' mother. But cf. M. Noth, *Die israelitischen Personennamen* (1928), p. 111, and H. Bauer, *Z.A.W.*, N.S. x (1933), pp. 92 f.

Yahweh " begin (Num. xxi. 14 ; I Sam. xviii. 17) wars
which groups forming the backbone of the convenant-
league prosecuted in offensives, not always successful,
against Canaanite communities. " Arise O Yahweh,
that their enemies may scatter and they that hate thee
flee before thee " (Num. x. 35) ; so runs the battle
cry, when Yahweh's emblem [1] is carried before, presumably the holy shrine as symbol of the presence of
the God worshipped. Victory is Yahweh's, defeat
means Yahweh's wrath. " Who among the Gods is
like unto thee, Yahweh? Thou art praised as the
fearful one that doeth wonders ! " (Exod. xv. 11.)
With the acceptance of the name of Yahweh began
the religion of Israel as a warlike and exclusive
allegiance to the God who guided, as an active
submission to His will (cf. also Joshua xxiv. 16 ff.).

5. *The provenance of the Divine Name*

Whence came the name of this powerful God?
The tradition in Exodus iii answers " From God's
own mouth "—and thereby shows the ambiguity of
the procedure when the divine expresses itself in the
form of human speech. But was this form merely
created by the founder of the religion, or did he adopt
it from some tradition? No one can answer these
questions with certainty. If the answer to the first is
in the negative, then some sort of probability must be
established in reply to the second ; but that has not
yet been convincingly achieved.

The possibility of a Yahweh outside and before
Israel, which had been raised by a certain discovery

---

[1] This is found as late as Exod. xvii. 15, Yahweh's *nissî* ; but
perhaps the reference is to a throne ; cf. *kesyāh* as *Kethîbh* in
verse 16.

among Accadian personal names [1] and attracted much attention, has been raised again by texts from Ras Shamra,[2] a Syrian coastal resort which certainly goes back to a date before Moses (1500-1200 B.C.). The circumstance that a divinity *yaw* occurs there, whose name bears an undeniable affinity to the form of *Yahweh* common in proper names, which is also found independently in inscriptions, is scarcely to be explained by the theory that it is a question of philological coincidence,[3] although there is some superficial probability that this may be so. Conjecture could also turn towards Egyptian religion, especially to Amun Re' the "King of the Gods" who resided in Thebes,[4] if it were worth while to trace a religious tradition which might conceivably have bequeathed some inheritance to the Yahweh-tradition or could explain the origin of the name. But such conjectures lead to no settled conclusions.[5]

[1] Cf. the collection of material in J. Hehn, *Die biblische und die babylonische Gottesidee* (1913), pp. 230 ff. ; G. R. Driver, "The Original Form of the Name Yahweh" (*Z.A.W.*, 1928, pp. 7 ff.). Well-attested identity of divine elements in names compounded with Yahweh is rare, and does not as yet extend back beyond the era of the prophets. For the specially suggestive name *Ya'u-bi'di*, see Noth, op. cit. p. 110. [See also J. W. Jack, "The Ras Shamra Tablets", O. T. Studies No. I (1935).]

[2] Cf. O. Eissfeldt, *Zeitschrift der deutschen Morgenländischen Gesellschaft* (1934), pp. 173 ff. ; R. Dussaud, *Les Textes de Ras Shamra et l'Ancien Testament* (1937).   [3] See Bauer, op. cit. pp. 92 ff.

[4] K. Sethe, *Amun und die acht Urgötter von Hermopolis* (*Abhandlungen*, Berlin Academy, 1929, no. 4), bases his conjecture of an Egyptian precursor of the conception of Yahweh upon passages which connect Yahweh with *rûaḥ* (pp. 119 f.) to which he assigns the very name of Yahweh (see n. 3, p. 56 *infra*). But these passages would have to be more strongly emphasised in the proclamation of Yahweh and to be assignable to an earlier date, to make the idea of Amun's being a precursor acceptable.

[5] There is a collection of further hypotheses, some of them fantastic, in A. Schleiff, *Zeitschrift der deutschen Morgenländischen Gesellschaft* (1936), pp. 683 ff.

The same is true of the so-called " Kenite-hypo-
thesis " [1] which has achieved a certain importance as
the relatively most concrete filling of the vacuum.
Based upon the account of the marriage of Moses with
the daughter of Jethro, the priest of the Midianites
(Exod. iii. 1—another name is found in ii. 18), and
his assistance with the organisation of government
among the tribes of Israel (Exod. xviii. 1 ff.), it supposes that Yahweh was the God of the nomadic tribe
of the Kenites, to which, according to Judges i. 16
(cf. also iv. 11) Moses was bound by oath. This thesis
draws a certain amount of support from the traditions
connecting Yahweh with the mountain of Sinai (J)
or Horeb (E). To it was led the host of Moses,
migrating out of Egypt (Exod. xix. 3 f.), there is His
temenos, His " holy ground " (Exod. iii. 5, J). From
there He sets forth with the people for the struggle for
Canaan (*bā' missînai*, Deut. xxxiii. 2). Less precisely
it is stated in the Song of Deborah (Judges v. 4) that
Yahweh went out from Seir, and marched from the
field of Edom [2] to wage war. These texts speak of
Yahweh as domiciled in the territories bordering upon
Canaan to the South—of Elijah too it is reported that
he sought and found the presence of Yahweh on Horeb
(I Kings xix. 8 ff.). Thus if Yahweh had really been
a god of the nomads bivouacking in the open country,
then the history of His name would turn up out of the
prehistoric past of those tribes. [3]

But to speak with enough certainty to lead to definite

[1] First put forward in detail by B. Stade, *Z.A.W.*, xiv (1894),
pp. 250 ff., later expressed with great confidence by H. Schmökel,
" Jahveh und die Keniter ", *Journal of Biblical Literature*, lii (1933),
pp. 212 ff.

[2] Note the harmonising gloss in verse 5 : " That is Sinai ".

[3] A. Alt, *Der Gott der Väter* (1929), p. 6, n. 2, refers to *'ahiyyû* in
Nabatean names in the third century.

conclusions is in every respect denied, and to fill up the gaps with conjectures about Moses' personal contribution to the form of the divine name [1] is completely useless. All we can cling on to is the possibility that the god Yahweh was an object of worship tied to some locality, like many others, so that the foundation by Moses also signified a reformation in the sense that it filled a very old form of epiklesis with new content.

6. *The form and meaning of the name Yahweh*

In these circumstances it would be of great importance to know the original meaning of the name Yahweh, since from that, even though it should not have been always present to the minds of those who spoke and heard it, one could probably arrive at important conclusions about the root and original colour of the view of god entailed in the name. But there are difficulties in the tradition with regard to the mere form of the name which prevent us, or rather ought to prevent us, from reading the word in its full tonal form without the occurrence of objections.

(a) There is not even an unambiguous tradition for the make-up of the consonants. The so-called tetragram YHWH, occurring 5,321 times in the O.T., alternates with the digram YH, which occurs 25 times, and the relationship between the short form and the long form is not clear (*vide infra*, p. 57, *ad fin.*). The Elephantine Papyri write YHW, for which— presumably in error—YHH is also found. YHW [2] which also appears epigraphically, occurs in alternation with YW at the beginning of proper names, cf.

---

[1] Cf. Schleiff, op. cit. p. 696.
[2] [The Hebrew consonant W is also used as the vowel Ô or Û.]

Yᵉhôyāqîm, Yô'ēl, etc., at the end of names it alternates
with YH, cf. *'ēliyyāhû, yᵉsha'yāh*, etc.   It is not possible
to be certain which of these forms is the original.
The earliest known is *YHWH*, which appears on the
ninth century *stēlē* of King Mesha of Moab in old
semitic script, which completely excludes the doubt
which so easily arises in the square script about such
ambiguous letters as *YW* and *H*.[1]

This combination of consonants admits neither of a
fixed reading nor of an unambiguous interpretation,
since even in the Masoretic text the vowels added to
the tetragram vary and in any case show themselves to
be a foreign addition to the word.   Alongside the most
frequent form *Yᵉhôwāh* we find, in conjunction with an
'ᵃdhônāi before or after the tetragram, the reading
Yᵉhôwih.   In old and important manuscripts with
tiberian vocalisation (as e.g. in Codex B 19 a Lenin-
gradensis (sign L), which is the basis of the third
edition of *Biblia Hebraica* by R. Kittel and P. Kahle),
we frequently find *Yᵉhwāh* (without a *hôlem*),[2] while
texts with Babylonian pointing regularly refrain from any
vocalisation of the divine name or else follow the tiberian
tradition.[3]   From this changing situation it must be de-
duced that the vocalisation is not essential to the word in
this or that instance, but denotes that the *Qᵉrê* was periphrastic.   *Yᵉhôwāh* was to be read as *'ᵃdhônāi* " Lord of
all ", *Yᵉhôwih* as *'ᵉlôhîm*, " God ", *Yᵉhwāh* as *shᵉmā'*, " the
name ", with the proper name for god itself disappearing

[1] Mesha Inscription, line 18 ; cf. M. Lidzbarski, *Handbuch der
nordsemitischen Epigraphik* (1898), pp. 415 and 286 . . . .

[2] J. Fischer, *Biblica*, xv (1934), pp. 50 ff., establishes the pointing
Yᵉhwah (without *hôlem* and with *pathaḥ*) in a scholastic source;
qāmeṣ is completely unknown in the manuscripts ; cf. *Werden und
Wesen des A.T.* (= *Z.A.W.*, Beiheft 66), pp. 198 ff.).

[3] P. Kahle, *Der masoretische Text des A.T. nach der Überlieferung
der babylonischen Juden* (1902), p. 11.

out of reading and meditation.[1] It is *shēm hamᵉ-phôrash*, " the expressive name ".[2]

(*b*) Thus attempts to arrive at the original complete form and the inherent meaning of *ĬHWH* cannot count upon assistance from the biblical tradition, but must depend solely upon philological combinations. Even Exod. iii. 14, as will be seen shortly (p. 61, *ad fin.*) contributes nothing, so that from the very start there must be no expectation that any of the results of such deliberations will attain a degree of certainty sufficient for definite conclusions to serve the interpretation of the usage of *ĬHWH*. Nevertheless much ingenuity has been devoted to these attempts in pursuing the two possibilities of (1) a basic root *HWH*, (2) a formation upon some other basis.

(*a*) The vowel-less tetragram *ĬHWH* appears to be either a verbal or a substantival form of the root *ĬWH*. The most probable hypothesis seems to be a verbal inflexion, especially when account is taken of the report of Theodoret of Cyros,[3] that the Samaritans said ’Ιαβέ and that of Clement of Alexandria,[4] that the name was ’Ιαουε. True, the question immediately arises as to what the subject of the verb might be. On the analogy of many verbal names of persons, e.g. *Yaᶜᵉqōbh*, *Ĭiṣḥāq*, one might think of an *hypocoristicum* which has excluded the element forming the subject of the verbal clause.[5] In that case the intrinsic meaning of the name

[1] When the tetragram appears outside the Canon, e.g. in the Targums, the masoretic editing is taken as authentic.

[2] Geiger, op. cit. p. 264 ; Bousset-Gressmann, op. cit. p. 309, n. 2.

[3] *Quaestio* 15 in Exod. 7 (Migne, 80, p. 244 a, b).

[4] *Strom.* V, 6, 34 : τὸ τετράγραμμον ὄνομα τὸ μυστικόν, ὃ περιέκειντο οἷς μόνοις τὸ ἄδυτον βάσιμον ἦν · λέγεται δὲ ’Ιαουε.

[5] The once widely misunderstood Accadian person's name *jawilu*, or *jawi-Dagan*, in which *jawi* is not a name but a verb, shows the philological possibility with especial impressiveness. Th. Bauer, *Die Ostkanaanäer* (1928), pp. 56, 61, 63, 74. (H. Bauer, op. cit. p. 93, still maintains the old interpretation.)

would only be half preserved in the surviving phrase. But although this scheme of name-forming is often used for names of persons linked with gods, for divine names, on the other hand, it cannot be instanced with any certainty, if it were to be proposed that the verbal meaning should be held back in favour of the substantival.

But if *YHWH* is a noun with a prefixed *Y*, its meaning must still depend upon the root *HWH*, which seems to be less at home in Hebrew than in Aramaic. The two meanings that confront us in the O.T. (*a*) " to fall ", and (*b*) " to be ", have so little to do with one another that one does well not to mix them.[1] Job. xxxvii. 6, *h^ewē' 'ereṣ*, " fall to the earth " corresponds exactly to the Arabic *hawa'*, " to fall ".[2] If *YHWH* is he who " falls ", then lightning or meteors could be meant, and the sphere of a storm-god be given.[3] But if we consider the Aramaic *HWH*, " to be " (cf. Gen. xxvii. 29 *h^ewēh g^ebhîr l^e'aḥeykhā;* Isa. xvi. 4), then *YHWH* could mean " he who is ", or " being " personified—which is incidentally much too abstract to carry conviction.

(β) Uncertain as these conclusions may be, the other possibility, interpreting *YHWH* from its shorter form (which leaves the root *HWH* less clearly discernible),

[1] E. König, *Hebr. und aram- Wörterbuch z.A.T.* (1910), pp. 76 f. s.v. *HWH* attempts a very violent conflation, comparing the Latin cecidit and accidit. He sees the meaning " to be " as a metaphysical spiritualised conception of " to fall ". This is hardly conceivable.

[2] Cf. *hawwāḥ* (also *hōwāḥ*) " fall ", in the Psalms *passim*, for the deed which leads to a fall—also metaphorically of folly. [Rev. Islwyn Blythin says the Arabic root ends with a Yôdh, not an Āleph, so points it *haway*.]

[3] The derivation from the Arabic *huj*, to blow, has a certain significance for Sethe's conjectures (p. 51, n. 4); unfortunately it is not " absolutely certain " (op. cit. p. 120), but is inconclusive, as are all other attempts to find the original meaning.

also leads to no evidence. The shorter form which occurs in the Bible text—chiefly in the liturgical formula *halᵉlû-yāh*—is *yāh*.[1] In the Elephantine Papyri the divine name occurs as *YHW*—which out of wilfulness or carelessness occasionally appears as *YHH*. As a termination of god-linked personal names (*Yirmᵉyāhû*, etc.) the masoretic text expresses it as *yāhû* and as *yᵉhô* at the beginning of such names (e.g. *Yᵉhônāthān*) or, with elision as *Yô* (e.g. *Yôḥānān*).[2] There is further the transcription 'Ιαώ, in numerous, even pre-christian, texts,[3] even though many of these must be excluded as evidence for the biblical name of God, for writers as early as Irenaeus (*Haer.* I, 30, 5) and Origen (*Cels.* VI, 32) recall that *'Iao* (or *Iaoth*, or *'Iaώ* was clearly used by the Gnostics, as a result of borrowing, as the name of a god or *daemon*. Thus *YHW* can be pronounced either *Yāhû* or *Yāhô*.[4]

(γ) The relation between the short and the long form constitutes an inexplicable problem. If one sees in the short form *yāh*, an interjection [5] found also in Arabic, a " god-cry ", this is based on a correct calculation, that proper names originated from a practical desire, namely to be able to call upon someone.[6] But this consideration can contribute nothing to the interpretation in face of the fact that *yāh*, as much as

[1] Transcribed *'Ia* in Origen, *In Celsum.* VI 32, v. l., in Jerome, *Breviarium in Psalmos* on Ps. 146 (Migne 26, p. 1253b), also in Θ.

[2] Inscriptions give similar evidence. Cf. Lidzbarski, op. cit. p. 286.   [3] Diodorus Siculus I, 94, 2.

[4] Jerome, op. cit. on Ps. 8 (p. 838a) also gives evidence for *Yaho* in a very instructive sentence. " Nomen domini apud Hebraeos quatuor literarum est, yod, he, vᵒu, he, quod proprie dei vocabulum sonat ; et legi potest Iaho, et Hebraei ἄρρητον, id est, ineffabile opinantur."

[5] Driver, op. cit. p. 24.

[6] Cf. Buber, op. cit. p. 236 ; R. Otto, op. cit. conjectures a dervish cry, referring to the *nᵉbhî'îm*.

the tetragram, is a name applied to the divine person.
The monosyllabic call is completely colourless and constitutes no name, even if one brings in a *hû'* (meaning
" he ") to fill it out. A he is no thou.[1] Then the
long form, the tetragram, must also be thought of as
originating from some kind of learned process,[2]
against which is not only the early instances *YHWH*
(p. 54, n. 1) but also the inflexions with *-yama* in
accadian yahwistic personal names which are based
upon the longer form.[3] The possibility that the longer
and short forms before us are quite separate words
deserves some attention, in view of the difficulty of explaining the relationship.[4] But in this direction also
the way forward is uncertain.

7. *The reasons for the reticence in using the name*

We have shown that in the last resort it cannot be
stated with certainty what *YHWH* means. All attempts at etymological interpretations, which always
at the same time of course are seeking to convey the
religious content of the word and are influenced by
definite theories about this, suffer from its ambiguity.
The greatest difficulties in this direction arise from that
fence which the biblical tradition has erected around
the name of God as a result of the realisation of the

---

[1] The name Jehu suggests that a *hû'* is not contained in the name
Yahweh ; cf. Th. Bauer, op. cit. p. 31.

[2] This must be the view of K. G. Kuhn, who sees Yahweh as
a verbal inflexion of a nominal plural. (*Orientalistische Studien*, E.
Littmann-Festschrift (1935) pp. 25 ff.)

[3] See the list in Driver, op. cit. p. 13, and also O. Eissfeldt,
Z.A.W. (1935), pp. 65 ff. who, through *Yᵉhabhyāh* in Jewish-
Babylonian names of the seventh century A.D. (= *YHWH*)
supports the interpretation of *-jama* as *YHWH*, and at the same
time supposes a much longer survival of unrestrained pronouncing
of the name Yahweh than hitherto accepted.

[4] Cf. Schleiff, op. cit. p. 699 ; H. Grimme, *Biblische Zeitschrift*
17 (1926), pp. 29 ff.

dangers inherent in the existence of a proper name for God. This arose partly from a feeling of taboo, partly—as we must be careful not to overlook—from a mature insight into the being of God.

(a) To a naïve sensibility a name for god naturally inspires a certain awe, which is to some extent intelligible from the very fact of name-giving, especially in ancient times. The name puts the personality of its bearer into a usable formula, it embraces his being.[1] " As is his name, so is he ", can be said sarcastically of someone and yet also quite seriously (I Sam. xxv. 25). Thus God's being is concentrated in His name. The name is both the quintessence of His person and the bearer of His power, the pronouncing of His name gives a concrete form to all that can be perceived in the god. But not least is there the specifically divine, the holy and awe-inspiring (*pil'î*, Judges xiii. 18), visible and efficacious in it. Thus the name of God is a numinous force, *nikhbādh*, " mighty ", and *nôrā*', " feared " (Deut. xxviii. 58), as is God Himself.[2]

(b) This, however, is a one-sided approach to the name, in that in the God of Israel it is not only dynamic and fearful qualities that are discernible. True, we must also reckon fully with the fact that the vast majority of the biblical authors, as they wrote down the tetragram in their texts, must have had in their minds a style of speech which made bold to pronounce the name as it was without hesitation. That is true at least of those who began their prayers with the word *YHWH* in the vocative as the most personal expression of trust and hope.[3] They experienced in the name the positive, protecting, element of divine

[1] Cf. J. Pedersen, *Israel* (1926), pp. 245 ff.
[2] Because the name is feared its pronunciation is avoided ; Amos vi. 10 (cf. Zeph. i. 7) ; Hab. ii. 20.
[3] Cf. Ps. xxvii. 4 : the presence of Yahweh is ecstasy.

presence and reality, not just the negative element that rejected and endangered men. Correspondingly, we seldom find in the O.T. writers themselves a tendency to diminish the use of the name, except in E. and Ecclesiastes.[1] Even where 'ᵉlôhîm is found, there is mention of the " name " as the power of God: " O God, help me through thy name and grant me justice through thy power! " (Ps. liv. 1). It is hard to believe that these authors are under the spell of the numinous awe which certainly dominated the redactors, when, for example, in Lev. xxiv. 11, in a narrative of the cursing of God, they inserted the " name " as the object of the curse,[2] or the Greek translator of Exod. iv. 24 wrote ἄγγελος κυρίου for Yahweh.[3] True, the feeling of distance is a definite feature of the Yahweh-religion from its beginning and even constitutes one of its basic elements (cf. Exod. iii. 6, where Moses fears to look towards God, and especially Isa. viii. 13: " It is He that fills you with fear and terror ").[4] But, as a result of a revival of ancient dynamic modes of heathen thought which came perhaps to Judaism through close contact with ceremonies of swearing allegiance, the feeling of distance was overcome, as may be seen in the Masoretes' treatment of the name of God and the use of shēm by the Samaritans.

(c) But a fundamental and spiritually powerful criticism of the name of God, a determined challenge towards its myth-based construction preceded these narrowly-channelled anxieties and probably involuntarily promoted the growth of their parasitic tendrils. This criticism is to be seen in the procedure of the

[1] Cf. Bousset-Gressmann, op. cit. pp. 307 f.; B. Jacob, *Im namen Gottes*, pp. 164 ff.

[2] Baudissin, *Kurios*, vol. ii, pp. 174 ff.

[3] See further Geiger, op. cit. pp. 264 ff.

[4] See also Joshua xxiv. 19 ; Lev. x. 3.

so-called elohistic recension of the Hexateuchal
narratives in dealing with the name of God, and then in
the confirmation of the development of those thoughts
in the so-called elohistic psalter, Ps. xlii to lxxxiii.[1]

Whatever answer we give to the still open question
of the literary independence of the elohistic narratives
it cannot be denied that in them the first large-scale
attempt is made to break with the use of the proper
name Yahweh.[2] Yet the tradition that this name had
a decisive significance in the foundation of Moses
proved a hindrance to this attempt. The result of
that tradition is to be seen in the text as it stands in
that in those parts of the narrative which follow after
the theophany to Moses in Exodus III the name
Yahweh is gradually introduced. But the fact that
this happens only irregularly leads to the supposition
that the use of Yahweh in E is entirely due to the altera-
tions of redactors, whereas the original author always
used *'elôhîm*.[3]

Whatever reasons he had for this procedure, he at
least showed unmistakably that the person of God
cannot be distinguished from other individuals by the
normal method of using names, since divinity is the
possession not of several but only of One.[4]

8. *The divine name in the narrative of Yahweh's revelation
to Moses, Exodus, iii. 14*

(a) This well-known holding back by E from the
name Yahweh is especially noticeable when he comes

---

[1] Cf. H. Gunkel, *Einleitung in die Psalmen* (1933), pp. 447 ff.

[2] Baudissin, *Kyrios*, ii, p. 171, disagrees.

[3] See J. Wellhausen, *Die Composition der Hexateuchs*[2] (1889), p. 72.

[4] R. Kittel, op. cit. p. 258, sees in the use of Elohim not a mono-
theistic tendency but only a pre-Yahweh form linking on to
Canaanite terminology. If E really proceeded so much on the
correct lines of the *Religionsgeschichtliche Schule*, he must have done
it with some educative purpose : what was that?

of necessity to speak of the name, in the story of the revelation of Yahweh to Moses in Exodus iii.[1] That the climax of this narrative was the imparting of this divine name is shown, quite apart from the obviously added verse 15,[2] by the Priestly account of the same event in Exod. vi. 2 f. Nevertheless the key words in Exod. iii. 14 do not contain the tetragram; but to the question what information Moses is to give about the name of God speaking to him, God answers Moses " I am that I am. And he said, Thus shalt thou say to the sons of Israel, ' I am ' has sent me to you." These enigmatic words are either to explain the name Yahweh by an alliterative description of its meaning, or else, in approaching near to the form of the name, expressly to avoid it and allow its use to seem problematical.

(b) It is at first sight tempting to interpret the clause giving God's answer as an ingenious attempt at an interpretation of the meaning of the name Yahweh which is nowhere otherwise discussed; and this is usually what happens. In that case the clause would be analogous to the attempt to explain *hawwāh* from *hayyîm* (Gen. iii. 20) or *Abraham* out of *hāmôn* (Gen. xvii. 5), i.e. as a very free connexion with the given word-picture, as narrators like to do, and thereby guide the attention of their hearers to the symbolic content of the name. The fact that there is no small number of philologically unacceptable etymologies in the Bible stories is a strong argument for supposing that that is also the case here, when we have to reckon with the naïve determination of all those attempts to arrive at the meaning of the names, however different may be the moods in which they are made.[3] In the

[1] To E belong verses 1, 4b, 6, 9-14.

[2] " And God spake *further* to Moses. . . ."

[3] Cf. on Jacob, Gen. xxvii. 36 with xxv. 26, and the satirical play upon the words Edom and Seir in xxv. 25, and the spiteful puns about Moab and Ammon in Gen. xix. 37 f.

present instance the moral would be indubitable: the name of God is intended to express something like existence (*hāyāh*).[1] But how would that be meant? Surely every name, also every divine name, obviously embraces an expression of existence, in that it denotes a concrete phenomenon.   And what is the point of the relative clause " that I am "?

To this there is no certain answer, and this circumstance therefore attracts interpreters since Rashi until today to continue discovering hidden meanings in this *'ehyeh*.   Thereby can much be said that is correct and unassailable about a conception of existence or reality, and many a speculation about the weaning of faith from magic,[2] about the " Deus revelatus " and " Deus absconditus ", be indulged in.   But even so the results are as speculative as the LXX with its ἐγώ εἰμι ὁ ὤν,[3] which certainly has but little to do with *'ehyeh 'asher 'ehyeh*.[4]

(*c*) The speculative hidden meaning of a ὁ ὤν in the Hebrew text is in the last resort impossible to define.   The words lose their unfathomability as soon as one refrains from regarding them as aetiological etymology.   For the supposition that they are such becomes very questionable, owing to marked formal

---

[1] Cf. Job iii. 16, *lô' 'ehyeh*, " I do not exist ", Gen. i. 2 (?), ii, 18.

[2] Cf. Buber, op. cit. p. 85.   An interpretative periphrasis suggests " I exercise power " (J. Hempel, *Gott und Mensch im A.T.*).

[3] That might conceivably be a translation of *'ehye 'asher yihyeh* ; cf. P. Haupt, *Orientalische Literaturzeitung*, xii, pp. 211 ff.   W. F. Albright, *Journal of Biblical Literature*, xliii (1924), pp. 370 ff.

[4] For the nota relationis *'asher* is ambiguous.   The probability that *'asher 'ehyeh* could fulfil the static function of a participle is slight.   For where in Hebrew the participial function of a verb is envisaged in a relative clause, its participial form is entirely usual, cf. *'asher yôshēbh* (Deut. i. 4) or *'asher mebhaqeshîm* (Jer. xxxviii. 16), etc., and a participle corresponding to the speculative Greek ὤν does not exist in Hebrew.

and material gaps which are not explicable by the general strangeness of O.T. etymologies.

Against the etymological interpretation, is (i) the fact that the consonants forming the tetragram are ignored in so far as it is a question of *hāyāh* instead of *HWH*, which might have been expected. But *HYH* and *HWH* sound different to the ear, however closely they may be connected.[1] (ii) The imperfect form *'ehyeh* leaves out the preformative *yôdh* which is decisive in the formation of the tetragram. The necessity of using the first person in a narrative context would have stopped an author desirous of explaining the form *YHWH* from any explanation along these lines. (iii) Nowhere else in the O.T. literature is *HYH* cited as the root of *YHWH*. For it is impossible to interpret every occurrence of the form *'ehyeh* or something like it on God's lips[2] as an echo of Exod. iii. 14. (iv) The " revelation-style " is by far the least suitable form for etymology. " Etymologies are not revealed." [3]

(*d*) In that case the situation is either that the words *'ehyeh* *'asher* *'ehyeh* and *'ehyeh* by itself constitute an incursion into the original text such as was later called a *tiqqûn sôpherîm*,[4] and constitutes nothing other than a refusal to enquire into the name of God, or that the author himself intended this refusal.

(*a*) Under the former alternative, the coming into existence of the phrase would have been something like this; the narrator, setting aside all reflexion of his own, and following the tradition before him, had recounted how God had given His own name as

---

[1] In Isa. xxxviii. 11, *yāh yāh* is vocative of the short form in litany-style repetition.

[2] Cf. e.g. Hos. i. 9 ; Ezek. xiv. 11, xxxiv. 24, etc.

[3] H. Gunkel, *Genesis* [5] (1922), xxii.

[4] For this concept cf. E. Ehrentreu, *Untersuchungen über die Massora* (1925), pp. 8 f.

authentication of what He said.   But this authentication also pointed unmistakably to the polytheistic background of the whole narrative, namely the in itself problematical fact [1] that the Israelites could be in doubt which of the divinites who might conceivably be regarded as God the Father (cf. Josh. xxiv. 14 f.) had imposed his charge upon Moses.   It is easy to comprehend how in these circumstances a so pointed mythical declaration about the revelation of a divine name at the most important passage of the tradition of redemption could be objected to.   It would be felt as an authentication as Father-gods of the " other gods " mentioned in Joshua xxiv.   Thus a redactor, at the same time influenced by elohistic propensities, could easily have omitted the name from the divine answer because at this particular juncture, and in the text of a divine saying, the whole complex of questions connected with the name was felt to be too difficult.[2]   The violence of the alteration is glossed over in masterly fashion by turning to account the phrase already present in verse 12, 'ehyeh 'immākh—" I am beside thee ". Almost unnoticeably the HYH has been heightened into an existential function and the mystery of divine being set forward as the most significant element in all invocation.   With the context the author of the tiqqûn is not further concerned.

(β) Less easy than this supposition of an early redaction is the interpretation of the text as a rejection of the question directed to God on the part of the narrator himself.   It is in that case given in the form of an inconsequential tautology " I am I ".   One might make this conjecture since the divinity striving with

---

[1] On this cf. A. Alt, op. cit. pp. 12 ff.

[2] A possible analogy is shîlôh in Gen. xlix. 10.   There may have been a name for the Messiah in the text there which for some reason it seemed advisable to conceal.

Jacob in Jabbok refused him his name (Gen. xxxii. 29): " Why askest thou my name? " The messenger of God who met Samson's parents answered similarly and added the reason that his name was *pil'î* " belonging to God " and therefore unattainable by, or dangerous for, men (Judges xiii. 18). But the supposition that an analogous desire to suppress the name may have influenced the narrator comes up against the difficulty that in the entire picture of the rencontre there is not the very slightest suggestion of a refusal on the part of God. On the contrary, the second part of verse 14—" thou shalt say to the children of Israel, ' *'ehyeh* ' has sent me ", looks like an accession to the request.[1] The refusal would then be expressed only in the word *'ehyeh*, a stylistic difficulty which would be very noticeable in this highly prominent passage, and which is also not present in the two passages which support this thesis. For that reason we may assume that alternative (α) is the more likely.

9. *The name Yahweh as the Foundation of the Old Testament proclamation about God*

The O.T. texts about Yahweh take many forms, and vary in the intensity of their faith and in their forms of expression according to the ability and character of many great and lesser authors; sometimes they are boxed up curiously in strange thoughts, but mostly expressed in clear and ordered terms. The link with history, with the here and now, takes very many forms, but never loses its basic motif—that Yahweh is Lord. Man has no power over him; any influence he may exercise is limited to that allowed to a slave over his lord. But no man can adjure Yahweh to do what he wants, and anyone who tries to has felt

---

[1] Buber, op. cit. pp. 237 f. ; Grether, op. cit. p. 22.

no breath of His spirit. The texts cohere together
into a consistent picture of God in such a way that its
complete interpretation springs from the apprehension
of the Thou who speaks to man. This power is
experienced not so much as something total, as something whose vitality showed itself in the will directed
to the salvation and consummation of existence—that
is the revelation for whose sake the history of Yahweh
with Israel, its beginning, its zenith and its passing
over into the history of God with the world has been
collected together in the canon of the O.T. Its
content might be summarised by saying that the name
of Yahweh is the basic mould of all O.T. predications
about God, or that the figure of Yahweh is the mould
of biblical revelation.

(a) This judgement, it is true, is immediately confronted by the difficulty that the God who bears the
proper name Yahweh is thereby labelled as one God
among many: indeed important early sources of faith
in God, such as the two-fold traditions of the decalogue
(Exod. xx. 3 ff. and Deut. v. 7 ff.) or Psalms such as
lviii and lxxxii, narratives such as Joshua xxiv. 14 f.,
prophecies like Amos v. 26, confirm that in the worship
of Yahweh there was always a distinction between
Yahweh and the gods which was explicitly understood
as well as implicitly felt. True, that was mostly by
way of rejection of the other gods, but there are also
definite instances of mythical thought. In a strange
land it is impossible to sing Yahweh's songs (Ps.
cxxxvii. 4), it necessitates the service of other gods
(I Sam. xxvi. 19); in Damascus Rimmon is lord
(II Kings v. 18) in Moab Chemosh (Judges xi. 24;
II Kings iii. 27). Foreign soil is impure: Amos vii.
17; Hos. ix. 3 f. But the surest proof of the vitality
of mythical thinking in the congregation of Yahweh is
the fact that the rivalry of the " other gods " did not

cease from producing new crises of faith from generation to generation. The narrative in I Kings xviii.
17 ff. shows it in the ordeal staged by Elijah in order
to prove that his God was the right one for the inhabitants of the Carmel district to worship.[1] Here
too, as almost always, the crisis was resolved as a result
of political development in which the shifting of power
among the gods seems to have found expression. State-
gods of foreign powers, " the whole host of Heaven "
(II Kings xxi. 3) at times found an official place alongside Yahweh;[2] Ishtar, " the Queen of Heaven "
(Jer. vii. 18), Adonis, the Syrian vegetation-Baal (Isa.
i. 29 f.) attracted the women. " According to the
number of thy cities are thy gods " is the verdict of
Jer. ii. 28. Nearly every page of the prophets testifies to opposition to faith in Yahweh and threats to its
unity.

(*b*) Besides deviations into foreign mythologies there
are also signs of lack of feeling for the numinous
altogether. In quiet times and in secure strata of the
people Yahweh was accepted with a certain official
matter-of-factness which led to reserve in face of
mythical conceptions. The political cleavage of
Yahweh's people led, especially in the Northern
Kingdom, to a receptivity towards alien myths, which
leads one to infer an ominous lack of poise and instinct
in religious questions. " They sacrificed unto the
Baalim, and burned incense to images " (Hos. xi. 2).
They cry unto Yahweh " not with their heart " (Hos.
vii. 14), incapable of stomaching His demands (Jer.

[1] A. Alt, *Das Gottes Urteil auf dem Karmel*, Beer-Festschrift
(1955), pp. 1 ff., explains the events as a political *force majeure*
of the State-God of Israel against the Phoenicians.
[2] Ezra viii. 10 ff. probably refers to Egyptian cults. Official
syncretism appears since Solomon. Cf. R. Kittel, op. cit. ii,
pp. 192 ff.

vi. 10). The child-sacrifices of Manasses' and Ahaz' times are like acts of despair, enheartening people without roots. On the other hand, we find a vulgar contentedness of which prophets can only speak in scorn and disgust. The Holy One of Israel is despised and spurned (Isa. i. 4) since their wills are not responsive, but they are led on merely by animal impulses so that the symbolic gods seem a more natural object of worship. In undisturbed enjoyment of bourgeois prosperity they are like " wine left on the lees " (Jer. xlviii. 11), " lying upon the lees " (Zeph. i. 12) unmoved by the fear of God: " Yahweh does neither good nor evil "—i.e. his activity is fundamentally doubtful. " He will not make investigations ", Ps. x. 4; cf. Jer. v. 12). What is " Yahweh's work "? (Isa. v. 12). Only scorn accompanies the phrase, " Let Him hasten with His work that we may yet experience the counsel of the Holy One of Israel! " (Isa. v. 19).

Thus does the comfortable bourgeois seek to ridicule the god-inspired speaker and call him mad (Hos. ix. 7; Jer. xxix. 26); the fear of God is a mere human tradition learned by rote (Isa. xxix. 13), no real experience. Even the patriarchal narrators have not resisted the temptation to introduce a frivolous feature of this kind into the story of Jacob, who in his extremity dares to support his lies with Yahweh's name while cautiously disassociating himself from it. (" Yahweh, thy God ", Gen. xxvii. 20.)

Such aberrations, it is true, are not solely explained by mythical thinking, for which " God " means a changeable and therefore crippled authority. But the history of religions corroborates the inference that the indifference of sly self-seeking is wont to be bolstered up by mythical ideas of God: the power of a God so limited is also curtailed. It was decisive in Yahwism that the figure of Yahweh, however belarded with mythical *traits*, was no special god with a limited sphere, but infused unlimited authority into every sphere of life. " Seek me and ye shall live " (Amos v. 4); so challenge and promise are fused, and the mythical form of speech and thought about Him lose their human values and become the monumental means of expression of a cosmic will.

(c) Thus, Yahweh, in the minds of His proclaimers, is never a mere abstraction, nor an euhemeristic concept, but stands before them and compels them as an audible, visible and felt personality. They do not get the impression of dreaming when His hand lays hold of them, Jeremiah speaks stern words about such an imagined reception of revelation (Jer. xxiii. 28). They see Yahweh and yet are unable to describe Him. The picture seen by the inmost eye has nothing of the naïveté of mythical conception, it is in every respect compulsive and imposing. Especially instructive is the theophany described in Ezekiel. A miraculous picture is sketched, consisting of a complex of animals and wheels and beating wings, and not till later is the attempt made to say what is essential in carefully composed words: there was something there which seemed like an image of the majesty of Yahweh. The prophet almost recoils from the fact that he has previously said that what sat upon the likeness of a throne looked like a man. So he repeats, correcting himself, the whole proclamation, leading it up to *kābhôdh*. *Kābhôdh*, the royal *plērōma*, comes in as substitute for person or man (Ezek. i).[1]

In the light of passages such as this there is no ground for attaching decisive importance to the frequent

[1] The apocalyptist of Dan. vii, speaking of the " Ancient of days " and His white hair, himself shows, albeit unconsciously, that he is using a temporal conception to express authority, when he speaks of God as being old.

human and mythical features in the picture of Yahweh, where our object is to ascertain the essence of faith in Him. It is a mere figure of speech to say that Yahweh has a mouth or a heart, that His lips are full of wrath, or that His arm is stretched out like that of a giant. The necessities of artistic imagination are the prime cause of the use even in religious poetry, of such forms, as seem to be the only possibility for the portrayal of voluntary and masculine *motifs* in religious experience. The astringent originality of personal experience expresses itself in them, regardless of possibilities of interpretation which could lead one astray from the central experience of revelation. The strong resolution of the prophets, just as the hymnodic or pathetic fervour of the poets, is born out of the contact with the personal will of Yahweh. That is the real genesis of the conception of divine grandeur and power which infuses with commanding power each mind that traces the traditional manifestations, so that out of even the humblest and most scanty sources about the cult of Yahweh, the question of its reality arises automatically and no reader is freed from the existential judgement over the divine Person and His will.

(*d*) The great poetical attempts to see the divine action of Yahweh in the dimensions of time (Ps. xc) and space (Ps. cxxxix) projected into infinity also lead us up to the limits of human understanding of personality, but nevertheless do not give up the revealed knowledge of the divine personality and so do not diverge from the lineage of biblical religion. The unusually speculative *traits* of these meditations are neither resigned nor quietistic, but arrive out of the feeling of responsibility of man addressed by God, which threatens to rise to the level of purely numinous awe. If the poet seeks " knowledge " (Ps. cxxxix. 6) concerning the secret of divine existence he comes

up against a " wonder " (*pele'*), and the knowledge
that Yahweh is ever beholding him and enfolding
him gives rise in his mind to a creaturely anxiety:
" Whither shall I go from Thy spirit, whither
flee from Thy countenance? ". The threatening
words of Amos (ix. 2 f.) live in his mind and the desire
to flee from God induces a basic feeling of the " religion
of holiness ",[1] such as the poem of Job has especially
pictured in words of helpless anguish born of the dark
depths of experience.   It sounds like a bitter travesty of
Ps. viii. 5 when Job vainly seeks to escape from God:
" let me alone! What then is man, that Thou
dost make him so great and workest Thy will upon
him, inspecting him every morning, testing him every
moment?   Wherefore dost Thou not look away from
me for one moment? " (Job. vii. 16 ff.).   Then his
feeling of guilt stifles him in a mood of panic: " Whether
blameless or wicked, it matters not—He destroys "
(Job. ix. 22).   But Ps. cxxxix. like Ps. lxxiii. 13 ff. is
an example of how so crippling a feeling, of being the
victim of demonic arbitrariness, finds its way back to
the peaceful mood of the hymn to the Lord and
expresses itself in the prayer " lead me in Thy eternal
way! "

(*e*) Naïve mythical thinking is more easily to be
seen in the Priestly texts about man as the " moulded
image " and " similitude " of God (Gen. i. 26, ix. 6).
It is discernible in the " we-style " of God's speech and
is most strongly expressed in the word *ṣelem*.   It is
further significant that the attached asyndetic form
kidhᵉmûthēnû " corresponding to our similitude " attempts to turn away the massive realistic expression
in the direction of allegory.   But in strict logic, without
any abstraction or spiritualisation, the sentence " We

[1] J. Hänel, *Die Religion der Heiligkeit* (1931), i, pp. 317 ff.

will make men as our moulded image, corresponding to our likeness " is saying two things: (1) that the God who speaks has a shape, like all gods, which man can portray as ṣelem, and can therefore imagine; and (2) that by looking at man's figure we may arrive at the conclusion " God looks something like that ".[1] That the text must be spiritualised follows not so much from that it goes on to say that God made them as man and woman, for both these are " man ", as from the context of the narrative, of which it can fairly be said that it " demythologises its material as far as possible ".[2]

(f) The same observation is justified about the few relatively tangible pieces of evidence about the early phases of the cult of Yahweh. The definitely masculine picture of God which evolved from the tradition beyond the pioneer work of Moses, determined that O.T. piety shall be basically not only obedience and loyalty, but also love, not because the myth was especially imposing, but because in it the unknown power of the Holy was transformed into the purposeful will of the leader-God, binding man to obedience and loyalty. Yahweh " the man of War " (Exod. xv. 3) is no berserk: He fights not for the sake of fighting but for the sake of the victory of His resolve to give this people which bears the name " God fights ", and is bound to Him by oath, its inheritance, the necessities of life, and joy. To understand how much more than

[1] That the shape of His body is meant is shown by V, 3. A silver coin of about the fifth century B.C., coming probably from Gaza, with the letters *YHW*, shows a bearded man sitting upon a winged chariot. Reproduction in J. Hempel, *Die althebräische Literatur* (1930), p. 111. Is Yahu here portrayed as territorial God of a heathen province, or heathen god as territorial God of an Israelite province? Cf. H. Gressmann, *Z.A.W.* (New Series), ii (1925), pp. 16 f.

[2] G. von Rad, *Die Priesterschrift im Hexateuch* (1934), p. 168.

theoretical the loyalty between God and people was, their mutual *ḥesedh*, it is of special significance to note how great a part is played by impulsive emotion from this powerful figure of God. In the Decalogue and elsewhere, Yahweh is called a jealous God—*'ēl qannâ'* (Exod. xx. 5, etc.).[1] As this can even be His " name " (Exod. xxxiv. 14) a description of the mystery of His person, the importance of the term for the knowledge of Yahweh is also prominent in the tradition. Its influence upon the whole biblical message must not be overlooked. The precise meaning of the word is that Yahweh wills to be loved by those He loves, that loyalty to Him must be unlimited, because mutual. There is scarcely any stronger expression for the personal, emotion-born relationship of God to man, which is only half-seen if one looks at the negative character of threatening. An inmost sphere of God's life is shyly pointed to when there is talk of an elemental emotion which, as painful reaction against an alien invasion into this sphere, moves with compelling power. As *'ēl qannâ'* Yahweh is no Baal at rest in himself, because love makes itself felt in Him. It is a feature of the virile seriousness of this message from God that its expression is veiled in negation and must be felt. *Qin'āh*, used of men, is wounded love, the raging " gnawing at the bones " (Prov. xiv. 30) correlative of *neqāmāh*, vengeance, the affronted sense of justice and honour. The jealous, avenging God (Nahum i. 2; Ps. xliv. 1) is thus He who can be wounded at heart, is person in the full sense as bearer of sensitivity,[2] to be

---

[1] The thought appears so spontaneously that it stands out sharply from its context in the decalogue's text. It belongs to the old kernel of Yahweh's message. Through its use as a paraenetic threat in Deuteronomy, its already veiled kernel, love, is so clamped down as to be scarcely discernible.

[2] Cf. *Ka'as*, Ps. lxxxv. 5, etc., and the verb *hikh'îs*.

provoked by suspicious doubt as to His serious demands. His advice and actions are steeped in emotion, and so fully and unreservedly that He appears to need that men whom He trusts should act in accordance with His directions.   Thus one might say that the '*ēl qannā*' is a young God, since only an old man such as the dogmatic Eliphaz (Job. v. 2) finds jealousy foolish.   The emotional witness of the conception and its logical adequacy become clearer if one attempts to develop its consequences in an ordered manner, as happens with those glosses on the text of the decalogue which attempt to make it support a theory of retaliation.[1]   The concept can only be understood within the framework of the general picture of Yahweh, the man who is no man but a God.   In other words the imponderable which is dynamic and demonic takes form in the imponderability of the person of the Holy.   In face of it, man is only in doubt when he tries to evade it.   Then he incurs the wrath.[2]   But the feeling yet teaches man that it is better to fall " into the hand of Yahweh " than into the hand of man, " for His mercy is great " (II Sam. xxiv. 14).

(*g*) It is in His guiding that Yahweh is seen and recognised as Lord.   It is total, covering the whole of life, as even the classic basic text of the torah, the Decalogue,[3] suggests.   The " I " of the speaking God

---

[1] Exod. xx. 5 f. ; Deut. v. 9 f. is theologically naïve, and therefore itself had to submit to a further unhappy correction (" who love me ", " who hate me ").

[2] Wrath is also a periphrasis for the operations of the Holy, which presupposes its being expressed in personal feelings. Wrath is never intended as the essence of God in the O.T., as it is elsewhere (cf. R. Otto, op. cit. p. 123), but it denotes a definite emotional reaction of His.   *Paḥadh yiṣḥāq* (Gen. xxxi. 42) is not Yahweh, but a Baal of Beersheba.

[3] To the attempts to trace the origins of the Decalogue back to Moses it has rightly been objected (most recently by L. Köhler,

addresses a " thou ". Who is thus addressed, a
community or an individual, remains at first sight
obscure. What is clear, however, is the practical
pointedness of the address: " I am Yahweh, thy God ",
in the phrase " other gods shall not be present for thee
in despite of me ". If other gods were present for
thee, that would mean not a theoretical recognition
of their existence, but practical willing adoption
of their powers, " service " in the broadest sense.
That sort of thing is not to happen " in despite of me ".
Thus this is no informative declaration on the existence
or non-existence of gods, as distinct from God: the
theological term monotheism has only a subordinate
significance when applied to the biblical religion, since
it is not practically effective in life. The God who
speaks " to thee ", who declares His will authoritatively
and intelligibly to human understanding, is God for
those who hear Him. That this relationship with
authority excludes all others at all similar, that is the
clause, felt to be self-evident, which impelled the biblical
belief in God inexorably beyond all limits of people
and myth. The prohibitive form " thou shalt have
none other gods " (to which most of the other clauses
of the Decalogue also point) makes clear that the
sovereignty of the clause as a way of life is exclusive.
The extent of its infusion into the mythical formative
impulses of the religions of race, even into the ever-
luxuriant growth of myth in religious thought in
general, may now be measured by surveys over the
field of the history of religion. But the men to whom

Theologische Rundschau, New Series I (1929), pp. 161 ff.) that they
can lead to no certainty, nor even to a probable result. The two
texts are self-subsistent, which means that they are in any case older
than any of the great narrative sources of the Hexateuch, into
which they have been inserted at an important juncture, the
account of the constitution of the community.

the sentence was originally spoken felt themselves at first merely reminded of the will of their God Yahweh in a way that was binding and saw themselves obliged to adjust themselves to His will. The strongest germ of religious life, the moving contact of the experience of God with the will, has here emerged.

And here we see what God's lordship is. Overcome both in will and feeling, man receives the unconditionally valid guidance which gives his life significance, balance and purpose, and demands an obedience which is not exhausted in an elegiac cult of a feeling of creatureliness, but shows itself in concrete actions, especially towards other men in the fulfilment of an imposed obligation of loyalty. " We act and we hear " (Exod. xxiv. 7) is the answer of those gathered on the mountain of God to the reception of the law. The realisation that the revelation of God's ways is binding upon men, and not at all just theoretically or generally, but always to the most concrete action, for which it gives the simple and great norms—this may be called the greatest legacy of the O.T. to its readers. It was through the moral demands that the divine experience of Yahweh's congregation was first realised to be universally valid. " O man, you have been told what is reasonable and demanded of thee by Yahweh: do justly, love loyalty, go thy way humbly together with thy God " (Mic. vi. 8). The collective term " man " comes to the prophet unreflectingly out of the dynamic of his divine mission, as with Amos his threatening words against Damascus and the other foreign powers (Amos i. 3 ff.) were born from the unconsciously dawning realisation that the peoples cannot do, and leave undone, what they will, but must pay their accounts to the same divine power whose deep tones had resounded in his ear from Sion (Amos i. 2; cf. ix. 12).

10. *The confessing of allegiance to Yahweh in Deuteronomy* vi. 4

The history-of-religions formula " monotheism " can only be properly applied to O.T. religion in so far as it constitutes a theoretical appraisal of its total contribution to religious perception. But a need to speculate is itself alien to the belief in Yahweh.[1] That is also true of the beginning of the so-called *sh^ema^c* of Deut. vi. 4, which might be interpreted as a speculative declaration, if the form of the confession and its context did not show that here too the purpose is not to stimulate or justify thought, but, by means of an emotional declaration about God to energise the will of His confessors. The love towards Yahweh expresses itself in order to foster the community's love for him. The fact that so extensive a value, both in worship and theology, has been assigned to the four brief words *Y^ehôwāh 'elôhênû y^ehôwāh 'eḥādh* is justification for a special examination of their much disputed meaning.

The style of the phrase, introduced by a paraenetic formula " Hear, O Israel ", customary only in Deut. (v. 1, ix. 1, xx. 3, xxvii. 9) appears for that very reason to be a quotation of an already-existing formulation. It might well be from an hymn, as it shows the pregnant brevity of hymnody, which is not the style of the rest of Deuteronomy. It contains—and here lies the difficulty—either two clauses, or only one. Grammatically it is easier to suppose that these are two substantival clauses. The first, " Yahweh is our God ", is a kind of basic confession by the people of God, monolatrous, like the first clause of the Decalogue. Beside it comes

---

[1] Ecclesiastes is perhaps an exception ; cf. the obscure phrase about the " one shepherd " (xii. 11).

a second, perhaps also from a hymn, but much more didactic and far-reaching: " Yahweh is one ". If one interprets it on the analogy of a completely similar construction such as Gen. xli. 25, *ḥᵃlôm par'ôh eḥādh hû'* (i.e. it is a question of a single dream, not two), then it would mean that Yahweh is a single person, not several. That would be a pedestrian platitude, but one which can only come into being if one stresses *'eḥādh* and thus arrives at a numbering which is pointless.[1] But the surprising and therefore effective part of the mathematical refinement lies unmistakably in the emphatic stressing of the name, which thereby receives the value of a denotation of species. "Yahweh is one " means that in Yahweh is all that He is, in the last resort exhaustively and exclusively present.[2] Thus the second clause is analytic, not synthetic: it would transcendentally connect the meaning of the first with e.g. Isa. xlv. 6, *'ᵃnî YHWH wᵉ'ên-'ôdh* and should be rewritten, after clauses such as Deut. iv. 35, *YHWH hû' hā'ᵉlôhîm 'ên-'ôdh milᵉbhaddô*, or Deut. vii. 9, viz. no one is that, which Yahweh is, God.

This interpretation, however, runs into difficulty in the combination of the two clauses: the question why the more far-reaching clause has the narrower beside it can only be answered by envisaging the possible presence of hymnody in the whole sentence. But the supposition that the second clause does not go beyond the first results in the platitude that *YHWH 'eḥādh* is in fact a numbering which does not become any more

---

[1] The author of Zech. xiv. 9 has obviously interpreted it so. To that corresponds the questionability of his empty sentence, with which he intends to say something quite different from what he actually says.

[2] There is a similar inflexion in e.g. Job xii. 2, *'attem 'ām:* " you are the species man exclusively ".

tolerable if one sees in it a polemic against a " poly-Yahwism " which attempted to introduce into Yahwism the many-sidedness of Baal.[1]

No very definite meaning, however, results from seeing the words hitherto construed as two clauses as one. In that case *'elôhênû* would be in apposition to *YHWH*, after which the subject *YHWH* would be taken up again: " Yahweh, our God, Yahweh is one ".[2] This analysis, however bad the style, is more satisfactory than the other, which puts *YHWH 'eḥādh* in apposition to *'elôhênû*. The feeling that a numeral does not consort with a proper name must then prompt periphrastic inflexions such as " Yahweh is our God, Yahweh as the one and only ". Thereby the highlight of the monolatry is preserved at the expense of verbal clarity.

Thus our result is that it is not possible to determine the meaning of these words in unassailable logical clarity. This fact, together with the rhythmical force of the passage and the unmistakable grandeur of the theme, makes the phrase an unique testimony to the power of the trust in Yahweh, maintained and yet restlessly pressing. It seems to stand at a water-shed. The energising power of the national cult makes use of an expression that is by now inadequate, and so the questing depths of perception probe the secret of the real content of the Yahweh-revelation. Yahweh,

[1] There have indeed been instances of that (cf. Gen. xvi. 13, xii. 7, xviii. 1 ff., xxviii, and the divine triad in the temple of Yeb) but there can be no doubt that it is not in place here, and so doctrinaire a conception could not possibly have arisen in the brevity of two words.

[2] So the LXX: κύριος ὁ θεὸς ἡμῶν κύριος εἷς ἐστιν. Upon the early Christian formula εἷς θεός there was probably no influence from Deut. vi. 4, unless some Greek form of the *shema'* (I Cor. viii. 4 ff. (?) ; Jas. ii. 19) deriving from the LXX, supplied that text ; cf. E. Peterson, *Εἷς θεός* (1926), pp. 293 ff.

as the epitome of all religious experience, is, according to this confession, the source of one single and consistent historical revelation. How many, and how similar, revelations there may be remains, of course, a question. But what has been learned should be heard.

IV. "LORD" IN LATE JUDAISM

1. *The choice of the word Κύριος in the LXX*

AT this juncture we must discuss the reason for the
choice of the word κύριος in the LXX. Baudissin [1]
has established that the meaning of the O.T. '*ādhôn* is
" being superior to ", in contrast to the exercising of
power over a thing or person. This " being superior
to " could result in the exercise of power over, but is to
be distinguished from it. '*ādhôn* is applied to God in
the O.T. so as to signify that He is the superior being
who " belongs " in this capacity to the speaker
(Baudissin, ii, p. 244). The meaning of κύριος in the
LXX is similar. But Baudissin's argumentation is
not convincing at this point. When he mentions in
support of it that in the O.T. the address '*ªdhônî* is also
used by the independent person who wishes merely to
convince the person addressed by using this term that
he honours him and wishes to enter into relationship
with him (Baudissin, ii, p. 246), he forgets that such a
mode of address in this context involves the self-
designation of the speaker as " servant " and expresses
the dependence—even when not meant to be taken
literally—of the speaker upon the person addressed: it
is expressive of subjection. The fact that *gᵉbhîrāh*, used
of the queen, is not translated κυρία, as elsewhere,
but by expressions which definitely indicate rule
(Baudissin, ii, p. 253), does not depend upon the fact
that κυρία is only an expression of superiority and not
of rule over someone, but upon the fact that κυρία is
not specially appropriate to the queen: in most of the
passages here cited by Baudissin (loc. cit., n. 1) κυρία

[1] Op. cit. ii, pp. 241-57.

would not convey the meaning sufficiently clearly, since the queen is also κυρία in relation to her slaves.

It is much better to start from the Greek meaning of the word κύριος in the time of the LXX. Since κύριος was not as yet used as an epithet for God in paganism, the ethnic use of it depicted by Baudissin is not relevant for the LXX. Κύριος then, where the specifically hellenistic use of it had made headway, meant " he who can legally dispose ". The element of legality must be stressed all the more because of the uniform substitution of κύριος for the tetragram in the whole LXX, so that it goes back to the first beginnings of this translation. With the choice of κύριος rather than δεσπότης (which was also possible and was even more ready to hand in the Greek of those days) the LXX strongly and consciously affirms that the lordship of God is legitimate. Now this affirmation can be based on the historical fact of the election of Israel: He who has saved her from the " smelting-furnace of Egypt " has thereby a legitimate claim upon His people. But the affirmation can also be based on God's creatorship: He who created the universe and mankind is the legitimate Lord. Baudissin supports the former of these alternatives: a main argument for this, apart from that already mentioned, is that κύριος occasionally translates 'ᵉlôhîm with the suffix (Baudissin, i, pp. 449 ff.). But here our comprehension of the motives for occasional divergences from the Hebrew text, like these, must always be very uncertain. It must also remain a question whether the LXX, in choosing a translation for ỲHWH (if it is not the case, as Baudissin has meticulously tried to show, that the LXX was influenced by 'ᵃdhônāi as a substitute for ỲHWH) confined itself to a term which simply denotes the superior, who gives himself over to those who honour him. Above all, the meaning of the LXX's κύριος which Baudissin assigns to it, from the Greek word and also from its use in the LXX, is most certainly not to be accepted without question, especially as the support of a definite pagan use of it was lacking. Indeed, such a linkage with pagan usage would rather have been a reason for the LXX to avoid its use. The permanent use of κύριος by itself directs our thoughts to the legitimate, unbounded and also invisible power of God to dispose—his ἐξουσία. Even if the motive of the LXX in choosing κύριος has not been correctly hit upon in the foregoing lines, if, for example, it were true that 'ᵃdhônāi was the pattern for κύριος in the LXX, even so there remains the fact of the far-reaching-ingness of this consistently chosen "translation". The sole word κύριος, without the addition of a divine name (as later on in ethnic use and before in Babylon and Egypt), the appropriate word, was in itself suf-ficient to denote one God—but that means *the one God*. That was bound to suggest to the hearer God's boundless power to dispose over all things. "In the one case (in the ethnic use) the title is added to the name, and the name distinguishes its bearer from numerous other gods and men, who may bear, or may have borne, the title. . . . In the other case (in the LXX) the title is substituted for the name, and the implication is that the bearer is 'sovereign' in the absolute sense. There is no exact parallel to this in earlier or contem-porary Greek." [1]

2. " Lord " in the Pseudepigrapha

Baudissin has produced many arguments against the widely held opinion that 'ᵃdhônāi as a substitute for the tetragram is older than the LXX. He dates the origin of this artificial form as late as the first century B.C. or A.D. Indeed the use of the tetragram outside

[1] C. H. Dodd, *The Bible and the Greeks*, p. 11.

scripture is perhaps not altogether avoided as late as the first century A.D., especially because of the vocative used in the prayer in *IV Esdras*, " dominator domine " (Baudissin, ii, pp. 189 ff.). The facts are these: A and *Σ* have kept the tetragram, written in Hebrew letters in their Greek translation: for the masoretic *'ᵃdhônāi* in the vocative, A once, and *Σ* often, has δέσποτα, otherwise κύριος, which Θ gives for *YHWH* and *'ᵃdhônāi*. The masoretic *'ᵃdhônāi YHWH* is variously rendered by these translations (Baudissin, ii, pp. 98 ff.). The Apocrypha use κύριος more or less frequently up to the time of I, III and IV Maccabees, so also the *Psalms of Solomon*, in which κύριος or (more seldom) ὁ κύριος and κύριε are more or less equally balanced by θεός or ὁ θεός (more frequent) and also ὁ θεός used as the vocative. In the somewhat later *Assumption of Moses* " dominus " is much more prevalent than " deus ", as is also the case, to a lesser extent, in the *Testaments of the XII Patriarchs*, whereas *IV Esdras*, has " altissimus " as its regular denotation for God, occasionally also " fortis ", once " excelsus ". In it " dominus " is only found in the vocative for God and (occasionally with " deus ") in contrast with angels. The *Syriac Baruch* has mostly " the Almighty " but " the highest " is also frequent. " Lord " occurs 8 times, " the exalted Lord " once, " God " (or " the almighty God " 6 times, " the exalted " once. In the vocative, however, we only once find " Almighty ", 7 times " O Lord, my God ", as many times " Lord ", and twice " my Lord ". A variegated picture greets us in *I Enoch*. In the oldest section, *The Vision of Beasts* (chapters lxxxiii-xc), the Lord of the Sheep in the parable is a designation for God, but occasionally we find simply " Lord " (lxxxiii. 2, lxxxix. 14, 15, 16, 18, 54, xc, 17, 21, 34; in the vocative, " My Lord ", lxxxiv. 6, once " God " (lxxxiv. 1). In the *Similitudes* the regular designation for God is "Lord of the Spirits ", more seldom simply " Lord ", " Our Lord ", " Lord of the World ", " Lord of Kings ", " the highest ",[1] still less frequently "God" (lv. 3, lxi 10, lxvii. 1). In the other sections of this collection of writings we find equally often " God " and " Lord ", also various periphrases, especially " the highest " (11 times), " the great one ", " the holy " and " Lord " with various genitives: " Lord of Heaven ", " of the world ", " of Creation ", " of glory ", " of judgment ," " of righteousness "; also " the God of glory ", the " King of the World ", " the King of Glory ". In *Jubilees*, finally, simply " God " is remarkably predominant (besides composite phrases such as " the highest God " " the God of Abraham " " our God ", etc.). The simple " Lord " is almost only found in the vocative, but we find " Lord " in composite phrases such as " God the Lord " " the Lord our God " (the last in the mouth of the angel of revelation), etc. The *Zadokite Fragment* [German *Damaskusschrift*] has usually 'ēl, once 'elyôn, three times hayyāḥîdh. In quotations from the O.T. it usually leaves out *YHWH* or replaces it by 'ēl. Forbidden are the oath with Aleph and Dāleth ('ᵃdhônāi) and with Aleph and Lāmedh ('ᵉlôhîm) xv. 1 (Schechter).

This evidence admits of another explanation from that which Baudissin gives, namely that the pseudepigraphists wanted their writings to be regarded as sacred and therefore wrote the tetragram as found in the O.T. but pronounced it 'ᵃdhônāi as they read the O.T. This would agree with the supposition that the LXX with its κύριος inclined to the already common

---

[1] " Lord " xxxix. 9, 13, xli. 2, lxii. 1, lxv. 6, lxvii. 3, 10, lxviii. 4 : " Our Lord ", lxiii. 8 : " Lord of the World ", lviii. 4, " Lord of Kings ", lxiii. 4, " Lord of Glory ", xl. 3, lxiii. 2 ; " the highest ", xlvi. 7, lx. 1, lxii. 7.

substitution of *'ᵃdhônāi* for the tetragram. The considerations which prompted the precise choice of
κύριος remain untouched by this, and precise certainty as to the dating of *'ᵃdhônāi* is hard to attain,
especially as the use of " Lord " in the *Pseudepigrapha*
reveals noticeable individual divergences. On the
other hand, the copious use of many substitute words
for the designation of God in, e.g. the *Ethiopian Enoch*
reveals a strong anxiety *vis-à-vis* simple terms for
God. In any case Josephus [1] and the sources of the
gospels show that *YHWH* and *'ᵃdhônāi* had vanished
from everyday speech. The substitute-words in the
Pseudepigrapha give us a good picture of the important
features of the picture of God in writers. In circles
close to Hellenism, from which the authors of the
Letter to Aristeas, of *III* and *IV Maccabees*, and the
Sibylline Oracles [2] spring, κύριος is absent, not from
religious awe, but because it was unintelligible for
Hellenism without the addition of divine names. Philo
was confronted by the fact that in his bible, the LXX,
θεός and κύριος stood side by side as the two chief
designations for God. He saw allegorically in κύριος
a pointer to the βασιλικὴ δύναμις, in θεός one to
the χαριστικὴ δύναμις.[3]

[1] Josephus often uses the adjective κύριος : *Contra Apionem*, I,
19 and 146, II, 177, 200 ; he calls the Romans οἱ κύριοι νῦν
Ῥωμαῖοι τῆς οἰκουμένης, *Contra Ap.* II, 41; he also knows that
κύριος corresponds to the Hebrew *'ādhôn*, *Ant.* V, 121. He
entirely avoids using it of God except in one prayer ; *Ant.* XX, 90
(δέσποτα κύριε . . . τῶν πάντων δὲ δικαίως μόνοι καὶ
πρῶτον ἥγημαι κύριον) and one quotation from scripture
(*Ant.* XIII, 68). But δεσπότης is common, and δέσποτα in
prayer-invocations to God. See A. Schlatter, *Wie sprach Josephus
von Gott, Beiträge zur Forderung Christliche Theologie*, xiv, 1 (1910),
pp. 8-11 ; and his *Theologie des Judentums*, pp. 25 f.
[2] The same is true of hellenistic-jewish writers such as Artapanus.
[3] *De Somniis*, I, 163. Further passages in Foerster, op. cit.
p. 119, n. 3 ; and see the next note, *infra*.

3. " Lord " in Rabbinic Judaism

In Palestine in the time of Jesus the literal pronunciation of the tetragram was an unusual occurrence.
The Rabbis also linked speculations on to the two chief
names for God in their bible, *YHWH* and *'elôhîm*, and
these concerned the two " measures " of God, the
measure of pity and the measure of judging, but they
assigned them to the names differently from Philo.[1]
In general speech *'ādhôn* has largely disappeared.
True, it is still occasionally used as a mode of address
1ogether with a title, *'ᵃdhônî hārôphē*';[2] to the king,
'ᵃdhônî hammelekh;[3] to the high-priest, *'ᵃdhônî kôhēn
gādhôl*;[4] *'ᵃdhônēnû wᵉrabbēnû* to the king.[5] Of Pharoah
it is said that he has called himself *'adhôn hā'ôlām*.[6]
Of God *'ādhôn* is still used in various ways, together
with *hā'ôlam, kol hā'ôlāmîm, lᵉkhol maʿᵃśîm, lᵉkhol bâ'ê
'ôlām, kol bᵉriyyôth*.[7] When the Rabbis discussed the
problem who was the first to call God *'ādhôn*, we see
the significance which they attached to this name.[8]
This makes clear the connexion between being " Lord "
and " Creator ". In general the Rabbis use for
" Lord " *rabh, rabbā', rabbôn, rabbônā', mârē'*, later also
qîrîs (κύριος) or *qîrî* (κύριε). *Mârē'* is " Lord "
in the most varied uses of this word: master of a slave,
owner of property, lord of the soul, i.e. of passions

---

[1] On this see A. Marmorstein, " Philo and the names of God "
in the *Jewish Quarterly Review* (New Series), xxii, pp. 295-306,
and the literature there cited.

[2] *Jer. Berakoth* 9b, Dalman, *Worte Jesu*, p. 349.

[3] Dalman, loc. cit.

[4] *Leviticus Rabba* iii, 5 on ii, 1; Dalman, loc. cit.

[5] Ibid.

[6] *Exod. Rabba* v, 14 on v, 2 ; Marmorstein, op. cit. p. 63.

[7] Instances in Marmorstein, pp. 62 f.

[8] First Simeon ben Jochai (*c.* A.D. 150) *Bab. Berakoth* 7b ;
Marmorstein, p. 62.

(corresponding to κύριος), as a mode of address (always with a personal pronoun) it is a courteous address from inferiors (servants and subjects) and also between equals, corresponding to 'ādhôn in the O.T.[1] Of God, mârê' is used together with sheᵐmayyā'[2] and 'álmā',[3] marî as a mode of address to God is found, e.g. Gen. rabba 13, 2, on ii. 5, the abstract mârûthā' deᵉ'álmā' occurs Gen. rabba 55, on xxii. 2.[4] Rabh is in general, even without suffix, the teacher,[5] but especially used in the suffix form rabbî as a mode of address to a teacher. The suffix soon lost its meaning.[6] But rabh also means lord in other respects, e.g. of the slave.[7] Rabbî is in any case a form of address showing unusual respect.[8] Besides rabh we find rabbôn (later ribbôn) which in the gospels is used as a mode of address and is also found in the Targums[9] for the biblical 'ādhôn where it does not refer to God. But later this word is practically used only for God, especially in the phrases rabbôn shel 'ôlām, rabbôn hâ'ôlāmîm.[10]

Another important word is ba'al, which denotes ownership[11] and in parables often means God, in the phrase ba'al habbayith.[12] Some further names of God compounded with ba'al must also be mentioned[13]—albeit

[1] Dalman, op. cit. p. 267, where texts are cited.

[2] Qoheleth Rabba on iii. 2.

[3] Genesis Rabba 99, on xlix. 27 : Marmorstein, p. 94, n. 46.

[4] Marmorstein, p. 93, n. 44.

[5] Pirqe Aboth I, 6, 16. On rabbi cf. also C. H. Moore, Judaism iii, pp. 15-17.

[6] Dalman, op. cit. p. 274.

[7] Bab. Taanit 25b ad fin.; Bab. Gittin 23b.

[8] Dalman, op. cit. p. 275.

[9] Dalman, op. cit. pp. 266 f.; Str.-B. ii, p. 25, on Mark x. 51.

[10] Texts in Str.-B. iii, pp. 671 f.; Marmorstein, loc. cit. pp. 98 f.

[11] Ba'al hatteᵉ'ênāh (= Aramaic mârê' ditᵉênta') Jer. Talmud Berakoth 5c, line 16.

[12] Marmorstein, pp. 77 f.

[13] Marmorstein, pp. 78 ff.

only "names" in a metaphorical sense. *ba'al dîn* (accuser), *ba'al hôbh* (creditor), *ba'al m'lā'khāh* (slave-owner), *ba'al hammishpāṭ* (judge), *ba'al happiqqādhôn* (him to whom a pledge is entrusted, in connexion with good deeds); also *ba'al hannehāmôth* and *ba'al hārah'mîm* and *ba'al hā'ôlām*.

In contrast to Greek usage, in Hebrew and Aramaic "lord" is never used absolutely without an attached noun [1] or suffix, and the address "O lord" is occasionally duplicated.[2]

The lordship of God is important for late Judaism in two connexions—one that God is Lord and Leader of the universe and its history, the other that He is Lord and Judge of the individual. Out of the number of designations for God which name Him in this two-fold insight proceeds the significance of the two spheres of thought. The former is especially (but certainly not exclusively) expressed in the *Pseudepigrapha*, which of course wish to indicate the certainty that the history of the universe, despite all opposing powers, has nevertheless its God-given goal.[3] Characteristic phrases in this connexion are *I Enoch*, ix. 4: σὺ εἶ κύριος τῶν κυρίων καὶ ὁ θεὸς τῶν θεῶν καὶ βασιλεὺς τῶν αἰώνων, and xxv. 3: ὁ μέγας κύριος ὁ ἅγιος τῆς δόξης, ὁ βασιλεὺς τοῦ αἰῶνος; cf. also xxv. 7, xxvii. 3, xci. 13. The prediliction of *IV Esdras* and the *Syriac Baruch* for the names "the highest", "the almighty" also links up with this. For the latter we are referred to the God-names compounded with *ba'al*

---

[1] Dalman, op. cit. p. 268. But there are exceptions—*Bab. Berakoth* 61b, *ad init.*

[2] King Josophat is supposed to have greeted every scholar with *'abhî 'abhî rabbî rabbî marî marî: Bab. Talmud, Makkoth* 24a; Dalman, op. cit. p. 268, *ad init.*

[3] How strongly the tension was felt is clear, e.g. from *I Enoch*, lxxxix. 57 f., lxx-lxxi, lxxv-lxxvii, xc. 3.

mentioned above, and should compare also *I Enoch*, lxxxiii. 11, " Lord of judgment ". The Lordship of God is absolute, but yet hidden. Every man can " do deeds of guilt " [1] and be remiss before the " Lord of the work " (*Pirqe Aboth* ii. 19), the kings of the earth can exercise their power against God and His people— that is a result of the sin of the people. If it were to keep a single Sabbath, it would be immediately re-deemed (*Jer. Taanit* 64*a*, ll. 31 f.). This determines the tenor of Judaism towards the powers of this world.

The reason why God is absolute Lord of this world and its course, and over the individual, is because He is " creator of all ": *I Enoch* lxxxiv. 2 f. " Praised art thou, O Lord, King, great and mighty is thy greatness, Lord of the whole creation of the Heaven, King of Kings and God of the entire world! Thy power, sovereignty and greatness endure for eternity and thy Lordship for all generations: all heavens are thy throne for ever and the whole earth the footstool of thy feet. For thou hast created all things and dost rule them." [2] This connexion with the thought of creation gives the lordship of God its final unshakable foundation, gives the ethical obligation its inevitability. *IV Esdras* viii. 60: " the creatures have dishonoured the name of Him who created them, and shown in-gratitude to Him who gave them life. Therefore my judgment is now imminent upon them." *Jer. Talmud, Berakoth* 7 d, l. 61,[3] *berā'thānû la'ªśôth reṣônekhā.* The election of Israel now ranks as far less important than these ideas, and is itself found essentially in the form that God is the Creator of Israel (*Apocalypse of Baruch*, lxxviii. 3, lxxix. 2, lxxxii. 2).

[1] Cf. the saying of Rabbi Akiba, *Pirçe Aboth* iii. 16.
[2] Cf. loc. cit. ix 4 f.
[3] Str.-B. iv, pp. 478 ff.

V. *KURIOS* IN THE NEW TESTAMENT

1. *The Secular usage*

In the New Testament, *kurios* denotes the Lord and owner of a vineyard (Mark xii. 9, par.), of an ass (Luke xix. 33), of a dog, (Matt. xv. 27); the master of the (free) steward (Luke xvi. 3, 5, and (?) 8) and the master of unfree slaves (often in the parables, also Acts xvi. 16, 19; Eph. vi. 5, 9; Col. iii. 22, iv. 1); also the person who controls and has to give the word—over the harvest (Matt. ix. 38, par.),[1] or the Sabbath (Mark ii. 28, par.). In oriental courtesy (regarding merely the verbal usage) Elizabeth can call Mary the " mother of my Lord " (Luke i. 43). The subservience of one who sets store by expressing it is expressed in *kurios*, as I Peter iii. 6 points out that Sarah calls Abraham *kurios* (a play upon the words in the LXX of Gen. xviii. 12) and in the quotation of Ps. cx in Mark xii. 36 f. par., and Acts ii. 34. Festus speaks of Nero as the *kurios* (Acts xxv. 26, cf. p. 29, n. 1 *supra*). Κύριος occurs in a stricter sense, implying legal but not actual ownership, inclining towards the adjective κύριος, in Gal. iv. 1: ἐφ᾽ ὅσον χρόνον ὁ κληρονόμος νήπιός ἐστιν, οὐδὲν διαφέρει δούλου κύριος πάντων ὤν. With few exceptions (Matt. xviii. 25, xxiv. 45; Luke xii. 37, 42, xiv. 23, cf. John xiii. 13 f.), this *kurios* is always followed by a genitive in the gospels and Acts, whether it be of a substantive or personal pronoun (also of objects, Luke xx. 13, 15)—a sign of the influence of Palestine usage, cf. *supra*, p. 90, n. 1). But a corresponding genitive is not found in the Epistles—Eph. vi. 5, 9; Col. iii. 22, iv. 1; I Peter iii. 6, also Acts xxv. 26. On Palestine soil

---

[1] Cf. A. Schlatter, *Mathäusevangelium* (1929), on ix. 38.

this *kurios* may translate *rabbôn*, *rabh* or *mârē'* (cf. *supra*, p. 88, *ad fin.*). *Kurie* is used often as a mode of address, not only when slaves are addressing their master (they use it exclusively in the gospels) but also by the vine-dresser to the owner of the vineyard (Luke xiii. 8), by the Jews to Pilate (Matt. xxvii. 63), by the son to his father (Matt. xxi. 29—a special case),[1] by Mary to the unknown gardener (John xx, 15), by the jailer at Philippi expressing his awe of his prisoners by calling them *kurioi* (Acts xvi. 30). *Kurie* is also used in addressing angels (Acts x. 4, Rev. vii, 14 (with μου) and the unknown apparition (Acts ix. 5, xxii. 8, 10, xxvi. 15, x. 14, xi. 8). A double *kurie, kurie* (Matt. vii. 21, 22, xxv. 11; Luke vi. 46) also corresponds to Palestinian usage (cf. *supra*, p. 90, n. 2). *Kurie* in the gospels corresponds to *mârî* with suffix, since in speaking of Jesus the evangelists have rendered *rabbî* differently and it was not commonly used in addressing one who was not learned. For *kurie* used in addressing Jesus, *vide infra*, p. 106, *ad fin.*). This *kurie* is never joined to a personal pronoun, nor are the vocatives *epistata* and *didaskale* (except John xx. 28 and Rev. vii. 14) although the vocative " lord " in Palestinian speech always had a suffix attached to it. The vocative " lord " was accorded to a greater number of persons than the designation " lord " and was therefore earlier outmoded. The use of the nominative with the article instead of the vocative (John xx. 28; Rev. iv. 11) [2] is semitic.

Of the genitive-constructions *kurios tēs doxēs* (I Cor.

---

[1] The other son uses no appellation. This sharpens the difference between the words and the deeds of the son who said yes, in that such an appellation upon the lips of a son to his father stresses his subordination. Cf. p. 10, *supra, ad fin.*

[2] Cf. F. Blass, *Grammatik des neutestamentischen Griechisch*, 5th edn., ed. A. Debrunner, § 147, 3.

ii. 8), *tēs eirēnēs* (II Thess. iii. 16a), the latter is supported by *ba'al hannehāmôth* (p. 90, line 5) while the former must be a semitic genitive in the place of an adjective.

Despotēs in the gospels is used in the vocative only in addressing God. It is used of the slave-owner I Tim. vi. 1 f.; Titus ii. 9; I Peter ii. 18; of the Lord and owner of a house II Tim. ii. 21. It is presumably a sign of more precisely chosen language (*vide supra*, p. 9).

2. *God the Lord*

(*Ho*) *kurios* is the name for God in quotations and reminiscences of the O.T., in which the LXX is generally followed: thus Mark i. 3, par., xii. 11, par., xii. 36, par., and Acts ii. 34 (in these cases the LXX has *ho kurios*, but in the N.T. passages the article has been omitted by B, with the support of some other manuscripts), Matt. xxvii. 10; Luke i. 46, and iv. 18, 19; Mark xi. 9, par., John xii. 38(twice); Acts ii. 20, 21, 25, iv. 26, xiii. 10 (most manuscripts omit the article, in contrast to the LXX), xv. 17 (in the LXX *ton kurion* is the reading of A alone, other manuscrips omit it completely), Rom. iv. 8, ix. 28 (the LXX, except for B, has *ho theos* instead of *kurios*), xi. 3 (*kurie* is added to the LXX text), xi. 34 (= I Cor. ii. 16) Rom. xv. 11; I Cor. i. 31 (the words *en kuriōi* are not in that form in the LXX), iii. 20, x. 22 (*ton kurion* is not in the O.T. original), x. 26, II Cor. iii. 16, viii. 21, x. 17; II Thess. i. 9, II Tim. ii. 19 (the LXX has *ho theos* instead of *kurios*), Heb. i. 10, vii. 21, viii. 2 (the LXX omits the article in the Hebrew), viii. 8-10, 11, x. 30, xii. 5-6, xiii. 6; Jas. v. 11, (B omits the article), I Peter i. 25 (LXX *tou theou*), ii. 3, iii. 12 (twice), Jude 9. *Kurios Sabaōth:* Rom. ix. 29; Jas. v. 4. *Kurios ho theos,* followed by a genitive: Matt. iv.

7, 10, par.; Mark xii. 29, 30, par.; Acts iii. 22 (omitting the LXX's personal pronoun), ii. 39 (adding *ho theos hēmōn* to the LXX). *Ho kurios* (LXX adds *pāsēs*) *tēs gēs*, Rev. xi. 4.

In the Markan and Q sources of the synoptics, God is not called (*ho*) *kurios*, except Mark v. 19 (peculiar to Mark), when Jesus says to the healed (pagan) Gergesene demoniac *apangeilon autois hosa ho kurios soi pepoiēken*, and Mark xiii. 20: *ei mē ekolobōsen kurios tas hēmeras* (Matthew and Luke have changed it, or have a different text). In the Gospels *kurios* is used of God in Matthew and Luke's prologues and Matthew's epilogue,[1] also in Luke v. 17, xx. 37—both peculiar to Luke. This shows that *'adhônāi* was not common in the original Palestine community.[2] The marked incidence of *kurios* in the Lukan birth-stories is bound up with the conscious biblical style, and betokens a link with the LXX rather than with contemporary Palestinian usage. Correspondingly, no essential distinction can be made between *kurios* with, and without, the article. Influence of the LXX is seen in the case of *kurios* in certain fixed conjunctions: *cheir kuriou* (Luke i. 66; Acts xi. 21, xiii. 11); *angelos kuriou* (Matt. i. 20, 24; ii. 13, 19, xxviii. 2, Luke i. 11, ii. 9. Acts v. 19; viii. 26, xii. 7 and 23); *onoma kuriou* (Jas. v. 10 and 14); *pneuma kuriou* (Acts v. 9, viii. 39), and the inflexion *legei kurios*, which is added as a formula in Rom. xii. 19; II Cor. vi. 17, and Rev. i. 8; and in Heb. viii. 8, 9, 10, has displaced the LXX's *phēsin kurios*. In these cases *kurios* is always without the article, but it is always with it in the case of *ho logos*

---

[1] Matt. i. 20, 22, 24, ii. 13, 15, 19, xxviii. 2 ; Luke i. 6, 9, 11, 15, 17, 25, 28, 38, 45, 58, 66 ; ii. 9, 15, 22, 23, 24, 26, 39.

[2] I therefore see no reason for Schlatter's contention (*Johannesev.* p. 42) that for Palestinians *kurios* without the article is *'adhônāi*, with it is *mârā'*, i.e. Jesus.

tou kuriou: Acts viii. 25, xii. 24, xiii. 48-9, xv. 35-6, xix. 10 and 20.[1] *Kurios* is also certainly used for God in I Cor. x. 9; I Tim. vi. 15 (with *tōn kurieuontōn*); II Tim. i. 18; Heb. vii. 21, viii. 2; Jas. i. 7, iii. 9 (with *ho patēr*), v. 11a, II Pet. iii. 8; Jude 5 and in Revelation, which in its grandiose style often makes use of the O.T. phrase *kurios ho theos* (plus *pantokratōr*) —i. 8, iv. 8, xi. 17, xvi. 7, xviii. 8, xix. 6, xxi. 22, xxii. 5. Unparalleled formulae occur in Rev. iv. 11—*ho kurios kai ho theos hēmōn*—and xi. 15 (*tou kuriou hēmōn*) and xxii. 6 (*ho kurios ho theos tōn pneumatōn*).

Thus (*ho*) *kurios* is not, especially on Palestinian soil, but also in the community which used the LXX as its bible, a designation for God much used apart from its origin in the Bible. And yet the content inherent in the word *kurios* can be actualised in all its richness at any moment. This is the case in some significant passages. First and foremost, Matt. xi. 25 (almost word for word the same as Luke x. 21): ἐξομολογοῦμαί σοι, πάτερ, κύριε τοῦ οὐρανοῦ καὶ τῆς γῆς, ὅτι ἔκρυψας ταῦτα ἀπὸ σοφῶν καὶ συνετῶν, καὶ ἀπεκάλυψας αὐτὰ νηπίοις. ναί, ὁ πατήρ, ὅτι οὕτως εὐδοκία ἐγένετο ἔμπροσθέν σου· here, the solemn mode of address is a vital component of the willing submission before the sovereignty of the divine *eudokia* and gives it an universal significance. The completely uncaused essence of the divine will is reverently assigned to the Lord over Heaven and earth. The voluntary assent to this good will shows that subservience to this Lord does not produce lack of will-power. A similar line of thought stands behind the parabolic expression *kurios tou therismou* (Matt. ix. 38,

---

[1] *Ho logos tou theou* in Acts is presumably equivalent to *ho logos tou kuriou*. Whether St. Paul in I Thess. i. 8, II Thess. iii. 1, also thought of *ho logos tou kuriou* as the word of God is perhaps not ascertainable and anyhow irrevelant. The point at issue is the influence of the LXX.

par.). The harvest is the great harvest of mankind, its Lord is thus Lord over the whole of world history. In connexion with the day whose dawning is known to no one, not even the Son, St. Paul speaks of God as *ho makarios kai monos dunastēs, ho basileūs tōn basileuo'tōn kai kurios tōn kurieuontōn,* thus declaring Him to be the director who is sovereign over all the powers which make history upon earth. In a significant passage in Acts, the speech before the Areopagus, St. Luke records St. Paul as seizing upon the word *kurios,* with the genitives *ouranou kai gēs,* to obtain roots for this lordship of God from pagan worship. In this context the lordship of God is traced back to His creatorship. The great part played in Revelation by the full phrase *kurios ho theos ho pantokratōr* is of course no mere accident, but no less important is the newly coined inflexion *ho kurios kai ho theos hēmōn* with which, in iv. 11, the twenty-four elders, who are surely to be thought of as not unconnected with all mankind, as God's creation, describe their relationship with God. In devotional invocations, too, *kurie* can be invested with a special tone, as e.g. Acts i. 24, *su kurie kardiognōsta pantōn.* Jas. iii. 9 must also be mentioned, where *kurios* is the ground for the obligation to sing praise.[1] But the content expressed by the word *kurios* is also found in the N.T., quite apart from the actual word: the personal, legitimate, comprehensive sovereignty of God.

3. *Jesus the Lord*

It will be well to start with St. Paul, whose use of *kurios* is clear. The other N.T. writings will then be added in support and by way of clarification and as tokens of the consistency of usage.

[1] In the foregoing lines those passages have been selected in which *kurios,* used of God, has a special tone and could not be replaced by *theos* without altering the sense.

In I Cor. xii. 3, St. Paul contrasts *anathema Iēsous*
with *kurios Iēsous*. The former is an expression of
what Acts calls *blasphēmein*—to speak of Jesus as being
opposed to God and so incur God's judgement. It is a
strictly religious attitude, opposing something for the
sake of God. A corresponding expression for its
opposite is lacking: it would be *eulogētos*, but in the
N.T. that is reserved for God. Thus *kurios Iēsous* is
not exactly parallel to *anathema Iēsous*, as the latter
predicate can be applied to much and many in some
sense, but not the former. But in any case it includes
a religious declaration for Jesus, " for the sake of God ";
this attitude is only possible and legitimate towards
One Person.

We are led further by the well-known, inexhaustible
passage in Phil. ii. 6-11, especially verses 9-11:
*dio kai ho theos auton huperhupsōsen kai echarisato autōi to
onoma to huper pan onoma, hina en tōi onomati Iēsou pan gonu
kampsēi . . . kai pāsa glōssa exomologēsetai hoti kurios
Iēsous Christos eis dōxan theou patros.* The name, which
the repetition of the article indicates to be a very special
one, can only be the name of *kurios*. It has been given
to Jesus as the divine answer (*dio*) to his mortal sufferings in obedience. At the name which Jesus, who took
upon Himself the form of a slave, has received, i.e.
in the presence of Him who was in history and has been
raised on high, the whole world bows. So too Revelation (v. 12) says precisely of the *arnion hōs esphagmenon*
that it is " worthy " to receive the book which comprises the liberation of mankind, to receive *dunamis*,
doxa and *eulogia*. The name of *kurios* involves equality
with God: the " bowing the knee " and the exclama-
tion *kurios Iēsous Christos* belong together, and, although
Philippians does not actually quote Isa. xlv. 23 f.,
the *exomologēsis*, especially in the LXX but also in the
masoretic text, so runs that *kurios Iēsous Christos* does

not link on to it, and yet there is a substitution of *en tōi onomati Iēsou* for *emoi* (sc. *kampsei pan gonu*) on the lips of God. But that this Jesus is acknowledged as *kurios* is to the glory of God. Thus the name of *kurios* comprises the exaltation. In the light of this there is no need to decide whether the *huper* in *huperupsōsen* relates to *en morphēi theou huparchōn*, or only means " beyond all measure ".

The whole N.T. uses *kurios* of Jesus as the resurrected. In Rom. x. 9, St. Paul expressly sets the confession of the lordship of Jesus side by side with the heart's faith that God has raised Him from the dead. Acts ii. 36 records St. Peter as saying at the end of the Pentecost sermon: *asphalōs oun ginōsketō pās oikos Israēl hoti kai kurion auton kai Christon epoiēsen ho theos, touton ton Iēsoun hon hūmeis estaurōsate.* The larger the share of St. Luke in the formulation of this passage, the clearer is the indication of the connexion in his mind between the resurrection and the *kuriotēs* of Jesus. The connexion between the suffering, resurrection and the divine status of Jesus which is expressed by *kurios*, appears often, without the word *kurios* being specially prominent: thus when Heb. ii. 6 ff. quotes Ps. viii. 5 ff., it is in verse 8 that it is first shown that the text cannot relate merely to man but rather (verse 9) relates to Jesus, who is crowned with *doxa* and *timē* because of his death-pangs: in this the lordship of Jesus is already pointed to, without the author going so far as to say expressly that the *panta hupetaxas hupokatō tōn podōn autou* has also been fulfilled in him. The same connexion between resurrection and lordship is also shown by the words of the Risen One in Matt. xxviii. 18: *edothē moi pāsa exousia en ouranōi kai epi gēs:* he who has *exousia* is *kurios*. Most clearly of all, however, is the connexion to be seen in the use of Ps. cx. 1. This passage is the sole basis for the idea of sitting at the right hand of God. It occurs nowhere else. But in this Psalm the sitting at the right of God is bound up with a being lord, in the Psalm with being David's lord. Acts ii. 36, lets St. Peter draw the consequence from this verse of the Psalm for Jesus with a "therefore". Sitting at the right hand of God connotes reigning with Him,[1] i.e. divine status, as does the mere sitting in the presence of God (Babylonian *Chagiga* 15a; Hebrew *Enoch* xvi. 3).

The echoes of this Psalm passage in the N.T. mostly show the connexion between resurrection and exaltation (cf. also Acts v. 31; Rom. viii. 34; Col. iii. 1; Heb. i. 3, 13, viii. 1, xii. 2; Rev. iii. 21—cf. Rom. i. 4) and between exaltation and universal lordship (cf. I Cor. xv. 25 ff.—where Ps. viii. 7 is also used) similarly Eph. i. 20 f., also I Pet. iii. 22 and Heb. x. 12 f.).

In I Cor. xi. 3, St. Paul mentions a series of ranks: *thelō de humas eidenai hoti pantos andros hē kephalē ho Christos estin, kephalē de gunaikos ho anēr, kephalē de tou Christou ho theos.* It is inconceivable that St. Paul means that woman is further from Christ than man. The whole passage deals with the natural superiority of man. The universe, of which the relationship between man and woman is a constituent, has no direct relationship to God, but only one through Christ. Without Him, the "world" could not exist before God. It is through Christ that the world can exist before God, it is He who exercises God's sovereignty towards the world. As the heavenly, earthly and subterranean powers bow their knees before Him (Phil. ii. 10) so (in Col. ii. 10) He is *kephalē* (the same expression as in I Cor. xi. 3) *pasēs archēs kai exousias*, He is *pro pantōn kai ta panta en autōi sunestēken* (Col. i. 17), and with reference to this cosmic [2] status of Christ in the foregoing

---

[1] Josephus, *Ant.* vi. 235.

[2] "Cosmic" here includes mankind.

verses Paul summarises (*oun*) by saying (Col. ii. 6) *hōs oun parelabete ton Christon Iēsoun ton kurion*. . . . Here *kurios*, with special emphasis on it (cf. the repeated article) summarises all that Paul has told the Colossians about Christ in the preceding sentences. That the world as it is cannot subsist in the sight of God depends upon its fallen nature; cf. Col. i. 20—*di' autou apokatallaxai ta panta eis auton, eirēnopoiēsas dia tou haimatos tou staurou autou, di' autou eite ta epi tēs gēs eite ta en tois ouranois*; cf. Eph. i. 20, f.; I Pet. iii. 22. The Son exercises God's sovereignty over the world in order to lay it— and with it Himself—at the Father's feet, after the overcoming of all opposing forces (I Cor. xv. 28). The lordship of Jesus, by which He exercises God's almighty sway over the world, thus has as its goal the putting of the reconciled and judged world in subjection to God.

In this process, however, the cardinal factor is mankind. Without detracting from the cosmic extent of His lordship sketched above, its centre of gravity is His lordship over men (Rom. xiv. 9—*eis touto gar Christos apethanen kai ezēsen, hina kai nekrōn kai zōntōn kurieusēi*. That is shown by the Pauline usage: [1] (*ho*) *Christos* is He who died on the Cross and has risen again (Rom. v. 6, 8, vi. 4, 9, xiv. 9; I Cor. i. 23 f., v. 7, viii. 11, xv. 3, 12 ff.; Gal. iii. 13, etc.); [2] the word appears when it is a question of the work of redemption (Rom. viii. 35, xv. 7; II Cor. iii. 14, v. 14, 18 f.; Gal. iii. 13); this work is in evidence when Paul exhorts through the *praütēs kai epieikeia tou Christou* (II Cor. x. 1, cf. I Cor. xi. 1). It is called *to euangellion tou Christou* (Rom. xv. 19; I Cor. ix. 12; II Cor. ii. 12, iv. 4, ix. 13, x. 14;

[1] Cf. the works of Stead, Burton and Dobschütz in the Bibliography ; also H. E. Weber, in *Neue kirchliche Zeitschrift* xxxi (1920), pp. 254-8.
[2] For what follows, cf. the tables in Foerster, *Herr ist Jesus*, pp. 237 ff.

Gal. i. 7, cf. I Cor. i. 6; II Cor. iii. 3) being crucified,
dead, with " Christ " (Rom. vi. 8, vii. 4; Gal. ii. 19)
baptised into Him (Gal. iii. 27). " Christ " has called
the Galatians into grace (Gal. i. 6), with the fullness
of the blessing (*eulogia*) of " Christ " Paul is certain of
coming to Rome (Rom. xv. 29), " Christ " has sent
him (I Cor. i. 17; Rom. xvi. 9; I Cor. iv. 1; Gal. i. 10;
II Cor. xi. 13, 23; the community is one body " in
Christ ", Rom. xii. 5; Gal. i. 22).

On the other hand, *kurios* looks towards the exalted
Lord who is authority (I Cor. iv. 19, xiv. 37, xvi. 7—
cf. Jas. iv. 15): it is the " lord " whom the faithful
serve (Rom. xii. 11; I Cor. xii.5; Eph. vi. 7; Col. iii.
23). Everyone stands or falls with his " lord " (Rom.
xiv. 4-8, cf. I Cor. vii. 32-5, Rom. xvi. 12, 22, II Cor.
viii. 5); that is also true of private life (I Cor. vii. 39).
Actions must be worthy of the " lord " (I Cor. xi. 27;
Rom. xvi. 2). It is the exalted Lord who dispenses to
each one the measure of his faith (I Cor. iii. 5, vii. 17).
It is the " lord " who is coming (I Thess. iv. 15 ff.;
I Cor. iv. 5, xi. 26; Phil. iv. 5) and who is the judge
(I Thess. iv. 6; II Thess. i. 9; I Cor. iv. 4, xi. 32;
II Cor. v. 11, x. 18). In this life Paul sojourns
" away from " the " lord " (II Cor. v. 6 ff.). He is
the lord of His servants, to whom He gives full authority
(II Cor. x. 8, xiii. 10) at whose work the community
members remain steadfast (I Cor. xv. 58) as, e.g.
Timothy (I Cor. iv. 17, xvi. 10). Paul's " work in
the lord " is the church at Corinth (I Cor. ix. 1-2);
in Troy Paul found a door opened " in the lord "
(II Cor. ii. 12). He is the one lord of all (Rom. x. 12),
" Christ " is proclaimed as " lord " (II Cor. iv. 5).
This exalted " lord " is the Spirit (II Cor. iii. 9) it is
to " the Lord " that Paul prays for release from his
sufferings (II Cor. xii. 8). The summary of all this is
found in I Cor. viii. 5 f.: *eiper eisin legomenoi theoi* . . .

*all' hēmin heis theos ho patēr . . . kai heis kurios Iēsous
Christos, di' hou to panta kai hēmeis di' autou.* " There
are many so-called gods in heaven and earth "—here
Paul is thinking of the fact that rulers too are equated
with gods. In fact, he adds, there are (more than
those who speak of gods in Heaven and on earth are
aware of) many gods (cf. Phil. iii. 19—*hōn ho theos hē
koilia*) and many " lords "—much upon which men are
dependent, and that consists of real powers. Thus
Paul makes no distinction between *theos* and *kurios* in
the sense that *kurios* denotes a mediator-divinity: there
are no instances of this in the environment of primitive
Christianity.[1] *Kurios* is here a term expressing relationship, it denotes that upon which men make themselves dependent or are in fact dependent. For the
Christians there is only one God with whom they have
to reckon, from and to whom all things exist (cf.
I Cor. xv. 28, p. 101, lines 10 ff *supra*), and only one
Lord upon whom they depend, to whom they owe
everything that makes them Christian. Here again it
is clear that *kurios* means He through whom God has
interposed into this world to save and to act.

Thus it is not the case that the distinction between
Christos and *kurios* is drawn according to some fixed
scheme. *Eis Christon hamartanete* (not *eis ton kurion*)
says Paul (I Cor. viii. 12) and thereby wishes to make
clear to the Corinthians that by their thoughtless
behaviour they are sinning against Him who died for

[1] Even Bousset, op. cit. p. 99, is obliged to supplement his contention that " while the Apostle, using the concept of *kyrios*, on the one
side places his Lord at the very side of God and yet also subor-
dinates Him in a certain manner, he thought there were analogies
for this differentiation within the Godhead in hellenistic religion ",
with his second note that it is not quite clear " what the Apostle
must have been thinking of when he presupposes that the difference of meaning between the words *theos* and *kurios* was well-
known ".

them and the brethren. It is the same with Rom.
xiv. 18: *ho . . . en toutōi douleuōn tōi Christōi.* On the
other hand, I Cor. xi. 26 has *ton thanaton tou kuriou
katangellete,* in contrast to the common usage, perhaps
because *achri hou elthēi* follows. In I Cor. vii. 22,
Paul, presumably upon grounds of style, changes the
expression: *ho gar en kuriōi klētheis doulos apeleutheros
kuriou estin* with *homoiōs ho eleutheros klētheis doulos estin
Christou.*

Besides the use of the simple *kurios,* or (*Iēsous*)
Christos, we find also varying conjunctions of the two.
Here too one has to reckon with a certain amount of
freedom of usage. The fact that 10 out of the 27 Pauline
uses of *ho kurios (hēmōn) Iēsous,* without *Christos,* are in
Thessalonians and 14 of the 18 non-Pauline uses are in
Acts is doubtless due to the youth of the Church in
Thessalonica and the missionary character of Acts.
The variation *ho kurios (hēmōn) Iēsous (Christos)* occurs
besides the simple (*Iēsous*) *Christos* or *kurios.* In Gal.
vi. 14 we find *kauchasthai . . . en tōi staurōi tou kuriou
hēmōn Iēsou Christou* alongside the numerous cases in
which, in this context, *Christos* stands alone, similarly,
e.g. Eph. iii. 11; Rom. v. 1, vi. 23, viii. 39; I Cor. xv.
57; I Thess. v. 9; and in contexts in which *ho kurios*
otherwise stands alone, the more detailed variation
occurs in Rom. xv. 30, xvi. 18; I Cor. i. 7, 8, 10; II Cor.
i. 14; I Thess. ii. 15, 19, iii. 13, iv. 2, v. 23; II Thess.
ii. 1; I Tim. vi. 14. It is clearly noticeable how the
longer form of the name of Jesus expresses a certain
emphasis and solemnity; so especially in the initial and
final greetings and decisive phases of the thought—
Rom. v. 1, viii. 39; I Cor. xv. 57; Rom. xv. 30. A
further element is introduced by the addition of a
personal pronoun, usually *hēmōn,* to *kurios.* The
general meaning is made clear by Phil. iii. 8—*hēgoumai
panta zēmian einai dia to huperechon tēs gnōseōs Christou Iesou*

tou kuriou mou—that of a personal allegiance. But it must be emphasised that it is not the allegiance of a lazy slave to his lord or between every slave and even the harshest master, whom his slave inwardly despises. The *hēmōn* in *ho kurios hēmōn Iēsous Christos* does not indicate a mere coupling together. " I never knew you " is the Lord's answer to " many " (Matt. vii. 23). Paul calls Him *Christos Iēsous ho kurios mou* (cf. Rev. xi. 8), because he is privileged to call Him his Lord, because He is the Lord who is for him, who " regards him as loyal " (I Tim. i. 12). The " our " which is always otherwise used refers to all Christians, not a single church, just as " your Lord Jesus Christ " never occurs. Christendom owes all that it is and has to the fact that it is " His " and He " its Lord ". Therefore it may be that with the " our " another element comes in, that of the sense of belonging together of the congregations which imposes obligations (Rom. xv. 30: *parakalō de humās dia tou kuriou hēmōn Iēsou Christou . . . sunagōnisasthai moi en tais proseuchais huper emou*—cf. I Cor. i. 10), which binds together (I Cor. i. 2), but which also separates them from others (Rom. xvi. 18: *hoi gar toioutoi tōi kuriōi hēmōn Christōi ou douleuousin*).

(*b*) In the N.T. Epistles and in Acts *kurios* is also used in a sense which we have not yet discussed, namely, for the " historical Jesus ": " I charge, not I, but *ho kurios* " (I Cor. vii. 10)—with these words Paul refers to a " word of the Lord ". Similarly in I Cor. ix. 14 and vii. 25, Paul says, in reference to the lack of any definite word of the Lord over this question *epitagēn kuriou ouch echō*. The same situation is behind I Cor. vii. 12—*legō egō, ouch ho kurios*. In I Thess. iv. 16, *touto gar humin legomen en logōi kuriou*, Paul is probably referring to a saying of Jesus which has not come down to us. Although in this passage one might think that *kurios* was used to denote authority, this point of view does not fit Gal. i. 19, nor I Cor. ix. 5—James the brother, and the brothers, *tou kuriou*. It is also the historical Lord who is in mind in Heb. ii. 3: (*sōtēria*) *hētis archēn labousa laleisthai dia tou kuriou hupo tōn akousantōn eis hēmas ebaiōthē*. An unrecorded word of the Lord is reckoned by Paul as one of the *logoi tou kuriou Iēsou* in Acts xx. 35: a recorded one is introduced in Acts xi. 16 with *emnēsthēn de tou rhēmatos tou kuriou*. This usage is also once paralleled in the gospels. Luke uses *ho kurios* thirteen times [1] always in L or in independent formulations, while John uses it similarly five times.[2] Otherwise *kurios* is only used in the gospels, except in the vocative, by Jesus in Mark xi. 3, par.: *kai ean tis humin eipēi: ti poieite touto? eipate: ho kurios autou chreian echei*, and, on the lips of Peter, in John xxi. 7: *ho kurios estin*. True, in Mark xi. 3, it is not quite clear whether in the Aramaic, in which "lord" is bound to have some suffix, the disciples must have said "our", "thy" or "his" (the donkey's) lord, or whether (cf. Mark v. 19) *ho kurios* is here a designation of God. The parallel with Mark xiv. 14, makes it probable that an "our", referring to the disciples, was linked as suffix to the original Aramaic word.

Modes of addressing Jesus demand separate treatment. In Mark it is only the Syropheonician woman who uses *kurie* (vii. 28), the disciples, Pharisees and people use *didaskale*.[3] Matthew has kept *didaskale* in Markan material only on the lips of Pharisees and Judas Iscariot and in ambiguous cases, and otherwise replaces it by *kurie*: thus for him *didaskale* as a mode

[1] vii. 13, 19, x. 1, 39, 41, xi. 39, xiii. 15, xvii. 5, 6, xviii. 6, xix. 8, xxii. 61 (twice); xvi. 8 and xxiv. 34 are omitted.
[2] iv. 1, vi. 23, xi. 2, xx. 2, 13, not counting xx. 18, 20, 25, xxi. 12, i.e. the passages which refer to the risen Lord.
[3] See Foerster, op. cit. pp. 216 ff.

of address connotes a definite reserve towards Jesus. Luke has kept *didaskale* in Markan material, or replaced it by *epistata*. In non-Markan passages he often has *kurie*, especially on the disciples' lips. In John *kurie* predominates. Mark and John have preserved original terms of address in *rhabbi* (Mark ix. 5, xi. 21, xiv. 45 (= Matt. xxvi. 49); John i. 38, 49, iii. 2, iv. 31, vi. 25, ix. 2, xi. 8 (and, in addressing the Baptist, John iii. 26)), and *rhabbouni* (Mark x. 51, John xx. 16). Both these are specifically translated as *didaskale* by John. Luke (always) and Matthew (generally) have reproduced this alien word by *kurie* (Matthew, Luke, e.g. xviii. 41 for *rhabbouni*) and *epistata*. In an unparalleled passage, Matthew xxvi. 25, Judas addresses Jesus as *rhabbi*. As to the meaning of this term, Mark and John must be regarded as its oldest and best interpreters. Even the independent Lukan translation (*epistata*) shows that a difference was felt between *rabbî* and *mârî*.

Thus in Mark Jesus is only once addressed as *kurie*, by a gentile woman, otherwise He is spoken to as *rhabbi* (only, of course, when some term of address is employed). The latter term has the sense of an address of honour, used especially to those learned in the law. The less frequent *rhabbouni* is closer to *mârî*, although John treats it as identical with *rabbî*. Luke reproduces it by *kurie*. It is unlikely that we ought to attach so much importance to the Marcan tradition as to conclude that Jesus was never addressed as *mârî*. For in Luke vi. 46; Matt. vii. 21 f., xxv. 11, the duplication of *kurie* is semitic—why not then the word as well? Moreover, in John xiii. 13, Jesus expressly refers to both the appellations *ho didaskalos* and *ho kurios*, and *mârî* is not impossible as a title used in addressing a scholar,[1] and was more common than *rabbî* as a mode

[1] Jer. Talmud, *Ketubboth*, 28d, l. 43. Dalman, op. cit. p. 267.

of address in general. That *mârî* is not mentioned in
Matt. xxiii. 7 ff. among the titles which Jesus forbids
to the disciples is bound up with the fact that the title
of rabbi was given to persons who had in any case no
right to it.

Didaskalos is also the word used to describe the relationship of Jesus to His disciples by Himself and by others:
by Jesus Himself Mark xiv. 14, par.; Matt. x. 24 f.
par, (xxiii. 8), cf. John xiii. 14; by others in Mark only
v. 35, par., also Matt. ix. 11, xvii. 24; John iii. 2, xi. 28.
Thus to a considerable extent Jesus was not addressed
as " lord " during His sojourn on earth, nor referred
to as such.

But this supplies the germ for the later usage of
referring to the historical Jesus as the *kurios*. The
designation of the members of the family of Jesus as
desposunoi (Eusebius, *Hist. Eccl.* i. 7, 14) harks back in
its style to Palestine. Here is no transmutation into
another species, but a heightening of the style found in
the Gospels. That it was later, in Luke's special
material and in John, that the possibility emerged of
referring to Jesus as the *kurios*, is linked with the fact
that the formulation of the Gospel material is influenced
by the needs of evangelism.[1]

This *kurios*, however, must be sharply distinguished
from that which confronts us in the Epistles. It may
perhaps be inferred from the speeches in Acts that the
name of Lord was not immediately used for the
Ascended (against this are Acts ii. 36 and x. 36: but
according to iii. 20, the name of Messiah was at first
prevalent). It is important to look not for the origin,
but for the roots, of the use of *kurios* most clearly observ-
able in Paul. Most decisive is the resurrection of
Jesus. Without it the disciples, looking back upon
their relationship with Jesus, might at any moment

[1] Foerster, op. cit. pp. 213 ff.

have described it by saying that He had been their Lord: but in fact it was a question of His being so still. The relationship of personal ties to Jesus which had characterised the dealings of the disciples with Him was now through the resurrection vitally renewed and sealed. The parables which describe the relationship of Jesus to His disciples under the guise of a lord and his slaves or servants now received their profoundest significance; now the disciples were the servants waiting for their lord. Since the disciples knew Jesus to be at the right hand of God, their relationship to Him now transcended all human analogies and became purely religious, i.e. founded upon faith. A further root which produced the use of Lord as a name for Jesus is the use which Jesus twice made of Ps. cx—Mark xii. 35 ff. par. and xiv. 62, par.[1] We have seen how strong was the effect of this psalm upon the N.T. (cf. *supra*, pp. 99-100, ff.). He who is David's lord is thereby also Israel's lord, and, in the faith of the early Church, lord of the New Israel. Perhaps the Palestinian original congregation went no further than that —for them " lord " had always a genitive or personal pronoun attached to it, " our lord " was there the name for Jesus. That is also indicated by the Aramaic word *maranatha*, which occurs twice in early Christianity—I Cor. xvi. 22 and the *Didache* x. 6. The interpretation is disputed, whether it should be transcribed as *māran 'athā'*, or *māranā' thā'*.[2] In any case the phrase is about " our lord " and it refers to Jesus. There is no ground for maintaining that the word did not originate with the Palestinian church, since all the Aramaic words preserved in the gospels did so and the retention of the foreign-sounding words is only significant

[1] See also E. Meyer, *Ursprung und Anfänge des Christentums*, iii, p. 218, n. 1.

[2] See E. Peterson. $Ε\hat{ι}ς\ θεός$ (1926), pp. 130 f.

if it derives from the first Christians and not from
some Aramaic-speaking congregation in Syria. In the
Greek-speaking congregations the personal pronoun
hēmōn, corresponding to the suffix, dropped off, as we
observed in the case with the gentile use of *kurios* for
gods (p. 27, lines 8 ff.). Thus *kurios*, used absolutely,
could express the comprehensive lordship of Jesus,
testifying that " the Father has given all judgment to
the Son " (John v. 22) and that to Him all authority
in Heaven and earth has been given (Matt. xxviii. 18).
If *kurios* expressed this, then the LXX passages which
mention *kurios* could be interpreted of Jesus: in Him
God acts in such a way as is said in the O.T. of the
kurios.

4. *Earthly Kurios-relationships*

In the N.T. a new look is given to earthly relationships of rank. This is clear from the relationship of
slaves to their masters: " Slaves, be subservient in all
respects to your *kurioi* in the flesh, not in *ophthalmodou-
liais*, as men-pleasers, but in singleness of heart, fearing
ton kurion. Whatever you do, work with your whole
soul as *tōi kuriōi* and not for men, knowing that you
will receive the reward of your inheritance *apo kuriou* "
(Col. iii. 22). It is a question of complete submission
to their lord, which also shuns *ophthalmodoulia*, superficial appearances of service, and is thus complete
loyalty. But this loyalty is only possible because
their service for their lords is their service of the
Lord, their service of God: thereby they can serve
their lords completely in their loyalty to Christ, free
from all human constraint. This focuses at one point
in relationships of rank the fundamental solution of
the whole problem raised by the word " lord ", a
problem which every people has sought to solve in its
own way.

I. INDEX OF WORDS AND REFERENCES

III. OLD TESTAMENT

GENERAL INDEX

(See also the Bibliography pp. ix – x)

II

GNOSIS

BY

RUDOLF BULTMANN

Translated from the German
first edition, Stuttgart, 1933
and with additional notes
by J. R. Coates

PREFACE

EARLIER manuals in this series have borne English titles, and formal consistency would suggest " Knowledge " for this one. But while that would indicate part of its contents, it would not obviously include what is in reality its main subject, viz. the Biblical doctrine of the knowledge of God in relation to non-Christian and heretical forms of Gnosticism.

The Greek word *Gnosis* finds a place in modern English dictionaries both because of its use in historical, philosophical and theological writings and because it is still claimed by successors of the Gnostics as " knowledge of spiritual mysteries ". This is the definition given in *The Concise Oxford Dictionary*, which also has the following equivalents for *Gnostic:* " Relating to knowledge, cognitive; having esoteric spiritual knowledge; of the Gnostics, occult, mystic; early Christian heretic claiming *Gnosis*."

It has long been evident to students of the New Testament that in some of its later Books there are references to Gnostic doctrines which were being widely taught in the second, third, and fourth centuries, both outside and inside the Church, and now there is a growing tendency to recognise the existence of these doctrines at a much earlier date, so that they have to be taken into account in the interpretation both of the whole of the New Testament and also of the Greek versions of the Old Testament. The latter is illustrated briefly by Georg Bertram in our fourth chapter, and in the rest of the volume Rudolf Bultmann, after comparing Greek and Hebrew theories of knowledge

and describing Hellenistic Gnosticism, presents the
case for a much fuller use of Gnostic material in the
exegesis of the New Testament, thus preparing the way
for an elaborate treatment of the subject in his new
Theologie des Neuen Testaments.

Much of what Dr. Bultmann has to say is summed
up in Martin Buber's aphorism, " All revelation is
summons and sending ", or in his longer statement,
" The Father and the Son, like in being—we may even
say God and Man, like in being—are the indissolubly
real pair, the two bearers of the primal relation,
which from God to man is termed mission and command, from man to God looking and hearing, and
between both is termed knowledge and love " (*I and
Thou*, 1937, pp. 115, 85).

This is no merely academic subject. Dr. A. D.
Galloway does well, in his chapter on the Gnostics in
The Cosmic Christ (1951), to emphasise the point that
" the primary concern of the main Gnostic schools
was not simply to solve certain theological problems.
Their primary concern was salvation." To understand them requires not only ʻhistorical knowledge
but also personal religious experience—and some
acquaintance with certain types of evangelical technique. No-one can fail to be impressed by the depth
of spiritual understanding shown in the hymn of
thanksgiving which concludes the crowning discourse
addressed *To Asclepius* by an Egyptian Gnostic teacher,
writing under the name of Hermes Trismegistus,
probably towards the end of the third century. By
the kindness of the Delegates of the Clarendon Press,
who published it at Oxford in 1924, we are allowed
to quote from Walter Scott's translation of this in
Hermetica, vol. I, p. 375.

> We thank thee, O thou Most High, with heart
> and soul wholly uplifted to thee;

for it is by thy grace alone that we have attained
to the light and come to know thee.

We thank thee, O thou whose name no man can
tell,

but whom men honour by the appellation ' God ',
because thou alone art Master,

and bless by the appellation ' Father ', because thou
hast shown in act toward all men and in all
things loving-kindness and affection such as a
father feels, nay, yet sweeter than a father's;

for thou hast bestowed on us mind, and speech, and
knowledge:

mind, that we may apprehend thee;

speech, that we may call upon thee;

and knowledge, that having come to know thee,
and found salvation in the light thou givest,
we may be filled with gladness.

We are glad because thou hast revealed thyself
to us in all thy being; we are glad because,
while we are yet in the body, thou has deigned
to make us gods by the gift of thine own
eternal life.

Man can thank thee only by learning to know thy
greatness.

Wilfred L. Knox, commenting in *St. Paul and the
Church of the Gentiles* (p. 176) on Col. iii, 15 ff., refers
to this and other Hermetic passages as examples of a
conventional use of thanksgivings for propaganda
purposes; but this hardly does them justice, for they
convey the thrill of an authentic vitality, and it is not
surprising that they should come to be used in later
days for magical purposes.

Whether Dr. Bultmann's views be accepted or not, his presentation of them in the following pages throws new light on many parts of the Bible, and makes us more eager than ever for the publication of the large store of Gnostic works recently discovered at Khenoboskion in Upper Egypt, said to be of first importance.

J. R. COATES.

CONTENTS

SELECT BIBLIOGRAPHY

G. ANRICH: Das antike Mysterienwesen, 1894.

E. BAUMANN: *yadha'* und seine Derivate, Z.A.W. XXVIII, 22 ff., 110 ff., 1908.

W. BOUSSET: Hauptprobleme der Gnosis, 1911; Pauly-W. VII, 1503 ff., 1912; G.G.A., 740 ff., 1914; [Kyrios Christos, 2nd edn., 1921].

H. JONAS: Der Begriff d. Gnosis, Diss. Marburg, 1930.

J. KROLL: Die Lehren d. Hermes Trismegistos, 350 ff., 1914.

R. REITZENSTEIN: Die Hellenistischen Mysterienreligionen, 3rd edn., esp. 66 ff., 284 ff., 1927; Hist. Monachorum u. Hist. Lausiaca, esp. 146 ff., 1916; [Poimandres, 1904].

A. SCHLATTER: Der Glaube im N.T., 4th edn., 214 ff., 316 ff., 388 ff., 1927.

B. SNELL: Die Ausdrücke f. d. Begriff des Wissens in d. vorplaton. Phil., Philol. Unters. 29, 1924.

[E. BEVAN: Christianity, 64-77, 1932.

F. C. BURKITT: Church and Gnosis, 1932.

C. H. DODD: The Bible and the Greeks, xii-xv, 99-248, 1935.

E. DE FAYE: Introd. à l'étude du gnosticisme, 1903.

A. D. GALLOWAY: The Cosmic Christ, 66-98, 1951.

A. HARNACK: History of Dogma (Eng. Tr. 1894-9).

F. J. A. HORT and J. B. MAYOR: Clem. Alex. Strom. VII.

W. R. INGE: E.R.E., I, 308-319, 1908.

W. D. NIVEN: D.A.C., II, 453-456, 1915.

E. F. SCOTT: Gnosticism, E.R.E., VI, 231-242, 1913.

W. SCOTT: Hermetica, 1924-26.]

Note.—Square Brackets indicate additions by the translator.

ABBREVIATIONS

B.D.B.	Brown, Driver and Briggs, Hebrew Lexicon, 1906.
Bill.	Strack u. Billerbeck, Komm. z. N.T. aus Talmud u. Midrasch, 1922-28.
C.B.	Cambridge Bible for Schools and Colleges.
Corp. Herm.	G. Parthey, Berlin, 1854.
D.A.C.	Hastings, Dictionary of the Apostolic Church.
Diels	H. Diels, D. Fragmente d. Vorsokratiker 4, 1922.
Ditt. Syll.	W. Dittenberger, Sylloge Inscript. Graec.
E.R.E.	Hastings, Encyclopædia of Religion and Ethics.
G.G.A.	Götting. Gel. Aus.
Herm.	W. Scott, Hermetica, 1924-26.
I.C.C.	International Critical Commentary.
J.T.S.	Journal of Theological Studies.
Kautzsch	Die heilige Schrift des A.T., 4th edn. Bertholet, 1921 ff.
Kittel	Theol. Wörterb. N.T., G. Kittel and G. Friedrich, 1933 ff.
LXX	Septuagint.
Moult-Mill.	Moulton and Milligan, Vocab. Gk. Test., 1915 ff.
M.P.G.	Patrologia, Series Graeca ed. Migne, 1844 ff.
Nauck	Porphyrii opuscula selecta, A. Nauck, 2nd ed. 1886.
N.G.G.	Nachrichten v. d. Kgl. Gesellschaft der Wissenschaften zu Göttingen, 1894 ff.
Pauly-W.	Pauly-Wissowa Realencyclop., 1892 ff.
Pr.-Bauer	Preuschen-Bauer Wörterb., 1928.
R.G.G.	Die Religion in Geschichte und Gegenwart, 2nd edn., 1927 ff.
S.A.B.	Sitzungsberichte . . . Akademie . . . Berlin.
S.A.H.	Sitzungsberichte . . . Akademie . . . Heidelberg.
Snell	See Bibliography.
Z.N.W.	Zeitschrift f. N.T. Wissenschaft.

Note.—Scripture references are to the English Bible; where Hebrew and/or Greek enumeration differs, this is shown throughout the book.

I. GNOSIS IN GREEK LITERATURE

In ordinary Greek γινώσκειν (earlier γιγνώσκειν) denotes the intelligent grasp of an object or a situation,
whether encountered for the first time or on some
subsequent occasion, or as something long known.
The inchoative form of the verb shows that the original
emphasis was on the ingressive experience of becoming
aware, but the loss of this is seen when οἶδα takes the
place of ἔγνωκα, and the meaning is simply to know or
understand—just as, on the other hand, γνῶσις or
γνώμη generally takes the place of εἴδησις.[1] The best
way of getting at the root meaning of γινώσκειν, and
of understanding the specifically Greek conception of
knowledge, is to differentiate it on the one hand from
αἰσθάνεσθαι, and on the other from δοκεῖν and δοξάζειν.
(a) The first means simply perception, with no
necessary emphasis on understanding, though this
may be present in an unreflective, instinctive form,[2]
and originally there was not much difference between
the two words. Epistemology, however, maintains
the distinction between αἴσθησις as perception and
γνῶσις, or ἐπιστήμη gained through γινώσκειν, as

---

[1] Cf. Snell (see p. xi), 30 f. For examples of the " ingressive "
see Hom. Il. XVII, 333 f. (perceive); Xenoph. Anab. I, vii, 4
(get to know); Soph. Antig. 1089 (learn). For wider usage see
Heracl. Fr. 97 (I, 97, 5f. Diels: " dogs bark at people if they
do not know them "); Plato, Crat. 435a (understand); Democritus, Fr. 198: II, 102, 6 f. Diels: " the beast knows (οἶδεν)
how much it needs, but man lacks this sagacity (οὐ γινώσκει) ".

[2] Ἀισθανόμενος means sensible, intelligent, capable of dis-
tinguishing between right and wrong. See Xenoph. Mem. IV.
v, 6; Thuc. I, lxxi, 5; and cf. Phil. i, 9 (αἴσθησις). Ἀναίσθητος
means dull, stupid, idiotic.

knowledge resulting from the exercise of reason, sometimes stressing the contrast and sometimes the connexion. (*b*) The other two words (δοκεῖν and δοξάζειν) mean holding an opinion (δόξα) without any guarantee of its truth, whereas γινώσκειν means grasping things as they really are—the ὄν or ἀλήθεια.[1] An opinion may certainly be true, but only he who knows (γινώσκειν) can be sure that he is right, that he has ἀλήθεια. Gnosis is connected with ἐπιστήμη, but differs from it (and from ἄγνοια) in not being used absolutely; it requires an Objective Genitive, and signifies the act of knowing rather than the knowledge itself.[2]

The attainment of knowledge is not bound up with a special organ, or limited to any particular method; it comes to man in the experience of intercourse with his environment, whether that be good or evil (Homer, Od. xxi, 35 f.; xv, 537; Plato, Rep. v, 466c; Xenoph. Anab. I, vii, 4), as he exercises the normal means of apprehension, seeing and hearing, study and reflexion (cf. γνῶθι σαυτόν: know thyself). Hence γινώσκειν can denote personal acquaintance and friendship with persons (Xenoph. Cyrop. I, iv, 27; Hist. Graec. V. iii, 9),[3]—a development specially seen in the adjectives γνωστός and γνώριμος. Further, it

[1] Heracl. Fr. (I, lxxviii, 11 f. Diels): " not knowing gods or heroes ". The object of knowledge is essential reality (τὸ ὄν) at Parm. Fr. 4, 7 f. (I, clii, 12 f. Diels) and Plato, Rep. V, 477a ff. (where δόξα is placed between γνῶσις and ἄγνοια). At Plato, Rep. IX, 581b it is truth. For the contrast with δοκεῖν or δοξάζειν see Heracl. Fr. 7 (II, lix, 17 ff. Diels); Plato, Men. 97a ff.; Rep. V, 476d ff.

[2] Isolated examples of the absolute use are Plato, Rep. VI, 508e (see p. 8); Epicurus (cf. Philodemus Περὶ κακιῶν ed. Jensen, col. 8, 33 f.); Plut. adv. Col. 3 (II, 1108e).

[3] Here belong Wettstein's ostensible parallels to Matt. vii, 23, which show that γινώσκειν (and γνωρίζειν) with the negative can actually mean to ignore.

is possible that " a knowing one " (γινώσκων) is the equivalent of " a wise one " (σοφός), though his schooling is merely that of life itself (Plat. Rep. i, 347d).[1] This development, however, is found much more in the case of εἰδέναι, which commonly has the sense of understanding and ability.[2]

The most important question is, which mode of knowing determines the primary Greek idea of knowledge. Since γινώσκειν denotes the knowing of what really is, it comes to mean verifying (konstatieren); and since the Greeks regard the eye as a more reliable witness than the ear (Herac. Fr. 101a (Diels I, xcvii, 15 ff.); Herodot. i 8), sight being higher in rank among the senses than hearing (Plato. Phaedr. 250d; Rep. vi 507c), verification depends upon personal observation, as has already been indicated by the linking of γινώσκειν with εἰδέναι, the latter meaning knowledge as the result of seeing for oneself.[3] This explains how γινώσκειν may be the result of considering

---

[1] Snell, 5 ff.

[2] E.g. in the use of weapons (Hom. Il. II, 718; XV, 525; VII, 236), the practice of friendship (Hom. Od. III, 227) or gratitude (frequently; χάριν γινώσκειν is also found), or things lawful or lawless (Hom. Il. V, 761; Od. IX, 189; cf. Theog. 1141 f.). Correspondingly γνώμη can mean reason, reasonableness, intelligence: Theogn. 1171 f.; Heracl. Fr. 41 (I, lxxxvi, 4f. Diels); Epicharmus, Fr. 4 (I, cxx, 17 ff. Diels); Herodot. III, 4; Thuc. I, lxxv, 1; Xenoph. Anab. II, vi, 9; Plato, Rep. V, 476d (contrasted with δόξα). It can also mean disposition, good or evil: Theog. 60, 396, 408 ; Pindar, Olymp. iii, 41; Aristoph. Fr. 355 ; Snell, 34. Later examples are Porphyry ad Marcellam 11, 20, 21; p. 281, 19; 287, 17; 288, 4, Nauck; Albinos, Is. 1, p. 152, Hermann; Ditt. Syll. 3rd ed., 983, 4 ff. Standing by itself it may connote a good idea, sound advice, a maxim or pronouncement (cf. the definition at Aristot. Rhet. II, 21, p. 1394a, 19 ff.). See also pp. 4, 56. [Alb. Is.: 2nd cent. Intr. to Plato.]

[3] See Snell, 20 ff. on the connexion between knowing and seeing.

the facts and circumstances of a case,[1] so that it means
comprehension; a conclusion has been reached, and
the matter is clear (δῆλον) or manifest (φανερόν).[2]
Knowledge amounts to close inspection, and is objective
in that its sole interest is in seeing its object at close
quarters. This does not apply merely to things and
facts immediately at hand; everything which can
raise a question can be an object of γινώσκειν—e.g.
the right time for doing something (καιρὸν γνῶθι),[3]
or the right thing to do (ἔγνω δεῖν);[4] and thus
γινώσκειν can mean giving a decision or a decree[5]
or even a legal verdict.[6] But the idea of visual
inspection is never absent.[7]

Ultimate truth for the Greeks means the reality
which underlies all appearances, and this determines
the nature of knowledge of the truth. The Greek ideal

[1] Democr. Fr. 283 (II, 119, 13 ff. Diels); Aristoph. Clouds 912;
Plutus, 944; Thuc. I, xxv, 1; xliii, 2; cii, 4; Plato, Apol. 27a;
Phaedo, 116c. etc.
[2] Philol. Fr. 11 (I, 313, 5 ff. Diels); Archyt. Fr. 1 (I, 334, 12,
Diels); Plato, Crat. 435a.
[3] Pittacus I (II, 216, 10, Diels).
[4] Xenoph. Hist. Gr. III, i, 12.
[5] Democr. Fr. 229 (II, cvii, 1 f. Diels); cf. Isocr. vi, 30;
Demosth. lix, 47.
[6] Plut. Ages. iii (1597a).
[7] Similarly γνώμη can be counsel, policy (Pindar, Nem. X,
89; Thuc. II, lv, 2), the decree of the popular assembly, the
judgment (Snell, 35; also in inscriptions and papyri); and
γνῶσις the legal verdict (Snell, 38, 2; cf. the German Erkenntnis).
But we must be on our guard against interpreting this in terms
of the modern idea of the will, remembering that the Greeks
always thought of it in terms of seeing. Cf. on this point E.
Wolff, Platos Apologie, Neue philologische Untersuchungen VI
(1929), 34 ff., and Snell, Das Bewusstsein von eigenen Entschei-
dungen im frühen Griechentum, Philologus, 85 (1930), 141 ff.;
and on γνώμη cf. Ed. Schwartz, Gnomon II (1925), 68; J.
Stenzel, G.G.A. 1926, 200 f. and Pauly-W. II, Reihe III (1927),
829; and see pp. 3, 56.

of knowledge becomes clear when it is understood
that knowing is a kind of seeing. Correspondingly,
reality belongs to forms and figures, or to the elements
or principles which they embody. That is why the
student and the philosopher must get to know them;
for it is the εἶδος (or ἰδέα) of things which makes
possible the knowledge of what they are.¹ Knowing
is thus seeing (cf. θεωρεῖν, σκοπεῖν, σκέπτεσθαι for
studying), and seeing is grasping or handling. This
explains both the importance of mathematics for
knowledge (cf. Plato, Gorg. 508a) and the fact that
γινώσκειν and γνῶσις can have the same meaning as
καταλαμβάνειν and κατάληψις. On the one hand that
which is real, as being comprehensible by knowledge of
this kind, is regarded as being seen by the eye of the
soul in its eternal unchangeableness. On the other
hand, the seer truly " has " this reality, and is thereby
assured that in knowing it he can make use of it.
Knowledge (ἐπιστήμη) differs from opinion (δόξα)
in that it is " bound " (Plato, Meno 98a); [it cannot
escape or be lost]; what it gives is a lasting possession.²
Now it is the character of the thing as known which
actually constitutes its reality. Therefore the knowledge of what really exists may be regarded as man's
highest possible achievement in this present life, for
in it he touches the eternal and shares in it; although
different views may be held on the question how far

¹ Of course it does not matter if the Pythagoreans speak of
ἀριθμοί instead of εἴδη (apart from Plato, cf. e.g. Antiphon, Fr. 1
(II, 292, 5 ff. Diels)), since it is these that make knowledge possible,
by giving things outline and form (Philologus, Fr. 3, 4, 6, 11
(I, 310 ff. Diels)) ; cf. also J. Stenzel, Zahl und Gestalt bei Platon
und Aristoteles, 2nd ed. (1932). Similarly the atoms of Democritus, which differ from each other in shape or form (Aristot.
Phys. I, ii, p. 184b, 21), serve to explain the qualitative differences
of things as differences of form, order and disposition; indeed he
seems also to have called the atoms " ideas " (II, xxvi, 35, Diels).
² Plato, Theat. 209e; Phaedo, 75d.

knowledge (γνῶσις) of this kind may be identical
with the ideal of the contemplative life (Βίος
Θεωρητικός);[1] for knowledge is concerned, not only
with the elements or ideas of the natural world, but
also with those of human life, individual and social,
such as virtue and beauty (e.g. Plato, Rep. V, 476cd:
he who can discern abstract beauty is he who " knows ").
Plato regards gnosis or philosophical knowledge as
being in the same relation to correct political action
as the vision of the artist is to his work of art (means to
an end); whereas Aristotle sees disinterested scientific
thought as man's highest occupation (an end in itself).[2]

[1] Cf. F. Boll, Vita contemplativa (S.A.H. 1920); W. Jaeger,
Über Ursprung und Kreislauf des philos. Lebensideals (S.A.B.
1928, 390 ff.).

[2] It is remarkable, perhaps a Semitism, that from the Hellenistic period γινώσκειν is used in the sexual sense. See p. 16, and
Moult.-Mill. and Pr.-Bauer s.v.

II. GNOSTIC USAGE

THE natural development of Greek usage, which we have briefly examined, prepares the way for that of the Hellenistic period, specially in the case of *gnosis*.[1] Here other sources have to be recognised, viz. the Mystery Religions, which impart the secret learning necessary for salvation, and Magic, which bestows supernatural powers on those who know it.[2] We are

[1] Empedocles and Plato described philosophy after the analogy of initiation into the Mysteries (for Plato, cf. Rohde, Psyche II, 281 ff.; Anrich, Das antike Mysterienwesen, 63); Plato was simply using an illustration, but Neo-Platonism meant it seriously (cf. Anrich, 66 ff.; P. Friedländer, Platon I (1928), 68 ff.; on the whole subject see J. Stenzel, Platon der Erzieher (1928)). It is truly Greek feeling that finds expression in what Plutarch says in Isis et Osiris i, 2 (II, 351de): the blessedness of God consists in wise understanding; it is his everlasting happiness to enjoy knowledge which never falls short of reality; without this immortality would not be life, but merely the lapse of time; the search for truth is a yearning after divinity; sobriety and worship lead to the *gnosis* of ultimate reality, which Isis offers in communion with herself.

[2] Cf. Reitzenstein, Hell. Myst. 295 f. ; 300 ff. ; Kroll, Die Lehren des Hermes Trismegistos, 326 ff.; esp. 366 f.; Anrich, Mysterienwesen, 78 ff.; W. Bousset, Pauly-W. VII (1912), 1521 ff. The connexion with the contemplation of Mysteries (cf. preceding note) is illustrated, e.g. by the secrecy of Gnosis and its characterisation as an incommunicable mystical word (Hippol. Ref. V, vii, 22). For the connexion with Magic see, e.g. Epiphanius, 31, 7, 8 (I, p. 397, 9); Preisendanz, Pap. Gr. Mag., II, 128: the magician has received as a gift the *gnosis* of the name of a god, and is himself addressed as the blessed initiate of holy Magic (ib. 127); Philo, Spec. Leg. III, 100, calls immediate apprehension (ὀπτικὴ ἐπιστήμη), which is identical with γνῶσις, "a true Magic". The two are almost synonyms.

7

concerned here, of course, with *gnosis* in its technical sense, not with its ordinary use, which retains all its old variety of meanings.[1] This special kind of knowledge constitutes the goal of that Hellenistic type of piety, both outside and inside the Church, which we call Gnostic. The three main characteristics of Gnosticism are as follows.

I. KNOWLEDGE OF GOD

Gnosis here means not only the act of knowing, but also knowledge itself, and can be used absolutely, without a qualifying Genitive. This does not mean knowledge or science ($\dot{\epsilon}\pi\iota\sigma\tau\dot{\eta}\mu\eta$) in general, but is limited to knowledge of God. Formally this resembles Plato's assertion that the idea of the Good is superior to *gnosis* (used absolutely!)[2] and truth. But though it is obvious that his gnosis, in arriving at ultimate reality, attains to the divine, the Gnostic sources represent God in more exclusive fashion against a background of dualism.[3] The former conceived of the Godhead as beyond the world in the sense that it was the ground of all existence, but for the latter it was the wholly other, not apprehended within the world by means of recollection, but by looking away from it, cf. Corp. Herm. X, 5. Thus the knowledge with which the Gnostics were concerned differed from that of the earlier Greeks in being separated from all other kinds of knowledge, just as " truth " and " substance " ($o\dot{\upsilon}\sigma\dot{\iota}a$) were predicated of God alone.

[1] The Stoics said that all men have a natural knowledge of God's existence. See Bultmann in Kittel s.v. $\ddot{a}\gamma\nu\omega\sigma\tau\sigma\varsigma$.

[2] See p. 2.

[3] Cf. W. Bousset, Kyrios Christos, 2nd ed. (1921), 183 ff.; also in N.G.G. (1914), 706 ff. and Pauly-W. VII (1912), 1507 ff., 1518 ff.

2. A GIFT

Whereas the older Greeks regarded knowing as the developed methodical activity of mind (νοῦς) or speech (λόγος), fulfilling itself in science and specially in philosophy, to the Gnostic it was—both as process and as result—a gift (χάρισμα) from God to man, illumination, something fundamentally different from rational thought.[1] For God is inaccessible to men in their natural state; but he knows them (the pious) and reveals himself to them.[2] Such *gnosis* is ecstatic or mystical vision,[3] still a kind of seeing, but very

[1] The numerous cases, in which gnosis is traced back to Mind or Speech, do not point to human ability but to the supernatural power which flows into man and enlightens him, e.g. Corp. Herm. I, 2, 22 f. ; IV, 3 ff. (the divine Mind is here differentiated from the human Speech). In such cases Mind or Speech takes the place of Spirit; cf. Reitzenstein, Hell. Myst. 328 ff.

[2] Corp. Herm. I, 31; VII, 2; X, 4, 15: " God does not lack knowledge of man, but knows him perfectly and wishes to be known "; Asclep. 29b (Hermetica I, 370, 6 f. Scott); Clem. Al. Exc. ex Theod. 7; Porphyry ad Marcellam, 13, 21 (p. 283, 9; 288, 14, Nauck); Clem. Al. Strom. V xi, 71; Odes of Sol. VI, etc. [See A. Mingana, D.A.C. II, 101 (1918).] For gnosis as a gift of the Spirit, cf. R. Liechtenhan, Die Offenbarung im Gnosticismus (1901), 98 ff.; E. Norden, Agnostos Theos. (1913), 287 f. ; Kroll, Die Lehren des Hermes Trismegistos, 354 and esp. Reitzenstein, Hell. Hyst. 285 ff. with the thanksgiving in Asclep. III, 41b (Scott, Herm. I, 374 ff. [see p. xi]); and see H. Schlier, Religionsgeschichtl. Unters. zu d. Ignatiusbriefen (1929), 58 ff.

[3] For a description of the vision see Corp. Herm. I, 30; X, 30; X, 4-6; XIII, 13 ff.; Stobaeus, Ecl. I, 486 (Scott, Herm. I, 418, 12 ff.); Kroll, Die Lehren d. H.T., 355 f. On the synonymous use of ὁρᾶν, θεᾶσθαι, etc. cf. Kroll, op. cit. 352; Reitzenstein, op. cit. 352. Plotinus avoids altogether the use of *gnosis* for the mystical vision. He calls it θέα, using γνῶσις for the preparatory scientific learning (Enn. VI, vii, 36). His gnosis is built upon forms (εἴδη VI, ix, 3) and in the vision of the One the

different from that of the older Greeks. The Gnostic does not come into possession of what he sees; he has to pray to be kept in a state of *gnosis*,[1] which means both the culminating point of the Vision of God and also, preferably, the way which leads to the goal of Θεωρία in the sense of ecstatic, mystical vision.[2] This process naturally involves the acquisition of a mass of traditional mythology and philosophy so that in some of its types Gnosticism is hard to distinguish from speculation. Philo and Plotinus, e.g. pursue a course of genuine scientific philosophy on their way to the mystical vision, but in the resultant *gnosis* the fiction is maintained that all that preparatory learning is a gift of divine revelation communicated to the believer through tradition. Gnosticism is a form of occultism, learned in a mystical way rather than a philosophical. Its teaching demands faith rather

soul must be independent of them (VI, iv, 7). The One itself cannot have knowledge without consequently having ignorance (VI, ix, 6). But of course the scientific grasp of the idea of the One can be called knowledge (VI, ix, 5). Cf. Norden, Agnostos Theos, 89, 1.

[1] Corp. Herm. I, 32; Scott, Herm. I, 376, 12 ff.; Clem. Al. Strom. VII, vii, 46. According to Clement of Alexandria *gnosis* can become a habit through practice (Strom. IV, xxii, 139; VI, ix, 71, 74, 78: " when perfected in the mystic habit, it abides infallible through love ").

[2] Clem. Al. Strom VI, vii, 61. On gnosis as the way, cf. Corp. Herm. IV, 8, 11; VII, 1 ff. ; X, 15 (gnosis as the ascent to Olympus). In the Naassene Hymn (Hippol. Ref. V, x, 2), the Redeemer says, " With the seal will I descend, travel through all Aeons, disclose all mysteries, show the forms of the gods; the secrets of the holy path which are called gnosis I will impart ". [Trans. E. F. Scott, E.R.E. VI, 231.] Jamblichus, Myst. X, v, 291, 7 ff. (Parthey, 1857): Gnosis " saves our true life by leading it up to its Father "; it is also the way of blessedness, a door into the presence of God the creator of all. Cf. Kroll, op. cit. 380 ff.; Reitzenstein, op. cit. 295; Bultmann, N.Z.W. 29 (1930), 173 ff.

than hard thinking.[1] At a primitive stage the knowledge gained through the sacred tradition guarantees
the soul of the Gnostic access to heaven after death;[2]
at a later stage the initiate is born again through the
operation of the mystical or magical formula of the
regenerating word (λόγος παλιγγενεσίας).[3]

The doctrine consists of cosmology and anthropology,
viewed entirely from the standpoint of soteriology.
It comprises things on earth, things in heaven, and
whatever may be above heaven, particularly the secrets
of astrology; [4] but all learning serves the knowledge
of the self, which is the condition of redemption and
the vision of God. This, however, is not identical
with Socrates' self-examination (Plato, Apol. 38a),
which means looking into the mind and its powers.
It is knowledge of the soul's Whence and Whither,[5]

[1] For the place of faith in Gnosticism cf. Corp. Herm. I, 32;
IX, 10; XI, 1; esp. IV, 4 f. 9; Asclep. III (Scott, Herm. I,
p. 366, 7, 9, 20; 370, 12, 15); Porphyry ad Marc., 21, 22, 24
(p. 288, 7, 22 f. ; 289, 18 ff. Nauck). See Reitzenstein H.M.
234 f.; 385 ff.

[2] Irenaeus I, xxi, 5 (M.P.G. VII, 665 ff.).

[3] Corp. Herm. XIII.

[4] Cf. Kroll, Lehren d. Herm. Trismegistos, 367 ff.

[5] Clem. Al. Exc. ex Theodotus, 78: " It is not baptism alone
that sets us free, but also knowing (*gnosis*) what we were and what
we have become, where we were or where we were driven, where
we are hurrying, from what we are cleansed, what birth is, and
what re-birth ". According to Hippolytus, Ref. V, xvi, 1, it is
said by the Perates [an Ophite Gnostic sect, see E. F. Scott in
E.R.E. VI, 238; IX, 500]: " We alone know the necessity of
birth, and the ways by which man enters the world, and so being
fully instructed we alone are able to pass through and beyond
decay " (περᾶσαι τὴν φθοράν); and Ref. V, vi, 6: " they think
knowledge of man the beginning of the possibility of knowledge of
God, calling the one the beginning of perfection and the other the
end ". Cf. Acta Thomae, 15, p. 121, 12 f.; Corp. Herm. I,
19, 21; IV, 4f.; M. Lidzbarski, Das Johannesbuch der Mandäer
(1915), 170, 18; 171, 17; 180, 15 f.; Norden, Agnostos Theos,

and of the tragic journey from its original home in the
world of light into entanglement in the world of matter:
he who knows that he came originally out of the world
of life and light will ultimately return to it. This kind
of gnosis certainly includes cosmological speculation,
but it is far from being a mere acceptance of theory and
dogma, for it involves a definite act of the will, and
leads to a definite attitude towards life. Knowledge
of the ideal (καλόν) no longer serves the shaping of the
world as Plato taught, but requires its abandonment.
The man who truly knows himself is the opposite of
the man who loves his body, misled by desire. Gnosis
is a form of piety,[1] and ignorance (ἄγνοια, ἀγνωσία) is
not only lack of knowledge, but also wickedness.[2]

102 ff.; Kroll, Lehren d. Herm. Tr. 372 ff.; Bousset, Kyrios Chr.
201 f.; Reitzenstein, Hell. Myst. 291; G. P. Wetter, N.Z.W. 18
(1917-18), 49 ff.
    A philosophical turn is given to this thought of self-knowledge,
e.g. by Hierocles of Alexandria (d. A.D. 485) in his commentary on
Pythagoras' Carmen Aureum (ed. F. W. A. Mullach, 1853), 137 ff.
esp. 141, 2 ff.; 142, 1 ff.; and at Plotinus, Enn. VI, ix, 7; cf.
V, i, 1; Porphyry Abst. III, 27 (p. 226, 15 ff. Nauck): "the
wicked man yields to the mortal side of his nature until he loses
all true knowledge of himself". The moral aspect is also presented at Clem. Al. Paedagogus III, iii; Strom. III, vi, 44.
    [1] Corp. Herm. I, 22, 27; IX, 9; X, 21; Herm. Fr. in Lactan-
tius Div. Inst. II, xv, 6 (Scott Herm. I, 536, 10): "Piety is
knowledge of God". Cf. Clem. Al. Strom. II, x, 46; III, vi.
43 f. (gnosis and the management of life); VII, xii, 71 (gnosis as a
rational death, ending the régime of the passions); VI, 9 (gnosis
as "apathy"); IV, vi, 39 (the gnosis of the princely is cleansing
of the soul and the working of inner goodness); Chairemon in
Porphyry Abst. IV, 6 (p. 237, 3 f. Nauck): "To abide for ever
with gnosis and inspiration delivers from envy and from passion
and leads to a life that is unified ". So also among the Mandaeans
cf. Lidzbarski, Ginza, 58, 36 f.; Kroll, Lehren, etc. 353 f.;
W. Jaeger, G.G.A (1913), 584, 587.
    [2] Cf. Acts xvii, 30; I Cor. xv, 34; Eph. iv, 17 f.; I Pet. i, 14;
and see Bultmann's art. on ἄγνοια in Kittel, Wörterb. I, 117-120.

3. POWER

Just as knowledge, being the investigation of truth, brought the ancient Greek close to the Godhead, so that he himself became real in his intimate contemplation of the ultimate reality, so Gnosis endows the Gnostic with the divine nature, i.e. primarily, with immortality; his vision transforms him from man into God.[1] The *gnosis* itself, which leads to this result, is understood to be a divine power ($\delta\acute{\upsilon}\nu\alpha\mu\iota\varsigma$), which gets into a man and, along with other powers, drives death out of him. It is true that Plato called knowledge ($\gamma\nu\hat{\omega}\sigma\iota\varsigma$), or science ($\dot{\epsilon}\pi\iota\sigma\tau\acute{\eta}\mu\eta$), a " power " ($\delta\acute{\upsilon}\nu\alpha\mu\iota\varsigma$),[2] but he meant a possibility peculiar to man, a " faculty "; whereas the Gnostic meant something magical,[3] a mysterious divine fluid (mana), like the Spirit, identical with Life and Light.[4] Gnosis thus

[1] Corp. Herm. I, 27-29; IV, 4 f. 11b; VII, 1-3; X, 4-6; XIII (rebirth); Iren. I, 21, 4 (M.P.G. VII, 665a): " gnosis redeems the inner man "; Plotinus, Enn. V, 8, 10; VI, 9; Porph. Abst. II, 34; Hierocles (see p. 12) 180 f.; Clem. Al. Strom. IV, 6, 40; IV, 23, 149; V, 10, 63; cf. Kroll, op. cit. 360 ff.; Reitzenstein, H.M. 288 ff. 302 ff. (on the Christian Gnostic); Bousset, Kyr. Chr. 165 f. It is characteristic that, in the terminology of relationship to the object, verbs of touching and handling are prominent, rather than $\kappa\alpha\tau\alpha\lambda\alpha\mu\beta\acute{\alpha}\nu\epsilon\iota\nu$ (grasping).

[2] Rep. V, 477d ff.

[3] Corp. Herm. XIII, 7 ff.; Jamblichus, Myst. x, 5 (Parthey, 292, 1 ff.) on gnosis as power. Cf. K. Müller, N.G.G. (1920) 181 f.; the " name " is also synonymous with power, Acta Thomae, 27, p. 142, 13 f. Cf. Müller, op. cit. 225: " Gnosis is wherever the divine presence is: indeed one may say it is the divine presence ". [Cf. M. R. James, Apocryphal N.T. (1926), 376.] For gnosis as Aeon among the Barbelognostics see Iren. I, 29, 3 (M.P.G. VII, 693a). The Gnostics are the illuminati ($\pi\nu\epsilon\upsilon\mu\alpha\tau\iota\kappa o\acute{\iota}$), cf. Reitzenstein, Hell. Myst. 289, 292, 301, 305.

[4] Corp. Herm. XIII, 7 ff. esp. in the hymn, XIII, 18: " O holy gnosis, illumined by thee, by thee praising the light of the mind,

gives its devotee authority (ἐξουσία) and sets him free from fate (εἱμαρμένη).[1] In this sense it is a possession or mysterious quality of the substance of the soul, always in danger of being lost and requiring asceticism for its preservation—not like the knowledge which consists in the mastery of a subject.

. . . O life and light, from you and unto you moves the hymn ". See also Asclep. 41b (I, 374 ff. Herm.). Cf. Kroll, Lehren d. H.T. 375 f.; Reitzenstein H.M. 292.

[1] See Reitzenstein, Hell. Myst. 300 ff.; Kroll, op. cit. 382 ff.; Jamblichus, Myst. 10, 5.

III. OLD TESTAMENT

IN order to understand the use of *gnosis* in the New Testament, we must also take into account the usage of the Septuagint and the idea of knowledge in the Old Testament. The latter is expressed by the Hebrew word *yadha'*, usually represented in LXX by γινώσκειν or εἰδέναι, and, like them, indicating perception, not by the use of a special organ, but in the course of ordinary experience.[1] The Hebrew word, like the Greek εἰδέναι, can also denote ability,[2] and (like γινώσκειν) knowing what ought to be done.[3] This wider usage is, however, more frequent in the Old Testament than in Greek literature, and expresses finding out by experience rather than objective visualisation.[4] Thus the verb *yadha'* can govern objects seldom if ever found after γινώσκειν, such as blows (I Sam. xiv, 12), childlessness or disease (Isaiah xlvii, 8; liii, 3), divine punishment or vengeance

[1] E.g., through intercourse: Exod. i, 8; Deut. ix, 2, 24; I Sam. x, 11, etc.; through good or bad experience: Is. xlii, 25; Jer. xvi, 21; xliv, 28, etc. In both cases LXX has γινώσκειν or εἰδέναι. The passive part., like the Greek γνωστός, can thus mean acquaintance, friend, confidant, e.g. Ps. xxxi, 11 (12); lv, 13 (14); lxxxviii, 8, 18 (9, 19).

[2] Gen. xxv, 27: a cunning hunter (LXX εἰδὼς κυνηγεῖν); I Sam. xvi, 16; I Kings ix, 27; Is. xxix, 12 (LXX ἐπίστασθαι). The active part., with *da'ath* as object, like γινώσκων, means a man of understanding, Prov. xvii, 27; Dan. i, 4. But the verb can be used absolutely, Ps. lxxiii, 22; lxxxii, 5.

[3] Judg. xviii, 14; I Sam. xxv, 17 (LXX γινώσκειν).

[4] Characteristic is *yadha'* in its causative form, with God as subject: he makes men know his power, in punishment or in grace—Jer. xvi, 21; Ps. lxxvii, 14 (15); xcviii, 2; cvi, 8 (LXX γνωρίζειν).

15

(Jer. xvi. 21; Ezek. xxv, 14). LXX usually has γινώσκειν in these cases, where αἰσθάνεσθαι would be better Greek,[1] characteristically making no difference between the two words. The use of *yadha'* for sexual intercourse is to be understood in this connexion, both of the man (Gen. iv, 1, 17, 25) and of the woman (Numb. xxxi, 18, 35; Judg. xxi, 12).[2] It is true that *yadha'* can denote merely having accurate information,[3] and that the noun *da'ath*, specially in the Wisdom literature, can mean the investigation and understanding of the sage.[4] But the Old Testament does not take the view that reality is most purely apprehended when things are seen objectively in a disinterested way; on the contrary, it is characteristic of its writers to emphasise the subjective aspect; knowledge being a matter of hearing rather than of seeing, and vision itself closely associated with prophetic ecstasy. That is why there is no place for pure science in the culture of ancient Israel. It also explains why the Hebrews found reality, not in eternal forms and principles, but in the events of historical time. The latter, however, are not understood as the outcome of preceding causes, but as the behaviour of God or of man in relation to God. God is not thought of as everlasting, but as exercising will, having a definite aim, demanding,

---

[1] Αἰσθάνεσθαι is relatively rare in LXX; for *yadha'* only Is. xlix, 26 (elsewhere γινώσκειν). The noun αἴσθησις is, however, frequent in Prov. for *da'ath*.

[2] [See J. Skinner, Genesis (1910), 101; G. J. Spurrell, Notes on Gen. 2nd ed. (1896), 49; and cf. O. Piper, Sinn u. Geheimnis d. Geschlechter (1935), 47-51, etc. (Trans. " The Christian interpretation of sex ", Nisbet & Co. 1942; Times Lit. Sup. Review, August 15: " it is the incompleteness of the one sex which, in his view, gives religious significance to sexual ' knowledge ' ". Cf. Luke i, 34 and see pp. 6, 18, 26.)]

[3] Ps. xciv, 11; cxxxix, 1.

[4] Prov. i, 4; ii, 6; v, 2; Eccles. i, 18.

blessing, judging. When knowledge is referred to in a special sense, it, means knowledge of God, not as existing for ever, but as making a demand, whether through commandments or through mighty acts, claiming honour and obedience with recognition of his power and grace and call. Knowledge is therefore more than appropriated information; it must realise itself in appropriate action. The contemplative life is as foreign to the Old Testament as the ideal of a city or a universal society, planned by philosophy for men to build; and, of course, the Hebrews never think of a mystical vision of the Godhead.

Knowledge in the Old Testament, therefore, means perception accompanied by emotion, or rather by a movement of the will, so that lack of knowledge is an offence as well as a mistake. This is clearly seen in passages where " to know " signifies " to take care of ", since it includes apprehension of the meaning and challenge of what is known—and this can be said of God as well as of man.[1] But above all *yadha‘* is used to indicate recognition of the acts of God.[2] Knowing that Yahwe is God means the same thing (Deut. iv, 39; viii, 5; xxix, 5; Isaiah liii, 10; Ps. xl, 10(11). To know him or his name means to recognise him, to confess him, to give him honour and do his will (I Sam. ii, 12; Isaiah i, 3; Jer. ii, 8; ix, 2-5; Ps. ix, 10 (11); xxxvi, 10 (11); lxxxvii, 4; Job xviii, 21; Dan. xi, 32). " Knowledge of God " or even " knowledge "

---

[1] Of man: Gen. xxxix, 6, 8; Deut. xxxiii, 9; Prov. xii, 10 ; xxix, 7; Job ix, 21; Ps. ci, 4 (obj. " evil "); cxix, 79 (obj. " thy testimonies "). LXX mostly γινώσκειν or εἰδέναι, also ἐπίστασθαι ; but Prov. xii, 10 οἰκτείρειν ! Of God: Ps. i, 11; lxxxiii, 11; cxliv, 3; LXX γινώσκειν. Specially significant are the cases in which the character of *yadha‘* is illustrated by a parallel, e.g. Jer. viii, 7 (*shamar*, observe); Prov. xxvii, 23 (*shith libbᵉkha*, pay good heed). Cf. Ps. i, 6; xxxi, 7 (8); xxxvii, 18.

[2] Deut. xi, 2; Is. xli, 20; Hos. xi, 3; Mic. vi, 5.

alone (Hos. iv, 1, 6; vi, 6; Isaiah xi, 2, 9; Prov. 1, 7;
ix, 10) is almost identical with " fear of God " (both
together at Isaiah xi, 2) and implies doing what is just
and right (Jer. xxii, 16). The same word can be
used for man's acknowledgement and confession of
guilt (Jer. iii, 13; Ps. iii, 3 (5)) and for God's acknowledgement of man's innocence (Job xxxi, 6). "Known"
men are those who are respected, held in high esteem
(Deut. i, 13, 15;[1] Prov. xxxi, 23). Finally, the part
played by the will in the act of knowing (*yadha'*)
is specially clear when God is said to know, for it is
his knowledge which first gives its meaning to that
which is known, and this is equivalent to choosing or
electing it as an object of attentive care.[2]

[1] [L. Koehler, Lexicon in V.T. (1950), 365, says *yᵉdhu'im*
means " mit den Dingen bekannt, sachkundig, *experienced* ".
So Moffatt. LXX συνετούς.]

[2] Gen. xviii, 19; Exod. xiii, 12; Am. iii, 2; Hos. xiii, 5; Jer.
i, 5. I doubt whether the sexual reference is to be found here,
so that Am. iii, 2 might be translated, " With you alone is my
marriage bond " or Hos. xiii, 5, " Thee only have I wedded ",
as K. Cramer holds, Amos (1930), 32, 57, 60. In any case the
meaning is made clear by the use of phrases containing *yadha'*
or alternatives such as *qara' bhᵉshem* [call by name] Is. xliii, 1
[followed by " thou art mine " !]; xlv, 3 f.; xlix, 1; or *laqah*
and *bahar* [" take " and " choose "]. LXX in such cases has not
only γινώσκειν or εἰδέναι but frequently συνιέναι.

IV. SEPTUAGINT USAGE

THE Greek translators sometimes use the verb γινώσκειν in a special way: e.g. in Leviticus it occurs only six times, whereas there are eight examples of the Hebrew *yadha'*, and they are all connected with sin. This is a usage which prepares the way for a conception of knowledge as a challenge to man, threatening his very existence and yet, if it is taken up, leading to repentance and salvation. Apart from many cases in which the Greek is simply following the Hebrew in this usage, LXX sometimes independently anticipates revelations which contradict human hope and expectation, e.g. by means of an introductory Imperative (" Know thou ")—emphasising beforehand the irrational element in such knowledge (Judges iv, 9; Job xix, 3, cf. Heb. ver. 6; Job xxxvi, 5; Prov. xxix, 20; Is. viii, 9;[1] xliv, 20;[2] xlvii, 10; li, 12). The same idea underlies the LXX misreading of *yad$^{e'}$ah* for *yar$^{e'}$ah* at Is. xv, 4;[3] and salutary self-knowledge is demanded at Is. xxx, 15 with no Hebrew equivalent. Knowledge as the awakener is the exact opposite of that ignorance which is the reproach of sinners and the heathen (Wisdom ii, 22; v, 7). LXX also introduces the latter at Zech. vii, 14, where the Hebrew refers

---

[1] LXX read *d$^{e'}$u* instead of *ro'u* from *ra'a'*.

[2] LXX read *d$^{e'}$i* instead of *ro'eh* from *ra'ah*.

[3] LXX also reads *d* for Heb. *r* at Hos. ix, 2. Guthe in Kautzsch adopts this—surely wrongly [should this not be " rightly " in view of the sentence which follows ?]. To say that the threshing-floor and the wine-press will know the chosen people no more, brings home the meaning of the divine judgement. [This is paralleled by *y$^{e'}$khaḥḥesh* in the next clause.] Cf. Jer. ii, 16; I Sam. x, 24.

merely to peoples unknown to the Jews, and thus gives
a propagandist turn to a passage which says that distant
nations shall serve the Jews, emphasising God's
power and Israel's coming greatness. The same note
is struck in Aquila's reading at Ps. xviii, 44 (xvii, 43).
The verb γινώσκειν is used by LXX at Is. xxvi, 11
as a technical term for the terrifying recognition of the
wrath of God; the Hebrew word for " see " (ḥazah),
which it represents, is connected with the thought of
salvation, according to H. Guthe, who omits " and
be ashamed ".[1] The situation is different where the
natural man is denied all knowledge of divine providence,
as happens frequently in Ecclesiastes (cf. Wisdom ix,
13, 17). It is from this point of view that LXX puts
γινώσκειν for tikken (pi.) at Isaiah xl, 13,[2] though it
is generally identified with kun and rendered by
ἑτοιμάζειν, κατευθύνειν, etc. Going on from the idea
that God cannot be measured to the idea that he cannot
be known, the Greek changes the Hebrew theological
statement into an anthropological one. Similarly at
Job xxxviii, 31 (A) the Greek indicates man's ignorance
instead of his powerlessness in comparison with the
Creator. The question in the Hebrew is purely
rhetorical—and we may doubt whether the Greek
question was always answered in the negative by
Hellenistic Jews who were under the influence of
astrology.[3]

---

[1] H. Guthe, in Kautzsch, 3rd ed. ad loc., differing from Duhm.
LXX elsewhere occasionally uses γινώσκειν for verbs of seeing and
hearing (see p. 16): for ra'ah, Numb. xi, 23; Judg. ii, 7 (cf. also
Gen. xxxix, 23 and Exod. xxii, 10; xxxiii, 13) in the sense of recognising a beneficial revelation; for shama' Is. xlviii, 8, as synonym
of the following ἐπίστασθαι (yadha'). Cf. Neh. iv. 15 (9), Aq.

[2] [See J. Skinner, in C.B. (1929), ad. loc. and B.D.B. s.v.
takhan.]

[3] Cf. A. Jeremias, Handb. d. altorientalischen Geisteskultur,
2nd ed. (1929), 213 and Index under Plejaden; Bill. IV, 1046,

Often γινώσκειν or γινώσκεσθαι denotes God's self-revelation as such. More than once this is the meaning of the word in LXX when it is the translation of *ya'adh*, though quite different renderings of this are also found; thus, at Exod. xxix, 42 f., it is surely a mistake to assume with Bibl. Hebr. (R. Kittel) that *yadha'* lies behind the LXX in ver. 42: the translator intentionally gives two different renderings of the same Hebrew root because he is presenting three stages of revelation from the human point of view, as being known, met, and sanctified, although the Hebrew tense (Niph'al) indicates the divine initiative.

Passages in which man is the subject of the verb are far more numerous than those in which he is said to be known by God. The latter may mean approval of the way in which man stands the divine test (Gen. xxii, 12; cf. Prov. xxiv, 12), or the election of the righteous (Numb. xvi, 5; Ps. i, 6; xxxvii (xxxvi), 18; Hos. xi, 12). In the last example LXX, differing as it does from the Hebrew text (xii, 1), expresses the idea of election, and not that of the divine knowledge which threatens a sinful people with judgement.[1] The same thought is found at Hos. v, 3; Am. iii, 2; Nah. i, 7. Closely related to this is the thought of the divine omniscience, which is bound up with the idea of the Creator's love for his creatures, as it is in the cases where knowledge involves election: Gen. xx, 6;[2] II Kings xix, 27; I Chron. xxviii, 9; Ps. xl, 9 (xxxix,

1048 (Zodiac allegory in Pesiqta rabbati 203 a 31, and its cultic application in Tanchuma, *ha'azinu* 27b, 33). From here to an astral analogy-magic is but a short step, which a Gnosis, falsely so called, was ready to take at any time. [Cf. C. H. Dodd, The Bible and the Greeks (1935), 17 f., 138-141, 155.]

[1] [See W. R. Harper, Amos and Hosea (I.C.C. 1905), 374, 376; and B.D.B. s.v. *rudh*.]

[2] At Gen. xviii, 19, LXX substitutes the idea of omniscience for that of election (see p. 18, n. 2).

10); xliv, 21 (xliii, 22); 1 (xlix), 11; lxix, 5, 19
(lxviii, 6, 20); ciii (cii), 14; cxxxviii (cxxxvii), 6;
cxxxix (cxxxviii); cxlii, 3 (cxli, 4); Am. v, 12; Baruch
ii, 30. In such cases, specially in the Psalms, trust in
God's mercy goes along with the thought of the judge
and saviour who marks what is wrong and effects
reconciliation.

The noun, " gnosis ", occurs in LXX much less
frequently than the verb, but is used relatively much
more often in a religious or ethical sense for the revealed
knowledge which originates in God himself or in
Wisdom. God is the God of knowledge, *de'ah*,
γνῶσις, I Sam. ii, 3; Ps. lxxiii (lxxii), 11 (Symm.
ἐπίγνωσις, cf. Ecclus. xxxii, 8; Prov. iii, 20, Aq.?).
His strict yet gracious treatment of his creatures is
based on his omniscience.[1] From him springs the
gnosis of the pious; it is a spiritual possession due to
revelation: Prov. xxiv, 26; Ecclus. i, 19; Job xxxii,
6;[2] Prov. xvi, 8 (diff. from Heb.); Prov. ii, 6; Wis.
vii, 17; cf. x, 10; Ps. xciv (xciii), 10; cxix (cxviii), 66.
The representative and teacher of gnosis is the pious
sage, the Servant of the Lord (Is. liii, 11 [Aq. Theod.]),
the righteous (Wis. ii, 13; xvi, 22), the sage (Ecclus.
xxi, 13; Prov. xv, 7 Symm.), the clever (πανοῦργος,
Prov. xiii, 16;[3] xiv, 18[4]), the understanding (Prov.

[1] I Chron. iv, 10 (for Heb. *mera'ah* LXX reads *madda'* or
modha'ath, using γνῶσις in the sense of a favourable judicial
verdict; another trans., Cod. 53, has βόσκησις, reading *mir'eh*);
Wis. i, 7; Add. Esth. xiv, 15(14); II Macc. vi, 30; Is. xl, 14
(Aq., Symm., Theod.; LXX has κρίσιν).

[2] Aq. Theod. γνῶσιν; LXX ἐπιστήμην. Cf. xxxii, 8; xxxiii,
3 f.

[3] Heb. obviously means worldly wisdom. But LXX inserts
Prov. ix, 10 (in a form differing from Heb.) in xiii, 15, and so
reaches a religious understanding of it.

[4] Heb. *'arumim yakhtiru dha'ath*: LXX πανοῦργοι κρατήσουσιν
αἰσθήσεως; Aq. ἀναμένουσι γνῶσιν; Theod. στεφθήσονται
γνῶσιν—the usual interpretation.

xiv, 6 Aq., Symm. Theod.; xix, 25 Aq., Symm. Theod.).
It is true that the O.T. Wisdom Literature is mainly
concerned with worldly wisdom, and the word *gnosis*
is generally used in this sense. But LXX shows a clear
leaning towards a religious reference. This is also
seen where the capacity for gnosis is denied to the
worldly-minded, sinners and the godless: Prov. xiii,
19;[1] xxix, 7; i, 22 Symm.; Ecclus. xxi, 14, 18;
Prov. i, 22 Aq.; xix, 20. When the holy nation turns
away from God, it falls under the same condemnation.[2]
Finally this is the judgement passed upon the idolators
(Wis. xiv, 22), those who are far from God (Jer. x,
14; li (xxviii), 17), and also upon those whom this
world counts wise (all the Greek translators agree in
this interpretation of Job xv, 2).[3] Gnosis appears
here as a technical term expressing the opposite of
secular wisdom. But the linguistic usage is not consistent. Gnosis and Wisdom often stand side by side,
and occasionally the latter has the precedence, e.g.,
IV Macc. i, 16: " Wisdom is knowledge of things
divine and human and of their causes " (cf. Prov, viii,
12).[4] Gnosis is certainly divine revelation, objective
in character, but there is no mistaking the subjective
element of deep religious knowledge, in the mystical

[1] Again a misreading of *mera'* as *madda'*. Aq. ἀπὸ κακοῦ.
The same mistake occurs in Ecclus. xl, 5.

[2] The call for conversion at Hos. x, 12 (" Break up your fallow
ground for it is time . . .") appears in LXX as " Enlighten
yourselves with the light of knowledge ", but the change of
we'eth into *da'ath* by Guthe, after LXX, hardly corresponds to the
original sense of the Heb.

[3] The continuation of the passage in LXX shows tha⁺ the first
clause of Job xv, 2 means that the wise of this world cannot
answer with true *spiritual* knowledge; it has nothing to do with
the wind.

[4] Cf. R. C. Trench, Syn. N.T. 188 ff. where almost the same
definition is quoted from Clem. Al. Paed. II, ii, 25, 1 ff.; cf.
Strom. I, v, 30, 1 f.

Gnostic sense, due to the influence of Hellenism. Thus it appears as insight into the divine world-plan at Dan. xii, 4 (Theod. with Heb.; LXX substitutes *ra'a'* for *yadha'*). Gnosis is knowing about God and his work, which is beyond man's conceiving, Ps. cxxxix (cxxxviii), 6, and is communicated to the believer through the whole creation, Ps. xix (xviii), 3.

V. JEWISH USAGE

I. RABBINIC, ETC.

THE Old Testament conception of knowledge was maintained in Judaism, and this largely modified the meaning of γινώσκειν etc. in LXX and the rest of Graeco-Jewish literature—with the exception of Josephus. Apart from Philo, knowledge as such is not a problem for the Jews. When the Rabbis use the word *dey'ah* absolutely, they mean acquaintance with the Law, acknowledgement of the claim of its commandments,[1] as they do when they glorify " knowledge " (*da'ath*),[2] although they sometimes use these words in a general sense. A man who has knowledge may be (*a*) a thinker as contrasted with a child or a weak-minded person; or (*b*) a gifted person as contrasted with one who is stupid; or (*c*) one who has acquired learning as contrasted with one of the common people ('*am ha'areç*) who has never been to school. Since, however, the source and content of education are confined by the Rabbis to the Law and the tradition, all knowledge tends to be looked at in the same way; and since God's commandments can only be fulfilled when they have been studied, the distinction between learned and unlearned becomes equivalent to that between saints and sinners. Obedience, as the foundation of knowledge, being the leading idea in the Old Testament equation of the knowledge of God with the fear of God, the Rabbis thus gave priority to knowledge

---

[1] Bill. I, 191 f.; Test. Levi xiii, 3.
[2] Bill. III, 378 on I Cor. viii, 1.

25

as the basis of obedience. At the same time Judaism did not lose the specific Old Testament idea of the knowledge of God,[1] for in its liturgy it gives thanks to God as the bestower of knowledge, being followed in this by Christianity.[2]

This usage is also found in Hellenistic Judaism, e.g. Wis. xv, 3: "To be acquainted with (ἐπίστασθαι) thee is perfect righteousness, and to know (εἰδέναι) thy dominion is the root of immortality". The recognition of God's power and mighty acts is mentioned at Ecclus. xxxvi, 5, 17; Bar. ii, 15, 31; I Macc. iv, 11; II Macc. i, 27; Tob. xiv, 4 (Sin.); Judith ix, 7; Sib. iii, 693; and knowledge of his way or ways, etc. at Wis. v, 7; ix, 10; x, 8; Bar. iii, 9, 14, 20; cf. Ecclus. xviii, 28; xxiv, 28.[3] At the same time a modification is introduced, as in Isaiah xl-lv, through the stress laid on monotheism in the conflict with heathenism, so that knowledge of God means equally or emphatically, knowing that there is only one God and that the heathen gods are not gods (Judith viii, 20; Ep. Jer. 23, 29, 51, 65, 72; Wis. xii, 27; Sib. iii, 31 f.). This again raises the question, foreign to the Rabbis, whether God can be known: cf. II Macc. vii, 28; Test. Napht. iii, 4 and specially Wis. xiii-xv, and all the apologetic and propagandist literature of

[1] Cf. Schlatter, Matt. 384; Bill. III, 776, 778. To know God means to hear him, Bill. III, 34. Knowledge can also mean recognition, both of a person (Bill. I, 469 on Matt. vii, 23) and of guilt (Test. Sim. ii, 13 f.; iv, 3; Test. Iss. vii, 1; Test. Jos. iii, 9). The sexual connotation also came to be more widely used: Bill. I, 75 f.; Schlatter, Matt. p. 24; Judith xvi, 22; Wis. iii, 13; Test. Jud. x, 3 f. etc.; Philo de post. Caini, 33, 134. (See p. 16.)

[2] For Rabbinic ref. see Bill. III, 378; cf. Bousset, N.G.G. (1915), 466 ff. on Apost. Const. VII, 33-39; Didache ix, x (based on Jewish liturgy); cf. prayer for knowledge in 4th benediction of the Sh'moneh-'Esreh [see I. Abrahams' note in Companion to (Jewish) Daily Prayer Book (1932), pp. lxi f.]

[3] For ἐπιγινώσκω see Index.

Hellenistic Judaism.[1] The idea of knowledge, like the idea of God, thus becomes partly hellenised, in either a Stoic direction or a Gnostic.[2]

2. PHILO

Philo's idea of knowledge and use of γινώσκειν are thoroughly Hellenistic, i.e. either rationalist or Gnostic. He can speak generally of knowledge (ἐπίγνωσις) of the truth,[3] and also of knowing ultimate reality (γνῶναι τὸ ὄν);[4] but what he really means is knowledge of God. On the one hand he contrasts the knowledge of the one and only God with polytheism (De virt. 178 f.; De ebr. 44 f.) or with scepticism (De ebr. 19), using the Stoic theory (De virt. 215 f.; De post. C.167). On the other hand for Philo such argument can only prove the existence of God, or attest his mighty works[5]

---

[1] Cf. Lietzmann on Rom. i, 20 and Excursus on i, 25, and cf. Bultmann in Kittel I, 122 n. 3. The Rabbis do not discuss the problem (Bill. III. 33); when they say God cannot be known, they mean that his mighty working cannot be fully traced out. See Bill. III, 294 f.

[2] For Stoic influence see preceding note and cf. Epist. Arist. 195, 210, 254; for Philo see Bultmann, Z.N.W. 29 (1930), 189 ff. The proximity of " innate knowledge " and " innate law " in Apost. Const. VII, 33, 3 is symptomatic. Gnostic influence is seen in the combination of knowledge with life and immortality in the Eucharistic prayers (Did. ix, 3; x, 2); cf. R. Knopf ad loc. in Handb. z. N.T., Ergänzungsband. Perhaps the same influence accounts for the frequent use of γινώσκειν for secret eschatological knowledge in the Testaments of the XII Patr. (e.g. Dan v, 6; Napht. iv, 1; Gad viii, 2; Asher vii, 5) and for the " light of knowledge " in Levi iv, 3; xviii, 3; Ben. xi, 2. But there are examples of the genuine Jewish idea of knowledge as well, e.g. Levi xviii, 5, 9; Gad v, 7. Josephus only uses gnosis in the sense of the knowledge of secular events (Ant. 8, 171, etc.).

[3] Omn. Prob. Lib. 74.   [4] Virt. 215.

[5] Spec. Leg. I, 43 ff.; Fug. 165; Mut. Nom. 17.

—it cannot deal with the ultimate question (führt . . .
nur zur Erkenntnis des Dass Gottes, nicht des Wie).[1]
There is, however, a knowledge of God which goes
further than this, an immediate vision of God, described by Philo as an ecstasy, in which the soul is
both seeing and seen (De somn. ii, 226). It is not
gained through study, but is a gift from God.[2] This
is the Gnostic view, which appears again in the
expression, γνῶσις εὐσεβείας (De Abr. 268), indicating
that it is bound up with a dualistic type of piety (Leg.
All. iii, 48; Deus Imm. 4, 143). Such a view involves
the depreciation of man, and so Philo can also adopt
Old Testament ideas, according to which gnosis is
equivalent to worship (Leg. All. iii, 126:τιμὴ τοῦ ἑνός).
A good illustration of the way in which Philo mixes
up Greek philosophy, Gnosticism and the Old Testament is seen in his interpretation of the saying, γνῶθι
σαυτόν (know thyself). He not only takes it to mean
self-examination (De fug. et. inv., 46 f., cf. Leg. Gai. 69),
but also, and more frequently, introduces it dualistically
as the negative side of knowing God, so that it means
turning away from what is of the earth (De migr. Abr.
8 f. 137 f.; De spec. leg. i, 10, 44, 263 ff.; De mut.
nom. 54, 186) and so the Old Testament motif makes
its appearance (Deus Imm. 161; Quis; Rer. Div. 30),
specially at De Somn. i, 54-60 (cf. 211 f., 220), where
self-knowledge leads to renunciation (ἀπογινώσκειν),

---

[1] Somn. I, 231; Spec. Leg. I, 32 ff.; Praem. Poen. 39, 44.
[2] Op. Mund. 70 f.; Abr. 79 f.; Praem. Poen. 37, 41 ff. etc.
Cf. Bousset-Gressmann, Die Rel. d. Jud. 3rd ed. (1926), 450 f.;
Bousset, Kyrios Chr. 167; H. Windisch, Die Frommigkeit
Philos (1909), 60 ff.; Reitzenstein, Hell. Myst. 317 f.; H.
Leisegang, Der heil. Geist, I (1919), 223, 4; Bultmann, Z.N.W.
29 (1930), 189 ff. Like Plotinus (see p. 8, n. 3), Philo inconsistently
avoids γινώσκειν and γνῶσις for this vision of God, preferring
ὁρᾶν, ὅρασις, θέα etc.; and also speaks, not of γνωστικοί, but of
ὁρατικοί and φιλοθεάμονες.

and that is followed by knowing the one who is (γινώσκειν τὸν ὄντα). Similarly syncretistic is the use of ἄγνοια (ignorance), which sometimes has the thoroughly Greek connotation of the cause of misfortune (Leg. Gai. 69, cf. De ebr. 6) and sometimes that of the cause of all sins (De ebr. 154 ff.; De. somn. i, 114) as in Gnosticism and the Old Testament.

VI. EARLY CHRISTIAN USAGE

1. COMMON SPEECH

CHRISTIANS in the early days largely used the verb γινώσκειν and the noun γνῶσις in the everyday sense of knowing, without raising any question of theoretical implications peculiar to the Old Testament, to Greek thought, or to the New Testament. Thus γινώσκειν can have the following meanings.

Feel (Mark v, 29; Luke viii, 46).

Observe (Mark viii, 17; xii, 12; Matt. xxvi, 10; II Cor. ii, 4; John v, 42; viii, 27).

Perceive, discern, recognise (Luke vii, 39; Matt. xii, 15; xxii, 18; Gal. iii, 7; James ii, 20; John iv, 1; v, 6; vi, 15).

Learn, discover (Mark v, 43; xv, 45; Luke ix, 11; Acts xvii, 13, 19; Phil. i, 12; ii, 19; John xi, 57; xii, 9; I Clem. xii, 2; Ign. Tr. i, 1 f.; Passive: Matt. x, 26 and par.; Acts ix, 24; Phil. iv, 5).

Make certain (Mark vi, 38; xiii, 28 f.; Luke i, 18; I Cor. iv, 19; II Cor. xiii, 6; John iv, 53; vii, 51; Didache xi, 8; 1 John iii, 19, etc.).

Be aware of (Matt. xxiv, 50 and par.; Luke ii, 43; xvi, 4; Heb. x, 34; Rev. iii, 3; John ii, 24 f.; vii, 27; I John iii, 20; Ign. Rom. v, 3).[1]

---

[1] There is no difference in meaning between γινώσκειν and εἰδέναι, e.g. Mark xii, 15 and viii, 17; Mark xv, 10 and Matt. xxvii, 18; Matt. vii, 23 and xxv, 12; Acts i, 7 and Mark xiii, 32; John viii, 55 and vii, 28, viii, 19. The two verbs are interchangeable at Mark iv, 13; I Cor. ii. 11 f.; II Cor. v, 16; Gal. iv, 8 f.; John vii, 27; xiv, 7; xxi, 17; I John ii, 29.

Be acquainted with (Matt. xxv, 24; Luke xii, 47 f.; xvi, 15; Acts i, 7; Rom. ii, 18; vii, 1; II Cor. v, 16, see p. 34; John i, 48; vii, 49; I Clem. xxxi, 3; xxxv, 3).[1]

Comprehend (Luke xviii, 34; Acts viii, 30; I Cor. xiv, 7, 9; John iii, 10).

Be expert in (Matt. xvi, 3 interpolation: Luke xii, 56 has οἴδατε; II Cor. v, 21 probably belongs here, echoing O.T., though Rabbinic has no parallel, acc. to Bill.).

Be familiar with (Rom. vii, 7; Hermas Mand. ii, 1).

Decide (Josephus Ant. v, 22; xv, 284; Philo, De Spec. Leg. i, 176; Quod Det. Pot. Ins. 27; cf. γνῶσις, De Spec. Leg. iv, 63, 70; not found in the New Testament [unless Luke xvi, 4 be an example]).

Ἐπιγινώσκειν is largely synonymous with γινώσκειν. In Greek literature the preposition can be emphasised, indicating observation; but this is equivalent to perception. Generally the two words have the same meaning also in the Papyri, where the compound does not connote testing, as Preisigke suggests, but making certain. The preposition has its proper force when the verb means recognising (again), or, legally, adding another decision. But these and other special meanings, found in the Papyri, hardly belong to the early Christian vocabulary. LXX often makes no difference between the two: e.g. Hab. iii, 2; Ezek. xxv, 14 and Is. xliii, 10; Hos. xiv, 10 and Jer. iii, 13; Ps. lxxix (lxxviii), 6 and lxxxvii (lxxxvi), 4; I Macc. iii, 42 and 11, etc. Occasionally the compound seems to be used purposely for perceiving, discerning, recognition (Gen. xxvii, 23; xxxi, 32;

---

[1] At Acts xix, 15 γινώσκειν and ἐπίστασθαι both connote acquaintance.

Judg. xviii, 3, etc.; cf. Josephus Bell. v, 262; Ant. vi, 138; viii, 417, etc.). Presence or absence of the preposition often differentiates readings of MSS. of LXX (Gen. xlii, 8; Exod. xiv, 4; Hos. vii, 9; Jer. iv, 22; I Macc. xvi, 22, etc.). Philo also uses the compound with no perceptible difference from the simple verb (Quod Det. Pot. Ins., 176; De Somn. i, 231 and i, 60), and similarly the noun (Leg. All. iii, 48 and 126). Identity of meaning in early Christian literature is illustrated at Mark ii, 8 and viii, 17; Mark v, 30 and Luke viii, 46; Mark vi, 33 [some MSS. ἔγνωσαν] and 54; Matt. xiv, 35 and Luke ix, 11; Matt. vii, 16, 20 and Luke vi, 44; Matt. xi, 27 and Luke x, 22; Luke xxiv, 31 and xxiv, 35; Col. i, 6 and II Cor. viii, 9. The same alternation is found in Hermas Sim. iv, 3; ix, 18; Diogn. xii, 6, and in the various readings at Acts xxiii, 28; xxiv, 11. The alternation at I Cor. xiii, 12 is simply rhetorical, the compound here being equivalent to the simple verb at viii, 3 and Gal. iv, 9. See also Rom. i, 32 and ii, 18.

Generally the compound means *perceive*, and only in rare cases is it used consciously instead of the simple verb: e.g. Luke i, 22; xxiv, 16, 31 (but cf. 35); Acts iii, 10; iv, 13; xii, 14; Hermas Vis. v, 3 f. Other meanings are as follows: *learn* (Luke vii, 37; xxiii, 7; Acts ix, 30; xxii, 29); *comprehend* (II Cor. i, 13 f., where the addition of the words, " unto the end ", shows that the compound has in itself no fuller connotation than the simple verb); *understand, know* (Acts xxv, 10; II Cor. xiii, 5). The rhetorical antithesis at II Cor. vi, 9 must not be understood in too restricted a sense: " known " means " understood " both by man (cf. i, 13 f.) and by God (cf. v, 11). It is possible that the compound is used purposely in some places to mean *make certain* (Luke i, 4; Acts xxii, 24; xxiii,

28; xxiv, 8). Other meanings, corresponding to those of the simple verb, will be mentioned later.[1]

2. INFLUENCE OF THE OLD TESTAMENT

Proceeding now from early Christian use of γινώσκειν etc. in their ordinary Hellenistic meanings to that which grows out of the Old Testament and Judaism, we may begin with those cases in which a warning is given, by means of the imperative, to pay special attention to something. Nothing peculiar may seem to be involved; and yet we have here an example of the tendency to move away from the Greek point of view in the direction of the Hebrew; knowing is an act of the will (" let it be said to you "); what is involved is not making certain of something objectively, but accepting the consequences of what is perceived: e.g., Matt. xxiv, 43 and par.; Luke x, 11; Eph. v, 5; James i, 3; v, 20; II Tim. iii, 1; II Pet. i, 20; iii, 3; I Clem. vii, 4; lix, 1; II Clem. v, 5; ix, 2; xvi, 3; Barn. xix, 11; Pol. iv, 3; Herm. Vis. III, vi, 7; Mand. VI, ii, 3, 5. See also ἐπιγινώσκειν at I Cor. xiv, 37. None of this offends against Greek usage;[2] nor does Acts ii, 36, though here the O.T. idea of acknowledgement is included.

Other passages clearly imply the Old Testament idea of knowledge: insight into law or grace as the will of God, which is primarily acknowledgement, with submission, in obedience or gratitude, to that which is known.[3] This is naturally found in the

---

[1] See pp. 34-38. Cf. Moult.–Mill. s.v. and Armitage Robinson, Eph. (1904), 248 ff.

[2] Similarly, Epictetus, e.g. Diss. I, xxv, 24; II, xviii, 5; IV, i, 13; ix, 2; and Philo, Cherub. 29; Ebr. 160; Somn. I, 54 ff.

[3] Γινώσκειν also means to recognise or acknowledge in some cases where the object is not God or his will: Heb. xiii, 23 (?);

quotations at Rom. iii, 17 (Is. lix. 8) and Heb. iii, 10
(Ps. xcv, 11). Luke xix, 42, 44 and Rom. x, 19
are to be understood in the same way; on II Pet. ii,
21, see p. 35. Knowledge of God's will is mentioned
at Rom. ii, 18 and Acts xxii, 14;[1] of salvation through
Christ at II Cor. viii, 9 (cf. the compound at Col. i,
6); and of special divine grace at Gal. ii, 9 and Rev.
iii, 9.[2]

The same force attaches to the knowledge of God
himself at Rev. ii, 23 (cf. Heb. viii, 11, quoting Jer.
xxxi, 34). Elsewhere the early Christian conception
of the knowledge of God is differentiated from that
of the Old Testament. Whereas the prophets of
Israel were preaching against the practical denial of
God among their own people, the Christian mission
was to the heathen, who did not yet worship the one
God, and therefore had to include the element of
awareness along with, or even before, that of recogni-

I Clem. lxi, 1; Ign. Pol. 5 (" if he—the ascetic—be known "
[Lightfoot: " if it be known "]). Similarly ἐπιγινώσκειν, I Cor.
xvi, 18; (εἰδέναι I Thess. v, 12). Heb. *yadha'* often means " to
care for, be concerned about ", but this does not occur in the
early Christian use of γινώσκειν except in so far as it may be involved in acknowledgement or recognition. The sexual use is
found at Matt. i, 25; Luke i, 34. (Cf. p. 16.)

[1] When Epictetus (Diss. IV, vii, 17) says he knows God's
commandments, he means that he is aware of them (cf. Mark x,
19); nevertheless he is " letting it be said to him ".

[2] Didache v, 2 and Barn. xx, 2 may be included here, since the
parallel verbs involve the exercise of the will; cf. II Pet. ii, 15.
Acknowledgement of guilt is meant at Hermas Sim. VIII [not IX],
x, 4; ἐπιγινώσκειν has the same meaning at VIII, vi, 3; xi, 2.
On the other hand at II Cor. v, 16 " knowing " does not, at least
primarily, mean acknowledging but simply being aware of, with
a suggestion of understanding. Paul is concerned, from i, 13 f.
onwards, with the question how he is to be understood as an
apostle, how he can be " made manifest " to the community
(v, 11): he must be known, not according to the flesh, but as a
minister of life (ii, 14-16; iii, 7 ff.; iv, 7 ff.).

tion in its idea of the knowledge of God. The blending
of the two into one is very clearly shown at Rom.
i, 18-23: N.B. ver. 21 and cf. I Cor. i, 21; Gal.
iv, 8 f. (see p. 43). That there is no thought of a
speculative knowledge of God also appears at Rom.
xi, 34; I Cor. ii, 16; both quoting Is. xl, 13 and showing that γινώσκειν can certainly mean theoretical
comprehension. Christian knowledge of God is
service of God (I Thess. i, 9), and yet includes a
theoretical element (I Cor. viii, 4-6), though this is
not predominant. The same is true at John i, 10
(see pp. 45 ff.). Conversion to monotheism includes
the theoretical with the practical at I Clem. 59:
" Open the eyes of our hearts that we may know thee,
who alone art the highest " etc. The practical is
to the fore at Didache 5 and Barn. 20, where sinners
are those " who know not him that made them "
(cf. Hermas Sim. 4). The theoretical receives more
emphasis at II Clem. iii, 1; xvii, 1, where the knowledge of God means conversion to Christianity, as it
does at Hermas Sim. ix, 16 and 18; Vis. iii, 6;
cf. Kerygma Petri.[1] Similarly ἐπιγινώσκειν is used
at I Tim. iv, 3, with " truth " as its object; cf.
Hermas Sim. ix, 18, which uses both simple and
compound forms, and Col. i, 6; whereas II Pet. ii,
21 unifies the theoretical and practical elements in
conversion by employing the compound for both.
Cf. further Epictetus Diss. I, vi, 42 ff.; ix, 11;
Maspero Papyrus iv, 9 (A.D. sixth century), where
the compound is followed by " the invisible God ".

The corresponding reference to divine knowledge as
meaning election, characteristic of the Old Testament,
occurs a few times in the New Testament, most clearly
at II Tim. ii, 19 (from Numb. xvi, 5; cf. Matt. vii,
23), but also at I Cor. viii, 3; xiii, 12; Gal. iv, 9

[1] [See M. R. James, Apocr. N.T. (1926), 16.]

(see p. 43). This is the least Greek of Biblical usages and was later abandoned.

The noun, *gnosis*, has the same Old Testament force as the verb; i.e. knowledge of God is obedient recognition of his will. When Paul, at Rom. ii, 20, characterises the Jew as " having in the Law the form of knowledge and of the truth ", *gnosis* stands for the Hebrew *da'ath* and means knowledge of God's will, recognition of his demand as set forth in the Law, accompanied by the theoretical knowledge of monotheism, which is emphasised by adding the word " truth ", because the Jew is here contrasted with the heathen, who dwells in the darkness of polytheism. Obedience is the plain meaning of gnosis at Barn. v, 4; xxi, 5; and the confession of Christ as the way to the knowledge of God is equated in II Clem. with doing what he says (iii, 1, 4). We have already noted (pp. 26 f.) that the Christian liturgy took over the Hebrew and Jewish idea of *da'ath* (Didache ix, 3; x, 2; Const. Apost. vii, 33-39. In the New Testament itself the idea is found at II Cor. ii, 14; iv, 6; x, 5, though with a special nuance. Whether gnosis is used in the O.T. sense at Luke xi, 52 instead of the Kingdom of heaven (Q: cf. Matt. xxiii, 13) is not certain; it might refer to the Hellenistic idea of theoretical knowledge of God. But there can be no doubt about the O.T. sense at Luke i, 77, where the knowledge of salvation is equated with the forgiveness of sins; this can be no mere communication of a theory: it must mean either the divine awakening of man to the new order of salvation (cf. Is. lix, 7 f.; Luke xix, 42, 44; see p. 34) or, more probably, the actual inner experience.[1] It is God himself who possesses gnosis

---

[1] Cf. Ps. xvi (xv), 11; xcviii (xcvii), 2. On the " knowledge of salvation " see Lidzbarski, John II, p. xvii, n. 2.

at Rom. xi. 33, and this is best understood on the analogy of the use of *yadha'* in the Old Testament, as meaning choice or election, although there is no direct parallel;[1] the reference is to God's gracious will, directing the course of history according to his plan.

Curiously enough, the compound ἐπίγνωσις, like the compound verb, is almost a technical term for the decisive knowledge of God which is involved in conversion to the Christian faith. (See pp. 35 f.) This is not the case at Rom. i, 28, but clear examples of it appear in the Pastoral Epistles: I Tim. ii, 4; Tit. i, 1; II Tim. ii, 25; iii, 7 (in the last two the reference is to true doctrine as opposed to false). The same thing occurs at Heb. x, 26, where "truth" is the object, whereas this is God (and Christ) at I Clem. xl, 2; Mart. Pol. xiv, 1; II Pet. i, 3, 8; ii, 20.[2] The theoretical element comes to the fore in all these cases but it is always presupposed that Christian knowledge includes a corresponding attitude in life.

Judaism frequently uses the compound (verb and noun) for knowledge of God: Exod. xiv, 4; Hos. ii, 20; iv, 1, 6; Ezek. xxv, 14; Ps. lxxix (lxxviii), 6 [B; some MSS and Rahlfs have γινώσκοντα];

---

[1] For the divine transcendence and inscrutability, see Is. xl, 12 ff.; lv, 8 f.; Prov. xxx, 1 ff.; Job ix, 1 ff.; xxviii, 23 ff.; and for the same in Judaism, Baruch iii, 29 ff.; Ecclus. xlii, 18 ff.; xliii, 15 ff.; Wis. ix, 13 ff.; cf. Bill. III, 294 f. on Rom. xi, 33. Analogous heaping up of expressions for knowledge and wisdom in the Old Testament and Judaism: Exod. xxxi, 3; xxxv, 31 (both with a secular meaning); Deut. iv, 6; Is. xi, 2; Prov. i, 4; ii, 6; viii, 12; Eccles. i, 18; ii, 26; Bar. iii, 14; Ecclus. i, 19; Sifre Numb. 41 on vi, 25; Barn. ii, 3 (cf. Windisch in Handb. z. N.T., Extra Vol.); xxi, 5. Cf. also in N.T. Phil. i, 9; Col. i, 9; Eph. i, 17.

[2] Philo, Om. Prob. Lib. 74, and Epict., Diss. II, xx, 21, are only formal parallels; what they mean is knowledge of what is generally true or real.

Prov. ii, 5; Ecclus. xxiii, 27; xxxiii (xxxvi), 5;
Test. Napht. iv, 3; II Macc. iii, 28; ix, 11; Judith
ix, 14; Wis. v, 7 (var. lect.); xii, 27; Sib. iii, 557;
Philo Leg. All. iii, 48; De Somn. i, 230; Quod Omn.
Prob. Lib. 74.

It is, however, impossible to say that there is any
difference between γνῶσις and ἐπίγνωσις, either in
N.T. or LXX, in Philo (see p. 31) or Justin iii, 5 or
Iren. I xxi, 4 (M.P.G. vii, 665a). The compound
noun at Rom. i, 28 corresponds to the simple verb at
ver. 21. There is no difference of meaning between
the compound noun at Phil. i, 9 and the simple at
I Cor. i, 5; Rom. xv, 14. Our interpretation of
γνῶσις as the actual inner experience (p. 36) is
identical with the sense of ἐπίγνωσις at Rom. iii, 20;
as the obedient recognition of God's will (p. 36), it
corresponds to the compound verb at Rom. x, 2
(cf. ver. 3 and xi, 30-32). Origen tries in vain to
prove that there is a difference between the two
in his comment on Eph. i, 15 ff.[1] referring to Ps. xxii,
27 (xxi, 28).[2] Epictetus uses the compound for knowledge of God at Diss. I vi, 42; ix, 11, but the simple
verb for the same purpose, e.g. at I, iii, 2; and, like
Philo, he uses ἐπίγνωσις with " truth " in the general
sense (p. 37, n. 2). See also Aristeas 139; Chrysippus
(III, 60, 28 von Arnim); Irenaeus I, 21, 4 (M.P.G.
vii, 665a); Julian Conv. p. 336c; Porphyry de
abstin. ii, 53.

Consistently with its character, largely due to the
Old Testament, as a combination of the grateful and
obedient recognition of God's actions and demands
with the mere awareness of his existence and activities,

---

[1] See J.T.S. III (1902), 399, 26 ff.
[2] Cf. M. Dibelius, N.T. Studien f. G. Heinrici (1914), 176 ff.,
and in his commentary, 2nd ed. (1931), on I Tim. ii, 4; and H.
Windisch on Heb. x, 26.

Christian knowledge of God is not something gained once and for all; it continues to grow through obedience and meditation. Gnosis in the New Testament is thus a gift of grace which distinguishes the utterances of Christians (I Cor. i, 5; xii, 8;[1] II Cor. viii, 7; I Clem. i, 2; the absence of a following Genitive does not necessarily mean that the reference is to the technical Hellenistic usage). The word is used in its ordinary Greek sense, and can always be translated " knowledge ", but the practical consequences are always involved along with the theoretical element. It is also characteristic that the main interest is not in a Christian form of science, but in the building up of the community, which demands for its furtherance the service of every member's gnosis (Rom. xv, 14; I Cor. xiv, 6; I Clem. xlviii, 5; Did. xi, 2). Meditative study is clearly shown to be involved (Phil. i, 9 f.), but being based on love it leads to doing what is right. Similarly in the case of Philemon (ver. 6), the faith in which he shares must become effectual in his realisation of all the goodness that is bestowed on the believer and of that which strengthens union with Christ when it is brought into the light; the words which follow show that such a knowledge of what is good leads to appropriate action. The knowledge of his will leads to walking worthily of the Lord (Col. i, 9 f.). The new man, who puts away the vices of the heathen, is renewed unto knowledge (Col. iii, 10). Christian husbands live with their wives according to knowledge (I Pet. iii, 7).

[1] I find it impossible to differentiate precisely, as regards form or content, between λόγος γνώσεως and λόγος σοφίας at I Cor. xii, 8. In any case it seems to me wrong to distinguish both kinds of " word ", as forms of teaching, from apocalypse and prophecy, as C. Weizsäcker does in Das apostol. Zeitalter d. christlicher Kirche, 3rd ed. (1902), 580 [Eng. Trans. (1895) II, 262]. No strong distinction is made at xiii, 2; xiv, 6.

Ethical instruction is a special kind of gnosis and teaching (Barn. xviii), and the description of the way of light which follows (xix) begins by saying, This is the gnosis given to us that we may walk in it: thou shalt love him that made thee, etc. See also II Pet. i, 3, 5 f.; iii, 18; Barn. ii; xxi.

But gnosis can mean specifically theological knowledge, with more emphasis on the theoretical side. This may grow, e.g., out of the study of Scripture. The simple verb is used in this sense at Gal. iii, 7; James ii, 20; Barn. vii; xiv; xvi; and gnosis in Barnabas, after referring at the beginning to Christian knowledge in general, goes on to mean the knowledge gained from the allegorical interpretation of Scripture (vi; ix; xiii) ; for the latter cf. also I Clem. xxxii, 1; xl, 1; xli, 4. The understanding of the mysterious little book in Hermas Vis. II, ii, 1 is called gnosis. The simple verb, γινώσκειν, is used for understanding parables (Mark iv, 13 [with εἰδέναι as parallel]) or allegories (Hermas Vis. III, i, 2; iv, 3; Sim. V, iii, 1; IX, v, 3, etc.). But the conviction that faith includes knowledge of the mysteries of the Kingdom of Heaven (Matt. xiii, 11 and par.; cf. Wis. ii, 22) leads to the thought of gnosis as a kind of systematic theology. Paul introduces his theological interpretation of baptism at Rom. vi, 6 with the significant words, " knowing this ". The testimony of the Epistle to the Colossians is that faith leads to knowledge of the mystery of Christ, in whom are all the treasures of wisdom and gnosis hidden (ii, 2), and the author of the Epistle to the Ephesians desires such gnosis for his readers (i, 17; iii, 19; iv, 13), himself offering more than one specimen of it (p. 57).

3. GNOSTIC INFLUENCE

This theological type of gnosis was a necessary development in the early Church because it was in conflict not only with polytheism, but also, to an even greater degree, with the heathen gnosis, closely associated with mystery religions, which was its rival in preaching. Christian evangelism was thus faced from the beginning with the danger of absorbing not only pieces of Gnostic terminology, but also Gnostic types of problem and speculation, and the danger was increased by the fact that Jewish circles were already infected. [The evidence may be examined under three heads: (*a*) Paul, (*b*) John, (*c*) Matthew xi, 27.]

(*a*) The battle was joined with Gnostic teachers who had made their way into Christian communities before we come to Jude, II Peter and I John; the author of the Apocalypse was not the first to oppose those who claimed to know the deep things of Satan (Rev. ii, 24);[1] it is not first in the Pastoral Epistles that the enemy is named explicitly " the gnosis that is falsely so called " (I Tim. vi, 20); nor are the Epistles to the Colossians and the Ephesians the first to show the influence of Gnosticism on their vocabulary.[2]

---

[1] It should be clear that here we have a formula of Gnostic teaching. Probably those under reproof were taking the Satan mythology seriously (Ophites, Cainites), and drawing licentious conclusions from their Gnosis. This is better than supposing that their phrase was " of God " and that the writer twisted this into " of Satan ". See the commentaries.

[2] Col. is contending against syncretistic and Gnostic false teaching. This not only affects its terminology, but also influences the development of Christology along the line of cosmological speculation. In Eph. there is no polemic, and the terminology is given a different application, serving the ecclesiological interest which here takes the place of the cosmological; cf. esp. Dibelius,

Long before, a movement of Gnostic illuminati made its way into Christian circles at Corinth, and Paul had to counteract their influence. His enemies are proved to have been Gnostics by the way in which they strove after speculative wisdom (I Cor. i, 17 ff.), boasting of their gnosis and of the authority which it gave them in matters of personal behaviour (I. Cor. vi, 12 ff.; viii, 1 ff.); and to proofs drawn from the spiritual sphere (II Cor. x-xiii) may be added a certain tendency towards asceticism (I Cor. vii), and the denial of a bodily resurrection (I Cor. xv). In his opposition to them Paul held fast to the special quality of genuine Christian knowledge, but at the same time appropriated to a certain degree Gnostic terms and ways of presenting problems.[1] A good example is the absolute use of the word *gnosis* at I Cor. viii, 1, 7, 10 f.; xiii, 8. But this just shows the contrast in a specially clear light. Paul admits (I Cor. ii, 6 ff.) that the Christian also possesses a form of wisdom, which enables him to know the divine plan of salvation that is hidden from the " rulers " of this age, a knowledge penetrating into the deep things of God because it depends on his gift of the Spirit; and he admits that the spiritual man is superior to the psychic, and is judged of no man. But such knowledge has for its content nothing but God's saving act (I Cor. ii, 12); it is no vague speculation. It is a reality only in one whose way of life is in accordance with the Spirit (iii, 1 ff.). The Gnostic is not in possession of some mysterious quality

Komm. z. d. Gefangenschaftsbr. 2nd ed. (1927), and H. Schlier, Christus und d. Kirche im Eph. (1930). [Cf. A. D. Galloway, The Cosmic Christ (1951).]

[1] Reitzenstein, Hell. Myst. 258 ff. ; 333 ff.; Bousset, Kyr. Chr. 2nd ed. 113 ff.; 130 ff. A different view is given in K. Deissner, Paulus u.d. Mystik s. Zeit, 2nd ed. (1921); A. Schweitzer, Die Mystik d. Apost. Paulus (1930).

for his enjoyment (I Cor. viii, 1 ff.). The passage just cited makes three points clear: (i) knowledge of the one God is not a theoretical speculation which gives its possessor liberty to live as he likes (ver. 9), but is only genuine when accompanied by love; (ii) love of God is not a mystical relationship, but expresses itself in brotherly love; (iii) true gnosis is not something achieved by man, but has its root in God's knowledge of man (note the startling substitution of the Passive for the Active in ver. 3). There can be no doubt that the last point provides an example of dependence on the Old Testament, and that God's knowledge is his gracious choice. See also Gal. iv, 9: since " knowing God " here refers to the knowledge communicated to faith by missionary preaching, quite apart from mysticism, it is clear that " to be known by God " can mean nothing but what is elsewhere called election or calling. Opposition to Gnosticism appears also in I Cor. xiii, where it is admitted that *gnosis* is bestowed on the believer, not in its Old Testament sense, but (as shown by its absolute use in ver. 8) on the Gnostic analogy as an inspired faculty of knowledge; but the admission is accompanied by two qualifications, viz. (i) it stands on a lower level than love, without which it is completely worthless, and (ii) it is only preparatory, inadequate, and bound to pass away, whereas faith, hope and love remain. Gnostic piety is surpassed by Christian love and eschatological faith; gnosis is not full intimacy with God; that must wait until we have passed beyond earthly life. When Paul uses the compound verb at the end of I Cor. xiii, 12, he is certainly using Gnostic language,[1] but he deprives

---

[1] A rabbi would have spoken of seeing God (though not in the sense of an ecstatic, mystical vision; cf. Bultmann, Z.N.W. 29 (1930), 186 ff.), and Paul puts " now we see ", but by resuming

it of Gnostic meaning by adding the words, " as also
I have been known ", which are to be understood as
at I Cor. viii, 3; Gal. iv. 9.[1]

Similarly it could be shown that in II Cor., in his
polemic against the Gnostic illuminati, Paul borrows
their way of stating problems, and poses as a propa-
gator of *gnosis*; but the Genitives which he adds to
this word indicate that its primary meaning for him
is recognition (II Cor. ii, 14; iv, 6; x, 5). When he
speaks of the knowledge of Christ Jesus as the characteristic of a Christian (Phil. iii, 8 ff.) he is clearly
using Gnostic terminology, as he does elsewhere in
this passage. This gnosis corresponds to the resolve
to abandon confidence in the flesh (ver. 4 ff.), being
the knowledge of Christ as Lord, the existential
character of which appears in the fact that this resolu-

with " now we know " he shows that the chapter is a discussion
of the Gnostic problem.

[1] Reitzenstein (Hell. Myst. 383 ff.) seems to me to be right in
saying that in I Cor. xiii, 13 Paul is contending against a formula
of Gnostic origin, in which knowledge was counted in with faith,
hope, and love as divine powers constituting the spiritual man
and guaranteeing his immortality. Paul neither thinks of those
three as powers or elements, nor allows *gnosis* a place among them.
See further, Reitzenstein, Historia Monachorum und Hist.
Lausiaca (1916), 100 ff. ; 242 f.; Hist. Zeitschr. 116 (1916),
189 ff.; N.G.G. (1916), 367 ff.; (1917), 130 ff.; Norden,
Agnostos Theos (1913), 352 ff.; Harnack, Preuss, Jahrb. 161
(1916), 1 ff.; Dibelius, Wochenschr. f. klass. Phil. 30 (1913),
1041 f.; P. Corssen, Sokrates, N.F. 7 (1919), 18 ff. On the other
hand Reitzenstein is obviously wrong in tracing the correspondence
of knowing God and being known by him to the language of
mysticism. Corp. Herm. X, 15 (see p. 9) is no analogy, for
the assertion that God is not ignorant of man is quite general,
and does not, as with Paul, indicate the act of God which, as an
act of calling in the concrete, is the foundation of the knowledge
of the individual. Porphyry ad Marc. 13 is no real parallel,
since the divine knowledge there depends on the behaviour of the
wise man.

tion is not made once for all, but is continually renewed (ver. 12 ff.). Christian gnosis is explained (ver. 9 f.) as meaning " to be found in Christ ", i.e. to be drawn into God's saving act through faith, which never possesses that which is its object, but looks on the one hand to what God has done, and on the other to the future. Knowing him (ver. 10), therefore is not a withdrawal from historical earthly existence, but the experience of the power of his resurrection and the fellowship of his sufferings in the very midst of historical life (cf. II Cor. iv, 7 ff.), the quality of history being changed for Christians by God's saving act, for it now has the resurrection standing in the background. Finally, the un-gnostic character of all this is seen in the fact that Paul does not concern himself with individual occurrences but with the character of the Christian life as a whole.

(b) The simple verb, γινώσκειν, plays a bigger part in John and I John than in all the rest of early Christian literature, but they do not use the compound ἐπιγινώσκειν or, perhaps intentionally, the noun, γνῶσις. In addition to its everyday use, it is employed to indicate in an emphatic way man's relation to God and to Jesus as a personal fellowship, in which each is perfectly defined in his essential being through the other. Just as the relation between the Father and the Son is a reciprocal knowledge, elsewhere described as " being in " (John x, 38; xiv, 11; xvii, 21; N.B. I John ii, 3, 5; v, 20) or even as " being one " (John x, 30), so also is the relation of his own to Jesus (John x, 14 f., 27; cf. vii, 29; 8, 55), which can also be described as " being in " (John xv, 1 ff.; xvii, 21). But when the one who knows has his true nature defined by the one whom he knows, then the nature of the latter determines what knowledge is. Since God and the Son are and have life, to

know them is eternal life (xvii, 3); to be shown the
Father is enough (xiv, 8). Thus it is clear that the
proper business of life in this world—its highest
achievement—is to know; and it is equally clear
that this means to love. God is love, and he who is
related to God is related to him as one who loves
(I John iv, 8, 16), so that the practice of love is the
criterion of knowing God (I John iv, 7 f.; cf. iv, 20 f.)
—as it is of belonging to Jesus (John xiii, 35). Indeed
love, like knowledge, defines the relation between the
Father and the Son (John iii, 35; x, 17; xv, 9; xvii,
23 f., 26; xiv, 31) and also that between Jesus and his
own (xiii, 1, 34; xiv, 21 ff.; xv, 12, 17). This makes
it clear that the knowledge of which John speaks is not
an awareness due to study and reflexion; it is no
speculation; neither is it mystical vision, with liberation from the bonds of history and of this world's
business: these, on the contrary, are the field in which
it finds fulfilment. God's own love for the world
expresses itself in the sending of his Son (John iii,
16; I John iv, 9 f.), and in the love of Jesus in obedience
to the Father and in service to the world or to those
who belong to him (John xiv, 31; xiii, 1 ff.; xv, 9,
12 f.). Since correspondingly the knowledge of
Jesus and of God expresses itself in love, the keeping
of the commandments (of which love is the content)
can stand as a criterion of Christian gnosis (I John ii,
3-5; cf. iii, 6). At the same time the true knowledge
means being singled out by the love of God or of
Jesus, and therefore is realised not only in loving
activity, but also in the consciousness of being loved:
both meanings are included in such sayings as " Abide
in my love " (John xv, 9; cf. xvii, 26; I John iv, 16).
Indeed being loved and knowing it is the very foundation of love (I John iv, 10). " As I have loved you "
(John xiii, 34; xv, 12) means " On the ground that,

etc." All this means that knowledge, in its primary connotation of the recognition and acceptance of love, is equated with faith. But that shows again that the knowledge which, as directed towards God, brings life to man (xvii, 3; xiv, 8; see pp. 45 f.) and is the object of the Son's mission (i, 18; xvii, 4 ff.), is not an immediate intimacy with God, but has to do directly with Jesus as the revelation.

There is no such thing as direct knowledge of God (John i, 18), and every claim to knowledge of him is challenged by the appearance and claim of Jesus (v, 37 f.; vii, 28 f.; viii, 19). Outside revelation there is no God (*ist Gott nicht da*);[1] but Jesus is the revelation for the sinful world; he who sees or knows him sees the Father (xiv, 7-9; cf. xiv, 20; I John v, 20). But to know Jesus does not mean to have accurate historical information about his earthly life (vi, 42; vii, 28); it means to be aware of his one-ness with the Father (x, 38; xiv, 20; xvi, 3); and that again does not mean having a mystical relationship with Jesus, but understanding him in his obedience and his love, the " Holy one of God ", i.e. sent by God and sanctifying himself for the sake of the world (xiv, 31; vi, 69; xvii, 3, 18 f.). He appears as such in the preaching of the community, so that it is equally true that " he that knoweth God heareth us : he who is not of God heareth us not " (I John iv, 6; cf. iii, 1); and the same applies to " the other Paraclete ", i.e. the Spirit of Jesus at work in the preaching of the community: the world knows him

---

[1] This is absolutely true, and is the meaning of John i, 1 ff.: God was never without the Word, so that from the beginning it has been true to say that " the world knew him not " (ver. 10). Since " the Word became flesh ", this has the special meaning: God cannot be known apart from Jesus. Cf. Bultmann, Zwischen d. Zeiten, 6 (1928), 11 ff. [and Theologie d. N.T. 2 (1951), 386 ff.].

not; the community knows him, because he makes it what it is (John xiv, 17: *ihr Sein bestimmt*).

Since γινώσκειν means acceptance of God's act of love in Jesus and obedience to his demand, it might appear that in Johannine usage it were the counterpart of *yadha'* in the Old Testament. The relationship is certainly there, but a true appreciation of Johannine thought depends on seeing that—paradoxically—it starts from the Hellenistic, Gnostic, conception of knowledge and not from that of the Old Testament. This conclusion is based on four main considerations, as follows:

(i) Γινώσκειν combines, or alternates, with verbs of seeing: e.g. John xiv, 7-9, 17, 19 f.; I John iii, 6; iv, 14. It is obvious that the author is arguing against people who lay claim to a vision of God and a knowledge of him apart from history,[1] and that he accepts their way of stating the question: their goal, he says, is reached—but how differently!

(ii) An ostensibly dogmatising style, which speaks of "knowing that" such and such is the case, turns, e.g. the teaching of John vii, 16 f. into a controversy over the dogma that Jesus is the Son of God (vii, 26; x, 38; xiv, 20; xvi, 3; xvii, 7 f., 23, 25, etc.). The real subject is the historicity of the revelation, but this leads to the stumbling block of a knowledge that is dogmatic—a characteristic from which Johannine knowledge is never free.

(iii) Obedience (i.e. love) is indicated as the criterion of knowledge, and not as being of its very essence (like *yadha'*). The thesis for which the writer contends, specially in 1 John, that knowledge is fulfilled in obedience, is a paradox in relation to his theory of knowledge.

---

[1] I John shows that these are gnostic.

(iv) There is a peculiar connexion between believing and knowing. Knowledge represents the perfect relation between subject and object; this is shown by the fact that it, and not faith, is given as describing the mutual relation between the Father and the Son. Faith is man's first step towards God, or the revelation of God; if it is maintained, it will be rewarded with knowledge (John viii, 31 f.; x, 38; cf. xiv, 20). Faith, which Jesus is always demanding, is that doing of God's will which leads to knowledge (vii, 17). Knowledge is impossible where the word is not heard (viii, 43), i.e. where faith is withheld (cf. v, 24; vi, 60 with vi, 64, 69; xii, 46-48; xvii, 8: " hearing " or " receiving " means " believing "). John's " faith " corresponds to the " knowledge " of the Old Testament, whereas his " knowledge " lies beyond, not including obedience or thankful submission, but promised as their reward.[1] Of course this does not mean that faith and knowledge have different objects, or that knowledge stands on a higher level or is in possession of that which is known. The normal sequence (vi, 69; viii, 31 f.; x, 38) can be reversed, knowledge giving new strength to faith (xvi, 30; xvii, 7 f.; cf. I John iv, 16; cf. Tobit xiv, 4, Sin.). True faith, which " abideth ", as such

---

[1] John therefore differs from Paul in not using $\gamma\iota\nu\dot\omega\sigma\kappa\epsilon\iota\nu$ in the sense of divine calling, though he is familiar with the idea (vi, 70; xiii, 18; esp. xv, 16, 19). The wording of x, 14 f., 27 (note the difference in tense from Paul) does not represent Jesus as the pioneer, going on before; his knowledge is contemporary with that of his disciples: the relationship is one of mutual knowledge. This is obviously connected with Gnostic usage (see p. 9 and Bultmann, Z.N.W. 24 (1925), 117 f.). Knowledge in the O.T. sense might be indicated at viii, 32 ; xiv, 31; xvii, 23 (but not elsewhere): the world will one day realise to its horror (cf. the work of the Paraclete, xvi, 8-11) that Jesus is the revealer; cf. perhaps Is. xli, 20; xliii, 10, and see p. 17.

contains knowledge (cf. I John ii, 4 and 6) as one of
its components; this is faith's own understanding,
identical with that joy which has no more need to
ask (xv, 11; xvi, 22-24), because the word of Jesus
is no longer parabolic, but perfectly plain.

John's peculiar conception of faith-knowledge enables him to vary his use of the traditional identification of conversion with knowledge of the truth, and
so to deepen it (I John ii, 13 f., 21; v, 20; II John,
1 f.; cf. pp. 34 f.).

(c) There has been much dispute over the meaning of Matt. xi, 27 (par. in Luke x, 22 differs only
in style). Speaking of the Son in the third Person,
this verse (apart from Mark xiii, 32) stands alone
among the Synoptists, its affinities being with
Johannine usage; it can hardly have been connected originally with its present context (Matt. xi,
28-30 have no par. in Luke).[1] The text is doubtful,
the order of the sentences varying in the tradition.
[In Justin and Irenaeus and Codex N (sixth century)
knowledge of the Father comes first.] Perhaps the
saying that no-one knoweth the Son save the Father
is a later addition. If it is original, then the description of the relation between Father and Son agrees
with that of John, and the idea of knowledge
must be identical. But also if it is secondary, the
compound ($\dot{\epsilon}\pi\iota\gamma\iota\nu\dot{\omega}\sigma\kappa\epsilon\iota\nu$) can only be understood
in the sense of the Johannine $\gamma\iota\nu\dot{\omega}\sigma\kappa\epsilon\iota\nu$, because the
words, " and he to whomsoever, etc." rule out its
association with the knowledge of Yahwe in the Old
Testament. The verse thus presents us with Gnostic
language, and the question of its authenticity must be
discussed on the analogy of that of the relation between

[1] Bultmann, Die Gesch. d. Synopt. Trad. 2nd ed. (1931),
171 f.

the Johannine and the Synoptic reports of the words
of Jesus.[1]

[1] It is characteristic that Bill. has no parallels for Matt. xi, 27;
and the rabbinical parallels in Schlatter, Matt. 384, only illustrate
the Hebrew and Jewish idea of knowing Yahwe. C. G. Monte-
fiore, The Synoptic Gospels, 2nd ed. II (1927), 175 f. feels strongly
the Hellenistic nature of the knowing in this verse. Dalman,
D. Worte Jesus I, 158 f. [tr. D. M. Kay, the Words of Jesus (1902),
193 f.], who takes " neither the Son, but the Father " to be a later
addition at Mark xiii, 32, feels that the absolute use of " the Son "
and " the Father " at Matt. xi, 27 is un-Jewish, and holds that
" no-one knoweth, etc." is a general statement of what is always
the case, here applied to Jesus and his Father. Impossible!
Perhaps there is a reference to Gnostic terminology in the words
" All things have been delivered unto me "; cf. Corp. Herm. I,
32: " Blessed art thou, Father; thy Man seeks to share thy
holiness, even as thou hast given him all authority ". Besides
the commentaries, cf. Harnack, Sprüche und Reden Jesu, in
Beitr. z. Einl. in d. N.T. II (1907), 189 ff.; Norden, Agn. Th.
277 ff.; J. Weiss, N.T. Stud. f. G. Heinrici (1914), 120 ff.;
Bousset, Kyr. Chr. 2nd ed. 45 ff.

VII. LATER DEVELOPMENT

No special contribution is made by the Apologists. Where they are not quoting from the Old Testament, they use both verb and noun, simple and compound, γινώσκειν, γνῶσις, ἐπιγιν., ἐπίγν., in the common Greek sense of theoretical knowledge, primarily of God or truth or Christ,[1] and generally of biblical [2] or theological knowledge.[3] The conflict with Gnosis and the effort to come to terms with Greek philosophy led the Christians of Alexandria to transform the idea of gnosis, differentiating it from faith, not in the Johannine manner, but regarding it as a higher stage of Christian life (the Gnostic is the perfect man)— a peculiar and obscure combination of the Greek humanities with the Gnostic view of the vision of God.

There are many examples of the linking of faith with knowledge, in which the differentiation of the two finds no expression (Corp. Herm. IV, 4; IX, 10; Porphyry ad Marcellam, 21-24; Justin Dial. lxix, 1); that was introduced by the Christian Gnostics, who wanted to maintain their position within the Church, and therefore had to recognise their non-Gnostic brethren as those who had faith but not knowledge. Connected with this was the new status indicated by

[1] Aristides xv, 3; Athenagoras, Suppl. xiii, 1; Justin, Apol. I, xix, 6; Dial. xiv, 1; xx, 1; xxviii, 4; lxix, 4, 6; cxxx, 4; Tatian, Or. Gr. xii, 4; xiii, 1; xix, 2; xlii, 1; cf. Justin, Apol. II, ii, 2 (the lessons of the Christ); Dial. xxxix, 5 (absolutely, of Christian knowledge). On the possibility of philosophical knowledge of God, cf. Dial. iii ff.

[2] Justin Dial. xxvii, 4 ; lxix, 1; xcix, 3; cxii, 3.

[3] Cf. Justin, Dial. lxxi, 3: " those who know this saving mystery, i.e. the passion of the Christ ".

the word ψυχικός (psychic), which now came between
πνευματικός (spiritual) and σαρκικός (fleshly), whereas
formerly it was the opposite of πνευματικός. Clement
of Alexandria (Strom. II, iii, 10) suggests that the use of
" faith " and " knowledge " to mark successive stages
goes back to Valentinus. Clement and Origen accepted
them in order to establish the right to pursue their
scientific and speculative theology within the Church.
Faith is a summary knowledge of urgent truths, and
knowledge a demonstration of what has been received
through faith, being itself built upon faith (Clem. Al.
Strom. VII x, 57; cf. 55 f.). Faith is the first
inclination towards salvation (ib. II, vi, 31), but
knowing is more than believing (ib. VI, xiv, 109) ;
although progress is from faith to knowledge, yet
neither is completely devoid of the other (ib. II, vi,
31; V, i, 1), so that it is possible to speak of gnostic
or scientific faith (ib. VI, ix, 76; II, xi, 48). Gnosis
leads to fulfilment, i.e. to vision (ib. VI, vii, 61; xii, 98)
and when it is said that it leads to love (ib. VII, x, 55,
57), this " gnostic love " (ib. VI, ix, 73, 75) is identical
with contemplation (Θεωρία). This knowledge can
never be lost (ib. VII, xii, 70).[1]

[1] On the mysterious interpretation of *gnosis* in Clem. Al. see
pp. 9-14, and cf. Anrich, Das antike Mysterienwesen, 133 ff.;
in actual practice it is theological science or speculation carried
to the highest degree of vision in accordance with tradition
(Strom. I, i, 15). Origen, who distinguishes, like Clem. Al.,
between faith and knowledge (e.g., Comm. Johan. XIX, iii,
16 ff.), stresses still more the scientific character of *gnosis*. Cf.
the discussion on whether knowledge or faith comes first in Basil
Ep. 235 (M.P.G. xxxii, 872).

'Επιγινώσκειν has already been treated: see Index. Καταγινώσκειν means to remark, notice, observe, discover, detect, be perfectly sure—specially of something wrong in somebody—condemn, esteem lightly, despise, and is found in the Papyri, where it also means self-condemnation (see Moulton and Milligan s.v.).[1] LXX has few examples: e.g. Deut. xxv, 1 (for *rasha'* Hiph., contrasted with δικαιοῦν, " acquit "); Ecclus. xiv, 2 (for *ḥasadh* [? *ḥaṣar*] Pi.); Prov. xxviii, 11 and Ecclus. xix, 5 (" despise "); it is used for self-condemnation at Test. Gad v, 3, as at Ecclus. xiv, 2 and Job. xlii, 6 Symm. (for *ma'aṣ*); Ezek. xvi, 61 Symm. (for *kalam*), and this occurs in the New Testament at I John iii, 20 f., where the context shows that the word retains the element of knowledge; see also Acta Thom. 94.[2] The exact meaning at Gal. ii, 11 is hard to determine; the Old Latin has *reprehensus*, Jerome, .Vulgate and Ambrosiaster *reprehensibilis*; we may take it to mean " detected " or, better, " condemned " or " judged " —not officially, but as at Rom. xiv, 23 (John iii, 18 is different), cf. Josephus, Bell. ii, 135; Diognetus, 10.

'Ακατάγνωστος does not occur in Greek literature, but is used in inscriptions and Papyri of the imperial

[1] Cf. Deissmann, Neue Bibelst. (1897), 28 f.; Nägeli, 47; F. W. Mozley, Expositor, 8, Ser. IV (1912), 143 f.; Dibelius on Tit. ii, 8.

[2] Acta Thomae, 94, p. 207, 11 f.: " Blessed are the saints whose souls have never condemned themselves ". An instructive parallel is in Stobaeus Ecl. III, 558, 1 f.: " Demonax [Cynic, *c*. A.D. 100], being asked when he became a philosopher, said, When I began to condemn myself ".

period (Nägeli, 47), once in LXX (II Macc. iv, 47) and once in the New Testament (Tit. ii, 8), always meaning " unblameable ".

Προγινώσκειν usually means " to know before-hand ".[1] Human foresight and skill make this possible (Eur. Hipp. 1072 f.; Thuc. II, lxiv, 6; Plato, Rep. IV, 426c; Hippocr. Progn, 1), but a real foreknowledge of destiny is forbidden to men (Hom. ad Cer. 256 f.). Prophetic foreknowledge is ascribed to Wisdom in LXX at Wis. viii, 8 (cf. Philo de Somn. i, 2), and by a peculiar use of the Passive she is said to let herself be known beforehand to those who long for her (Wis. vi, 13; cf. xviii, 6).

The New Testament asserts God's foreknowledge, equating it with the election or predestination of his people (Rom. viii, 29; xi, 2) or of Christ (I Pet. i, 20);[2] see pp. 18 and 35 f. Mere foreknowledge is indicated at Herm. Mand. IV, iii, 4 (cf. II Clem. ix, 9). Believers have foreknowledge based on prophecy (II Pet. iii, 17; cf. Herm. Sim. vii, 5). Reference to the immediate past, at Acts xxvi, 5, is paralleled in Demosthenes, Aristotle and Josephus. Justin says that believers are foreknown to God (Apol. I, xlv, 1, etc.), but the polemic against determinism (Dial. cxl, 4) shows that this does not include the idea of election; he also ascribes simple fore-knowledge to Christ and the prophets, as Tatian (Or. Graec. xix, 3) does to Apollo, showing that the Greeks understood the idea.

Πρόγνωσις was a medical technical term from the

---

[1] See L. Edelstein, περὶ ἀέρων (Problemata IV), 1931, 60 ff.; E. F. K. Müller, Die göttliche Zuvorersehung u. Erwählung (1892).

[2] See commentaries of R. Knopf, 7th ed. (1912), H. Windisch, 2nd ed. (1930) [E. G. Selwyn (1947)], ad loc. and cf. II Esdr. vi, for apocalyptic background.

time of Hippocrates (b. 460 B.C.), and is used in the LXX for God's predetermining knowledge at Judith ix, 6. Among Greek Christians it means a gift of foreknowledge analogous to divination (Justin Dial. xxxix, 2; Clem. Al. Strom. I xxi, 133; Tatian, Or. Graec. i, 1; Pseudo-Clem. Hom. ii, 11; cf. K. Preisendanz, Pap. Graec. Mag. VII, 294).

Συγγνώμη at I Cor. vii, 6 must mean forbearance or concession, in line with general Greek usage,[1] though the context might seem to suggest personal opinion (the word for that would be γνώμη).

Γνώμη. See pp. 3 f. notes for general Greek meanings. Most of these, except " reason ", occur in Jewish and Christian writings. The English word " mind " covers most of the nuances, which fall under three main headings, viz. (a) disposition or will; (b) determination; (c) opinion. These are illustrated respectively at I Cor. i, 10; Acts xx, 3; I Cor. vii, 40.

Γνωρίζειν. (a) " To make known " (mostly for yadha' Hiph.) occurs frequently in LXX in a secular sense (e.g. I Kings i, 27; Neh. viii, 12; Prov. ix 9), but also in certain cases with an emotional tone. The subject of the verb may be priest, teacher or prophet (I Kings vi, 2; x, 8; xxviii, 15; Ezek. xliii, 11), or God himself, exercising his power or his grace (see p. 17), as at Jer. xvi, 21; Ps. xvi (xv), 11, etc., or proclaiming his will, at Ps. xxv (xxiv), 4; Ezek. xx, 11, etc., or bestowing secret knowledge, at Jer. xi, 18; Dan. ii, 23, etc. The same verb is also used for cultic proclamation of Yahwe's mighty acts at I Chron. xvi, 8 (ἀπαγγέλλω at Ps. cv. (civ), 1) and for confession

---

[1] Both verb and noun frequently mean " pardon ", e.g. Jos. Ant. vi, 144; Polybius XII, vii, 6 (trans. Shuckburgh) " Those who make untrue statements in their books from ignorance ought, I maintain, to be forgiven and corrected in a kindly spirit ". Cf. Euripides, Ion 1440: συγγνώσεται γὰρ ὁ θεός.

of sin at Ps. xxxii (xxxi), 5. In Daniel (Theod.) it is used for the interpretation of dreams or visions.

New Testament usage resembles that of LXX. The secular sense occurs frequently, e.g. I Cor. xii, 3; xv, 1; Col. iv, 7, 9. Here again the subject of the verb is often God, exercising his power and salvation (Rom. ix, 22 f.; Acts ii, 28, from Ps. xvi (xv), 11), or making them known (Luke ii, 15). But above all, this word indicates the communication of the mystery of his secret plan of salvation: Col. i, 27; Eph. i, 9; iii, 5, 10; vi, 19 (though the more usual term is Φανεροῦν, Rom. xvi, 25 f.; Ign. Eph. xix, 2 f. etc.). It can also mean the human proclamation of what God has done (Luke ii, 17), specially by means of preaching (Rom. xvi, 26; II Pet. i, 16), and making our requests known to God (Phil. iv, 6, as in Philo De Sacr. 132; Quod Det. Pot. 56; cf. Cong. 18; Fug. 38). John makes Jesus himself, as revealer, the subject (xv, 15; xvii, 26).

(b) " To know or perceive " is found in LXX, as in the Papyri [and in classical writers]. Both Active and Passive are frequent in this sense in Philo and Josephus —though in the Passive it is often impossible to distinguish between " known " and " made known ". There is only one example in the New Testament, viz. Phil. i, 22. Γνωρίζειν is used for knowing God in Philo, De Post. Caini, 167; De Mut. Nom. 17; Corp. Herm. X, 15 (here also of God knowing); and in the Epilogue to Herm. Asclep. 41b (Scott, Hermetica I, 376);[1] Diogn. viii, 5.

Γνωστός in Greek literature can mean both knowable and known, and it occurs in inscriptions and Papyri, though as a more refined word. LXX uses it for acquaintance, confidant or kinsman. Philo uses it, but not Josephus. Rabbinic distinguishes between

---

[1] Reitzenstein, Hell. Myst. 286.

kinsfolk (*q*^e*robhin*) and acquaintances (*m*^e*yudda*ʿ*in*) and this is found at Luke ii, 44, while at Luke xxiii, 49 the latter includes the former. " Acquaintance " is obviously the meaning at John xviii, 15 f.

LXX and Acts often use it for " made known ". Perhaps at Acts iv, 16 it means " clearly recognisable". The latter is certainly the case at Rom. i, 19, though it may be doubtful whether the translation should be " what may be known of God "[1] or " the God who is knowable " (cf. ver. 20; I. Cor. iv, 5; Rom. ii, 4, etc.[2] (See p. 35.)

[1] Cf. Blass-Debrunner, Gramm. d. n.t. Gr. 6th ed. (1931), § 263, 2.

[2] Cf. Ps. lxxxvi (lxxv), 1; Is. xix, 21; Exod. xxxiii, 13.

INDEX OF WORDS AND REFERENCES

59

III

BASILEIA

BY
K. L. SCHMIDT
H. KLEINKNECHT
K. G. KUHN, AND
GERHARD VON RAD

Translated from the German, with
additional notes, by H. P. Kingdon

PREFACE

THE chief aim of this volume—which is the seventh in this series of English translations of Kittel's famous New Testament *Wörter-buch*—is to clarify the meaning of the often enigmatic phrase " kingdom of God " in the New Testament. The tradition so far followed by my distinguished and much-lamented predecessor, the late Professor J. R. Coates, has been to transliterate Hebrew and Aramaic words, but to leave Greek words occurring in the German text in their original lettering. I have followed his example in the case of Hebrew and Aramaic words, and also in the case of Greek quotations mainly of interest to experts in that language ; but in the belief that this volume will be of special value also to many pastors and students who do not easily read Greek in the original but have a nodding acquaintance with many of the terms most common in the New Testament, I have trans-literated many Greek, as well as all Hebrew, words into English letters, and occasionally translated them into English, and still more rarely both ; the presence of transliteration is always indicated by the use of italics, and where these are used for Hebrew words I have distinguished Greek words by leaving them in the original lettering. It seemed best, however, not to adhere to any very rigid rule in other cases ; thus a Greek word that occurs especially often has occasionally been transliterated, occasionally not. This is partly for aesthetic reasons, but it may incidentally give practice to those who do not read Greek easily.

These considerations have particularly influenced me in the New Testament section, where students whose knowledge of Greek is so slight that they stand in special need of such studies as this in their preparation of sermons and lessons will specially look for guidance in this so central subject. Here, too, the German text usually has the traditional translation " Reich " for *basileia*, and I have mostly translated it " Kingdom " ; but those who use mainly this part of the book are asked to remember that it has been earlier established that " Herrschaft "—dominion or sov-reignty (cf. p. 32 ad. fin.) is the root meaning of the word ; but to reiterate this too much in the most familiar texts might seem pedantic. In view of this, however, the word *Basileia* has been left as the title of the book ; the German original is at the same time on *basileūs*, and other cognate words.

The few additions I have ventured to make to the text or notes are always in squar brackets ; a very few of the notes in the original have been abbreviated or omitted. So also with some books in the German Bibliography—where it is also pointed out that almost all books dealing with the origins of Christianity are relevant to the theme.

Since the publication of the first volume of the *Wörterbuch* in 1932-3, there has been much discussion among New Testament scholars as to the extent to which the " last things " (*ta eschata*) mentioned in the Gospels may be said to have been already realised in the earthly life of Jesus—how far " eschatology " (a word more honoured by use than by precise definition) has been " realised ". Professor J. Jeremias, on page 157 of the English translation of his great book on the *Parables of Jesus*, sums it up by saying that " they are all full of ' the secret of the Kingdom of God ' (Mk. iv, 11) that is to say, the recognition of ' an eschatology that is in process of realisation ' ", and he adds a footnote saying that this formulation has the agreement in principle of Professor C. H. Dodd—who first used the phrase ' realised eschatology '. I have added a footnote on page 43 to call attention to this now widely accepted modification of earlier interpretations. But we may do well to remember that it is often a *telos*, rather than an *eschaton*—or any ' -ology '—that is referred to as being realised in the New Testament.

Another field of recent deepening of our understanding of the New Testament is the greater realisation of the part played by extreme Jewish nationalism—what came to be called zealotry [1]— from 50 B.C. to A.D. 73, and its probable link with the " false Christs " and brigands mentioned in Josephus and the Gospels, against whom Jesus warned His disciples. The prevalence of their contaminating teaching about the Messiah and Kingdom— which led to the destruction of the Temple, as foretold by Jesus— is perhaps a main reason for the absence of the term *basileia* in Josephus,[2] who also mentions Messiahship with reluctance, and also for the disassociation of the term *malkûth* from Messiah in Rabbinic Judaism.[3] These insights, and the Dead Sea Scrolls,

---

[1] E.g. Oscar Cullmann, *The State in the New Testament* (Eng. tr. 1957).

[2] See p. 26, infra.

[3] See p. 20f. Chronologically this chapter on Rabbinic Judaism should come last in the book, as its sources were not written down till A.D. 200 and may well have been as much influenced by the Gospel teaching as *vice versa* ; but they are of course of help in determining the meaning of Gospel terms, and are therefore treated first.

provide new material for the not yet published Kittel articles on *Christos* and *Pseudochristoi*.

For the rest, although the statement (p. 47) that " whoever concentrates wholly upon ethics centres his logic upon the single individual " may seem to smack too much of a mode of thought specially characteristic of German protestantism in the beginning of the Nazi era (though certainly not of the Nazis) it is my hope that this volume will not only correct Anglo-Saxon misunderstandings of German evangelical scholarship but prove a permanent enrichment to our own.

Of the German authors of this article, Professor K. L. Schmidt, of whose career and publications a summary is given in his companion volume in this series on *The Church*, died on 10th January, 1956. The present editor of the Wörterbuch, Professor G. Friedrich, now of Erlangen, tells me that Professor Kleinknecht is at Münster, Professor Kuhn and Professor von Rad at Heidelberg.

H. P. KINGDON

CONTENTS

ix

BIBLIOGRAPHY

I. Greek Usage

Pauly-W., III (1899), s.v. ' Basileus '

E. Lohmeyer : *Christuskult und Kaiserkult* (1919), pp. 11 ff., etc.

A. Deissmann : *Licht vom Osten*, pp. 310 f.

Aristotle : *Politics* III, 14, p. 1284b, 35 ff.

II. O.T. Usage

H. Gressmann : *Der Messias* (1929).

E. Sellin : *Die israelitische-jüdische Heilandserwartung* (1909) ; *Der alttestamentliche Prophetismus* (1912).

S. Mowinckel : *Psalmenstudien* II: *Das Thronbesteigungsfest Jahwes und der Ursprung der Eschatologie* (1922).

A. von Gall : *Basileia tou theou* (1926).

R. Kittel : *Die hellenistische Mysterienreligion und das A.T.* (1924).

Bousset-Gressmann : *Die Religion des Judentums im Späthellenistischen Zeitalter* (3rd edn. 1926).

III. Rabbinic Literature

G. Dalman : *Worte Jesu*, i, pp. 75-119 (cf. 2nd edn. 1930, 375, ff.) [Eng. translation, 1902].

Strack und Billerbeck : *Kommentar zum N.T. aus Talmud und Midrasch* (1921), i, pp. 172-184 and *passim*.

G. F. Moore : *Judaism* (1927, ff.), I, 401, 432, ff. ; II, 346 f., 371-5.

V. New Testament

See above. Besides this we only add the latest literature on *basileia* in the N.T. owing to the immense amount that has been written, including the references to the subject in all comprehensive works on primitive Christianity ; cf. P. Feine, *Theologie des N.T.* (1931), 73 ff. (he gives a good bibliography); also K. L. Schmidt, *Jesus Christus* in RGG (2), iii, 110-51. For further detailed research see W. Mundle : *Reich Gottes* RGG (2), iv, pp. 1817-22. For discussions see the Report on the first British-German Theologians' Conference in Canterbury : *Das Wesen des Reiches Gottes und seine Beziehung zur menschlichen Gesellschaft* (Theologische Blätter, vi (1927), pp. 113 ff. (N.T. contributions by C. H. Dodd, E. C. Hoskyns, G. Kittel, A. E. J.

Rawlinson, K. L. Schmidt). [The English edition was entitled *Mysterium Christi.*]

German monographs :

G. HOLSTEIN : *Die Grundlagen des ev Kirchenrechts* (1928), 5 ff.

W. MICHAELIS : *Täufer, Jesus, Urgemeinde, die Predigt Jesu vom Reiche Gottes vor und nach Pfingsten* (1928).

J. KÖSTER : *Die Idee der Kirche beim Apostel Paulus* (1928).

G. GLOEGE : *Reich Gottes und Kirche im N.T.* (1929).

H. E. WEBER : " *Eschatologie* " *und* " *Mystik* " *im N.T.* (1930).

H. D. WENDLAND: *Die Eschatologie des Reiches Gottes bei Jesus* (1931).

OTHER LITERATURE

[E. F. SCOTT : *The Kingdom of God* (1931).

T. W. MANSON : *The Teaching of Jesus* (1931).

C. H. DODD : *The Parables of the Kingdom* (1935).

E. T. GUIGNEBERT : *The Jewish World in the Time of Jesus* (1939).

C. J. CADOUX : *The Historic Mission of Jesus* (1941)—with bibliography.

R. OTTO : *The Kingdom of God and the Son of Man* (revised 1943).

S. H. HOOKE : *The Kingdom of God* (1949).

T. W. MANSON : *The Sayings of Jesus* (1950).

T. W. MANSON : *The Servant-Messiah* (1953).

R. H. FULLER : *The Mission and Achievement of Jesus* (1954).

J. JEREMIAS : *The Parables of Jesus* (1954).]

Square brackets, here and elsewhere, indicate additions by the translator.

ABBREVIATIONS

Ditt. Or.   W. Dittenberger, Orientis Graecae Inscriptiones (1902 ff.).

Ditt. Syll. W. Dittenberger, Sylloge Inscriptionum Graecarum (3rd edn. 1915 ff.).

I.G.   Inscriptiones Graecae (Preussische Akademie 1873 ff.).

Moore   G. F. Moore, Judaism (1927 ff.).

Pauly-W.   Pauly-Wissowa, Realencyclopedie der klassischen Altertumswissenschaften (1892 ff.).

RGG.   Die Religion in Geschichte und Gegenwart (2nd edn. 1927 ff.).

S-B.   H. L. Strack und P. Billerbeck, Kommentar zum N.T. aus Talmud und Midrasch (1922 ff.).

Z.A.W.   Zeitschrift für die alttestamentliche Wissenschaft (1881 ff.).

Z.N.W.   Zeitschrift für die neutestamentliche Wissenschaft (1900 ff.).

I. GREEK USAGE

THE word *basileus* [1] denotes the king as the legal, and usually hereditary priestly ruler of the people in a good sense. In later political practice and theory it is contrasted with the *turannos* as usurper.[2] In the well known passage in the *Odyssey* XIX, 108 ff., Homer gives a legendary picture and a paean of the good king and the blessings attendant upon his reign. The justice or injustice of a *basileus* shows its results in the life of his people, who share in his penances or prosperity. The king's power is traced back to Zeus (*Iliad* II, 197) a relationship characterised by the common adjective *diotrephes* (*Iliad* II, 196, etc.) " fostered by Zeus ". In Hesiod, where the King is conceived of essentially as a figure of knightly chivalry, we find a standard developed doctrine of kingly wisdom. Kings as well as bards are inspired by the Muses—Kalliope βασιλεῦσιν ἅμ᾽ αἰδοίοισιν ὁπηδεῖ (*Theogony* 80). To speak with certitude (ἀσφαλέως ἀγορεύειν 86)—that is the ἱερὴ δόσις of the Muses to kings. This early Greek ideal of the king gives birth to the philosophical discussion of the ideal king in Plato's *Politicus :* the knowledge of the " ideas " is the kingly art, and its possessor the kingly man (*Politicus* 292 e; cf. the famous sentence Plato, *Republic* V, 473d: ἐὰν μὴ . . . ἢ οἱ φιλόσοφοι βασιλεύσωσιν ἐν ταῖς πόλεσιν ἢ οἱ βασιλεῖς τε νῦν λεγόμενοι

[1] It is generally accepted that *basileus* is borrowed from the pre-Greek " Aegaean " language (Debrunner, *Real-lexikon für Vorgeschichte* IV, 2 (1926), p. 526). See also attempts at its earlier etymology in Pauly-W., op. cit. 55 f.

[2] Cf. Aristotle, *Nicomachean Ethics* VIII, 12, p. 1160 b 3 and Suidas' definition s.v. Pindar speaks of the priest as *basileus*, *Olympian Odes* I, 23, *Pythian Odes* 3, 70, as *turannos*, *Pythian Odes* 3, 85.

καὶ δυνάσται φιλοσοφήσωσι γνησίως . . . οὐκ ἔστι κακῶν
παῦλα . . . ταῖς πόλεσι, δοκῶ δ' οὐδὲ τῷ ἀνθρωπίνῳ γένει . . .)
Thus Plato, reacting against a long development, is at
the same time precursor of Hellenism with its quite
new concept of the king. It developed the idea of the
" Benefactor King " [1] who moves god-like over the
heads of men, and tends them like a shepherd his sheep.
He knows no law except the personal law of his will,
which is not subject to any communal constitution:
and his will is the norm not only of a definite country
or state but of everything. The being and the office
of the king can be summed up by saying that he is
benefactor to the entire world.[2] From these philosophical ideas of the fourth century developed, under
the influence of the towering figure of Alexander the
Great, the hellenistic " divine kingship ". The primitive Greek faith in the divinity of the politically
creative personality fused in Hellenism with the special
God-king conceptions of different oriental cultures.
Thus *basileūs* is used for the hellenistic God-king, the
basileūs megas or later occasionally the *basileūs basileōn*,
as e.g. Antiochus I of Commagene: *basileūs megas
Antiochos theos*. . . . Ditt. Or. 383, 1, as also the Roman
Caesars.[3] His *basileia* is an *anupeuthunos archē* (Suidas
s.v.).

[1] *Euergetēs* is a specially popular and significant eponym of the
hellenistic kings, as e.g. Antigonus and Demetrius were hailed as
theoi sōtēres kai euergetai.

[2] E. Lohmeyer, op. cit. p. 12. Cf. Plato, *Politicus* 267 d, 275 b,
Aristotle, *Politics* III, 13, p. 1284 a 13—the picture of the ideal ruler
who cannot be placed beneath the *nomoi* because he is himself *nomos*;
and the ideal *pambasileia*—III, 10, p. 1225 b, 32 ff.; Xenophon,
Cyrop VIII, 2, 14—a comparison of the king with the shepherd.
For further examples of the stoics' and cynics' consequent pictures
of the king, see Lohmeyer, op. cit. pp. 48 f., notes 28-9.

[3] For its use as a style and divine predicate of hellenistic kings at
the end of the B.C. era, see Deissmann, *Licht vom Osten* (1923),
pp. 310 f.

Besides the use of *basilēus* for earthly or divine kings, the term is used for the ancient gods, especially frequently of Zeus as the *theōn basilēus* or just *basilēus* (Hesiod, *Theogony* 886, *Opera et dies* 668: here it is an epithet, or sometimes a cultic appellation (I.G. VII, 3073, 90; Ditt. Syll.[3] 1014, 110—Erythrae). For further *basilēus*-divinities (e.g. Hades in Aeschylus *Persae*, 627; I.G. I, 872; Poseidon, Apollo, Dionysus, Heracles) see Pauly-W. op cit. 82.

II. MELEK [1] AND MALKÛTH IN THE O.T.

1. KINGSHIP OF PEOPLE AND CITY

Kingship came to Israel in the great emergency caused by the attacks of the Philistines. Saul, who was at first, like his predecessors, a charismatic leader, was elected King over Israel. After his death, his mercenary general David was at first King of Judah until invested with the royal honours of Israel, which bound itself together with Judah in the form of allegiance to a common person. From the throne of his newly-won city-kingship over Jerusalem David ruled over the two kingdoms and protected the complicated constitution from disintegration, as a result of the transition from the traditional Israelite designation of the Leader by Yahweh to the ties of a dynasty. He saw the perpetually valid legitimisation of the Davidic house in the Davidic Covenant which Yahweh had made with him and his successors. [2] After the dissolution of the personal union at the death of Solomon, the Northern Kingdom knew only passing dynasties: the designation of the King by Yahweh became predominant. In Judah the house of David survived for four centuries on the throne, and in theory his lineage was traced to much later times still.

The relationship of the monarchy to the religious thought of Israel is conditioned by the circumstance that the monarchy emerged at a time when Israel's faith had developed in a highly unique fashion. In contrast to most of the old oriental peoples it did not

[1] *Melek* is common to all the semitic languages ; the verb *mâlak* must be denominative. The original meaning of the root is doubtful—possessor or arbiter. It is used but seldom in the O.T. in a purely metaphorical sense (Job xviii. 14).

[2] 2 Sam. vii and xxiii. 1-7.

grow up as an institution alongside religion and so become a fundamental element in religion, but was secondary, and came into a relationship with the already firmly established religious inheritance. Yahwism confronted it with a firmly founded criticism and very definite claims, but it received it tension-wise into its religion and especially into its hopes for the future.

In the early oriental courts, in whose centre stood a divine-human personality, the preconditions for the development of a court-style were conspicuously present, that is of a traditional ceremonial mode of addressing the king, greeting him as he ascends the throne, paying him homage with high-flown prayers and psalms, etc. In this sphere a quite definite repertory of stereotyped titles, similes, epithets and formularies had developed, and today we see clearly how strongly Israel had also participated in these common oriental forms.[1] When in the so-called Royal Psalms (Ps. ii. xx, xxi, xlv, lxxii, ci, cx, cxxxii) the King is promised divine sonship, the inheritance of the ends of the earth, when he is hailed as the King in whose reign a new era of peace and justice is dawning, here Israel has taken over many thoughts and formulations and incorporated them into her Yahwistic ideology. The King, in ancient eyes the very incorporation of the people, must of course, in Israel be pre-eminently the object of the gracious promises of Yahweh. But it is important to notice that the Israelite religion was stronger than the originally adopted forms: the King remains human: the O.T. knows nothing of any deification of the King, such as was the kernel of the court-styles of Babylon and Egypt.[2]

[1] Perhaps via old traditions of formerly Canaanite Jerusalem. Cf. Ps. cx.

[2] The only vestige that has escaped the severe censorship is Ps. xlv. 7. The declarations of divine sonship are formulas of adoption.

2. The Redeemer King

But now we must make a sharp distinction between the most extravagant utterances of the Israelite court-style and the belief in the Messiah. None of the Royal Psalms is messianic, for the ruler is everywhere thought of as present, it is present enemies who are addressed, etc.; there is nothing to indicate the eschatological expectation of a Redeemer King. And yet the court-style—so much we can now see—is the bridge to the messianic faith. The whole complex of religious-political concepts bound up with the actual king, what was expected of him, how he was addressed, the miracles attributed to him, all that became to a high degree the nursery of the messianic hope. This connection is not surprising, for the expected king is also a son of David. But problems still arise over the eschatological element infiltrating into the simple court-style. Why it was in Israel that that mystery-fraught projection into the *eschaton* appeared, for that we still have no satisfying explanations.[1] We need to remember that Babylon and Egypt, classical countries for the court-style, know no eschatology and no expectations of a Redeemer King at the end of time.

Although the belief in a Messiah feeds upon the ideology of the court-style for its form, its content links on to, and derives from, the person of David and especially the Davidic Covenant (2 Sam. vii). It is not David who will build a house for Yahweh—Yahweh will build David a house, and the latter's kingship is to last for ever. Here was a great promise whose complete, Yahweh-worthy, realisation (so it was increasingly realised) was still outstanding. It could not

[1] The unique Israelite conception of God, the belief in a powerful and dependable God, who is in a position to help Israel, is the root foundation of the religious hopes.

fall to the ground; if the present situation did not correspond, then it was carried forward into the future. Thus the hope of salvation in the re-establishment of the " fallen huts of David " in Amos (ix. 11) is implicitly based on the not yet fulfilled prophecy of Nathan (2 Sam. vii).

Now although the *terminus a quo* for the awakening of the messianic faith is David, that hope yet contains elements whose germs are not in the actual kingship. As early as the obscure prophecy in Gen. xlix. 8 ff. there are motifs of paradise involved (cf. Amos ix. 11-15). It is in no sense to be understood as a miserable formula of accommodation, for these tones are at their strongest in Isaiah, the messianic prophet *par excellence*. The shoot out of the stump of Jesse in Isa. ix and xi ushers in a new age of justice and of the peace of paradise. It is preceded by the annihilation of enemies, its essence consists of supernatural gifts. A similar expectation of a saving son of David is in Micah (v. 1 ff.). Rather less vigorous, yet clearly sketched, is Jeremiah's hope in the shoot (xxiii. 5 f.) and Ezekiel's expectation of the cedar-sprig (xvii. 22 ff., xxxiv. 23 ff., xxxvii. 24 f.). Deutero-Isaiah (xlv. 1 ff.) considered the Persian Cyrus, Zech. (vi. 9 ff.) the Davidic Zerubbabel, to be the King of the last age. This later projection of the messianic hope upon already existing historical characters represents an important change in eschatological conceptions. With the failure of this hope, specifically messianic prophecies become infrequent, and are almost entirely absent from the post-canonical literature,[1] until they come to life again immediately before the N.T. era.

[1] The Messianic hope seems to have been remarkably lively in the levitical circles which gave birth to Chronicles: cf. G. von Rad, *Geschichtsbild des Chronistischen Werkes* (1930), pp. 119 ff. Zechariah ix. 9 is hardly datable. In Dan. vii. 13, there was probably mention of a Messiah in the mythological material, but the editor

If one disregards the enthusiastic phraseology of the court-style and the already mentioned specifically Israelite element of the eschatological, both of which are part and parcel of the Hebrew messianic hope, one comes upon a very considerable remnant of mythological conceptions, which are certainly not an original contribution of the prophets, but which are far from easy to derive from ancient Hebrew religion. In particular, the indications of a pretemporal existence of this Saviour-King [1] and the indissoluble link of this personality with an age of paradisal fruitfulness lead to the conjecture that certain non-Israelite mythical elements [2] of a returning primeval King or of some paradisal *Urmensch* have become fused with the firm promises of the Davidic Covenant. Although the expectations linked with the Messiah take many forms, yet all the evidence points to the fact that the Messiah appears as a Prince of Peace for his own people, so much so that his advent is remarkably unconnected with the wars and capturings of enemies that precede his era. The transition to the new age is not fought for by him,[3] but he stands over beyond this last battle as the ruler in a paradisal era. Another peculiarity of most of the texts about the coming of the Messiah is the shunning of the title *melek:* " in it lurks something impious, all too human, violence and pressure ".[4]

has changed his material. There is no Messiah mentioned in the Servant-songs of Deutero-Isaiah, cf. *Z.A.W.* 47 (1925), pp. 90 ff.; 48 (1926), pp. 242 ff.; 50 (1928), pp. 156 ff.; 51 (1929), pp. 255 ff. Incidentally, the O.T. does not know of *mâshîach* as a title for the eschatological King.

[1] Esp. Mic. v. 1; cf. Sellin, *Prophetismus*, pp. 178 f.

[2] R. Kittel (op. cit. pp. 64 ff.) looks for the origins of the isaianic picture of the Messiah in the Egyptian myth of Osiris.

[3] Isa. xi. 4 is hardly an exception: without touching a weapon, and with the breath of his lips he combats his adversaries miraculously.

[4] W. Caspari, *Echtheit, Hauptbegriff und Gedankengang der messianischen Weissagung Jesaiah* ix (1908), p. 14.

Opposition to the empirical monarchy seems to be a feature of most of the messianic prophecies.

3. YAHWEH AS KING

It is clear, however, that the hope of a Messiah is by no means paramount in the O.T., but occurs relatively seldom in it. There is much more evidence for the belief in another supernatural kingship which directs the present and future—the sovereignty of Yahweh. The relationship of these conceptions to a messianic kingdom cannot be reduced to a simple formula.[1] It is not possible to draw out two independent traditions, for Isaiah, the most powerful of the messianic prophets, speaks of Yahweh as King, and so do Micah and Jeremiah; on the other hand the Psalms, which know nothing of the eschatological king, provide the most copious and the weightiest evidence for the kingship of Yahweh.[2]

The use of the term *melek* of the godhead is a characteristic of the ancient East (cf. among Israel's neighbours, Melkart, Milcom, Chemoshmelek)—indeed this divine epithet is probably of semitic origin. It provides the best description of the relationship between God and man: God is Lord, He demands obedience, but in return gives His people protection and help. In Israel the emergence of this designation can be traced fairly precisely. The references are to be found, as one might expect, after the advent of the empirical

[1] Unfortunately this problem has hardly been touched upon in the recent lively discussion over O.T. eschatology. Caspari, op. cit. pp. 12 ff., shows convincingly that the messianic figure of Isa. ix is no independent ruler. The terms *sar* and *yôçêr* indicate that he is responsible to power above. In Jer. (e.g. xxiii. 5) and Ezek. (xxxvii. 24) the Messiah is *melek*.

[2] A special attitude is shown in this as in other respects by the deuteronomic theology: it knows neither the conception of Yahweh's kingship nor a messianic hope.

Kingship: Num. xxiii. 21; Deut. xxxiii. 5; 1 Kings xxii. 19; Isa. vi. 5, must be the earliest examples.

The conception of Yahweh's Kingship has, however, very various shades of meaning in the O.T. There are passages which stress the timelessness of Yahweh's sovereignty, which comprehends past and future alike (Exod. xv. 18; 1 Sam. xii. 12; Ps. cxlv. 11 ff., cxlvi. 10), others accentuate the element of expectation (Isa. xxiv. 23, xxxiii. 22; Zeph. iii. 15; Obad. 21; Zech. xiv. 16 f.). The present is not enough to do justice to these claims, the concept of Yahweh's kingship gets drawn into the stream of eschatology, towards which it had always shown a propensity[1]: it is hoped that Yahweh will show Himself as King hereafter. But even the most pointedly eschatological passages do not for one moment suggest that Yahweh's kingship is not already a present reality. It is only the final manifestation of the complete sovereignty that is awaited. A third group of prophecies is to be found in Ps. xlvii, xciii, xcvi, xcvii, xcix (the number could probably be increased) and their peculiarity is pin-pointed in the verb *mâlak* (used of Yahweh—" Yahweh has become King "). These are the Coronation Psalms, which are obviously the high point of a festival which celebrated ceremonially (and dramatically?) Yahweh's ascent of His throne.[2] These Psalms proclaim no eschatological event, but a present actually experienced in the liturgy.

A really concrete picture of Yahweh's sovereignty is to be found only in the last-named group, and the officials of this ceremonial may in fact have considered the expectation of an eschatological king as a contradiction of their faith. On the other hand, the other

[1] O. Eissfeldt, *Jahwe als König*, *Z.A.W.* 50 (1928), pp. 81 ff.
[2] Cf. Mowinckel, *Psalmenstudien* II. But he greatly exaggerates the significance of this festival, and the ingenious derivation of Israelite eschatology from it has since been invalidated by his later dating of it. (*Z.A.W.* 52 (1930), p. 267, note 3.)

passages belong far more to the traditional poetical
style which could on occasion combine without great
tension with the belief in a coming Messiah. That the
two conceptions, which originally no doubt grew up
quite independently, were later able to come together
in harmonious fusion can be seen in Chronicles, which
strongly picks up Yahweh's not yet fulfilled promise to
David: David's descendant rules in Yahweh's *malkûth*:
that is the sense of the Davidic Covenant, as understood
by the later Chronicler (1 Chron. xvii. 14, xxviii. 5,
xxix. 23; 2 Chron. ix. 8, xiii. 8).

The exact nature of Yahweh's Kingdom, however,
is not discernible from the majority of the passages.
The many predications in the hymns are mostly silent
as to whether Yahweh is understood to be King of
Israel or King of the world.[1] Nevertheless the pre-
exilic passages mostly describe Yahweh as Israel's King
and promise help, deliverance, justice and joy for the
chosen people,[2] whereas in the exilic and post-exilic
eras there are also pointers to Yahweh's kingship over
the world.[3] Thus the designation of Yahweh as king
certainly seems to make expressly clear and concrete
his power, majesty and helpfulness, but these conceptions were so common and so little bound up with the
specific concept of king that there was no hesitation in
combining it with quite other thought-forms. Micah
mingles it with the figure of the shepherd (v. 3) and
Deutero-Isaiah speaks in parallelism of creator, redeemer and King (xliii. 14 f.). The essence of God's
malkûth is seldom more precisely sketched. But the
reason why that can be stated is that it is always

[1] Jer. xlvi. 18, xlviii. 15, li, 57; Ps. v. 3, xxiv. 7 ff.; Dan. iv. 34.
[2] Num. xxiii. 21; Jer. viii. 1; Zeph. iii. 15; Mic. x. 12 f.,
iv. 6 ff.; but also Isa. xli. 21, xliii. 15, xliv. 6.
[3] Jer. x. 7, 10 ff. (Jer. x. 1-16 is hardly jeremianic); Zech.
xiv. 9, 16 f.; Mal. i. 14; Ps. xxii. 29, xlvii. 3, 8.

described as immanent. Even in such late passages as Isa. xxiv. 23 and Zech. xiv. 9, 16, Yahweh is to reign over the whole earth, have His throne in Jerusalem and be worshipped there by all peoples (cf. Obad. 21).[1]

4. MALKÛTH

The noun *malkûth* is one of the few older Hebrew abstract terms, from which the large number of later conceptions derived. Its initial meaning is kingship; its use in the sense of royal sovereignty, in relation to the concrete sphere of power, is a simple inflection from the root meaning.[2]

[1] This problem is dealt with by Martin Buber in his large-scale work on the Kingdom of God—*das Königtum Gottes* (1932). His thesis, however, is original in so far as the O.T. evidence for Yahweh as King has not received the interpretation among theologians in general which Buber assumes. Even if one declines to follow Eissfeldt (op. cit. p. 104) in regarding Isa. vi. 5 as the first instance, on the ground that he is being too lexicographical, it remains true that Yahweh is in no case described as King before the era of the monarchy. In any case there is no exegetical basis in the texts for interpreting the Sinai covenant monarchically. In general the predication of Yahweh as King belongs far more to the poetical exaggerations of an exalted style rather than to any specially significant evidence for a basic belief. Buber sharply contrasts the *malk*, the " Führer-god " with the Baal. Had he said " Yahweh " instead of " *malk* ", one would agree; but when, it may be asked, in the bitter struggle versus Baal-worship—e.g. in Hosea or Deuteronomy—is Yahweh referred to as " *malk* "? Buber cites many passages which, in one way or another, declare that Yahweh has " led " Israel: yet the theological term " *malk* ", in the sense maintained, is not mentioned. Rather is the specific importance of those other passages where it does really belong (i.e. in the ceremonial or eschatological sense) thereby diminished.

[2] *Mamlākah* differs little from *malkûth*; similarly *melûkah* also means sovereignty. The latter term is used only in a *religious* sense in Ps. xxii. 29 and Obad. 21 of Yahweh's kingly power in the present and at the end of time.

The term *malkûth* is nearly always used in the O.T. in a secular sense, meaning political kingship (1 Sam. xx. 31; 1 Kings ii. 12). Religious thought before Daniel made little use of this term. However, in keeping with the naming of Yahweh as a *melek*, God's sphere of sovereignty is occasionally described as His *malkûth*.[1] A slight anticipation of the frequent eschatological use of it in the post-canonical writings is to be found in the slight corrections of the inherited text in the work of the Chronicler. In 2 Sam. vii. 16, David was confirmed in his *mamlâkah*, which word was understood in a much more secular sense than in 1 Chron. xvii. 14, where David appears as set over Yahweh's *malkûth*. In 1 Chron. xxviii. 5, Solomon sits upon the throne of the *malkûth* of Yahweh. This manner of speaking is not to be understood eschatologically. The Davidic Kingdom is here understood as Yahweh's *malkûth*: on the "throne of Yahweh" (1 Chron. xxix. 23; 2 Chron. ix. 8) sit the descendants of David. But these nuances are significant, for the Chronicler, living in an age when the Davidic monarchy could be but a distant memory, betrays an interest in the realisation of Yahweh's *malkûth*, which although not eschatological, was none the less actual and real.

The sharp apocalyptic distinction between the present and future ages, first found in Daniel, brings with it a much more incisive definition of the term "Kingdom of God". Although in Dan. vii each of the transcendent-born kingdoms is described as *malkû*, this term, when used of the last, the "Kingdom of the Saints" has its special colouring. God can pass on the *malkû* to whomsoever He will (Dan. ii. 44, iv. 22); He gives it to His people and thereby establishes an eternal

[1] Ps. ciii. 19, cxlv. 11, 13; Dan. iii. 33. Cf. *melûkah* in Ps. xxii. 29.

Kingdom (Dan. vii. 27). But this passage does not speak of God's *malkûth*, and Yahweh is not King: it is a question of a succession of human kingdoms until the *malkû* of the saints comes as the last—so is the coming " Son of Man " interpreted (Dan. vii. 16 ff.). This strongly nationalist hope for the *malkû* occurs very frequently in subsequent apocalyptic [1] literature (1 Enoch lxxxiv. 2, xc. 30, xcii. 4: *Assumption of Moses*, x. 1 ff., and *passim*).[2]

[1] For the use of *malkûth* in rabbinic Judaism, see pp. 16 ff.
[2] Cf. Bousset-Gressmann, op. cit. pp. 214 ff.

III. MALKÛTH SHÂMAYIM IN RABBINIC LITERATURE [1]

1. *Its Origin*

THE late Jewish conception of *malkûth shâmayim* [Kingdom of the Heavens] owes it genesis to the general tendency in late Judaism to avoid verbal references to God, such as are used in the O.T., and to replace them by abstract formulations. It is, therefore, closely connected with the term *sheʿkînah*. Just as the latter is simply a substitute for the O.T. sentence *shâkhan Yahweh* " God dwells " . . . " God is present ",[2] so the expression *malkûth shâmayim* appears in late Judaism in place of the O.T. " *malk Yahweh* ", " God is King ", cf. supra, pp. 9 ff.[3]

Thus the Targums frequently replace the O.T. term by *malkûthaʾ deʿY.*—" the Kingdom of God "; for example the *Onkelos Targum* to Exod. xv. 18 has *Y malkûtheh qâʾêm*, " God's Kingdom stands firm " for the O.T. *Yahweh yimlôk*—" Yahweh reigns "; that to Isa. xxiv. 23 has " God's Kingdom is revealed " for the O.T. " The Lord is King ". So also in Isa. xxxi. 4, xl. 9, lii. 7; Mic. iv. 7; Zech. xiv. 9.[4] On the other hand the Targum keeps the actual O.T. expression in

[1] *Melek* in the rabbinic literature calls for no special treatment, as here (unlike the O.T.) all the significance of the word-group is to be found in *malkûth:* hence everything of importance about the former in late Judaism (God as King, the Messiah-King) is included in this section, in so far as it has not already been said in the O.T. section.

[2] Cf. S-B, ii. p. 314. *Sifre*, Num. i or v. 3, etc.

[3] A third similar late Jewish abstract formation is the Targum term *mêmraʾ deʿY.* (rearrangement of the sentence " *ʾâmar Yahweh* ") and no more—no " hypostasis ". Cf. S-B, ii, pp. 302 ff.

[4] Cf. Dalman, *Worte Jesu*, i, pp. 79 and 83.

Ezek. xx. 33; Ps. xlvii. 9, xciii. 1, xcvi. 10, xcvii. 1, xcix. 1, cxlvi. 10.

Since in late Judaism the name *Yahweh* was replaced by *ᵃdônây* in liturgical use (scripture reading in the synagogue), the Targums quite logically write *malkûth' deY*, which was read as *m da 'ᵃdonây*. In ordinary conversation, however, the name of God was avoided by means of replacing it by *shâmayim*, "Heaven". Hence in the rabbinic literature, apart from the Targums, one always finds the expression *malkûth shâmayim*, of which the slavishly literal translation into Greek is βασιλεία τῶν οὐρανῶν (Matt.) but the actually correct rendering is βασιλεία τοῦ θεοῦ (Mark, Luke). In the rabbinic vocabulary even *shâmayim* was later—probably round about A.D. 100—itself replaced as a name for God by *hammâqôm*, "the place". Only in some stereotyped expressions [1] does *shâmayim* survive as a name for God, as also in *malkûth shâmayim*.

From this origin of the expression it is at once clear that *malkûth shâmayim* can never mean "the Kingdom of God" in the sense of the territory ruled over by Him. The expression describes simply the fact that God is King, thus meaning always the "being King", "Kingship" on the part of God.[2]

Malkûth shâmayim is therefore from the very start a purely theological conception formed in late Judaism, not a transference of the secular term *malkûth* to the

[1] Listed in S-B, i, p. 172, under A; and i, pp. 862 ff.

[2] Cf. Dalman, *Worte Jesu*, i, p. 77 ("King's *régime*, not king's realm"). But he establishes the point merely empirically: "An oriental *Reich* is no State in our sense, no 'constituted' people or land, but a rule which embraces a definite area." Actually the point lies in the meaning of the term itself. To turn the conception into a "more or less" as in RGG (2), iv. 181 (Mundle), "denotes *less* the geographical conception of an empire *than* the fact of the royal power of a king" is incomprehensible.

religious sphere.¹ In the rabbinic literature *malkûth*
by itself always means the secular government, the
Roman Empire,² by which is meant not so much the
State as such as the Roman suzerainty as seen from the
point of view of a subject of this State, " the authority
which exercises power over him ".³   With this secular
malkûth the *malkûth shâmayim*, which developed later out
of quite different roots, long after the term had been
coined, is, on occasion, contrasted.⁴ The unique,
original meaning of *malkûth shâmayim* (namely the
abstract counterpart of the clause " God is King ")
was, nevertheless, always clearly understood by the
Rabbis.   This is shown by the fact that in the rabbinic
literature those Bible passages in which God is called
" King " are described as *malkîyôth* i.e. " *malkûth*-
verses ", " Kingship-verses ".⁵

2. *Its Use*

The detailed development of the conception calls for
no comprehensive survey, as all the rabbinical material
about *malkûth shâmayim* has often been collected.   Here
we must above all set out the essential insights for the
understanding of the coverage of the term.   The first
point to notice is that the expression is rare in the
rabbinic literature and not nearly as important as, e.g.
in the preaching of Jesus.   The phrase occurs chiefly

¹ The transference actually took place much earlier—in the
time of David—with *melek*.   (Cf. supra, p. 9, ad fin.)

² S-B, i, p. 183, gives many instances.

³ In the case of this *malkûth*, the " more or less " of note 2 above
is in place.

⁴ Only in three passages, which (according to the authors named)
date from the third century A.D. is the *malkûth shâmayim* contrasted
with the *malkûth hâ'âreç*—Genesis *rabba* ix (7b), *Pesikta* 51 a (and
parallels): Babylon *berakoth* 58 a (S-B, i, pp. 175 f. under h).

⁵ Cf. *Rosh Hashana*, iv. 5; *Sifre*, Num. 77, on x. 10.   See on
this Moore, ii, pp. 210, 373.

only in two modes of speech which both cover its
theologically important range.   One is *qibbêl 'ôl malkûth
shâmayim*—" to take the yoke of God's sovereignty
upon oneself ",[1] i.e. (exactly corresponding to the
definition of the phrase given above) " to recognise God
as King and Lord over oneself ", " to recognise one
God as King and reject all other gods ".   The expression thus indicates acceptance of Jewish monotheism, as every believing Jew daily expresses it in the
shema' (Deut. vi. 4: " Hear, O Israel, the Lord our
God is One ").   So *qibbêl 'ôl malkûth shâmayim* often
means simply " to recite the *shema'* ".[2]

Thus *malkûth shâmayim* here means something for or
against which man must decide in a free choice.   For
there is always also the possibility open to him of
rejecting God as King and Lord (" casting off the yoke
of God's sovereignty "); and from this possibility it
follows that God's sovereignty is not patently apparent
—otherwise it would be a question merely of recognition, whether voluntary or not, on the part of all men
that God is King.   On the other hand there is only real
decision (i.e. decision which everybody must make and
which is at the same time binding and valid) when the
possibility of decision is limited, or has an end.   And
here we come to the second mode of speech in which
malkûth shâmayim commonly occurs.   For this end,
qêç—τέλος, which terminates the possibility of accepting or rejecting God's Kingship through a free act of
will, is of course the manifestation of God's sovereignty.
This manifestation is the oft repeated prayer of Judaism,[3] and in the same way the Targums speak frequently of the end of time when the sovereignty of God

[1] Cf. S-B, i, pp. 173 ff. *passim*.
[2] S-B, i, pp. 177 ff. under n.
[3] Cf. the two prayers out of Tractate *Soferim* in S-B, i, p. 179;
other instances are also cited.

becomes manifest.[1] Thus *malkûth shâmayim* is obviously, in the theology of late Judaism, a purely eschatological phrase, in the strictest sense of that word.

3. *Its divorce from national hopes*

Now it is especially worthy of notice that from all this thought the " people of Israel " is completely absent. In this case nationality is in no sense an element of significance for the religious attitudes of man. Here man stands before God as an individual (who must make a decision) just as " man ", not as a citizen of some country. In this there has reached its terminus in the rabbinic theology a development of religious thought which had its starting point in the O.T. prophets. But the other channel of O.T. piety —religion determined by nationality—which is above all alive in Law and Liturgy, has certainly not vanished in the rabbinic theology. On the contrary, the Rabbis always stressed the religious prerogative of the people of Israel, according to which nationality is determinative for man's position in the sight of God.[2] This thought has also a certain part to play in the conception *malkûth shâmayim*. Often in Jewish prayers, God is addressed as King of Israel.[3] The same thought occurs when it is stated that the patriarch Abraham made God King upon earth [4] in that he was the first to recognise the One God as King and Lord, or when it is said that Israel—the people as such—on

---

[1] Cf. the passages cited above p. 15; also Moore, op. cit. ii, p. 374, n. 3. *Sibylline Oracles* iii. 47 f. (φανεῖται) and Luke xix. 19 (μέλλει ἡ βασιλεία τοῦ θεοῦ ἀναφαίνεσθαι).

[2] Tractate *Sanhedrin* x. 1. All Israel shares in the world to come.

[3] S-B, i, p. 175 under e. Cf. *Psalms of Solomon* v. 18 f. and xvii. 3. The connection with the ceremonial piety of the Royal Psalms is clear.

[4] Cf. *Sifre*, Deut. 313, on xxxii. 10 (S-B, i. p. 173 under c).

the Red Sea or on Mount Sinai, through the confession
of the true God and through the acceptance of His
Torah " took upon itself the yoke of God's sovereignty ".[1]

Both these channels—religion determined by nationality and the religion of the individual—run side by
side and independently in all late Judaism. This
antinomy arose from the fact that each channel of
statements, present in various O.T. writings, as a result
of the canonicity of the O.T. for later Judaism, was
the word of God, and equally so. But the remarkable
thing is that there is not ever any indication sanctioned
in the Holy Scripture to correlate the two channels side
by side into one complete theological system. Such a
tendency is completely absent : the rabbinic writers
did not feel this antinomy as a tension or embarrass-
ment.

Thus, in considering *malkûth shâmayim*, the position
is that the occasional connexion with popular thought
noticed is merely a traditional link with the relative
O.T. quotations,[2] whereas the liveliness and significance
of the idea in late Judaism depends upon the strongly
religious sequence of thought first developed above.
Thus *malkûth shâmayim* is one of the few, if not the only,
quite strong and pure conceptions in late Judaism :
the ἔσχατον of the " manifestation of the *malkûth
shâmayim* " as that which demands the decision of each
individual to " take upon himself " or " reject " " the
yoke of the *malkûth shâmayim* ".

4. *Its relationship to the Messiah*

Thus we reach the clear definition of the conception
vis-à-vis the expectation of a Messiah-King at the end
of time. Whereas *malkûth shâmayim* as a phrase is

[1] S-B, i, p. 172, d and p. 174; *Sifre*, Lev. xviii. 6.
[2] Cf. p. 19, note 3.

purely eschatological and has not arisen in the course
of an historical development, so the expectation of a
Messiah-King developed gradually out of the at first
purely secular expectation of an Israelite King, who
would restore the Kingdom of Israel in the whole
extent and the glory of the ideal Davidic Kingdom,
into an eschatological hope—but not strictly eschatological. The " coming of the Messiah " is placed
rather *before* the ἔσχατον in Jewish thought.[1] The
difference may be reduced to this : the concept of a
Messiah in late Judaism was always an expression of a
hope for the end of time which knew God in the first
instance as the King of Israel and therefore regarded
as the goal of God's plan of salvation the eventual
inauguration of the Kingdom of the people of Israel
with the Messiah as King, of a King to whom all other
peoples are subject ; in *malkûth shâmayim*, on the other
hand, the purely religious concept of the ἔσχατον is
expressed in all its exaltation (" God all in all "),
wherein there is no longer any place for the special
national idea of the link with Israel.

Thus the two conceptions are quite heterogeneous.
True, they appear not seldom side by side as the two
points towards which the hope of the pious Jew, the
national and the purely religious hope, is directed.[2]
But nowhere are they closely related. Nowhere do we
find the thought that the Kingdom of the Messiah is
the *malkûth shâmayim* or that the Messiah inaugurates it
through his actions, or vice versa. Such a connexion
with the conception of a Messiah is impossible if one
starts with the definite concept of the *malkûth shâmayim*.

[1] Cf. S-B, iv, pp. 968 f.
[2] E.g. at the beginning of the Kaddish prayer: " May he set
up his royal sovereignty . . . and bring with it his Messiah."
For the whole train of thought see above all Moore, ii, pp. 371-5.

IV. BASILEIA (*TOU THEOU*) IN
HELLENISTIC JUDAISM

In essentials the LXX agrees with the Hebrew, or Aramaic (Daniel), originals in the few passages where God's Kingdom is mentioned. But in the LXX there are also a few passages which are specifically Greek or hellenistic, and have no Hebrew original in the canonical O.T.—e.g. Wisd. vi. 20 : *epithumia sophiās anagei epi basileian*. This passage summarises the high value and the accessibility of Wisdom : to aspire after her leads to leadership. True, in this sixth chapter of Wisdom there are also references to the *basileia tou theou* : in vi. 4 the Kings of the earth are addressed as the *hupēretai tēs autou* (i.e. God's) *basileiās;* in x. 10 it is said of Wisdom that she showed the righteous man " God's Kingdom ". But the use of *basileia* by itself (vi. 20; cf. x. 14) points to the sovereignty of the wise. This connects with 4 Macc. ii. 23—God has given man a law, by following which he βασιλεύσει βασιλείαν σώφρονά τε καὶ δίκαιόν καὶ ἀγαθὴν καὶ ἀνδρείαν: the *basileia* is identified with the four main virtues.

Yet more clearly and comprehensively is this popular-philosophical ethicalisation of the concept of *basileia* carried to its furthest lengths in Philo. So far as the general use of the term is concerned, there is no question but that the predominant meaning here is monarchy, royal sovereignty, and leadership in general. The actor puts on the *parasēma* (token) *tēs basileias*. This meaning also occurs in the plural; beside those invested with royal dignity stand those invested with generalship—οἱ τῆς βασιλείας καὶ ἡγεμονίας ἀναψάμενοι, *De Plantatione*, 67. Nimrod had Babylon as the ἀρχὴ τῆς βασιλείας, *De Gigantibus*, 66. On various occasions

Philo gives a definition of the term: *basileia* is linked
in hendiadys with *archē* (*De Mutatione Nominum*, 15, *De
Vita Mosis* I, 148, *Quod omnis probus liber sit*, 117); it
stands next to *politeia* (*De Plantatione*, 56); it is more
than *ochlokratia*, *De Fuga et Inventione*, 10; the earthly
basileia has two tasks, ποιμενικὴ μελέτη καὶ προγυμνασία
(*De Vita Mosis* I, 60). Furthermore, *basileia* is repeatedly linked, even identified, with *archē*. The
basileia of Moses, meaning his leadership, is parallel
with his *nomothesia*, *prophēteia* and *archierōsunē* (*De
Praemiis et Poenis*, 53), with his *nomothetikē hexis*, *hierōsunē*
and *prophēteia* (*De Vita Mosis* II, 187). The same is
found if one looks back to the first book of the *Vita* of
Moses, which shows that the whole of this first book
treats of the *basileia* of Moses (i. 333 f.; cf. ii. 66). In
a special discussion the difference between *basileia*
(secular Kingship) and *archierōsunē* (high-priesthood) is
clarified in such a way as to give precedence to the
latter over the former, because the latter is as good as
theou therapeia, and *basileia* as good as *epimeleia anthrōpōn*,
so that both terms are distinguished according to their
objects (*theos* or *anthrōpoi*)—*Legatio ad Gaium*, 278; cf.
De Virtutibus, 54. *Hierōsunē* is worthy of an *eusebēs anēr*,
and to be preferred to freedom, even to *basileia* (*De
specialibus Legibus* i. 57). In a definition of *basileia*, of
which the *dogmata* and *nomoi* are to be observed, we
find: " *basileian*. . . . *sophian einai legomen, epei kai ton
sophon basilea* (*De Migratione Abrahami*, 147). Similar
is the inflexion *hē tou sophou basileia* (*De Abrahamo*, 261;
cf. *De Somniis* ii. 243 f.). Correspondingly Saul is to
learn from Samuel *ta tēs basileias dikaia* (*De Migratione
Abrahami*, 196). That the first man gives their names
to the animals is understood to be *sophias kai basileias to
ergon* (connexion of wisdom and power) (*De Opificio
Mundi*, 148). Meanwhile the precise meaning of *basileia*
is defined as being merely royal sovereignty as seen in

the rule of the wise as the true king (*De Sacrificiis Abelis et Caeni*, 49). In respect of the wise King Abraham *aretē* (virtue) is defined as *archē* and *basileia* (*De Somniis* ii. 244). Similar language is used of *nous*: the operators of *nous* bring it to *tēn hēgemoniān kai basileiān tōn anthrōpeiōn pragmatōn* (*De Specialibus Legibus* i. 334). The opposite of all this is τὸ ἡδέως ζῆν, to regard which as *hegemonia* and *basileia* is a delusion (*De Ebrietate*, 216).

Does Philo speak in these passages of God's sovereignty, or at least also of God's sovereignty? Does he speak of God's sovereignty at all? Yes and no! *Tou theou* appears attributively once, in that the rule of a King is compared with the *basileia tou theou* (*De Specialibus Legibus* iv. 164), and also once predicatively —ἡ βασιλεία τίνος; ἆρ' οὐχὶ μόνου θεοῦ; (*De Mutatione Nominum*, 135). God's sovereignty may be in mind when the building of the tower of Babel is regarded as the *kathairesis tēs aiōniou basileias* (*De Somniis* ii. 285). God is clothed with *anantagōnistos* (invincible) *kai anaphairetos* (completely secure) *basileia* (*De Specialibus Legibus* i. 207). Abraham as true king, i.e. King of wisdom, comes from God, since God *tēn tou sophou basileian oregei* (*De Abr.* 261). Moses shows himself to be a being superior to the first cause who guides the world, χρώμενον αὐτεξουσίῳ καὶ αὐτοκράτορι βασιλείᾳ (*Quis Rerum divinarum Heres sit*, 301).

To a future *basileia* Philo gives only one hint when he once cites Num. xxiv. 7 (Balaam's messianic prophecy) in connexion with the LXX: ἡ τοῦδε βασιλεία καθ' ἑκάστην ἡμέραν πρὸς ὕψος ἀρθήσεται (*De Vita Mosis* I, 290). Here too the Kingship is conceived ethically. [1]

[[1] Philo also portrays the *substance* of a future 'messianic' kingdom which will come 'when men turn to God' in *De Praemiis et Poenis*, 85–126, also citing Num. xxiv. 7.]

Our summary of all the *basileia*-passages [1] in Philo makes it certain that the royal sovereignty is never understood eschatologically. Far more is *basileia* a chapter in moral teaching.[2] The true king is the wise man. Thus Philo agrees with the paeans to the wise man usual in ancient philosophy. The wise man as the true *basileūs* [3] transcends ordinary earthly kings and is thereby to be honoured as divine. This conception determines also Philo's philosophico-religious language about the *basileia tou sophou*. This interpretation derives ultimately from ancient philosophy, but its form comes from the Greek Bible, which Philo interprets and reinterprets in the same manner as has happened in some of the above-mentioned LXX passages. To be sure, it must be mentioned that behind this ethicalisation and anthropologising lie certain tendencies found in late judaism in general. But in spite of a clearly visible influence of this kind, apocalyptic and rabbinic judaism held firm to the thought of God's sovereignty depending upon God's free decision.[4] But Philo has completely changed the original *basileia*-concept, although as exegete (in contrast to Josephus) he has no hesitation in speaking of the *basileia tou theou*.[5]

[1] Cf. H. Leisegang's *Indices*, reading v. 14, 21 for v. 142, 1 and deriving τῶν βασιλείων not from ἡ βασιλεία, but from τὰ βασίλεια, in v. 230, 8.

[2] In the index to E. Brehier's *Les idées philosophiques et religieuses de Philon d'Alexandrie* (1908), there are many passages under " Vertu " but none under " royaume (de Dieu) "; cf. I. Heinemann, *Philons griechische and jüdische Bildung* (1932).

[3] Cf. supra, p. 1, ad fin.

[4] Cf. G. Gloege, *Reich Gottes und Kirche im Neuen Testament* (1929), 19 ff. In that section Philo is not valued more highly than is late Judaism.

[5] Cf. A. Schlatter, *Die Theologie des Judentums nach dem Bericht des Josephus* (1932), p. 49, note 1.

Josephus never uses the term *basileia tou theou.* Only in *Antiquities* vi. 60 is *basileia* mentioned in connexion with God. Whereas the Palestinian Judaism from which he sprang spoke of the *malkûth shâmayim* in the eschatological sense alongside its references to the present, Josephus used the word *theokratia* (*Contra Apionem* ii. 165) for the present situation of the congregation. Instead of *basileús* and *basileia* he says *hēgemōn* and *hēgemonia*, in that he ascribes to the Roman emperor not *basileia* but *hēgemonia*.[1] This situation is probably to be explained (i) by the fact that Josephus may (as he did in general) have refrained from speaking of the eschatological-messianic outlook of his people which is bound up with *basileia*, and (ii) from the circumstance that he, as an historian living and writing in Rome, was indebted to Hellenism and at the same time was completely dependent upon his sources.[2]

[1] So A. Schlatter, *Wie sprach Josephus von Gott?* (1910), pp. 11 f.

[2] Cf. G. Hölscher in his article on Josephus in Pauly-W. ix. 1955: "In his portrayal of Jewish history Josephus entirely renounced any independent use of the text of the Bible, whether in its Greek or Hebrew version, and his material is almost completely, even down to nearly all points of detail, taken from written sources."

V. *BASILEUS* AND ITS CORRELATES IN THE N.T.

A. BASILEUS

THIS word, meaning king, is used in the N.T. of men and God(s), and also of intermediate beings. Of theological importance is the fact that in the N.T., closely connected and in agreement with the O.T. and Jewish usage, both God and Christ (the Messiah Jesus) receive this title, and human kings receive a diminishing assessment of honour.

1. (*a*) *Earthly Kings* in general (unnamed) and special cases (named) in the N.T. are regarded explicitly and implicitly as contrasted with, or at least inferior to, God as King, or the Messiah-King. Those named king (as in the non-biblical literature) are Pharaoh (Acts vii. 10—then replaced by " another king ", Acts vii. 18; also Heb. xi. 23, 27); Herod the Great (Matt. ii. 1, 3, 9; Luke i. 5); also Herod Antipas—never strictly king—(Matt. xiv. 9; Mark vi. 14, 22, 25, 26, 27); Herod Agrippa I (Acts xii. 1 and 20); Herod Agrippa II (Acts xxv. 13, 14, 24, 26; xxvi. 2, 7, 13, 19, 26, 27, 30); also the Nabataean Aretas (2 Cor. xi. 32); further (according to oriental custom) [1] the Roman Emperor (1 Tim. ii. 2; 1 Pet. ii. 13, 17; Rev. xvii. 9 f.; cf. 1 Clement xxxvii. 3). All such kings are kings of the earth, of the nations— *tēs gēs* (Matt. xvii. 25; Acts iv. 26; Rev. i. 5, vi. 15, xvii. 2, 18, xviii. 9, xix. 19, xxi. 24); *tōn ethnōn* (Luke xxii. 25); *tēs oikoumenēs holēs* (Rev. xvi. 14). The description and appraisal of the "Kings of the earth" have been taken from Ps. ii. 2, lxxxviii. 28 [2], etc. As in the O.T.,

---

[1] Cf. Deissmann, *Licht vom Osten*, pp. 310 f.
[2 i.e. Ps. lxxxix. 28 in Hebrew and English.]

the earthly king is not given the rank of divine status
as in the old oriental court-style, since this status is
granted only to Yahweh or to his Messiah-King. In
the Apocalypse this contrast is further heightened, in
that in answer to the contemporary titles of the Roman
emperors and their oriental prototypes it is precisely
and only the One Almighty God who is designated
basileūs tōn ethnōn (Rev. xv. 3) and the Messiah-King is
called the great King, the King of Kings and Lord of
Lords (Rev. xix. 16; cf. xvii. 14). Earthly kings with
their power are subjected by God and Christ to the
sons of the Kingdom of God, who are taken out of the
realms of earthly royal power, who serve one another
as brothers (Matt. xvii. 25 f.; Luke xxii. 25). Before
hēgemones and *basileis* will Christians for Christ's sake be
led for judgement at the approach of God's Kingdom
(Matt. x. 8; Mark xiii. 9; Luke xxi. 12). *En tois
oikois tōn basileōn* (v.l. *basileiōn*) are to be found the
people clad in soft raiment, but no prophet like John
the Baptist (Matt. xi. 8). From earthly kings and even
prophets remain hidden the things which are clear to
the children of the Kingdom (Luke x. 24). Kings
occupied with war (Luke xiv. 31) are, like the Gentiles
and Jews, to hear the good news of God's Kingdom
(Acts ix. 15; cf. Rev. x. 11). At the end of days the
kings of the East are the rod of God's chastisement and
are then themselves annihilated (Rev. xvi. 12, cf. xvi.
14, xvii. 2, 9, 12, 18, xviii. 3, 9, xix. 18 f.). On the
other hand, the possibility also exists that they will
subject themselves in obedience (Rev. xxi. 24).

(*b*) No more and no less than an earthly king is also
an intermediate being like *Abbadon*, Lord of the Spirits
of the underworld (Rev. ix. 11).

(*c*) A special case is presented by the royalty of
earthly men like David and Melchizedek. No matter
how the monarchy appeared and maintained itself in

the Hebrew era (cf. Acts xiii. 21—the Israelites asked God for a King and received Saul), in the N.T. eyes David, as ancestor of Jesus Christ is a King forechosen by God (Matt. i. 6; Acts xiii. 22).[1] And Melchizedek, as King of Salem—of peace and righteousness (Heb. vii. 1-2) is, in the sense of the allegorical interpretation of Scripture, the " type " pointing to Christ.

2. (*a*) Hence it is obvious that in the N.T. it is Jesus Christ who is regarded as *the* King. First, as Messiah, Jesus is *basileūs tōn Ioudaiōn* (Matt. ii. 2, xxvii. 11, 29, 37; Mark xv. 2, 9, 12, 18, 26; Luke xxiii. 3, 37 f.; John xviii. 33, 37, 39, xix. 3, 14 f., 19, 21). But this usage is rather changeable. An uninterested contemporary of Jesus like Pilate knows nothing further than to take this title from his Jewish accusers (Luke xxiii. 2 f.). For the obdurate Jewish enemies of Jesus—in this connexion Pharisees and Sadducees go together—the title is a blasphemous claim of the deceitful messianic pretender. In Jewish eyes Jesus is a man who makes Himself a king (John xix. 12). The fickle mob, sensing but not understanding the messianic claims of Jesus—in whose ranks are to be found disciples in the school of Jesus—misinterpret the term " king of the Jews " more or less politically. The people want to make Jesus king, and do not perceive what they are actually about (John vi. 15). In a word, the fact that Jesus is designated as king merges into the messianic problem which is the very essence of Jesus' messiahship. If the messianic claim actually bound up with the royal title is to be underlined then Israel must be named instead of the Jews. In fact we also find—if but relatively seldom—the title *basileūs (tou) Israēl* (Matt. xxvii. 42; Mark xv. 32; John i. 49, xii. 13). In any

---

[1] The difficult passage about the Davidic sonship (Mark xii. 35-7, and parallels) makes no difference in this connexion.

case, the Jew who knew of the promises given to his
people was bound to speak of the King of Israel. To
the daughter of Zion, as the true Israel, comes the
promise of Zech. ix. 9; " See thy King comes to thee "
(Matt. xxi. 5; John xii. 15). This Messiah-King, at
God's behest, conducts the final judgement (Matt. xxv.
34, 40). According to Ps. cxviii. 26, Jesus, at His entry
into Jerusalem, is the blessed King who comes in the
name of the Lord (Luke xix. 38). Only so is Jesus the
Messiah-King (*Christos basilēus*), who stands in contrast
to the Roman Emperor, a contrast misunderstood by
Jews and Gentiles (Luke xxiii. 2).[1] It seems at first
sight remarkable that, apart from the Evangelists, the
individual N.T. authors use neither " King of the Jews "
nor " King of Israel " of Jesus. The designations are
absent from the earliest *kerugma* as we find it in Acts, and
also from St. Paul. To deduce from this that the
original Christian community, to whom the evangelists
also belonged, did not know or use the missing designations would be unconvincing. A hidden proof that
the royal title for Jesus was also not alien to the *kerugma*
can be found in Acts xvii. 7, where the Jews in Thessalonica denounce the Christians for high treason, for
maintaining that another was king, namely Jesus. At
the same time the marked reticence is revealing. We
may conjecture that the difficulty about the messiahship
of Jesus of Nazareth, already referred to as the messianic
problem, brought with it a certain uncertainty and

---

[1] On the subject of these contrasts within the framework of the
messianic secret much material is provided by the comprehensive
study by R. Eisler, Ἰησοῦς βασιλεὺς οὐ βασιλεύσας (1924-30),
esp. ii, pp. 374 and 688, with his acute, but often obscure and
unreliable detailed hypotheses. Eisler is criticised by H. Windisch, *Gnomon*, vii (1931), pp. 289-307. H. Lewy, *Deutsche
Literaturzeitung*, 21 (1930), pp. 481-94, and W. Windfuhr, *Philol.
Wochenschrift*, liii (1933), pp. 9 ff. [An English résumé of his
theories appeared in 1931, *The Messiah Jesus and John the Baptist*.]

therefore reticence. The situation also provides us with the evidence that the whole complex of the messianic secret, not properly comprehended by the first Christian community, is a vital component of the history of the Christ upon earth, that Jesus Himself, as the King of the Jews (or of Israel), regarded Himself as the Messiah of His people. The fourth evangelist here agrees entirely with the others, except that he goes further in the answer to Pilate's questioning by giving a christological definition of the Kingship of Jesus (John xviii. 37). The Book of Revelation takes up a special point of view in raising the royal title into a cosmological term. The eschatological messianic King bears sway over the entire universe. In the so-called synoptic apocalypse (part of Mark xiii, and parallels) the situation is the same. Here too fits St. Paul's description of Christ's judgement in 1 Cor. xv. 24, where Christ restores the sovereignty to God (the Father) at the end of time. In this sense is Jesus Christ (in 1 Tim. vi. 15—corresponding to the hymnodic style of Revelation) King of Kings and Lord of Lords.

In the Apostolic Fathers Christ is designated *basileūs megas* (Didache xiv. 3 after Malachi i. 14). He is preceded by a messianic-apocalyptic foe (an Antichrist) by a *basileūs mikros* (Epistle of Barnabas iv. 4; cf. Dan. vii. 24). When Christ is called King, it is in connexion with the heightening of the dignity of the incarnate, who is installed as King by God the King (Diognetus vii. 4). With regard to the result, and the ensuing example of the effect of the incarnation, Christ's title of *basileūs* is enlarged by the addition of the attribute *sōsas* (Polycarp ix. 3) and the title *didaskalos* (*ib.* xvii. 3).

(*b*) When the sovereignty is given back by His Christ to God, then St. Paul thinks of *God the Father as the eternal King*. This is clearly expressed in 1 Tim. i.

17 where God is *basileūs tōn aiōnōn* (cf. Tobit xiii. 6, 10).
For the rest, there is only one passage in Matt. (v. 35),
where God is praised as the *megas basileūs*. It is
noticeable that it is the First Evangelist, so specially
rooted in the O.T., who includes this reference. It
follows that he also passes down to us more parables of
God's Kingdom than the other evangelists. And in
some of these parables God is King in His diverse
functions: cf. Matt. xiv. 9, xviii. 23, xxii. 2, 7, 11, 13.

The Apostolic Fathers, naturally, like the philoso-
phically influenced Judaism of the Diaspora, include a
greater variety of epithets for God than does the N.T.
As in 1 Tim. i. 17, a passage which belongs even more
closely to the sphere just described, so in 1 Clement
lxi. 2, God is named *basileūs tōn aiōnōn* and praised as
despotēs epouranios. In Hermas v. 3, 9, 8, God is *ho
basileūs ho megas;* cf. Ps. xlvii. 3 (in lxx) and Tobit
xiii. 15. God is *basileūs* also in Diognetus vii. 4.

(*c*) According to the not specially well-attested
readings in Rev. i. 6, and v. 10, *Christians* also can be
called *basileis*.[1] In any case the verbs *basileuō* and
sumbasileuō are used of Christians.

B. BASILEIA [2]

1. *Its basic meaning*

As to the general use of this term, it must be said
that the word, which we mostly translate as *kingdom*,
realm, originally means only the *being, essence, situation,*

---

[1] A formal analogy to this transferred (inappropriate) use of
basileūs in the sense of someone who stands out from other people
occurs in Philostratus Vitae Sophistarum ii. 10, 2, where Herodes
Atticus occurs as *ho basileus tōn logōn*.

[2] Beside the expositions of Holstein and Gloege (see Bibliography, p. xi), it must be mentioned that an examination, in
method lexicographical, and true to the texts—as is here undertaken by way of acceptance and deepening of the article in

of a king. As it is a question of a king, we do best to speak of his *dignity*, his *power*. That is true of the earliest example of the word—τὴν βασιληίην (Ionian for *basileian*) ἔχε τὴν Λυδῶν (Herodotus i. 11). So also Xenophon *Memorabilia*, iv. 6, 12: βασιλείαν . . . καὶ τυραννίδα ἀρχὰς μὲν ἀμφοτέρας ἡγεῖτο εἶναι, διαφέρειν δὲ ἀλλήλων ἐνόμιζε (cf. the difference between *basileus* and *turannos* p. 1, note 2). Inevitably an often-found second meaning follows: the dignity of a king shows itself in the *territory* ruled over by him, in his *realm*.[1] Such a change of meaning is clear in the word " dukedom " and in the more general term " empire ". In kingship, on the other hand, the secondary meaning has not established itself, but the original meaning of the ending -ship, referring to position and dignity, has remained predominant. In *basileia* both meanings are present. In Rev. xvii. 12 and xvii. 17, the double sense seems to be indissolubly present.[2]

A survey of the O.T. (Hebrew and Aramaic and LXX; cf. supra pp. 4 ff.) of the Pseudepigrapha and Apocalyptic literature (with the rabbinic literature pp. 15 ff.) and the other hellenistic writers (above all, Philo: supra pp. 22 ff.) shows that the meaning *status*, or

H. Cremer's *Biblisch-theologisch Wörterbuch des N.T. griechisch*, 11th edn., revised by J. Kögel (1923)—is of special value for the examination of theological questions in the Bible. Questionable modern categories such as " dynamic ", " ultratemporality ", " anti-secularism " (especially used by Gloege) should be avoided. Exegesis should, moreover, not stand aside from the long struggle about the immanence and transcendence of the Kingdom of God—a struggle that has proved fruitless and was bound to do so—as may happen if it uses a newer, possibly better, terminology in contrast to one older and less good.

[1] Well explained by Suidas, s.v.: τὸ ἀξίωμα καὶ τὸ ἔθνος βασιλευόμενον.
[2] In modern Greek *basileia* means " monarchy ", " royal rule ", also " duration of reign "; for " royal realm ", *basileion* is used.

power, is in the foreground.   For the N.T. too, this
basic meaning is decisive.[1]

2. *The earthly Basileia*

(*a*) To the earthly *basileūs* (cf. pp. 1 ff.) corresponds
the earthly *basileia* as monarchy or King's realm.   The
two meanings established in the introduction are inter-
woven, but in some N.T. passages can be separated,
according to the context.   When in the Parable of the
Pounds we hear of a pre-eminent man who is reported
to have travelled to a distant land *labein heautōi basileian*
and returned *labonta tēn basileian* (Luke xix. 12, 15), on
both occasions it is a question of *royal status*.[2]   The
same verbal link is found in Rev. xvii. 12: *deka basileis
. . . basileian . . . oupō elabon*.[3]   To this fits the next
passage Rev. xvii. 17: *dounai ten basileian tōi thēriōi* [3]
and Rev. xvii. 18: *hē polis hē megalē hē echousa basileian
epi tōn basileōn tēs gēs*.[4]   In other N.T. passages the
meaning *King's realm* is natural.   Thus Matt. iv. 8
= Luke iv. 5, where the Devil at the temptation of
Jesus shows him " all the kingdoms of the world ".
From the fact that the plural is used and something
visible displayed, the meaning " royal realm " or just
" realm " follows naturally.[5] 'When Jesus in his

[1] Cf. some English statements: A. E. J. Rawlinson, *The Gospel
according to St. Mark* (1925), p. 111, speaks of " God's Rule or
Sovereignty, the Reign of God "; A. Deissmann, *The Religion of
Jesus and the Faith of Paul* (1923), pp. 108 ff., " Kingdom or
sovereignty, kingly rule of God "; J. Warschauer, *The historical
Life of Christ* (1927), " What we translate ' the Kingdom of God '
means thus rather His ' Kingship ', His ' reign ' rather than His
' realm '."

[2] So e.g. E. Klostermann, *Lukasevangelium* (1929), *ad loc.*

[3] E. Lohmeyer, *Apokolypse* (1926), *ad loc.* " monarchy ".

[4] Freely translated, op. cit., " The great city is queen over the
kings of the earth ".

[5] Klostermann's *Matthäusevangelium* and *Lukasevangelium*, *ad loc.*,
" Realms (*Reiche*) of the world ".

defence against the Pharisees says " πᾶσα βασιλεία μερισ-
θεῖσα καθ' ἑαυτῆς ἐρημοῦται " (Matt. xii. 25; Mark
iii. 24. and Luke xi. 17 are similar), the predicative
verb and the conjunction with a *polis* or an *oikia* (*oikos*)
indicate the translation " royal realm ". When we
find in the apocalyptic speech of Jesus " *egerthēsetai
ethnos ep' ethnos kai basileia epi basileian* " (Matt. xxiv. 7,
and parallels) the connexion with *ethnos* points to the
meaning *royal realm*. The same is true when the
tetrarch Herod promises his daughter " *heōs hēmisous
tēs basileias mou* " (Mark vi. 23) and in *egeneto hē basileia
autou* (sc. *tou thēriou*) *eskotōmene* (Rev. xvi. 10).

This sort of earthly *basileia* carries with it the circumstance that the contrast to, or at least the subjection
under, the *basileia* of God gets emphasised, just as the
kosmos (Matt. iv. 8 or the *oikoumenē* (Luke iv. 5) as the
basileia tou kosmou (Rev. xi. 15) is against God, because
it has sold its soul to the " Anti-King ", i.e. the Devil.
A special feature of this is the fact that the apocalyp-
tically interpreted (i.e. recognised as devilish) World-
power of the *imperium romanum* (the *thērion* in Revelation!) wishes to set up the *basileia* and so diffuse light
where it nevertheless lies in wickedness and deceit in
darkness (*eskotōmene* Rev. xvi. 10). That the Devil
claims to have a *basileia* follows from the facts that he,
as tempter, leads astray the *basileiai* of the world, and
that Jesus in speaking *vis-à-vis* the Pharisees in general
of an earthly *basileia* directs his words especially to the
basileia of the Devil.

(*b*) In the framework of this apologetic discourse the
phrase " the Devil's *basileia* " is actually used: πῶς
οὖν σταθήσεται ἡ βασιλεία αὐτοῦ (sc. τοῦ σατανᾶ). This
can mean either royal realm, or status (Matt. xii. 26
= Luke xi. 18).

(*c*) Over against such an earthly-human, in the last
resort devilish, *basileia* stands the *basileia* of the men

chosen by God and the people chosen by him. Legitimate proprietor, indeed representative, of the *basileia* is King David ; εὐλογημένη ἡ ἐρχομένη βασιλεία τοῦ πατρὸς ἡμῶν Δαυίδ (Mark xi. 10). It is only to Israel as the people of God of the Old and New Covenant (*Israel kata pneuma*) that the *basileia* belongs, for which Christ's disciples are asking and hoping : κύριε, εἰ ἐν τῷ χρόνῳ τούτῳ ἀποκαθιστάνεις τὴν βασιλείαν τῷ Ἰσραήλ; (Acts i. 6).[1]

3. *The Basileia of Christ*

Since, as has been shown above, Jesus Christ is in the N.T. (based on O.T.) the King of the true Israel, we find also mention of the *basileia* of Christ. The " Son of Man " will send out his angels, and they will collect *ek tēs basileias autou* all deceivers and evildoers (Matt. xiii. 41). Jesus says, " There are some standing here who shall not taste death until they see the ' Son of Man ' coming ἐν τῇ βασιλείᾳ αὐτοῦ " (Matt. xvi. 28). Of Jesus Christ as King we read *tēs basileias autou* there shall be no end (Luke i. 33). To his disciples this King promises " you shall eat and drink ἐν τῇ βασιλείᾳ μου " (Luke xxii. 30). To the suffering and dying Messiah-King His fellow-victim of crucifixion cries " Remember me when Thou comest εἰς τὴν βασιλείαν σου " (other reading : ἐν τῇ βασιλείᾳ σου : Luke xxiii. 42). Of the nature of His Kingdom Jesus says " *hē basileia hē emē* is not of this world " (John xviii. 36). The apostle of Christ tells of τὴν ἐπιφάνειαν αὐτοῦ καὶ τὴν βασιλείαν αὐτοῦ (2 Tim. iv. 1). He knows that his Lord will deliver him *eis tēn basileian autou ten epouranion* (2 Tim. iv. 18). To us Christians is granted the entrance *eis*

[1 Many scholars, however, would stress that these two references to the return of David's and Israel's, *basileia* do not represent the mind of Jesus Himself.]

tēn aiōnion basileian tou kuriou hemōn kai soteros Iesou Christou (2 Peter i. 11).

This *basileia* of Jesus Christ is at the same time the *basileia* of God. In various passages we find mention of the Kingdom of God *and* Christ. The unbeliever has no inheritance *en tei basileiai tou Christou kai theou* (Eph. v. 5). At the end of time the *basileia tou kosmou* becomes that of our Lord and His Anointed—τοῦ κυρίου ἡμῶν καὶ τοῦ χριστοῦ αὐτοῦ (Rev. xi. 15). Thus God and Christ stand side by side, now God, now Christ, being mentioned first. It is therefore certain that there can be no question of the *basileia* of Christ being mentioned apart from that of God. Jesus Himself says " My Father has bequeathed to me a *basileian* (Luke xx. 29). It is God who has delivered us unto the *basileian tou huiou tēs agapēs autou* (Col. i. 13). At the end of time Christ, who has similarly received the *basileia* from the Father, gives it back to Him (1 Cor. xv. 24). He can give to God only that which is already His own. And so we pass to consider the expression *basileia (tou) theou*, which dominates the entire N.T., about which is here already spoken implicitly in the foregoing pages; in what follows we shall at the same time have to speak explicitly also about the *basileia (tou) Christou.*

4. *The Basileia of God*

(*a*) *The terminology.* In surveying the terminology of the " Reich " (Kingdom) of God there are four main divisions: the juxtaposition of *basileia tou theou* and *basileia tōn ouranōn; basileia* used absolutely; attributive and predicative statements; synonyms.

The expression *basileia tōn ouranōn,* " Kingdom of Heaven ", is only found in Matthew in the N.T. except for the textually uncertain passage, John iii. 5; outside it also, and significantly, in the Gospel according to

the Hebrews fr. 11 (*regnum coelorum*). Furthermore,
Matthew has the phrase *basileia tou theou*, God's Kingdom, generally found in Mark, Luke and elsewhere,
certainly three times—Matt. xii. 28, xxi. 31, xxi. 43—
and probably also a fourth time (Matt. vi. 33, where,
it is true, *tou theou* is not in all the manuscripts), and
possibly also a fifth time, if *tōn ouranōn* is not the correct
reading, in Matt. xix. 24. The question arises, why
this double terminology in Matthew? Did the First
Evangelist make a distinction between his generally
used *tōn ouranōn* and his less frequent *tou theou?* In
general one must come to the conclusion that, as the
manuscripts and synoptic parallel passages change
about between both phrases, they are used indifferently
and mean the same. Whether Jesus Himself used one
or the other term in Aramaic, remains disputed. It
might be maintained that " Kingdom of Heaven " has
a special significance in that by it is meant the power
that comes from Heaven [1] and enters into the world.
Thereby we gain two important insights. We see
again, and clearly, that the essential meaning is not
realm, but *sway*. Bound up with this is the realisation
that such a power of Heaven can from its very nature
not connote a Kingdom that comes about as a result of
a natural development of earthly relationships or
human strivings, but through an intervention of God
from Heaven. As, moreover, in late Jewish speech the
word " God " can be replaced by " Heaven ", it
follows that the phrase *basileia tou theou* means precisely
the same as *basileia tōn ouranōn*. Not different is the
expression *basileia tou patros*, " Kingdom of the Father ",
Matt. xiii. 43, xxvi. 29. Cf. also Matt. vi. 10 (" May
thy, our father's, Kingdom come ") and Matt. xxv. 34
and Luke xii. 32 (" it has pleased your father to give
you the Kingdom ").

[1] The plural is a semitism.   Contrast 2 Cor. xii. 2.

A large number of passages speak of the *basileia* without any qualification, i.e. absolutely: Matt. iv. 23, ix. 35, xiii. 19, xxiv. 14 (*euangellion*, or *logos tēs basileias* viii. 12, xiii. 38 (*huioi tēs basileias*), Heb. xi. 33 (*dia pisteōs katēgōnisanto basileiās*), xii. 28 (*basileian asaleuton paralambanontes*), James ii. 5 (*klēronomous tēs basileiās*); perhaps also Acts xx. 25 (*kerussōn tēn basileiān*).[1] There is no need to prove that in all these passages the Kingdom of God is in mind, as is made certain by the contexts and by special attributes and predicates.[2]

Since any qualifications, whether expressed (by the addition of *tou theou, tōn ouranōn*) or not (used absolutely), are bound up with the Being and Acts of God, further direct attributes are very rare. Besides the already mentioned Heb. xii. 38 (*asaleutos*), there is also 1 Tim. iv. 18 (*epouranios*) and 2 Peter i. 11 (*aiōnios*). In the case of other aspects of God's Kingdom, other such attributes are more rhetorical and formal rather than realistically theological in their effect. The N.T. has also but few direct predicates. Whose is the *basileia tou theou?* Obviously God's—and men's, but only those men who are poor (in spirit) (Matt. v. 3; Luke vi. 20), who are persecuted for righteousness' sake (Matt. v. 10).

More detailed attributive and predicative statements bring us into a complex range of synonyms calculated to make clear the complexity of the proclamation of God's Kingdom. It makes no difference whether synonymous phrases are tacked on with an " and " (hendiadys) or whether they occur as predicates. It

---

[1] To which many manuscripts add *tou* (*kuriou*) *Iēsou*, or *tou theou.*

[2] This absolute use has led to a religious or religious-sounding, but really immanent-secular and pseudo-theological, use of the term realm (*Reich*). Cf. Religious-Socialism or the *dritte Reich* of the Nazis (linked with the faith in the old " Holy Roman Empire "—which in its turn looks back to the absolute use of *basileia*).

makes no difference in what order such expressions come, or in what order they are treated here. It is always a question of the many-sided and yet clear Being and Acting of God, and His call to and claims upon, men. Men are to seek God's Kingdom and His righteousness (Matt. vi. 33). This righteousness and peace and "joy in the Holy Spirit" build up the Kingdom of God (Rom. xiv. 17). This all means no innate, acquired or "to be acquired" quality, but is *palingenesia* ("being born again")—the word used in Matt. xix. 28 (cf. John iii. 3 ff.), whereas the parallel passage in Luke xxii. 30, has *basileia*. In this connexion the writer of Revelation speaks to his brother-Christians as their brother and companion ἐν τῇ θλίψει καὶ βασιλείᾳ καὶ ὑπομονῇ ἐν Ἰησοῦ (Rev. i. 9). To him has come ἡ σωτηρία καὶ ἡ δύναμις καὶ ἡ βασιλεία τοῦ Θεοῦ ἡμῶν καὶ ἡ ἐξουσία τοῦ χριστοῦ αὐτοῦ (Rev. xii. 10). Such a power (*dunamis*) of God is also spoken of when something like a definition of God's Kingdom has to be given. God's Kingdom comes *en dunamei* (Mark ix. 1); it does not exist *en logōi* (of men) but *en dunamei* (of God) (1 Cor. iv. 20).[1] Alternatively, to the Kingdom of God comes *doxa*—the glory of God (1 Thess. ii. 12); indeed *doxa* and *basileia* can be changed over, as Mark x. 37 shows with ἐν τῇ δόξῃ σου where the parallel passage in Matt. xx. 21 has ἐν τῇ βασιλείᾳ σου. The realm of Christ as sent from God coincides with His *epiphaneia* (2 Tim. iv. 1). Such a *basileia asaleutos* is for the believers grace (*charis*) (Heb. xii. 38); it is

[1] This Pauline passage would be entirely misunderstood if one were to see here only the well-known antithesis between word and deed, between talking and acting. The point here is that human work has no value *vis-à-vis* God's power. The following paraphrase gets the point: "Not in human deeds but in God's word is the Kingdom of God." The whole emphasis is on God's Kingdom, as the sovereign, unambiguous, logical subject of the sentence.

epangelia, as the manuscripts ℵ and A read for *basileia* in James ii. 5; it is life (*zoē*) into which one enters as into the Kingdom of God (Matt. xviii. 9) whereas in the parallel passage, Mark ix. 47, the text has *basileia*. The Scribes and Pharisees have wished to exclude from this Kingdom a man whom God has admitted to His Kingdom (Matt. xxiii. 13), replaced by the " keys of knowledge " (*gnōsis*) in the parallel passage Luke xi. 52; thus *basileia* (*theou*) is even the same as *gnosis* (*theou*)!

All these synonyms show that God's *basileia*, meaning God's ways with men, constitutes a soteriological entity, of which the explanation stands or falls with that of the general soteriology in the preaching of Jesus Christ and His apostles.

(*b*) The last sentence also means that in the Kingdom of God we are concerned with the entire preaching of Jesus Christ and His apostles. If the entire proclamation of the N.T. is *euangelion*, then this is the *euangelion* of God's Kingdom. For *euangelion tou theou* in Mark i. 14 many manuscripts read *euangelion tēs basileiās tou theou*. This summarising passage corresponds to other similar passages such as Matt. iv. 23, ix. 35; cf. also xxiv. 14. The verb *euangelizesthai* also refers to God's reign—Luke iv. 43, viii. 1, xvi. 16; Acts viii. 12. The same is the message of cognate verbs like *kērussein* (Matt. iv. 23, ix. 35; Luke ix. 2; Acts xx. 25, xxviii. 31), or *diamarturesthai* (Acts xxviii. 23), or *diangellein* (Luke ix. 60), or *peithein* (Acts xix. 8), or *lalein* (Luke ix. 11), or finally *legein* (Acts i. 3). As the *euangelion* of God's Kingdom, so also mention is made of the *mustērion* (or the plural *mustēria* = revelation!) of God's Kingdom (Matt. xiii. 11 and parallels) or the *logos* of God's Kingdom (Matt. xiii. 19) whereas in the parallel passages Mark iv. 15 and Luke viii. 12, we find *logos* alone, meaning the " word of God ". The whole of such preaching is expressly secured through the

much-stressed binding of word and deed in decisive
passages.   Together with the direction to His disciples
to proclaim God's Kingdom Jesus gives also the direction
to heal the sick (Luke ix. 2; cf. Matt. x. 7 f.; Mark iii.
13 f.) Jesus sees in the fact that he expels demons the
breaking in of God's Kingdom (Matt. xii. 28 = Luke
xi. 20).   Thus from this point there is not only the word
of God's Kingdom, but, coinciding with it, the deeds
of God's sovereignty.   That is expressly emphasised
in the summaries by the evangelists (tacked on to the
oldest *kērugma*); cf. Matt. iv. 23.

(c) What is the point of impact for this N.T. proclamation?   Jesus of Nazareth is not the first who has
spoken of God's Kingdom, nor John the Baptist.   The
preaching of both does not say " I proclaim unto you
that there is a Kingdom of God and it looks like so and
so " but rather " I proclaim unto you that the Kingdom
of God is nigh ".   The theme is thus well known to its
first hearers, the Jewish contemporaries.   This concrete
link with the situation is decisive.   The positive link
for the Baptist and for Jesus is given in the apocalyptic
and the rabbinic literature, partly agreeing with,
partly differing from each of these two themselves
differing movements, which on their part derive
originally from the prophets of the O.T.   Details of
these may be read in the articles on the O.T. and
rabbinic periods, which are here presupposed.   For
the N.T. authors, naturally writing in Greek, the Greek
translations of the O.T. are of importance.   When in
Heb. i. 8, in the middle of a long O.T. quotation,
mention is made of the ῥάβδος τῆς βασιλείας αὐτοῦ (LXX
σου) it is a question of the use of Ps. xliv. 7, out of the
Septuagint.[1]   On the other hand there are, in the

---

[1] The writer of Heb. argues entirely on the basis of LXX, writing
the " best " Greek of the New Testament. [The Hebrew—Psalm
xlv. 7—speaks of a sceptre.]

LXX, as we have seen, some specifically hellenistic passages; these are not of importance as a point of contact for the N.T. proclamation of the " Kingdom of God ".   The same is true of Philo and Josephus.

(d) If the " Kingdom of God " as has been shown from the terminology, means the existence of royal sovereignty, that is confirmed fully when we examine the details of the contexts.   The most important statement is that the Kingdom of God is near, has drawn near, has come to us, is coming, will manifest itself, shall come: $\mathring{\eta}\gamma\gamma\iota\kappa\epsilon\nu$ [1] (Matt. iii. 2, iv. 17 = Mark i. 15; Matt. x. 7; Luke x. 9, 11), $\mathring{\epsilon}\gamma\gamma\mathring{\upsilon}s$ $\mathring{\epsilon}\sigma\tau\iota\nu$ (Luke xxi. 31), $\mathring{\epsilon}\rho\chi o\mu\mathring{\epsilon}\nu\eta$ (Mark xi. 10), $\mathring{\epsilon}\rho\chi\epsilon\tau\alpha\iota$ (Luke xvii. 20), $\mathring{\epsilon}\phi\theta\alpha\sigma\epsilon\nu$ (Matt. xii. 28 = Luke xi. 20), $\mu\mathring{\epsilon}\lambda\lambda\epsilon\iota$ $\mathring{\alpha}\pi o\phi\alpha\mathring{\iota}\nu\epsilon\sigma\theta\alpha\iota$ (Luke xix. 11), $\mathring{\epsilon}\lambda\theta\mathring{\alpha}\tau\omega$ (Matt. vi. 10 = Luke xi. 2).

In the proclamation of Jesus of Nazareth to His disciples (which links closely on to that of John the Baptist), the nature of God's sovereignty is negatively and positively defined, and first and foremost negatively —and precisely thereby positively.[2]

Negatively, the Kingdom of God is contrasted with everything present and earthly, everything now and here; and thus it is something entirely miraculous. And yet somehow it is impossible to interpret God's Kingdom as a *summum bonum*, towards which man strives to reach, to which one can come gradually nearer.   From the clue provided at the beginning of

[1 C. H. Dodd in the *Parables of the Kingdom* (Nisbet), pp. 44 ff, maintains that this too means " has drawn nigh "—right up to us, rather than near at hand.]

[2] For what follows cf. R. Bultmann, *Jesus* (1926), pp. 28-54; K. L. Schmidt, *Jesus Christus*, in RGG., iii (2nd edn.), pp. 129-32; K. L. Schmidt, *Das überweltliche Reich Gottes in der Verkündigung Jesu*, Theolog. *Blätter*, vi (1927), pp. 118-20; K. L. Schmidt, *Die Verkündigung des Neuen Testaments in ihrer Einheit und Besonderheit*, Theolog. *Blätter*, x (1931), pp. 113 ff.

the reported proclamation of the gospel in the words
" μετανοεῖτε · ἤγγικεν γὰρ ἡ βασιλεία τῶν οὐρανῶν "
(Matt. iv. 17), may be seen the supreme question which
is inevitably at stake.   The question is not whether and
how we men can possess the Kingdom of God as a
sentiment in our hearts, whether we men as a fellowship
of disposition can " represent " the Kingdom of God.
For the Kingdom of God comes *to* us, and does so
without our help, without our actions.   But then comes
the question whether or not we belong to this Kingdom
of God.   To desire to attract the Kingdom of God to
ourselves is human precocity, self-justifying Pharisaism,
refined—zealotry!   Thus the hardest thing which is
demanded from men is patience, through which alone
the necessary condition for God's action is guaranteed.
The situation is thus as described in the preaching of
St. Paul, for whom soberness and " quenching not the
spirit " coincide (1 Thess. v. 8, 19).   The Parables of
the Kingdom were spoken to hammer home precisely
this point.   He who cannot show patience in being
" open " for God is like the man who sows seed and
then, like an impatient, inquisitive, child, will not
allow the seed—that grows he knows not how—to grow
up in silence (Parable of the self-growing seed, Mark
iv. 26-9).   Nothing less than a miracle is happening
before our eyes when, without our help, even without
our understanding, out of the smallest grain of seed,
the fruitbearing bush has grown.   That modern man
breaks up this miracle has nothing to do with the
tertium comparationis, which is decisive here.   The
Parables of the Mustard Seed (Matt. xiii. 31 f. and
parallels) and of the Leaven (Matt. xiii. 33 = Luke
xiii. 20 f.) are saying exactly the same.   The same
meaning rather more deeply hidden is to be found in
the other Parables of the Kingdom—only in these a
further point about which we shall speak later is also

playing its part—the Tares (Matt. xiii. 24-30), the
Treasure in the Field (Matt. xiii. 44), the Pearl of great
price (Matt. xiii. 45 f.), the Fishnet (Matt. xiii. 47-50),
the Wicked Servant (Matt. xviii. 23-35), the
Labourers in the Vineyard (Matt. xx. 1-16), the
Wedding Feast (Matt. xxii. 2-13), the Ten Virgins
(Matt. xxv. 1-13). The object of all these parables
is to make clear that the ordering of God's Kingdom
is different from ordinary human order, that the
Kingdom of God is unaccountably, overwhelmingly
present among the clues provided by the works of
Jesus Christ.

Positively, this Kingdom of God is a cosmic catastrophe which shows itself in certain events such as
comprise the eschatological drama of the Jewish
Apocalypses. Jesus stands among those of His Jewish
contemporaries who have not sold their souls to the
day-dreams of a political Messiah, but were waiting
for the " Son of Man " coming in the clouds of Heaven
(Dan. vii. 13). We must reckon with the possibility
that in this context many details (above all in the
so-called Synoptic Apocalypse, Mark xiii and parallels)
have crept in from the community intoxicated with
apocalyptic imagery. But in fact Jesus spoke of eating
and drinking in the Kingdom of God (Mark xiv. 25
and parallels). But the decisive point is not that Jesus
here shared the conceptions of His contemporaries, still
less went further than them. The decisive point is
really that in this respect He stopped short of His
contemporaries and did so deliberately. In contrast
to the genuine Jewish and early Christian apocalyptic
He declined to paint pictures of the last things or
to calculate the signs of their coming. The scorn of
the Sadducees, who put before Him a problem arising
from the apocalyptic and resurrection hopes which
they themselves (in contrast to the Pharisees) rejected,

failed to touch Him (Mark xii. 25 f.). Of special clarity is His rejection of all attempts to reckon up the future. In the passage peculiar to St. Luke (Luke xvii. 20 f.) we find that " the Kingdom of God does not come in such a way that one can assess its presence "— Luther translates here the *ou meta paratērēseōs* freely but aptly " not with external gestures "—" and one cannot say ' see here, or there '; for behold the Kingdom of God is in your midst "—Luther translates here the *entos humōn*, wrongly, " inside you ".

The whole point of this much-discussed and sorely vexed passage is to be found in its rejection of the contemplation of the signs of the future. The question whether there is any stress here upon the Kingdom of God being already present (immanent) at the speaking of this text is not the point at issue—for one thing in the aramaic original there is no word for " is " or " will be ". It is also worth remembering that the syriac translation demands a re-translation of the Greek word *entos* into the cognate aramaic which means " in the midst of you ". This agrees with the statement of Jesus about the time of the day of the " Son of Man " (Matt. xxiv. 26 f.; cf. Luke xvii. 23 f.). Those who surrounded Jesus often thought differently about the tokens and essence of the Kingdom of God. Thus the Sons of Zebedee, or their mother, asked after the best positions in God's Kingdom, and Jesus answered that this was a matter for God alone (Mark x. 40 = Matt. xx. 23). The apostolic proclamation of St. Paul, however, agrees entirely with Jesus; cf. Rom. xiv. 17—" The Kingdom of God consists not in eating and drinking, etc."

There is also another point in which Jesus lags behind the thought-development of His Jewish con-temporaries. Although national political hopes for the future do not stand in the forefront of His thoughts, where rather salvation for the whole world is expected from the end of time, yet in many passages the thought of a preferential place for the Jewish people remains important; Israel shall and will stand up anew in her ancient glory: her scattered people will stream together to the new Jerusalem along with the Gentiles. This hope is shared by Jesus. He confers upon his disciples, the " twelve ", as the representatives of the twelve tribes of the people of God, of the Holy People, the office of judges and rulers in the Kingdom of God (Matt. xix. 28 = Luke xx. 29 f.). But, like the Baptist, Jesus also stresses in this very point something negative; the Jew as such has nevertheless no special claims in the eyes of God; for he can and will, on the Judgement Day, be ashamed, even before the heathen. This rôle of Israel is conceived as it was afterwards by St. Paul (Rom. ii: the rejection of Israel; Rom. ix-xi: the salvation of Israel). Such care for the people of Israel is in no sense pointed against Rome. On this point the Jewish *Shemone Esra*, with its patriotic national strain, must be set beside the Lord's Prayer, with its setting of limits to the patriotic and national. Thus in the preaching of the Kingdom of God what is immanent is never proclaimed at the expense of what is transcendent. The Kingdom of God lies beyond ethics. Whoever concentrates wholly upon ethics centres his thought logically upon the single individual. But in the case of Jesus and his apostles it is not the individual as such who receives the promises, but only the congregation, as a member of which the individual receives salvation.

This proclamation of the Kingdom of God would be misunderstood if one were to overlook the contrast already sketched with Judaism. But it would also be misunderstood if this contrast were to be understood from the standpoint of Hellenism. Greek thought, in

which we are so much wrapped up, sees in mankind a
developing character, through which what is corporeal
and sensuous dies out and what is spiritual grows. But
it is also not permissible to replace individualism by
universalism. This ideal of mankind is also alien to
Jesus and his apostles, however well known it was in
late classical philosophy. Whoever regards the N.T.
preaching of God's Kingdom in the light of this
popular philosophical background is transforming that
preaching, and setting in place of human apocalyptic
phantasy and human political daydreams nothing
further than a refined humanism. But where God
breaks into life with His sovereignty, where God speaks
and acts, no spiritualism, no mysticism, no ecstasy can
prepare access to Him. Such refined human possibilities of a link with God, as Hellenism knows them,
are made impossible by the naïver Jewish pictures of
Heaven and Hell. Even more than a sublime philosophy, anthropomorphic conceptions of God and His
Kingdom leave God as the Lord, untarnished in His
transcendent majesty. But here we must remember a
yet further consideration: even expressions like " super-
naturalism ", " transcendence ", " cosmic catastrophe ",
" miracles ", become at once inadequate, when men
hope to feel at home in a superior world by their aid.
The negative point that God's Kingdom is a sheer
miracle must be held fast to, in stark negativity. This
negative, which sees God's Kingdom as the quite other,
the entirely supernatural and anti-secular, is much the
most positive statement that could possibly be made.
The realisation of God's sovereignty is future. And
this future conditions man in the present. To man
who is faced with God and His sovereignty comes the
call to repentance. Where man listens to this call with
faith, i.e. in obedience, then he comes into contact
with God's Kingdom, which comes without his doing

anything to it; there the gospel becomes a message of glad tidings that strikes home.

(*e*) A many-sided terminology shows in what way man can find himself in contact with God's Kingdom. The fundamental point is that he is " receiving " God's gifts. God gives His Kingdom: " it is the Father's good pleasure to give you the *basileia* " (Luke xii. 32). Jesus Christ promises to Peter as he makes his confession " I will give thee the keys of the Kingdom of Heaven " (Matt. xvi. 19). From the obdurate Jews the Kingdom is taken away and given instead to the faithful—" to a nation which creates the fruits of it " (Matt. xxi. 34). Christ bequeaths the Kingdom, as His Father has bequeathed it to Him: διατίθεμαι ὑμῖν καθὼς διέθετό μοι ὁ πατήρ μου βασιλείαν (Luke xxii. 29). God calls Christians into His Kingdom and into His glory (*doxa*) (1 Thess. ii. 12). God has transferred us into the Kingdom of the Son of His love: μετέστησεν εἰς τὴν βασιλείαν τοῦ υἱοῦ τῆς ἀγάπης αὐτοῦ (Col. i. 13). The faithful are made worthy of the Kingdom of God: καταξιωθῆναι ὑμᾶς τῆς βασιλείας τοῦ θεοῦ (2 Thess. i. 5). The Lord will deliver the faithful into His Heavenly Kingdom; . . . ῥύσεταί με ὁ κύριος . . . σώσει εἰς τὴν β. αὐτοῦ τὴν ἐπουράνιον (2 Tim. iv. 18). God has promised His Kingdom: ἐπηγγείλετο (Jas. ii. 5). God does not behave as do the Pharisees, who take it upon themselves to bar the Kingdom from men: οὐαὶ . . . ὅτι κλείετε τὴν β. τῶν οὐρανῶν ἔμπροσθεν τῶν ἀνθρώπων (Matt. xxiii. 13; cf. Luke xi. 52).

To these expressions correspond various correlatives on the side of the believing man. He *receives* God's Kingdom as a child: ὃς ἂν μὴ δέξηται τὴν β. τοῦ θεοῦ ὡς παιδίον (Mark x. 15 = Luke xviii. 17). Joseph of Arimathea is in the situation of one *prosdechomenos tēn basileian tou theou* (Mark xv. 43 = Luke xxiii. 51). *Paralambanein* (Heb. xii. 28), is similar. Especially frequent and, corresponding to the *diathēkē* of God's Kingdom, is the expression *klēronomein* (Matt. xxv. 34; 1 Cor. vi. 9, 10, xv. 50; Gal. v. 21); similarly *echei klēronomian en tēi basileiāi* (Eph. v. 5) and *klēronomous tēs basileiās* (Jas. ii. 5). To be thus chosen by God means *seeing* God's Kingdom. Some will be chosen to see God's Kingdom before their death (Mark ix. 1 and parallels). Only to him that has been born again will this insight be granted (John iii. 3). Another particularly frequent expression is that of *entering into* God's Kingdom: εἰσέρχεσθαι or also εἰσπορεύεσθαι (Matt. v. 20, vii. 21, xviii. 3 and parallels; xix. 23 f. and parallels; xxiii. 13—cf. Luke xi. 52; Mark ix. 47; John iii. 5; Acts xiv. 22); εἴσοδος (2 Peter i. 11). Next we come to the passages in which the phrase *en tēi basileiāi* is used: Matt. v. 19, viii. 11 = Luke xiii. 28 f.; Matt. xi. 11 = Luke vii. 28; Matt. xiii. 43, xviii. 1, 4, xx. 21, xxvi. 29 and parallels; Luke xiv. 15, xxii. 16, 30, xxiii. 42 (other reading *eis*), Eph. v. 5; Rev. i. 9. Before the self-righteous Pharisees, publicans and harlots have access into God's Kingdom: προάγουσιν ὑμᾶς εἰς τὴν β. (Matt. xxi. 31). The Jews should be *huioi tēs basileiās* (Matt. viii. 12), but as a result of their stubbornness they are not (cf. Matt. xiii. 38). The Scribe who is busy about the things of God is *ou makran apo tēs basileias tou theou* (Mark xii. 34). The true scribe, as God would have him, is *mathēteutheis tēi b. tōn ouranōn* (Matt. xiii. 52). Whoever really decides for God is *enthetos* (fit for) *tēi b. tou theou* (Luke ix. 62). When that is so, at the same moment comes the appeal to busy oneself properly over the things of God. We are to be like St. Paul's *sunergoi* (fellow-workers) *eis* [towards] *tēn b. tou theou* (Col. iv. 11). One must take care to notice that the phrase here is not *sunergoi tēs basileiās*. . . . Thus in spite of this expression it is not a case of synergism.

Thus, as faith is obedience towards God's commandments, so now there is demanded of us effort and striving. Through faith we are to fight for God's Kingdom like the chosen people of the Old Covenant: *dia pisteōs katēgōnisanto basileiās* (Heb. xi. 33). In a word, we are to seek after God's sovereignty, to *look* for it; *Zēteite . . . prōton tēn basileian* (Matt. vi. 33 = Luke xii. 31). This *zētein* is something different from *biazesthai* [use violence to] and *harpazein* [snatch] (Matt. xi. 12 = Luke xvi. 15).

To whom then does God's Kingdom belong? To whom will it be given? To whom has it been promised? To those who are poor (in spirit) (Matt. v. 3 = Luke vi. 20), to those who (Matt. v. 10) are persecuted for righteousness' sake! To children! (Matt. xix. 14 and parallels). The last-named passages above all make clear how great, how unspeakable is the decision laid upon us. It is a question of accepting invitations into God's Kingdom in *metanoia*, i.e. for His sake to bid farewell to all the other things of this world, riches and worldly fame, in other words, not to behave as did those invited to the Wedding Feast, who excused themselves with various pretexts (Matt. xxii. 1-14 = Luke xiv. 16-24). Once again there are various parables which stress what has been said with special force. For the sake of God's Kingdom, which is like the treasure hid in the field, or the pearl of great price for which a merchant gave all his fortune (Matt. xiii. 44-6), one must pluck out one's eye of temptation or cut off one's tempting hand (Matt. v. 29 f.). The crassest indication comes in the sentence that one must remember that many have made themselves eunuchs for the sake of God's Kingdom (Matt. xix. 12).[1]

---

[1] This demonstration, in contrast to one or two cases in the early Church (Origen!), should not be understood as a moral injunction but as a shocking, challenging appeal; we are to

In any case the result of a genuine facing of God's kingly power involves the deepest of decisions, the most searching selection of the few from the many (Matt. xxii. 14).[1] A sharp " either-or " demands irrevocable decision: " He who puts his hand to the plough, and looks back, is not fit for the Kingdom of God " (Luke ix. 62). Such a decision is no mere enthusiasm: it will not be made in a moment of intoxication, but is a matter of deliberate, sober consideration. As an architect makes a true estimate before building starts, as a king does not embark upon war without a plan of campaign (Luke xiv. 28-32), so must he who is bidden by God to enter His Kingdom deliberate as to the true acceptance of the summons. He who accepts without making clear to himself the nature of his undertaking, he who hears without due submission, is like the man who builds his house upon sand (Matt. vii. 24-7 = Luke vi. 47-9). Not everyone that says " Lord, Lord " will enter into the Kingdom of Heaven, but only he who does the will of God (Matt. vii. 21). The demand is for sacrifice up to the limit, right up to complete sacrifice of self, to hatred of one's own family (Matt. x. 37 = Luke xiv. 26). Who can really do that? Who ventures so far as to be to that extent submissive to the will of God? Nobody, except for—Jesus Christ Himself!

(*f*) With these words we arrive at the inescapable

reflect that men who have been completely in earnest about God's Kingdom, have now and then taken upon themselves even to go as far as to castrate themselves—which is thereby neither praised nor blamed, at any rate not praised. This interpretation of the difficult saying is surely preferable to the more pedestrian, although not quite impossible explanation, that here and there men have voluntarily refrained from sexual intercourse—as did John the Baptist and Jesus Himself.

[1] Cf. the words about the narrow gate and the broad way (Matt. vii. 13 f. = Luke xiii. 23 f.).

and very special relationship between God's sovereignty and Jesus Christ Himself.   It is not the case that precisely the same language is used of the Kingdom of Christ (cf. supra, pp. 36 f.) as of the Kingdom of God, but rather that certain passages presuppose the equivalence of the Kingdom of God and Christ. Whereas in Mark xi. 10 there is praise for " the coming Kingdom of our father David ", Matt. xxi. 9 and Luke xix. 38 (which are simply parallel to Mark xi. 9) speak simply of the person of Jesus Messiah.   Even clearer is the synoptic comparison of *heneken emou kai heneken tou euangelliou* (Mark x. 29), *heneka tou emou onomatos* (Matt. xix. 29) and *heineken tēs basileiās tou theou* (Luke xviii. 29): the name and message of Jesus Christ, and Jesus Christ Himself, are equated with the Kingdom of God. First and foremost, this equation is arrived at by way of the references to the " Son of Man " as the representative of the " people of God ": whereas Mark ix. 1 (= Luke ix. 27) speaks of the coming of God's Kingdom in power, the parallel passage in Matt. xvi. 28, speaks of the " Son of Man " coming in and with his Kingdom. This " Son of Man " and Lord is awaited by Christians just as is the Kingdom of God itself: cf. e.g. Matt. xxv. 1 with Luke xii. 35 f.   Exactly parallel is Acts viii. 12 (*euangelizomenǭ peri tēs basileias tou theou kai tou onomatos Iēsou Christou*) with Acts xxviii. 31 (*kērussōn tēn basileian tou theou kai didaskōn ta peri tou kuriou Iēsou Christou*.   Similarly there is a parallelism in *hē basileia tou theou hēmōn kai hē exousia tou Christou autou* in Rev. xii. 10.   Thus the language testifies to what is already clear from the general context: Jesus knows that the inrushing sovereignty of God has come into time and the world in His own person—what is expressed in the johannine sentence " *Ho logos sarx egeneto* " (John i. 14). That which is, and remains, future for the Christian, that for which he waits, is in Jesus Christ alone a

sēmeron (Luke iv. 21; cf. Matt. xi. 5 f. = Luke vii. 22)
[—a present reality]. Upon this decisive equation of
the Messiah Jesus made flesh, risen, and present in the
Church, with the future Kingdom of God depends the
christological *kērugma*, which sees the sending of the
Messiah as an *hapax*, or *ephapax*, event, as an unique
unrepeatable event—" once for all time ". Christ
apethanen hapax (Rom. vi. 10—cf. Heb. vi. ff. and
1 Pet. iii. 18). If one looks for an expression to
summarise the equation described, the term *autobasileia*,
coined by Origen (*Matthew Commentary*, xiv. 7—on
Matt. xviii. 23) (Lommatzsch iii. p. 283) suggests itself [1]
—without, to be sure, accepting the special interpretation put forward by Origen.[2] Before Origen,
Marcion, in his notorious " *Panchristismus* ",[3] had
written: *In evangelio est dei regnum Christus ipse*
(Tertullian, *Adv. Marcion* iv. 33) (iii, p. 532, 6 f.). Jesus
Christ alone obeyed the law, alone had faith (cf. Phil.
ii. 5 ff.), whereby He both proclaimed the message
of God's Kingdom and at the same time performed the
miracles as the signs of God's Kingdom (Matt. xi. 2 ff.
= Luke vii. 18 ff.).

From all this it becomes intelligible why the apostolic
and post-apostolic Church of the N.T. did not speak
often explicitly of the *basileia tou theou*, but always
implicitly stressed this *basileia* by pointing to the *kurios
Iesous Christos*.   It is not the case that the emphasis on
the Church has supplanted Jesus of Nazareth's preaching of the Kingdom of God.   Rather is it the case that
in the post-Easter experience of Christ the belief in the
Kingdom of God remained firm.

[1] So P. Feine, *Theologie des N.T.* (1910), p. 100 (5th edn., 1931,
p. 80).
[2] Cf. R. Frick, *Die Geschichte des Reich-Gottes-Gedankens in der alten
Kirche bis zu Origenes und Augustin* (1928), p. 101, note 2.
[3] Cf. A. von Harnack, *Marcion* (1924), pp. 223 ff.

5. *The Basileia and the Church*

However clear and distinct be the N.T. testimony of this *autobasileia* of Jesus Christ, the N.T. none the less understandably stops short of identifying the *basileia tou theou* with the believers in Christ.   Only one single passage can be found to suggest this: Christ *epoiēsen hēmas basileian*[1] (Rev. i. 6).   It is unnecessary to explain, or prove, that Christians can only be spoken of as being the *basileia* in a derivative sense—albeit derived from Christ.

[1] This text, quoted from the O.T., may safely be accepted rather than the other readings *basileion* or *basileis*.

VI. *BASILEIA* (*TOU THEOU*) IN THE EARLY CHURCH [1]

THE connexion between the texts in the Apostolic Fathers about the Kingdom of God with those in the N.T. starts with the fact that the Fathers quote a few N.T. passages—Matt. v. 3, 10 (Luke vi. 20) in Polycarp, ii. 3; Matt. vi. 10 in the *Didache*, viii. 2; 1 Cor. vi. 9 f in Ignatius, Eph. xvi. 1 Phil. iii. 3, *ad Pol.* v. 3.

The usage of " kingdom " and " kingdom of God " is in general as in the N.T. Besides *basileia theou* we often find *basileia tou Christou* 1 Clem. l. 3, etc.). *Basileia* stands alone in 1 Clem. lxi. 1, 2 Clem. v. 5. There are various expressions for man's relations with it, founded upon the N.T. basis—man receives God's gift. Of God, it is said: *edōkas tēn exousian tēs basileiās* (1 Clem. lxi. 1), etc. Man receives (2 Clem. xii. 1), touches (Barnabas, vii. 11), sees, inherits, dwells in it, is glorified in it, enters into it.

In this usage the Apostolic Fathers [2] agree with the N.T. God's kingdom is promised by the Apostles (1 Clem. xlii. 3). Its final coming is fulfilled in the return of Christ (1 Clem. l. 3). The entry of the Christian depends upon the sacrament (Hermas, *Simil.* ix. 16, 2) and upon good works (2 Clem. vi. 9). The ethical imperative is strongly stressed (2 Clem. xi. 7, Barnabas, xxi. 1) but it is always God who brings in His kingdom. Whereas this all agrees with the N.T. in form and content, there is a difference from it in that the coming of God's kingdom is made dependent upon the behaviour of the congregation; thus in 2 Clem. xii. 2 ff., when the Lord is asked when

---

[1] Cf. *basileūs* in the Apostolic Fathers, supra p. 31.
[2] Cf. R. Frick, op. cit. (p. 54, supra) pp. 27-35.

His Kingdom will come, He answers: " when the two shall be one, & the outside as the inside, and the male with the feminine neither male nor female." The apocryphal Egyptian Gospel is similar and typifies the ethicalisation of the conception of God's Kingdom in the direction of an ascetic and dualistic perfectionism. In this, faith and morality are not indeed divorced, but separated; in the list of virtues in the Similitudes of Hermas, ix. 15, 2ff. self-control and other virtues are named after faith.

The Apostolic Fathers are not unanimous in follow-ing the N.T.'s clear distinction berween Kingdom of God and Church. In Barnabas the Kingdom is purely eschatological and therefore not the Church; in viii, 5 the beginning of Christ's royal sovereignty is placed at His crucifixion, and there is an almost chiliastic mention of days of struggle and misfortune even in the Kingdom of Christ. In the *Didache* the Communion Prayers make a clear distinction between the Kingdom of God and the Church, and speak of the *ecclesia* which Christ is collecting up into His Kingdom, but 2 Clem. xiv. 3 says that the Church must be received all at once, exactly as the Kingdom of God. Similarly in Hermas the terms Church and Kingdom of God are very much the same thing.

The Christian Apologists,[1] steeped in the meta-physic of Plato and the ethics of the Stoa, seldom speak of the Kingdom of God. Their eschatology is domin-ated by the quest after the perfection of the individual Christian. The idea that God's *basileia* validates a claim to sovereignty over men is out of their ken. The Christian's task is to strive to be like God; he hopes for the *basileia meta theou* (Justin, Apology I, 11, 1). Athenagoras, Apology, xviii, 1, 2, conceives the *epouranios basileia* as the Creator's power over all

[1] Cf. R. Frick, op. cit. (p. 54, supra) pp. 35-45.

events—but this text stands alone in the Apologists, even in Athenagoras. Justin uses the word *basileia* chiliastically of the millenial Kingdom, not clearly distinguished from the eternal Kingdom. The Kingdom is promised as an eternal reward for the righteous, in contrast to the pains of Hell (Dialogue, cxvii. 3); in cxxxix. 5 *basileian klēronomein* is equivalent to *ta aiōnia kai aphtharta klēronomein*. But besides these unusual expressions *basileia tou theou* is often found in quotations in Justin's Apology and Dialogue. He cites the O.T. and *logia* of Jesus to make clear the relation between promise and fulfilment, and to clarify God's demands upon man. But the link with the proclamation of Jesus and his Apostles is more formal than real: the starting point is not the efficacious grace of God, but the freedom to live virtuously, coupled with the claim to reward. Thus the Apologists make a two-sided impression: on the one side Greek concepts of immortality, of (eternal) life, of attaining insight, bulk larger than the biblical *basileia tou theou*: but the words of Jesus and the Apostles, even though only quoted and not fully developed, also safeguard the Christian teaching from being metamorphosed into philosophy of religion.

This sets the stage for further developments in Church History and Dogma.[1] From the second century alongside the one-sided ethicalising of the *basileia*-concept, there was a one-sided eschatologising which expressed itself in early Christian apocalypses with their gnostic flavour, Acts of Martyrs, and above all burial inscriptions and catacomb pictures. In contrast, Clement of Alexandria sets Greek philosophy in the foreground; his *basileia*-concept is steeped in Platonism and Stoicism—he uses Stoic terms to define it (*Strom.* ii. 4, 19, 3 f.). Belief in gradual progress

[1] Cf. R. Frick, op. cit. (p. 54, supra) pp. 73ff.

(*prokopē*) displaces the biblical last judgement. Similarly, Origen's well-coined term *autobasileia* (p. 54, supra) leaves out at least part of the N.T. message of God's Kingdom. Different from this Oriental-Greek speculation is the Latin West, with its faith in the actual realisation of God's Kingdom upon earth: on this soil the development of the concept of the Kingdom of God culminates in Augustine's identification of it with the Church.

INDEX OF AUTHORS CITED

IV

APOSTLESHIP

BY

KARL HEINRICH RENGSTORF

Translated from the German
first edition, Stuttgart, 1933
with additional notes by
J. R. Coates

TRANSLATOR'S PREFACE

" I BELIEVE one holy catholic and apostolic Church."
The proper commentary on this confession is given
succinctly in the statement that " Behind the Apostles
of Christ is Christ himself, the Apostle of God; as
the Church is one because Christ is one, holy because
of his Holy Spirit, and catholic because he is the Lord
and Saviour of all, so the Church is apostolic precisely
because of Christ's own apostolic office." *

Apostleship belongs to the nature of the Church and
defines its function; and the problems of modern
Church life necessitate its reconsideration.

Reference to the article by Karl Heinrich Rengstorf,
here translated, has recently been made by British
writers on the Christian Ministry,† and no student of
the subject can afford to miss it.

Lightfoot's well-known adduction of the parallel
Jewish term *shali^aḥ* ‡ is here extended and deepened;
and special attention is given to the comparison of
Paul with Jeremiah. The special value of this essay
lies here. True apostleship is shown to involve the
same relation of man to God as is seen in the case of
the Hebrew prophet. " The sense of predestination
in Jeremiah's consciousness means the conviction that
the endowments of his whole nature, his physical and
moral environment, all the influences of heredity and
education that had shaped his life and made it what
it was, had worked together under the hand of God
to prepare him for the task to which he is now
summoned. He is not to be a mere mouthpiece of
the word of Yahwe, but a chosen vessel, fitted in every

* Harold Riley, *We are Witnesses* (1952), p. 7.
† Cf. *Expository Times*, LXII (1951), 271.
‡ See Bibliography, p. ix.

part of his being to be the medium of revelation to his
fellow men. . . . He stands wholly on the side of God
as the medium through whom He has chosen to reveal
His mind to His people. He is of course a self-conscious
medium ; his reason, his conscience, his perceptions of
spiritual and religious truth, are all actively employed
in the discharge of his duty. But there is no internal
schism, no reaction of any part of his being against the
word of the Lord." *

If it had been published before he wrote, K. H.
Rengstorf might well have strengthened his argument
by quoting from that profound and important work
on the subject, *Die Prophetie*, by Abraham Heschel.†
" The prophet must not be regarded, as sometimes
he is, as a mere messenger, fulfilling his task without
sharing its import" (p. 87). "They do not stand
forth as spokesmen of the people. Even when they
plead for justice, mercy and kindness to the poor, they
are not acting as champions of the people's rights.
. . . They always speak as God's delegates, carrying
out his commission. What moves them is not the fate
of their contemporaries, but the business of God"
(p. 174). " The Prophet's secret is sympathy with
the divine *pathos* " (p. 70).

But of course we are here concerned with a further
stage of revelation and a fuller conception of the
divine commission, as I Clem. xlii so well reminds us.
" The Apostles received the Gospel for us from the
Lord Jesus Christ ; Jesus Christ was sent forth from
God. So then Christ is from God, and the Apostles
are from Christ. Both therefore came of the will of
God in the appointed order. Having therefore
received a charge, and having been fully assured
through the resurrection of our Lord Jesus Christ

---

* J. Skinner, *Prophecy and Religion*, pp. 28, 217.
† Cracow, 1936 (Erich Reiss Verlag, Berlin).

and confirmed in the word of God with full assurance of the Holy Ghost, they went forth with the glad tidings that the kingdom of God should come."

Professor Rengstorf's examination of the elements involved in the New Testament sense of mission does more than satisfy the desire for accurate knowledge; it makes a very valuable contribution towards the reconciliation of what sometimes seem to be hopelessly divergent views on the subject of Apostolic Succession; and it expresses convictions which cannot fail to convey inspiration to readers who are seriously concerned to recover the power of the first envoys of the Lord Jesus Christ.

J. R. COATES.

CONTENTS

BIBLIOGRAPHY

P. BATIFFOL : Revue Biblique Nouvelle Série 3, 520 ff., 1906.

E. DE WITT BURTON : Galatians, 363 ff., 1921.

C. CLEMEN : Z.M.R. (see p. xi) 44, 225 ff., 1929.

K. DEISSNER : Zeitschr. Syst. Theol. 7, 772 ff., 1929-30.

F. HAASE : N.T. Abhandlungen IX, 1-3, 1922.

A. VON HARNACK : The Mission & Expansion of Christianity, Vol. I, 1904 (4th German ed. 1923).

G. HEINE : Synonymik d. N.T. Griechisch, 1898.

K. HOLL : Gesammelte Aufsätze z. Kirchengeschichte II, Der Osten, 44 ff., 249 ff., 1928.

F. KATTENBUSCH : in Festgabe z. Karl Müller, 322 ff., 1922.

S. KRAUSS : J. Q. R. (see p. xi) XVII, 370 ff., 1905 ; E. J. (see p. xi) III, 1929.

H. LIETZMANN : Kommentar z. Römerbrief, 3rd ed., 1928, on Rom. i, 1.

J. B. LIGHTFOOT : Galatians, 92 ff., 1890.

E. MEYER : Ursprung etc., I, 264 ff., III, 255 ff.

W. MUNDLE : Z.N.W. (see p. xi) 27, 36 ff., 1928.

E. NORDEN : Beitr. z. Gesch. d. gr. Phil., Jahrbuch f. Phil. Suppl. 19, 365 ff., 1893.

R. SCHÜTZ : Apostel u. Jünger, 1921.

W. SEUFERT : Ursprung u. Bedeutung d. Apostolates etc., 1887.

H. VOGELSTEIN : M.G.W.J. (see p. xi) 49, 427 ff., 1905 ; Hebrew Union College Annual 2, 99 ff., 1925.

J. WAGENMANN : Die Stellung d. Apostels Paul. neben den XII, etc., 1926.

J. WELLHAUSEN : Einl. in die 3 ersten Evangelien, 138 ff., 1911.

G. P. WETTER : F.R.L. (see p. xi) 26, 1916 : Der Sohn Gottes.

[C. H. DODD : The Apostolic Preaching, 1936.

R. N. FLEW : Jesus and His Church, 2nd ed., 1943.

A. HESCHEL : Die Prophetie, 1936 (Cracow ; Erich Reiss, Berlin).

W. F. HOWARD : Christianity acc. to St. John, 1943.

DANIEL JENKINS : The Gift of Ministry, 1947.

K. E. KIRK : The Apostolic Ministry, ed., 1946.

HAROLD KNIGHT : The Hebrew Prophetic Consciousness, 1947.

K. LAKE : The Beginnings of Christianity, V, 37-59, 1933.

G. W. H. LAMPE : Some Aspects of the N.T. Ministry, 1949 (S.P.C.K.).

T. W. MANSON : The Church's Ministry, 1948.

J. MUNCK : Studia Theol., III Fasc. i, 96-110, 1950 (Lund).

B. H. STREETER : The Primitive Church, 1929.

VINCENT TAYLOR : Expository Times LXII, 269-274, 1951.]

See also works listed under Abbreviations (p. xi).

Square brackets, here and elsewhere, indicate additions by the translator.

ABBREVIATIONS

B.G.U.	Agypt. Urkunden aus d. Kgl. Museen zu Berlin.
Bill.	Strack u. Billerbeck, Komm. z. N.T. aus Talmud und Midrasch, 1922 ff.
B.W.A.N.T.	Beitr. z. Wiss. v. A.u. N.T., 1908 ff.
C.I.L.	Corpus Inscript. Latinarum.
E.J.	Encyclopaedia Judaica, 1928 ff.
F.R.L.	Forsch. z. Rel. u. Lit. d. A.T. u. N.T., 1903 ff.
J.E.	Jewish Encyclopedia, 1901 ff.
J.Q.R.	Jewish Quarterly Review, 1905 ff.
M.G.W.J.	Monatsschrift f. Gesch. u. Wiss. d. Judentums, 1869 ff.
Moult.-Mill.	Moulton and Milligan, Vocab. of Gk. Test, 1915 ff.
N.G.G.	Nachr. v. d. Kgl. Gesellsch. d. Wiss. zu Göttingen, 1894 ff.
Pauly-W.	Pauly u. Wissowa, Realencycl. d. klass. Alt., 1892 ff.
Pr.-Bauer	Preuschen u. Bauer, Wörterb. z. N.T., etc.,[2] 1928.
P.S.B.A.	Proceedings of the Soc. of Bibl. Archaeol., 1878 ff.
R.E.J.	Revue des Études Juives, 1880 ff.
Z.M.R.	Zeitschr. f. Missionskunde u. Religionswiss., 1886 ff.
Z.N.W.	Zeitschr. f. d. N.T. Wiss., etc., 1900 ff.
Z.S.Th.	Zeitschr. f. syst. Theol.

The Index explains certain other abbreviations.

INTRODUCTION

KARL HEINRICH RENGSTORF's article on ἀπόστολος, of which the following pages are a translation, is preceded by a critical survey of the use of the ordinary Greek verbs for " sending " (ἀποστέλλειν, ἐξαποστέλλειν, πέμπειν and compounds) in classical and Hellenistic texts, LXX and New Testament. The main point which emerges from this is that, whereas the other verbs connote a sending as such, ἀποστέλλειν carries with it the ideas of special purpose, mission or commission, authorisation and responsibility. Examples from Epictetus (A.D. 50-130) show that it was a technical term for the divine sending of a teacher of philosophy (Epict. Diss. I, xxiv, 6). Other matters of importance for Bible study are that in LXX this verb, representing the Hebrew shalaḥ, generally emphasises the sender rather than the one who is sent; that Luke, like Josephus, often uses πέμπειν in the sense of commissioning (e.g. Luke vii, 6); and that John regularly uses πέμπειν to indicate God's sharing in the work of Jesus, and ἀποστέλλειν to assert Jesus' divine commission.

Useful material will be found in E. Norden, Jahrb. f. Phil. Suppl. 19, 377 ff., 1893; K. Holl, N. Jahrb. Klass. Alt. 29, 418 f., 1912; K. Deissner, Z.S.Th. 7, 783, 1929-1930.

I. GREEK USAGE

1. GENERAL

THE word ἀπόστολος rarely has in classical Greek anything like the meaning which it has in the N.T. In the older period it belongs to the vocabulary of seafaring, particularly on warlike occasions, indeed it is a technical term of political speech. Originally it was an adjective qualifying the word πλοῖον (Plat. Ep. VII, 346a), indicating a freight or transport ship, but later it was used for the same purpose without the noun (Pseud.-Herod., Vita Hom. 19). The close connexion with the verb ἀποστέλλειν is seen in the frequent use of the term for the sending out of a fleet or an army, originally always to make war, being simply a stronger form of the word στόλος (Lys., Or. xix, 21 ; Demosth. Or. xviii, 107) [1] ; then it comes to denote the fleet itself, and ultimately a naval expedition (Demosth. Or. xviii, 80, cf. iii, 5). [2] Subsequently the term can mean any group of men sent out for a special purpose, e.g. a band of colonists (Dion. Hal. Ant. Rom. ix, 59) ; [3] or it may mean the leader of an expedition, e.g. an admiral (Hesychius, s.v. Anecdota Graeca, ed. Bekker 217, 26). [4]

The passive character of all these meanings is quite clear. None of them include the idea of initiative on the part of the ἀπόστολος, or of authorisation. The only connotation of the word is that of being sent;

[1] Cf. Suidas: αἱ τῶν νεῶν ἐκπομπαί.
[2] At Demosth. Or. iii, 5, it can mean either the ships or the expedition.
[3] Almost a synonym for ἀποικία. Cf. Aeschin. Fals. Leg. 175.
[4] Pr.-Bauer, 156.

I

indeed one might go so far as to say that it is just a
technical term. This Passive characteristic shows
the adjectival origin of the word as controlling the
meaning long after it came to be used as a noun. Apart
from its impersonal root-meaning, it never came to be
a common expression among the Greeks for any kind
of messenger ; they had plenty of other words for that
(ἄγγελος, κῆρυξ, πρεσβευτής, etc.). The later Christian
use of the word therefore meant something quite new
for Greek ears and for all who were familiar with
the Greek language. Evidence for that may be found
in the fact that the Romans did not translate the word
but gave it a Latin form.[1] Even at the only two places
on Ionic soil where ἀπόστολος occurs or appears to
occur (Herod. I, 21 ; V, 38), it is perfectly clear that
the dominant idea is that of being sent ; the thought
of authorisation is completely in the background.[2]
We cannot therefore see in these passages any parallel
to the N.T. usage. Important witnesses against any
such thesis are LXX, Josephus and Philo, since they
provide no parallel usage in this case (see pp. 11 f.). The
only examples of any such parallel come from a much
later period and are derived from the Christian usage.[3]

The Papyri [4] show how far ordinary usage at the be-
ginning of the Christian era differed from that of the
N.T. ; they mean by ἀπόστολος a bill or invoice (Pap.
Oxy. IX, 1197, 13, etc.) [5] or even a passport (B.G.U.
V, 64 ; cf. VI, 1303, 26). These are obviously
developments from the classical usage ; there is

[1] See p. 13.
[2] Herod. uses the word as predicate of " herald " (See K. W.
Krüger, *ad loc.*).
[3] Preisigke, Wört., I, 195, gives only one example (8th cent.
Pap. Lond. IV).
[4] Cf. Preisigke, *loc. cit.* and Fachwörter 30.
[5] Ἐξ ἀποστόλου means " as per bill of lading " [Moult.-Mill.
s.v.].

nothing personal in them; the word has become thoroughly mechanised. It is not uninteresting to observe that in this late stage of its use it is still at home in the seafaring milieu in which it began.

2. HELLENISTIC MISSIONARIES

(a) There is very little in the Greek world corresponding to the Christian apostolate. There is nothing at all in the older period. Greek prophets are proclaimers of (an aspect of) truth and as such, in so far as they are connected with a shrine, speak for the divinity which they serve.[1] This is true of the Pythian priestess, who is simply a medium between the god and the believing enquirer;[2] that she has no independent personal significance whatsoever is shown by the fact that she is without name or date. The whole problem of authorisation remains completely in the background. That is obvious from the part which she plays and also from the fact that the communication is mediated through one of the messenger gods characteristic of the Hellenism of the Christian era (Schniewind, p. 237). The words ἄγγελος and κῆρυξ, which appear regularly in this connexion along with πρέσβυς, πρεσβευτής (cf. I. Tim. ii, 7; II Tim. i, 11), do not express the idea of a commission that can only be personally discharged, but that of a message which itself effects the desired contact, its bearer having no personal significance. The ultimate ground for this fact is to be found in the close connexion which Greek religiosity sees between inspiration and the office of divine messenger, so far as it is concerned at all with human intermediaries.[3] The same thing explains

[1] See E. Fascher, Προφήτης (1927) passim.
[2] Ib. 14, 68 ; J. Schniewind, Euangelion II (1931) 218 ff.
[3] For the Pythian see Dion Chrys. Or. lxxii, 12.

why the Hellenistic missionary does not develop a missionary consciousness or sense of personal authority; on the contrary, it follows of necessity that he must surrender his own consciousness and individual personality to the divinity.

(b) An obvious exception to what has just been said is presented by the teachers of the Cynico-Stoic philosophy in so far as the descriptions of the true Cynic drawn by Epictetus [1] are more than a merely ideal picture and give us historical fact. In this case we have an explicit assertion of the consciousness of being sent. The Cynic knows that he is "sent by Zeus", and Epictetus can even say that it is such knowledge which makes the true Cynic (Diss. III, 22, 23).[2] Even here ἄγγελος and κῆρυξ are the words in which the sending is described in relation to the content of the message (III, 22, 69); but apart from the fact that ἀποστέλλειν plays an important part as a technical term for the divine commission and authorisation,[3] there appears as a third function that of κατάσκοπος τῶν Θεῶν (heavenly inspector).[4] As such he has to investigate (κατασκέπτεσθαι) quite accurately (III, 2, 25), as a proper κατάσκοπος (I, 24, 3), what man's true situation is, and then proclaim the truth (III, 22, 25), like another Diogenes, who was the first "inspector" and the great example of a true Cynic (I, 24, 6; III, 22, 24).[5] Thus the Cynic observes men and seeks those points in their life at which he can offer his help as "doctor of souls, moral support, and

[1] Diss. III, 22.   Cf. P. Wendland, Hell.-Röm. Kult. 75 ff.
[2] See p. xii.   [3] See p. xii.
[4] Epictetus Diss. III, xxii, 69; I, xxiv, 3 ff.   Cf. Deissner, 783 and Norden, 377 f. (see p. ix).
[5] Antisthenes adopts the title, associating himself with popular ideas concerning mediators between gods and men (Norden, 373 ff., esp. 381).

saviour ".[1]   He thus becomes an overseer (ἐπισκοπῶν),[2]
so that Epictetus can call the true Cynic the examiner
of all human behaviour (III, 22, 77).[3]   He brings
help as the herald of the gods;[4] and thus proves
himself to be a true ἐπισκοπῶν, this term only having
meaning, if he really is a κατάσκοπος.

The situation therefore is that the Cynic is the
messenger of Zeus who sends him and stands behind
him.[5] To this quite passive feature, however, is
added, in the use of the term κατάσκοπος, the idea of
the messenger's initiative, resting upon the divine
commission and conveying the appropriate announce-
ment (" kerygma "), in which the Cynic to a certain
extent plays the part of the divine teacher.   It is
impossible to speak here, as in the case of the Greek
prophet, of a predominantly passive attitude.   That is
clear from the Cynic's relation both to his sender and
to the man to whom he is sent.   There can be no doubt
whatever that he regards himself as a being apart from
ordinary men, whom he sees before him as *massa
perditionis*, above whom he knows himself to be raised
by his commission and the freedom from worldly
ambition which that gives him; not in vain does he
call himself king and lord (βασιλεὺς καὶ δεσπότης Epict.
Diss. III, 22, 49).   He is under the control of a clear
consciousness of being different from ordinary men.
What distinguishes him therefore is not a feeling of
isolation, which might have been expected, but just

[1] K. Holl. Ges. Aufsätze II, 261 ; Pauly.-W. XII, 14.

[2] Norden 378.   κατάσκοπος and ἐπισκοπῶν are not identical ;
the former is a function of the latter.   Diog. Laert. VI, 102
is too late.

[3] Cf. III, xxii, 72, 97.

[4] Epict. Diss. III, xiii, 12 ; xxi, 13 ; xxii, 69 ; IV, v, 24 (Deissner
783).   For analogous non-Stoic usage see Pr.-Bauer, 674 f.

[5] Diogenes seems to have connected his name with his mission
(Norden, 380).

a strong sense of duty to the message (kerygma), and still more a strong sense of responsibility for men.[1] It might almost be considered an accident that the term debtor (ὀφειλέτης), as used by Paul at Rom. i, 14, is not used by Epictetus; the idea is certainly implied.[2] But this sense of responsibility for man is coupled with an equally strong sense of responsibility towards Zeus. The Cynic's perfect freedom in relation to all men is equalled by his devotion to Zeus (III, 22, 56, cf. 59); he is the servant [3] and minister of the gods (III, 22, 69, 82, 95). It is this combination which gives the Cynic his frankness (III, 22, 96), his right to be concerned with other people's affairs as if they were his own (III, 22, 97 ff.; cf. Horace Sat. II, 3, 19), and the assurance that he need not even fear the emperor if his duty concerns him (III, 22, 56). The word which combines the two ideas of commission and responsibility is κατάσκοπος. This both demands and defines the initiative of the Cynic. It is the only term which offers a real parallel to the N.T. ἀπόστολος. Both words are generally associated with the same terminology,[4] even though the identity is actually limited to form. In any case we may say that the Cynico-Stoic philosopher in his role as κατάσκοπος is the contemporary figure which stands nearest to that of the N.T. apostle.

The Cynic's missionary consciousness has its prototype in the figure of Socrates as presented by Plato in the Apology. He refers all his life-work back to the

[1] Deissner, 786 f. For the important 'medical metaphor see Epict. Diss. III, xxiii, 30 ff.; Diog. Laert. VI, 6; Wendland, Hell.-Röm. Kult. 82; Harnack (see p. ix), 129 ff. [and cf. Isaiah, Buddha, Jesus; see J. R. Coates, " The Saving History ", pp. 40-42].

[2] Deissner, 786.

[3] Cf. Diss. IV, iii, 9, etc. (Deissner, 784).

[4] See διάκονος, etc., in Kittel's Wörterbuch.

god of Delphi (Plato Ap. 23c), who has planned out his life and therefore claims his obedience (Ap. 29d). That is why his enemies and judges incur so heavy a responsibility when they try to get rid of him (Ap. 30e, 31a). The terminology here anticipates that of the Stoics, though ἀποστέλλειν is missing. Perhaps a certain difference between Socrates and the Stoics may be found in the fact that he thinks more of the end in view than of the origination of his activity, whereas Epictetus, e.g., makes a point of claiming the authority of God who sent him (Diss. III, 22, 56).[1]

The same may be said concerning the outward side of his activity; like the apostle he travels through the world seeking hearers for his doctrine, and like him is more or less dependent on the goodwill of those who welcome his teaching. Paul's appearance in Athens (Acts xvii, 16 ff.) exactly resembles that of Cynic and Epicurean philosophers and other contemporary missionaries who work among the people.[2] After his departure from Thessalonica his enemies apparently used this outward resemblance in order to cast on him the suspicion that he was actually one of these travelling preachers of the type that sought followers for the sake of honour and money rather than the propagation of truth.[3] The apostles therefore are no novelty on Greek soil; they are simply the representatives of a particular religion among the numerous missionaries of other forms of worship and belief in this classical age of religious propaganda.[4] The latter can therefore be disregarded as offering a parallel since, in spite of

[1] Plato refs. from H. Kleinknecht. Cf. P. Friedländer, Platon II (1930), 165 f. ; E. Wolff, Plato's Apol. (Neue philol. Unters.VI, 1929, 25 ff., 39 ff.).

[2] Wendland, op. cit. 92 ff.

[3] This may explain his so-called apology at I Thess. ii,1-13.

[4] See E. von Dobschütz, Thess. 2 ff. ; M. Gressmann, Heidn. Miss. i. d. Werdezeit d. Christentums (Z.M.R. 39, 1924, 14 ff.).

the use of the word ἀποστέλλεσθαι in connexion with
their authorisation,[1] they never produced a special
formulation of their missionary consciousness and the
claim which was bound up with it. This only happened
among the Cynics in the case of the κατάσκοπος. This
word describes very well the nature of the consciousness to which we have just referred. In so far as in it
the Cynic himself appears as the active subject, not
God as in the case of ἄγγελος,[2] it is clear that we are
dealing with self-consciousness and not with God-
consciousness. Outwardly this is shown in his arrogant
style of address, which frequently aroused opposition,[3]
and inwardly in the necessity which he felt of a religious
assurance of his authority as missionary. That can be
seen in the assumption of the formula " divine man "
(θεῖος ἄνθρωπος) as self-designation (see p. 5), specially
on the Stoic side,[4] though it also appears in the old
Cynic tradition, now carrying with it the mystic
feeling which it conveys in the language of the Mystery
religions.[5] It certainly cannot be separated from the
missionary consciousness of the philosophers (cf.
Plato Apol.), but the mere fact that it is used shows that
this consciousness lacks an ultimate metaphysical
ground, since it introduces an irrational element into
the otherwise rational philosophical piety, an element
which involves a certain approximation, though
within rational limits, to the " enthusiasm " of the
Greek prophets. Again, since this element is clearly
derived from pantheism, which always leads ultimately
to the absorption of the divine in the ego, it is not
along this line that the Cynico-Stoic philosophers are

[1] See p. 4.
[2] This is justified by the way in which Epict. speaks of " the
god ".   [3] Pauly-W. XII, 14 f.
[4] Dion Chrys. is typical. Cf. K. Holl, op. cit. 262.
[5] K. Holl, 262.

led out of self-consciousness into the missionary consciousness, which shows its theonomous character in the blending of an unlimited claim in the name of the god with an avoidance of over-emphasis of the importance of the highly favoured man. The tension between the missionary consciousness and the individuality of the missionary, which thus necessarily develops, could not be overcome by the Cynico-Stoic diatribe, just because that always remains ultimately a human programme, even when the missionary makes religious claims. The fact that these missionaries were called κατάσκοποι itself shows that they were conscious of this, for it implies that at the decisive point where the messenger of the gods becomes the herald everything depends on human initiative and judgement; the one who is sent (ἀπεσταλμένος) certainly belongs to the godhead as minister (ὑπηρέτης), but never figures as a slave in absolute dependence upon it;[1] on the contrary, he takes his stand as king and lord (see p. 5) and almost claims kinship with the gods.[2] The relation of the envoy to the godhead thus never has the character of an unconditional appointment which is laid upon him; it is more like an agreement between two partners.[3] That, again, is only possible because in these circles a clear thought of God and the consequent conviction of a final revelation of God's will is lacking, and that again provides the reason why the philosophical religiosity of the period never reached, in all its missionary self-consciousness, the clear statement of an absolute

[1] Cynic or Stoic could never be " God's slave ". See Deissner, 787.

[2] He is to a certain degree, like Zeus, father of all men (Epict. Diss. III, xxii, 81).

[3] When the Cynic is put to shame, he himself is to blame, never the one whom he is supposed to represent (Epict. Diss. III, xxii, 53 ff. ; cf. ibid. 22).

claim, which distinguishes all true religion and its
messengers.[1]

Finally, it may be added briefly that it is only natural
that in the Greek world legal elements play no real
part in the relation of the gods with men through a
human medium. That is perfectly obvious in the
case of the Cynics (see p. 9, note 3) : but it is so
elsewhere also. This follows inevitably from the
lack of the defining factor provided by a clear
idea of God and a historical revelation. Mythical
views of God and mystical union with God can find
no room for such concrete categories, or for that which
makes the substance of preaching or propaganda.
There is no need, therefore, to carry the matter any
further here.

[1] This again shows how appropriate it was for the Cynic to
call himself κατάσκοπος. It may be noted that this word and
ἀπόστολος are analogous formations from their respective verbs.

II. JEWISH USAGE

1. Among Greek-speaking Jews the word ἀπόστολος seems to have had little currency. The reason for that may have been that the Jews had very little to do with seafaring (see p. 1). Those who lived in Palestine had no need of naval expeditions, and those living in Egypt seem to have had very little to do with ships. Philo makes no use of the word.

In Josephus the word occurs twice, in one case not well attested. At Ant. 17, 300 it means a despatch of envoys,[1] thus taking its place between the original connotation (see p. 1) and that of the N.T., showing no kinship with Papyrus usages (see p. 2). One might connect the use of the word with the context in this particular case, for it should not be overlooked that the envoys were being sent to Rome and would have to cross the sea. Two points may be noted here, viz. the influence of ἀποστέλλειν on the word, so that it refers to the sending of men, and the traditional collective connotation. We cannot know how far Josephus is here making a quotation. The second passage (Ant. 1, 146) uses ἀπόστολος as synonymous with ἀποστολή,[2] unless the reading is corrupt;[3] it can have no bearing on the usage of Josephus.

The only occurrence of the word in LXX[4] is at I Kings xiv, 6, where it is attested by Codex Alexandrinus but not by Codex Vaticanus:[5] ἐγώ ἐιμι ἀπόστολος. These are the words of the prophet Ahijah to Jeroboam's wife, who comes to ask him about the issue of her son's

---

[1] It almost means " embassy ".

[2] There is evidence for this reading here.

[3] Probably ἀποδασμός should be read.

[4] See Hatch and Redpath, Concordance to LXX.

[5] This points to a later date.

sickness (Heb. *'anokhi shalu^aḥ*). The following points may be noted. First, ἀπόστολος is the equivalent of *shalu^aḥ*, which is obviously treated as a noun, though actually it is a passive participle,[1] which makes the Greek translation possible. But in this case ἀπόστολος acquires an individual character. This makes no difference to the fact that the Greek noun echoes the Hebrew verb. What is more important is that ἀπόστολος is here the messenger of God in the technical sense, so far as the word expresses the idea that Ahijah is commissioned with a word of God to the king's wife.[2] Here we see the influence of *shalu^aḥ*, which describes the authorisation of the prophet by God (see p. xii). The theological meaning of the verb has here taken the place of the secular, and this gives the noun its connotation. Further, it should be specially observed that the word is used of a prophet in a concrete situation, and here again the adjective σκληρός shows that the word has not yet reached a fixed connotation, but corresponds to the participle which would be the literal translation of the Hebrew. With this in mind, it can be said that this passage takes us a long way further than the two examples from Herodotus (see p. 2). It may be added that Aquila reads ἀπόστολος[3] at I Kings xiv, 6. Finally, Symmachus provides further evidence at Is. xviii, 2 where he has ἀποστόλους for the Hebrew *çirim*; this is the only place where ἀπόστολος is the equivalent of *çir*.[4]

2. Rabbinic Judaism carries us much further than what we have considered above. Here the term *shali^aḥ*[5] has its recognised place as a noun, and its

[1] Cf. Gesenius-Kautzsch, Hebr. Gramm. 27th ed. (1902), 393.
[2] She comes to the prophet, not the prophet to her.
[3] Wellhausen suggests that here Aq. is the source of LXX.
[4] Cf. Lightfoot, " Galatians ", p. 93.
[5] This is the usual form; for suffixes and plural *shalu^aḥ* is used (Bill. III, 2); the Aramaic is *sh^eliḥa'*.

usage provides the nearest parallel to that of the N.T. ἀπόστολος. Early Christian writers were impressed by the relationship. Jerome [1] speaks of Slias as the title borne by those Jews who may be compared with the apostles, and that is nothing else but the Latin form of sh⁻eliḥa'.[2] This correspondence in terminology is confirmed by the fact that in the Syrian church an apostle is called sh⁻eliḥa', while on the other hand, a Jewish inscription at Venosa, of the fifth or sixth century A.D.,[3] uses the word " apostuli ". The connexion between the two is thus confirmed from a non-Christian source; otherwise the use of the Latinised " apostulus " would be impossible.[4] The Greek word is not adopted by the Rabbis,[5] and this shows how firmly rooted the Semitic term must have been. Another reason may have been that from the middle of the first century the word had become part of the Christian vocabulary.

(a) *Legal.* The institution of the sh⁻eluḥim is ancient, probably going back before the post-exilic time (II. Chron. xvii, 7-9).[6] It is common to the sh⁻eluḥim

[1] On Gal. i, 1.

[2] Cf. messias from m⁻eshiḥa'. See S. Krauss, J.Q.R. XVII (1905), 370, n. 4.

[3] C.I.L., IX, 648 ; cf. R.E.J, VI (1882), 205 f.

[4] S. Krauss (*loc. cit.*), in his discussion with Harnack, was the first, after Lightfoot, etc., to treat fully the parallel between ἀπόστολος and shali⁻eḥ. But neither he nor H. Vogelstein (see p. ix) went beyond the comparison of formal details. It was P. Billerbeck (Bill. III, 2 ff.) who went deeper and made theological comparison possible, at the same time disposing of K. Holl's scepticism (Ges. Aufs. II, 51, n. 1).

[5] M. Jastrow (Dict. Targ. etc. I, 1903, 101) urges that 'phṣṭmoṣ burning the Law (Taanith 4, 6) means *apostolos*, and refers to II Macc. vi. But other explanations are more probable ; cf. S. Krauss, P.S.B.A. XXV (1903), 222 ff. ; J.E. II, 21 f.

[6] Krauss, J.Q.R. 382, says post-exilic ; Vogelstein, Heb. Un. Coll. Ann. II (1925), 100, says 419 B.C. (Elephantine Pap.).

of all periods that they have definite commissions to
discharge at a distance from those who employ them.
The designation emphasises neither the fact of their
being sent nor the nature of their task; it simply
establishes their authorisation. That is the decisive
point; the commission as such has no bearing on the
precise quality implied in *shali^aḥ*. It makes no difference whatsoever whether the business is that of proclaiming religious truths (II Chron. xvii, 7 ff.) or that
of transacting a financial matter (T. Qidd. 4, 2). The
shali^aḥ properly belongs not to the religious, but to the
legal sphere, and when the word has a religious meaning
that is not because he is a *shali^aḥ* but because, as such,
he is entrusted with a religious commission. This
usage is simply a theologically coloured application of
the meaning of *shalaḥ* (p. xii). The Rabbis found the
institution already present in the Law (Bab. Ned. 72*b*;
see below, p. 15).

Thus the legal element is involved in *shali^aḥ*.
Nobody can " send " one who is not at his disposal.
Therefore the commission of necessity involves responsibility; the one who is commissioned is always the
representative of the person who commissions him,
and as such exercises his right. The Rabbis summed
the situation up in the frequently quoted words " the
one whom a man sends is the equivalent of himself "
(Ber. 5, 5),[1] i.e. the sent is as good as the sender so far
as the commission is concerned. An example of this
is the case where a *shali^aḥ* performs the ceremony of
becoming betrothed to a woman (Qidd. 2, 1 ; T. Qidd.
4, 2; T. Yeb. 4, 4) on behalf of another, and his
performance is counted valid.[2] The same applies in
the case of divorce (Git. 4, 1), effecting a sale (T. Yeb,
4, 4), and the slaughter of the Passover lamb by a
slave (Pes. 8, 2, etc.).

[1] See Bill. III, 2.   [2] See Bab. Qidd. 41*a-b*.

Everything here depends on the conscientiousness of the one who is sent. There was nothing to hinder the sabotage of the commission through misuse of the delegated authority (Qidd. 3, 1). That means, however, that the system would only work properly when the will of the representative was entirely subservient to that of the one whom he represented. This Rabbinical institution is in fact not concerned with the mechanical fulfilment of a command, but with conscious agreement with the plan and commission of another person.[1] The recognition of this is not excluded by the fact that the situation is a legal one. It means no profaning of the institution, but on the contrary, its confirmation and cleansing by religion. It is well known that law and religion form an indivisible unity in Judaism. That can be seen, e.g., in the statement that God is well pleased with a *shaliᵃḥ* who lays down his life for the sake of his commission;[2] but it also becomes very clear in the wider use of this word.

All this has its foundation in the Semitic law of embassy, which is also pre-supposed in the O.T., where the ambassador fully represents the one who sends him, usually the king, and that is the original purpose of sending one who has authority. Honour due to his lord is given to him. This happens in the case of Abigail in her treatment of David's knights who come to take her to be his wife; by washing their feet she shows that she is ready, as his wife, to perform the same service to him (I Sam. xxv, 40 f.). On the other hand, shameful treatment of an ambassador affects his lord more than himself and therefore must have consequences. Thus the shaming of David's ambassadors by the Ammonites was the occasion of war to the

---

[1] This rather cumbrous definition is indispensable.
[2] Numb. Rabb. 16, 1 on xiii, 2 (H. Bornhäuser's ref.).

death (II Sam. x, 1 ff.). In all such cases we have
practical confirmation of the theory of the *shali^aḥ*, as
later formulated by the Rabbis (see p. 14); e.g. Bab.
B.Q. 113*b*, " a king's ambassador is as the king himself " (Bill. I, 590); Sifre Numb. 103 on xii, 9, " with
what is the matter to be compared? With a king of
flesh and blood who has a consul in the country.
The inhabitants spoke before him. Then said the
king to them, you have not spoken concerning my
servant but concerning me."

(*b*) *Ecclesiastical.* Hitherto this institution has been
treated as a relation between two men, as a transaction
under civil law. But that is not the end of the matter.
It is obviously possible for the *shali^aḥ* to represent
in the same way a number of people. In this case
the blending of law and religion in the person of the
envoy becomes much clearer than before, for he can
represent not only a particular circle of men but
also the community as such or a number of local
communities, when so authorised. In such cases the
institution affords a religious interpretation of previously existing offices.

No special importance attaches to the fact that a
court of law entrusts an individual with the conveyance
or even execution of its decisions. On the other hand,
it is important that this delegate is called *shali^aḥ*
(Git. 3, 6; cf. B.Q. 9, 5 and Yoma 1, 5).[1] Another
example is found in the case of the Rabbis authorised
by the great Sanhedrin to go to the Dispersion in
order to carry through in other places the intercalation
of days into the calendar which was appointed by the
Sanhedrin in Palestine (Yeb. 16, 7—Aqiba; T. Meg.

---

[1] *Sh^eli^aḥ beth din* thus comes to mean " agent of the lawcourt "
(Makkoth 2, 2 [i.e. for scourging]). In many cases it was necessary
for such agents to be themselves learned in the Law (e.g. Menaḥoth,
10, 3).

2, 5—Meir);[1] similarly the beginning of the new
month was made known to the Jews in Syria through
sh⁶luḥim (R.H. 1, 3, 4; 2, 2), and the news passed on
by means of fire signals to Babylon (R.H. 2, 4).
He who reads the prayers in the synagogue is the
authorised person in the local congregation (sh⁶liᵃḥ
çibbur); if he makes a mistake, that is a bad sign for
those whom he represents before God (Ber. 5, 5).[2]
The high priest is the authorised representative of the
priesthood, which is entrusted by the great Sanhedrin
with oversight over him and the correct performance
of the prescribed rites, and on the great Day of Atonement he represents the whole community (Yoma 1, 5).
This explains the care with which the Pharisees and
their following among the priests held fast to the ritual
in its traditional Pharisaic form (Yoma 1, 1 ff.; cf.
Bab. Yoma 19b).

The principal representatives of the scholars,
however, and (in their name) of Israel as a whole,
were those Rabbis who were sent out by the central
authority into the whole Dispersion; it was they who
bore the title of sh⁶luḥim as an official designation in
the proper sense (see p. 13). Their tasks were varied
enough, but always done under the authority of those
who stood behind them. After the year A.D. 70 these
envoys collected charitable gifts for the scholars of
Palestine who could not have continued their teaching
without this assistance. Without this help the work of
defining the Law (Halacha) would have been in danger
of discontinuance, and with it the religious life of God's
People. The collection of money was recognised as a

[1] These illustrate the function, though the term is not used.
Recognised scholars were needed for such important business,
affecting the unity of Judaism.
[2] So also in prayer for the sick, e.g. Hanina ben Dosa in Bab.
Ber. 34 b; Jer. Ber. 9d, 21 ff.; [Danby, Mishnah, p. 6].

religious service ; [1] otherwise Aqiba and other great
Rabbis of his time would hardly have been ready to
undertake it (Jer. Hor. 48*a*, 39 ff.). But such visita-
tions included more than the collection of money.
According to Jer. Ḥag. 76*c*, 31 ff. and other passages [2]
the Patriarch Jehuda II, about A.D. 250, " sent out "
three leading Rabbis into the districts of Palestine,
in order to appoint teachers of the O.T. and the Mishna.
Analogous activities, in which envoys maintain the
link between the spiritual authorities of the homeland
and the congregations of the Dispersion outside
Palestine, are to be found at a much earlier date. A
*shali*ᵃ*ḥ* of this kind is to be seen in Paul going to
Damascus with letters of commendation from the
central authorities (Acts ix, 1 ff.). An example of
such a letter is found in Jer. Ḥag. 76*d*, 3 f. (cf. Jer.
Ned. 42*b*, 22 f.). [3] It is written in commendation of
Rabbi Ḥiyya bar Abba to the patriarch Jehuda II
about A.D. 280, and speaks of him as being " sent "
as a *shalu*ᵃ*ḥ*. Obviously the letters gave details about
the person concerned and about his mission. It is not
without importance to recall in this connexion the
" false apostles ", with whom Paul had to contend
(II Cor. xi, 13) ; the use of letters of commendation
by the Jews suggests that false prophets were known
among them also.

These envoys, who were usually ordained Rabbis,

---

[1] In the course of time Jews of the Dispersion had to pay the
regular " Patriarchs Tax " along with the Temple Tax, instead
of making voluntary contributions, and its collection remained
in the hands of learned *sh*ᵉ*luḥim*, with the support of local courts
which were formerly responsible for collecting and transmitting
the Temple Tax. See Vogelstein, M.G.W.J. 49 (1905), 438 ff. ;
Bill. III, 316 ff.

[2] *Cf.* Krauss, J.Q.R. XVII (1905), 375 ff. ; E. J. III (1929), 5 ;
Vogelstein, *op. çit.* 437.

[3] Krauss, E. J. III (1929), 3 ; Vogelstein, *op. cit.* 435, n. 2.

seem to have been specially set apart for their task
by the laying-on of hands in the name of the community
which sent them. In this way their mission gets an
explicitly religious character and is an act of the
community.[1] Perhaps the last-mentioned feature is
emphasised by the fact that the envoys were not sent
out alone but in groups, usually two by two.[2]

Justin (Dial. 108) speaks of " chosen men who had
received the laying-on of hands ", meaning thereby
Jewish sheluḥim (cf. ibid. 17).[3] The laying-on of hands
(semikhah), with which, e.g. the High Priest was
designated for his duty on the Day of Atonement (Yoma
1, 1), and, what is more important for our purpose,
which regularly accompanied ordination (T. Sanh.
1, 1), seems to have been abandoned by the Jews (Bill.
II, 653 f.) in view of its appropriation by Christians.
Its earlier close connexion with the institution of the
sheluḥim shows all the more clearly the significance
of the latter.

Over against all that it must be most strongly
emphasised that Jewish missionaries, who were plenti-
ful in the time of Jesus,[4] were never called sheluḥim
and the words shalaḥ and ἀποστέλλειν play no part in
connexion with them. Their work was carried on
without authorisation through the community in the
strict sense, being personal in character, though
without losing substance or meaning thereby.[5] They

---

[1] Philo, Migr. Abr. 22, has χειροτονέω with ἀποστέλλω in
quite a different connexion.

[2] Cf. Venosa Inscription (see p. 13) ; Matt. xi, 2 ; Mark. vi, 7 ;
Luke x, 1 ; and see Schlatter, Matt. 325 f.

[3] Harnack (see p. ix) 65, n. 2, with other evidence for Jewish
" apostles ".

[4] Cf. Matt. xxiii, 15 ; Bill. I, 926.

[5] An outstanding example is the conversion of the royal house
of Adiabene through the Jewish merchant (a Pharisee, Bill. I,
926), Eliezer (Jos. Ant. 20, 17 ff.).

are not even called apostles by Justin (Dial. 108), although it would have been natural for him to use the term, all the more because he uses the verb ἀποστέλλειν to describe their authoritative despatch by the spiritual authorities in Jerusalem (17).[1] It may therefore be concluded that the term " apostle " was not simply the Greek equivalent of *shaliᵃḥ*, and above all, that it was not the Jews who drew the parallel.[2] In this connexion it should be noted that the Jews did not use the word ἀπόστολος in the N.T. sense before it was so used by the Church, and also that Jews, like Christians, transliterated ἀπόστολος into Latin (Venosa Inscription)[3] this being unnecessary in the case of *shaliᵃḥ*.[4]

It is thus impossible to speak of Jewish " apostles " in the time of Jesus ; the only correct term is " authorised agent ". Where the word " apostle " occurs, it is taken over mechanically from Christian usage into Judaism, in which there is really nothing to justify the use of the word ; it is certain that the older Judaism was already familiar with many different kinds of *shᵉluḥim*, but equally certain that this included no reference to missionary activity. This follows from the fact that the office of *shaliᵃḥ* grew out of the needs of daily life and had no reference beyond the bounds of the community. The institution is entirely secular in its origin and nature, and where it appears in a religious form (see p. 21), that is merely an application. In considering the provenance of the Christian apostolate in the strict sense we must avoid connecting it with Jewish missionary activity, and it is therefore a complete mistake to suppose that Paul was a

[1] See p. 19.

[2] Harnack, 340, n. 1, on the basis of a mistaken interpretation of Jos. Ant. 17, 300 (see p. 11).

[3] See p. 13.

[4] A suitable equivalent would have been *legatus*.

missionary called to preach the religion of his fathers
in foreign parts, before his conversion.[1]

The fact that there were no authorised Jewish
missionaries before A.D. 70 can only be explained by
Judaism's doctrine of election, which was expressed
in a form which subordinated the idea of God to that
of the religious self-consciousness, that element against
which Jesus set himself, specially in the Sermon on
the Mount. Holding this position, the Jews had no
interest in spreading their faith abroad; they were
content to let the others long after what they possessed,
but not themselves to offer it. Where missionary
activity took place, it originated in Pharasaic circles
and had its root in the idea of earning merit, not in
that of universal salvation.[2] The people as a whole
thought as little as their priests and spiritual leaders
of missions as a concern of Israel.[3] This situation
was not really changed after A.D. 70.[4]

(c) *Prophetic.* What has been stated above receives
special illumination from the fact that the rabbis
frequently applied the term *shaliᵃḥ* to one who was
commissioned and authorised by God. Two groups
are concerned, first the priesthood as a whole, and then
a small number of significant personalities, specially
Moses, Elijah, Elisha and Ezekiel.[5]

The priest is regarded as being commissioned by God
and not by the Jewish community when he offers
sacrifice (Rab Huna b. Jehoshua, about A.D. 350;

[1] With E. Barnikol, Die vorchristliche u. frühchr. Zeit d.
Paulus (1929), 18 ff.

[2] Midr. Shir 1 on i, 3: When anyone brings a creature under the
wings of the Shechinah (makes a man a proselyte), it is counted
to him (by God) as if he had created, trained and shaped it.

[3] Differing from the Maccabees and their successors, who had
special motives. See Schlatter, Gesch. Isr. 3rd ed. (1925), 132 ff.

[4] Cf. Bill. I, 926, where the failure is ascribed to circumstances.

[5] Bill. III, 5 f.

Bab. Qidd. 23*b*). This view is based on the whole conception of *shaliᵃḥ*, viz. that the one authorised is in the position of him who authorises him (see p. 14). If the priest were the *shaliᵃḥ* of the congregation, then the latter would necessarily have the right to offer sacrifice. But it has not this right, otherwise the priest would be superfluous; therefore the priest cannot be its agent, but only the agent of God. He is therefore called " envoy of the Merciful " (cf. Bab. Qidd. 23*b*, Yoma 19*a-b*). There is no contradiction here of Lev. xvi (cf. iv, 5 ff.), since his acting on behalf of the people is in no way prejudiced; on the contrary it finds here its justification.

Moses, Elijah, and Elisha, and even also Ezekiel, are reckoned as *shᵉluḥim* of God, since through them things happened, which elsewhere are reserved for God :[1] Moses brings water out of the rock (Bab. B.M. 86*b*); Elijah makes rain and awakens one who is dead; Elisha opens the mother's womb and also awakens the dead; and Ezekiel receives the key to the graves at the resurrection of the dead according to Ezek. xxxvii, 1 ff. (Midr. Ps. lxxviii, section 5, cf. Bab. Taan. 2*a*, Bab. Sanh. 118*a*).[2] What lifts these four above the rest of Israel is the ability which God gave them to perform miracles, doing that which at all other times he reserved for himself. Here, as in the case of the priests, the argument is *a posteriori*, from event to cause, and does not involve a deeper connotation of *shaliᵃḥ*. Perhaps in the background is the desire to avoid the suspicion of encroaching upon the divine right, by representing the four men as God's tools.

[1] Cf. Shemoneh 'Esreh, where God is praised as awakening the dead and as giver of dew and rain. I Clem. 17, 1 only mentions the first three by name.

[2] Angels, of course, are *shᵉluḥim*, e.g. Deut. Rabb. 9, 1 on xxxiv, 5 ; but they do not come in here.

Moses and Aaron, at Exod. Rabba 5, 14, on v, 1, in reply to Pharaoh's question, call themselves " envoys of the Holy One, blessed be He ". At first sight this might seem to point to the deeper meaning, viz. authorised agents of God. The context, however, shows that they mean no more than that " God sends us ", which was the only possible reply to Pharaoh's question (LXX ἀπεσταλμένοι). Cf. the angel of death (see p. 22, n. 2).

Finally, the prophets are not appointed by God as *sh͏eluḥim*, any more than missionaries are by the community. The Rabbis never regard a prophet as *shaliᵃḥ* of God,[1] although this would have been a good way of indicating his calling and authorisation by God. The reason may partly be found in the growing inclination of the Scribes to emphasise the Divine transcendence; this, however, does not fully explain it, since *shalaḥ* was the technical term for the Divine authorisation (see p. 14), so that *shaliᵃḥ* would have been the natural term to use. It cannot be denied that for Rabbinic Judaism God's " sending " of a man did not constitute him a *shaliᵃḥ*; in other words, *shaliᵃḥ* obviously was not among the Rabbis the right word to express the ultimate meaning of the prophetic office. Taking prophets and missionaries together we can only say that the ultimate reason for avoiding the term is to be found in the fact that they speak of God, in His name, but still do not represent Him, in so far as they perform no action. But the essential meaning of *shaliᵃḥ* is that he represents another in action.

A certain corroboration of this thesis that the prophet as speaker cannot be God's *shaliᵃḥ* is to be found in the fact that Judaism regarded the Holy Spirit as medium between the prophets and God; and it should not be

[1] Ezekiel is *shaliᵃḥ*, not as prophet, but as worker of miracle.

overlooked that the Holy Spirit is only a personal representation of God and serves to emphasise his transcendence. But if the Holy Spirit dwells in the prophets,[1] then they become his instrument, and lose that power of initiative [2] which belongs essentially to the *shali*ᵃ*ḥ*, even if that mean no more than the agreement of his will with that of his sender. No further proof is needed that the Rabbis seriously misrepresented prophecy by this mechanisation, in the interest of speculation; thus they destroyed the possibility of a true understanding of the prophetic vocation, which consists in the possession of his whole being by God's word and will. This rationally conditioned limitation of the Jewish view leads naturally to a consideration of the use of the word apostle in the N.T., which goes so much further.

[1] T. Sota, 13, 2 ; when the last prophets, Hag., Zech., Mal., died, the Holy Spirit disappeared from Israel.

[2] Cf. the common rabbinical formula: This is what the Holy Spirit said through (so-and-so). See Bill. I, 74 f.

III. N.T. USAGE

THE word ἀπόστολος occurs in the N.T. seventy-nine times, apart from a few secondary readings characteristic of Luke (e.g. Luke ix, 1; [1] Acts v, 34 [2]): Matthew, Mark, and John each have it once; Paul twenty-nine times including four in Ephesians, once in Colossians and five times in the Pastoral Epistles; Luke thirty-four times, twenty-eight in Acts and six in the Gospel; Hebrews, I Peter, and Jude each once; II Peter twice, Revelation three times. Thus Paul and his disciple and fellow-traveller Luke provide four-fifths of the examples and most of the material for studying the meaning of the word. An important point is the use of the word as a self-designation at the beginning of letters six times in Paul, three in the Pastorals, and in I Peter and II Peter. We should bear in mind the possibility that the non-Pauline addresses are dependent upon Paul's customary practice, not only in the adoption of his phrase " grace and peace ", but also in the use of the title of " apostle ".[3] This material provides us with the following meanings when considered in connexion with the history of word and idea, and also in the light of statements to be made in later chapters which are indispensable even for linguistic purposes.[4]

1. Non-Biblical usage, including Josephus, has now entirely disappeared. The word " apostle " never means in the N.T. the act of sending, or

---

[1] ἀποστόλους is here an ancient Alexandrine gloss. See J. Weiss, Das Ev. d. Lk. 9th ed. (1901), ad loc.

[2] See commentaries ad loc. (von Soden reads ἀποστόλους).

[3] Cf. p. 59, and see O. Roller, B.W.A.N.T. 4 Folge 9-10 (1933).

[4] For reasons of space the argument leading to these conclusions is given in the next chapter.

the business involved, but is always the designation
of a man who is sent as ambassador, and indeed, an
authorised ambassador.   The Greek word ἀπόστολος
merely provides the form ; the content and idea come
to light through the *shali*ᵃ*ḥ* of Rabbinic Judaism.   This
can be stated absolutely since the word is only used
in the N.T. for men, although in the course of time
(see p. 43, n. 1) women could also bear the title.   That,
however, would be a contradiction in itself since
*shali*ᵃ*ḥ* is a legal term and women in Judaism are not
only limited in their legal rights, and are above all
debarred from giving evidence (cf. Sifre Deut. 190 on
xix, 17) ; they come after the slave, in that he, as his
lord's property, is allowed legally to do his master's
will, e.g. when he slays the Passover lamb (see p. 14).
It is characteristic of the new situation that the word
μαθήτρια appears side by side with μαθητής for the
Christian woman, although Judaism knew nothing
of women disciples.   In this case, however, the pre-
suppositions were of an entirely different sort.

2. The complete identity of ἀπόστολος with *shali*ᵃ*ḥ*
is shown at John xiii, 16 : the Greek word here simply
represents the Jewish term and legally describes the
valid representation of another person and his business
(see p. 14).   This meaning is made certain by the use
of the synonymous parallel of the relation between
slave and master.   The slave is entirely under the
jurisdiction of his master and acquires his position
entirely from him.   But that is exactly what *shali*ᵃ*ḥ*
means.   Cf. Gen. Rabba 78 on xxxii, 26 : Rabbi
Simeon (about 150) said " From the fact that Genesis
xxxii, 26 has the word draw the conclusion that the
sender is greater than the one who is sent." [1]

[1] Bill. II, 558.   The word used is not the noun, *shali*ᵃ*ḥ*, but
the hithpael participle of the verb *shalaḥ* ; but this does not alter
the sense.   The saying of Jesus, characteristic of his own self-
consciousness, goes further than that of the Rabbi.

3. Corresponding to *shali*ᵃ*ḥ* (p. 16), ἀπόστολος means the one who is commissioned by a community. This is illustrated at II Cor. viii, 23, where Paul applies the term to those who conveyed the gift of the Greek communities to the saints [1] at Jerusalem. In exactly the same way Epaphroditus is the apostle of the Philippians to Paul (Phil. ii, 25). In these cases "apostle", having to do with expressions of love, is not only a legal, but also a religious term.

4. Generally speaking, "apostles" are the bearers of the N.T. Gospel. First of all the name is borne by the circle of the Twelve (the number being maintained after the disappearance of Judas, Acts i, 26; I Cor. xv, 5). The sender here of course is Jesus. This usage dominates Luke's writing in the Gospel and especially in Acts. The twelve appear here as "apostles", who constitute a limited *collegium*, beside which another body, that of the elders, can take its place (Acts xv, 2, 4, 6, 22 f; xvi, 4). The outstanding figure among them is that of Peter (Acts ii, 37; v, 29) and Jerusalem is expressly mentioned as the place where this circle has its abode (Acts viii, 1). Matthew x, 2 and Mark vi, 30 use the word "apostles" for the Twelve. The title is in all these cases absolute, carrying its meaning in itself, and always appears in the plural (see p. 51).

Further, "apostle" is the title given to the first Christian missionaries or their leading representatives, and also to men who always belonged to the wider circle of disciples. In Acts xiv, 4, 14 at least, Paul and Barnabas are called apostles, and here the expression must have been found by the author in his source.[2] The Twelve are "apostles" for Luke, but

---

[1] Cf. K. Holl, Ges. Aufs. II, 60.

[2] Some texts omit the word at ver. 14, showing that it was objectionable to later readers. J. Wagenmann, 76, n. 1 (see p. ix) omits it, without good reason, as we go on to show. Cf. W. Mundle, 38, n. 1 (see p. ix).

the circle is not limited to them. Above all Paul belongs to it and the Epistles show that he so regards himself. According to him it also included the Lord's brother James (Gal. i, 19) [1] who first joined the community, like Paul himself, after the death of Jesus. Two otherwise unknown fellow-workers with Paul, presumably of Jewish origin, Junias and Andronicus, are named at Rom. xvi, 7 as apostles; and a wider circle, including James, is indicated at I Cor. xv, 7.

In this connexion we may bring together the sending out of Barnabas and Paul by the congregation at Antioch (Acts xiii) and the more precise designation of an apostle as " apostle of Jesus Christ " in Paul's letters. Both elements here are obviously connected with the Jewish shali^ah. On the other hand, it is just at this point that we see the difference between these men and the first group. If there is no difference in designation, no reference to a wider and a narrower circle, then the ground of this must be found in the Apostleship itself, which is common to both and can be nothing else than an encounter with the risen Christ and the reception of a commission from him himself (see p. 42).

It will be observed that in spite of the naming of Barnabas (cf. I Cor. ix, 5 f.),[2] James, Junias and Andronicus as apostles, Apollos is never so designated, although one might have expected it at I Cor. iii 5 ff. Nor is the name applied to Timothy, although he took a lively and successful part in the missionary work at Thessalonica; he is called brother (II Cor. i, 1;

---

[1] Assuming that εἰ μή means " except " and not " but only ". For Junias and Andronicus see Th. Zahn and other commentators *ad loc.* On I Cor. xv, 7, see A. Schlatter, Erläuterungen z. N.T., for emphasis on the commission of the risen Lord.

[2] So H. Lietzmann *ad loc.* and J. Wellhausen, N.G.G. 1907, 5, n. 1; but not Ph.Bachmann, Cor. or K. Holl, Ges. Aufs. II, 51, n. 1

Col. i, 1 ; Philem. 1), slave of Christ Jesus (Phil. i, 1)
and even God's fellow-worker (I Thess. iii, 2) ; [1] but
these are not equivalents of the title of " apostle ".
It was the fact that they shared a common task which
prevented strong differences of opinion from leading
to a breach between Paul and those of Jerusalem under
James (Acts xv ; cf. Gal. ii, 9). Commissioning by
the risen Christ is expressly named at 1 Clem. xlii, 1 ff.
as the basis of apostleship. Paul himself connects his
apostolic consciousness with the memory of his meeting
with the risen Christ (I Cor. ix, 1 and specially xv, 8 ff). [2]

What has just been stated means that the apostolate
(I Cor. xii, 28 f.) is not an office created by the community or a synonym for its leaders, [3] but an appointment of Jesus creating the Church. For that reason
the apostles rank with the O.T. prophets (Eph. ii, 20 ;
iii, 5), whose office became a preparation for the coming
of Christ on the ground of their having been sent
(see p. xii). This is one of the most important aspects
of the apostolic self-consciousness, only possible in the
context of early Christian eschatology, as shown by
Paul.

That Paul means the Church as a whole at I Cor.
xii, 28 and not the Corinthian congregation, [4] is clear
from the context. Immediately before, he has been
speaking of the body of Christ. He never means
by that an individual congregation, but always the
whole organism, whose Head is Christ (Eph. i, 22 ;
cf. ii, 11 f. ; Col. i, 18, etc. ; cf. Rom. xii, 5). Besides,
if the individual congregation was meant, that would
brand Paul as the teacher of an interims-ethic, which

[1] This reading (D 33 Ambrosiaster) has strong internal support ;
cf. I Cor. iii, 9 and see p. 61 ; it is much too audacious to be late.

[2] Cor. xv, 8 ff. is more significant than ix, 1. Harnack, 335, n. 5
misses this. [For I Clem. see p. vi.]

[3] Pr.-Bauer, 156.   [4] As commonly regarded as obvious.

he certainly was not, for he never speaks of Christ
from the point of view of man or the community,
but always of them from the point of view of Christ.
Cf. also Eph. iv, 11.

5. Finally, Jesus himself is called the Apostle and
High Priest of our confession (Heb. iii, 1). " Apostle "
here can only mean that in Jesus the final revelation
of God through God himself has taken place (i, 2).

The phrase forms an obvious unity, the definite
article being omitted before " high priest ",[1] and
brings together, from the point of view of the reader's
conviction (ὁμολογία), what has already been said
about Jesus ; he is both the Son in whom God speaks
his final word (i, 1 ff.) and the High Priest who has
atoned finally for the sins of his people (ii, 5 ff.).   Thus
" apostle " is to be understood as infinitely surpassing
" prophet ", which is never applied to Jesus in Hebrews;
but, in view of the word " Son " (i, 2) used absolutely,
it would be explained best through the Rabbinic
shaliᵃḥ : in the Son God himself speaks and acts
(Hebrews avoids the name " Father ").   It has already
been shown that the idea of the shaliᵃḥ was applied
to ordinary priests (see pp. 21 f.).   Analogous thoughts
in the context (iii, 5 ff.) justify us in going back to this
conception.   If this interpretation is correct, the basis
of the unified expression is the acknowledgment of
the absolute authority which springs from the absolute
authorisation for word (Apostle) and work (High
Priest).   The phrasing is certainly unique, but it is
organically consistent with the rest of N.T. usage.

If this is not accepted, the only possibility which
remains is to take the phrase as setting forth Jesus as
surpassing Moses, the greatest O.T. bearer of revelation, and Aaron as the greatest of all the priests.
This, however, is a way of speaking which only appears

[1] E. Riggenbach, Heb. ad loc.

in Justin; it is never found in the N.T. or anywhere in the literature of the primitive Church. Justin calls Jesus " apostle " and " messenger " and " teacher " (Apol. 1, 12, 9, etc.),[1] adopting terms used in the Gnostic myths, according to which the final redeemer is called simply the one who is sent. An objection to this view, however, is that the word does not appear in the Gospel of John, in which this circle of ideas is echoed, or appears to be echoed;[2] Hebrews, on the other hand, has otherwise no reference to this speculation. Above all, this interpretation of " apostle ", separating it from " priest ", destroys the unity of the phrase, whereas the author wishes to emphasise their inseparability; he is anxious to show Jesus as the complete revelation, whose distinction is not in word alone or in priestly office alone, but in their combination.

[1] G. P. Wetter (see p. ix), 28.
[2] W. Bauer, Joh.-ev., on John iii, 17 ; R. Bultmann, Z.N.W. 24 (1925), 105 ff. See pp. 63 ff.

IV. CHRISTIAN APOSTLESHIP

1. JESUS AND THE FIRST GROUP OF DISCIPLES

(*a*) The origin of the apostleship must be associated with Jesus, quite apart from the fact that the circle of his disciples formed the nucleus of the Church, and was so regarded by himself.[1] The first point to be observed is, that outwardly there was no difference between this group and those which gathered around other teachers of the time. They too were known as " disciples ". The group around Jesus differs, however, from the rest in the manner of its attachment (Mark i, 17 ; ii, 14, etc.) and in what grew out of it ; its creation and shaping were not due to the special inspiration or initiative of the disciples, but solely to Jesus. It is characteristic of Jesus that he does not take this step immediately ; his followers must first become disciples, i.e. learners, although the situation itself was crying out for action.[2] The disciples refrained from taking any initiative, in spite of the circumstances, because they accepted the call to repentance for themselves with resolute sincerity.[3] Thus they learned what obedience is since Jesus showed them God both as the Holy One and as the Father.[4] This is the most important of all clues to the understanding of the innermost meaning of the N.T. apostleship. Here lie the ultimate reasons why it could never become hardened into an office, even when a community had

[1] Cf. A. Schlatter, Die Gesch. d. Christus, 2nd ed. (1923), 406 f.
[2] Frequently shown by the disciples' behaviour and finally by Peter's sword (John xviii, 10 and par.).
[3] A. Schlatter, *op. cit.* 312 f.
[4] Cf. the Sermon on the Mount as a whole and the great parables, esp. in Luke.

to be organised after the death of Jesus.[1]   That was impossible, since it grew up in a circle of believers, who knew themselves to be under the claim of God, and accepted the law of love as the only law of neighbourly intercourse.[2]   It follows from this that discipleship in the full meaning of the word was the necessary condition for sharing as servants in the work of Jesus.

This consideration makes clear the relation between " disciples ", " apostles ", and " the Twelve ".   The disciples constitute the larger community;   they provide the general term [3] which includes " apostles " and " the Twelve ".   Every apostle is a disciple, but not every disciple an apostle.   Thus the phrase " the Twelve Apostles " need cause no surprise (Matt. x, 2). There is no need to identify " the Twelve " with " the Apostles ";   the very linking together of the two expressions rules that out, all the more so because there is no place for a pleonasm in this passage.

(b) The activity of the disciples begins at the moment when Jesus decides to make them his fellow-workers.[4] No ground is given in the Synoptic Gospels for this decision.   Strictly speaking, nothing is said of any special decision by Jesus ; we are only told that he called the Twelve to him and " sent them out ".   Mark alone uses here the word $\dot{\alpha}\pi o\sigma\tau\acute{\epsilon}\lambda\lambda\epsilon\iota\nu$; Matthew and Luke, and Mark also in another saying, emphasise the point that Jesus bestowed on them the power or authority ($\dot{\epsilon}\xi o\upsilon\sigma\acute{\iota}a$) which he himself possessed.   It is clear that we have here a case of authoritative sending in the sense of the delegation of power.   The men so sent forth are throughout the narrative to be regarded as *sheluḥim* in the legal sense.   It is consistent with this

[1] Acts xv shows an organised community.   But cf. vi, 1.
[2] Cf. Matt. xxii, 37-40.
[3] R. Bultmann draws special attention to Luke's usage (Gesch. Syn. Trad. 390 f.).
[4] Matt. x, 1 ;   Mark vi, 7 ;   Luke ix, 1.

that they return later to report on their achievements
(Mark vi, 30 ; Luke ix, 10).

We cannot here enter into the question of the historicity of the sending out of the Twelve. The suggestion that it merely expresses the desire of the early
Church to place the appointment in the lifetime of
Jesus [1] is obviously wrong, because it presumes the
possibility, if not indeed the necessity, of identifying
the Twelve with the Apostles, and there is no ground
for this apart from expressions which can be explained
otherwise. It need only be said that the historical
circumstances become more obscure, if Jesus himself
was not responsible for sending out the Twelve ; it
would be difficult to find a motive for such a proceeding apart from the will of Jesus.

Besides the narrative of the commissioning, two pieces
of evidence may be adduced for the existence of the
institution of an apostolate resembling that of the Jewish
shali͆aḥ. The first is found at Mark ix, 38 ff. ; Luke ix,
49 f., where John complains about an exorcist casting
out demons in the name of Jesus without belonging
to the company of disciples. This complaint could
not have been made if it were simply a question of
prestige or a matter of competence concerning Jesus
himself. The indignation arises from the fact that an
outsider is appropriating that which does not belong
to him. The formula, " in thy name ",[2] indicates
that the stranger is using for his miracles the power
available to Jesus as if it were his own, but obviously
without being authorised. Authorisation is granted
only to the disciples of Jesus. This at any rate is
John's view, and is only possible if the authorisation
of the disciples [3] was not a mere ideal, but actually

[1] R. Schütz (see p. ix), 71 ff.

[2] Cf. linguistic parallels from Josephus in A. Schlatter, Luke 109.

[3] The evangelists, esp. Luke, use a general expression, not
" the Twelve ".

goes back to Jesus himself. The second reference is
to the words of Jesus concerning the meaning of men's
treatment of his disciples (Matt. x, 40 ff.; Mark ix, 41;
Luke x, 16). They illustrate the saying that a man's
ambassador is as himself and the action of his ambassador as his own action (see p. 14). This is only
possible if the corresponding authorisation has already
taken place. It makes no difference whatever that no
mention is made in this connexion of a miracle, or
indeed of any special action performed with the authority of Jesus; it is otherwise at Mark ix, 38 ff., etc.
Luke points to the preaching of the Word, but Mark
simply speaks of belonging to Christ, i.e. discipleship
(cf. Matt. x, 42). None of these passages uses the
word " apostle " or speaks of the " sending out " of
the disciples; reference is made only to the relation
of Jesus to God. All the same, there is here a close
parallel to the legal status of *shaliᵃḥ*. Both these
passages attest the personal authorisation of the disciples
by Jesus, and their evidence is all the stronger because
they take it for granted, and do not speak of an original
institution.[1] Their significance is increased by the
recognition, specially in the first, that Jesus is seen to
be purifying the ideas of the disciples. Although the
legal foundations of the apostleship are undeniably
present, Jesus rids them of every suggestion of a
consequent legal claim. When a disciple receives
authority " in the name of Jesus ", i.e. to speak and
act as he does, that gives him no new rights, but on the
contrary binds upon him the duty of service to the one
who authorises him. Further, the choice of examples
in the second passage signifies that the commission

---

[1] R. Schütz (see p. ix), 72 seriously misunderstands Jesus and
his relation to the disciples when he fails to mention his personal
authority and the underlying idea of God. Cf. J. Wagenmann
(see p. ix), 5 f.

to represent Jesus and his business involves lowliness
and not exaltation. Thus the words of Jesus not only
refer to the apostolate as such, but also cleanse the
idea of legal claims by connecting it with the thought
of service and humility, corresponding to Paul's
conception of the apostolic office. Jesus himself
thus rules out every attempt to make an office in the
community functioning in legal forms out of his
authorisation to speak and act. Putting the matter
quite sharply, one should avoid the word " office "
in this connexion, and use " commission " instead,
in the sense of an authorisation limited in time and
place, and concerned with the business in hand, and
not with the person discharging it, just as we find in the
case of the Jewish *shali⁽ᵃ⁾ḥ*. How little we are concerned
here with an " office " is shown by the fact that the
authorisation did not remain limited to the Twelve,
and no claim for such a limitation was ever made in the
interest of the so-called original apostles; otherwise
the mission of the seventy (Luke x, 1) could not appear
in the tradition. This story makes it obvious that the
commission of those nearest Jesus, viz. the Twelve,
to proclaim the coming kingdom, conveyed no special
personal pre-eminence. The idea of an office is also
contradicted by the fact that obviously the commission ended with the return to Jesus. The group of
disciples is no longer in action, because it is with Jesus
(Luke ix, 49 f.). We never hear of any activity on
the part of the disciples in the immediate neighbourhood
of Jesus; that is always preceded by a sending out.[2]
When they are with him they resemble the pupils of
the Rabbis, learning from him and ministering to him.[3]

[1] See A. Schlatter, Luke 274 ff.   [2] Cf. Luke x, 17.
[3] Cf. Matt. xix, 13 par.; xxi, 1 ff. par.; xxvi, 17 ff. par.;
but also John xii, 20 f. The foot-washing (John xiii) is only fully
understood against this background.

This is of decisive importance for the understanding of apostleship in the early Church, and closely bound up with *shali^aḥ*.[1] It should be clear that apostleship as such has no religious character, but is originally a formal term. These apostles receive their religious stamp only from the one who commissions them, and yet the commission itself always remains the chief thing and the apostles only its bearers, exactly according to the fundamental rabbinical saying: " a man's envoy is as himself " (see p. 14).

(*c*) Harder than the historical question which we have been discussing is the question whether the name of " apostle " was used among the first disciples of Jesus. It occurs a few times in the Gospels to indicate men commissioned to preach by Jesus (see p. 33). Matt. x, 2, speaks of the twelve apostles immediately after mentioning the twelve disciples (ver. 1). Between the two [2] come the commissioning and communication of authority, decided upon by Jesus. Similarly, at Mark vi, 30, we have the return of the " apostles " to Jesus, their commissioning and authorisation having been described at vi. 7. After this, both in Matthew [3] and Mark, the word " disciple " is always used.[4] This excludes the possibility that these evangelists regarded the apostleship as an office with an indelible character.[5]

What has just been said does not mean that Jesus himself did not use the word or give the commission, as if these ideas were introduced later. In the case of Luke, however, it is different. Here the word " apostle " occurs six times. At Luke xxiv, 10, the

[1] Commissioning two by two has Jewish parallels. See p. 19.
[2] Cf. p. 33.   [3] Matt. omits the return.
[4] J. Wellhausen's account of these things (see p. ix) can only be called a caricature.
[5] From this point of view critical objections to the word are justified.

inner circle is indicated by the definite formula " the apostles ", as it is at xxii, 14, referring to those who were present at the Last Supper.[1] Neither of these is concerned with sending forth. This actually points to an established usage, and this is confirmed by the absence of the word " twelve ".[2] The other passages connect the word with an actual mission. Thus at xi, 49, the word is coupled with " prophets " but does not refer to the disciples of Jesus. Luke ix, 10, speaks of the return of the apostles (Mark vi, 30). At xvii 5, in close connexion with Matt. xvii, 14 ff. and Mark ix, 14 ff., we must presume the authorisation of the disciples for their healing ministry,[3] although this failed through their lack of faith.[4] Finally, Luke vi, 12 f., records the choice of the Twelve and the bestowal of the name " apostles " in view of their coming mission (ix, 1),[5] from which they return as " apostles " (ix, 10).

Luke thus provides abundant evidence for connecting the noun " apostle " with the verb " to send ". This usage implies a situation in which $\dot{\alpha}\pi o\sigma\tau\acute{\epsilon}\lambda\lambda\epsilon\sigma\theta\alpha\iota$ is appropriate, not $\dot{\alpha}\pi\epsilon\sigma\tau\acute{\alpha}\lambda\theta\alpha\iota$ or $\dot{\alpha}\pi o\sigma\tau\alpha\lambda\hat{\eta}\nu\alpha\iota$; and this shows the later hardening of the word. This consideration makes it almost impossible to doubt that the term " apostle " goes back to Jesus, obviously not in its Greek form, but in Aramaic (sh*liḥa'). This word is free from the suggestion of an office, which was later associated with the word " apostle " through the position occupied by the Twelve. Luke vi, 13, says

[1] The reading " Twelve " at xxii, 14 is secondary.

[2] See p. 33.

[3] A. Schlatter, Luke 384 f. ; H. J. Holtzmann, Die Synopt., 3rd ed. (1901), 391. Th. Zahn argues for the Lucan context ; but see R. Bultmann, Trad. 384 ff.

[4] This occurs during the absence of Jesus (Matt. xvii ; A. Schlatter, Luke 385) just after the first prediction of the Cross.

[5] The chosen Twelve cannot be called apostles until they are sent forth ; cf. Matt. x, 1 f.

explicitly, " He chose from them twelve, whom also he named apostles ". The relative sentence is usually explained as an anachronism, perhaps even under the influence of a similar development in Judaism, or else it is simply rejected as unauthentic.[1] Neither of these is necessary, if " apostle " is regarded simply as an objective term, indicating a representative authorised for a particular task. This view (see p. 37) is not only possible but necessary, since otherwise we have a difficult description of the disciple in his relation to Jesus, which has necessarily led to strong contradictions in the narrative. Apart from that, this meaning is supported by the Gospel tradition itself.

A comparison of Luke vi, 12 f. with Mark iii, 13 ff. shows that there is a real parallel between the two. What follows in both Gospels shows that the real appointment to apostleship takes place later (Mark vi, 7 ; Luke ix, 1). The choice of the Twelve as an inner circle and their appointment as apostles do not coincide, as Matt. x, 1 also indicates. The choice of the Twelve is made by Jesus with a view to their sharing in his work. The form of Mark's statement points definitely to the future. Luke's relative sentence can only mean the same thing, unless the word " apostles " (without the article) is forcibly removed from the situation indicated by a comparison of Luke vi, 13 with ix, 1 ff. It is possible that Luke's sources suggested that Jesus discussed his plan with the Twelve when he chose them, this being the meaning of " naming " them apostles ; but this is pure speculation. It may be added that Luke's relative sentence is also found in many important MSS. at Mark iii, 14, though it has failed to gain canonical recognition because of Luke vi, 13. The difficulties connected with the term " apostles " may have played their part in the rejection.

[1] E.g. E. Klostermann.

Perhaps the words may have a better claim to retention in view of the considerations here advanced.

It can now be regarded as established, not only that the apostleship itself goes back to Jesus but also that he used the title of " apostle ". This does not get its meaning from the Greek word, or indicate an official position, but is to be understood as an application of the *shali*ᵃ*ḥ* institution to the relation between him and his disciples at the time when he communicated to them authority to take a full share in his work.

(*d*) The Gospels emphasise another feature which later became important, viz., the close association of the " apostles " with the activity of Jesus in proclaiming the Word. Mark (iii, 14) speaks of their commission as primarily to preach, and says that, on their return, they reported all that they had done and taught. Luke says that Jesus sent them out to proclaim the Kingdom of God and to heal (ix, 2) and Matthew reports the same charge more fully, with a clearer connexion with the work of Jesus (x, 7 f.). This gives a quality of absolute objectivity to the apostleship, avoiding the influence of idiosyncrasy upon the inner shaping of the commission. When a disciple is charged with the proclamation that the Kingdom of Heaven is at hand, he is thereby associated with Jesus, and so brought under the will of God, which completely destroys his autonomy [1] and leaves him simply to render full obedience.[2]

Inseparable from the commission to preach is authorisation by Jesus to perform actions. This follows naturally as an expression of the fact that the

---

[1] Cf. Matt. x, 9 ff., par. To this may be added much of what was said to the disciples as such, esp. Matt. xviii, 1 ff. par.

[2] Matt. xxv, 14 ff. ; Luke xix, 12 ff. It is noteworthy that the parable deals with a man going away and giving his servants work to do during his absence.

apostle is truly commissioned by Jesus as his representative. It is therefore significant of the humility
of the first apostles, taught and exemplified by Jesus,
that the miracles which they performed never led to
boasting, or a competitive spirit.[1] Similarly Luke
says that the Seventy returned with joy, and said,
" even the demons obey us in thy name " (x, 17) ;
here we have complete disinterestedness and devotion,
producing the joy which prevails when man leaves the
field to God and fills his life with service to Him.
Luke is here quite certainly not setting forth his own
ideal of apostleship ; he is simply quoting from his
source. This makes it all the more important that
the returning messengers give joyful thanks for their
success as the success of Jesus and, like all the other
returning messengers in the Gospels, say nothing about
the difficulties which attended work in the name of
Jesus, concerning which Jesus had doubtless spoken
(cf. Mark x, 11). The importance of this lies in its
emphasis, in the case of the first group of disciples,
on the same element which distinguishes the apostleship of Paul.

2. THE GIFT OF THE RISEN LORD

(a) The use of the word " apostle " and the experience of the disciples with Jesus have made it clear
that their commission to preach the nearness of the
Kingdom of God was limited to a definite period
(see p. 38). Nothing is reported concerning new
commissions to the Twelve, nor are they appointed
as his permanent representatives ; his departure found
them more like lost sheep than a body of his servants.

[1] Such thoughts may have provided the occasion for Matt.
xviii, 1 ff., par., though this is not necessary, since the subject
was always being discussed in the synagogue (A. Schlatter,
Matt. 543 f.).

All they had was his promise that he would not
remain dead [1] and that his fellowship with them would
endure.[2]   But this promise did not save them from
flight, [3] denial,[4] fear,[5] and hopeless grief.[6]   The Gospels
and the Book of Acts leave no doubt that it was the
fact that the Lord was risen which alone changed the
scattered circle of disciples into a community rejoicing
in hope and ready for work.[7]   But the fact of the Risen
Lord meant also the renewal of their commission as
apostles in its final form.[8]

Particular historical and geographical questions [9]
may here give place to what is fundamental.   All
that concerns us is the fact that the apostolate was not
taken over by the primitive Church from the time before
Easter ; what happened was that after his resurrection
Jesus first made the community, in the apostolate,
the preaching community.[10]   The apostles are witnesses
of the resurrection, though not all the witnesses became
apostles.[11]   The number of these appears to have been
comparatively small.   It may be specially noted that
so far no women were included, although women were
the first to see the Risen Lord,[12] and the Church con-

[1] Matt. xvi, 21 par. ; xvii, 23 par. ; xx, 19.

[2] Matt. xviii, 20 ; xxvi, 29 par.

[3] Matt. xxvi, 56 ; Mark xiv, 50.   [4] Matt. xxvi, 69 ff. par.

[5] None of Jesus' disciples takes part in his burial (Matt. xxvii,
57 ff.) ; only some of his women friends see where he is laid
(Mark xv, 47 ; cf. Luke xxiii, 55 f. ; Matt. xxvii, 61).   John xx,
19 is typical.

[6] Luke xxiv, 4, 13 ff.   [7] Cf. esp. Luke xxiv, 36 ff.

[8] Matt. xxviii, 16 ff. ; Luke xxiv, 48 f. ; Acts i, 8.

[9] Cf. J. Weiss, Das Urchristentum (1917), 10 ff.   For the
problem of " Galilee on the Mount of Olives " see Pr.-Bauer, 236.

[10] See A. Schlatter, Die Gesch. d. erst. Christenheit (1926), 10 ;
P. Feine, Der Apostel Paulus (1927), 222.

[11] Cf. Luke xxiv, 49 with 46 and esp. I Cor. xv, 8 ff., but also
K. Holl, Ges. Aufs. II, 51.

[12] Matt. xxviii, 1 ff., par. ; John xx, 11 ff.

tained prophetic women.[1] It is questionable whether
the " more than five hundred brethren " of I Cor. xv, 6,
became apostles as a result of the appearance of Jesus,
although verses 8 f. attest the early Christian linking
of apostleship with personal contact with the Risen
Lord, and the thought of the founding of the apostolate
is very prominent in the whole passage.[2] On the
other hand, James, the brother of Jesus, who was never
his disciple, but appears among the witnesses at 1 Cor.
xv, 7, is later one of the leaders of the Jerusalem
community (Gal. i, 19; ii, 9, 12), and is obviously
reckoned by Paul among the apostles,[3] though he
never gives him the title.[4]

It thus appears that, besides an encounter with the
Risen Lord, a personal commission was the only ground
of apostleship. The Twelve were the first to receive
this commission, because of their association with the
earthly life of Jesus, who specially prepared them to
continue his preaching, not in the same form, but rather
as the proclamation of Jesus as fulfiller of O.T. prophecy.[5] Two main elements are involved here. In
the first place, a number of men, specially those who
were close to him during his earthly life, received
authoritative appointment to be his representatives
inside the Christian community. But secondly, the
changed situation made them also missionaries, and
it was this part of their work which gave its stamp to
their office.

[1] Acts xxi, 8 f. In the Acts of Paul and Thecla the latter is
called apostle, but this is simply through assimilation with Paul.
[2] " The significance of the Easter story for Paul lies simply in the
fact that through it Jesus created his envoys." A. Schlatter,
Die Gesch. d. Christus 2nd ed. (1923), 532.
[3] Note " all the apostles " after " James " at I Cor. xv, 7.
[4] Cf. p. 28 and see Lightfoot on Gal. i, 19, where interpretation
remains doubtful.
[5] Cf. speeches in Acts and I Cor. xv, 3 f. ; Rom. i, 2 ; iii, 21

We do not know how many apostles there were in the early days, but they must have been fairly numerous. Paul and the Book of Acts show indirectly that all the apostles, including the Twelve, were missionaries. At the time to which reference is made at Gal. i, 18 ff., there were no apostles in Jerusalem except Peter and James (the Lord's brother) who never belonged to the Twelve, although it was a long time since the scattering of the community connected with the murder of Stephen.[1] The apostles alone, not the Twelve, appear at Acts xv, 1 ff., and this suggests that James, the son of Zebedee, was put to death before the so-called Apostolic Council (Acts xii, 1 f.). Paul attests missionary activity, specially on the part of Peter, at 1 Cor. ix, 5, if we may interpret " lead about " as referring to apostolic journeys ; [2] here again the Lord's brothers are not included in the phrase " the rest of the apostles ". Perhaps Peter as a missionary had a special connexion with Babylonian Judaism.[3] Further, it is surely significant enough that we know nothing about the fate of almost all the other apostles after Pentecost. Matt. xxviii, 19 f., seems to show clearly what became of them, for the Church would hardly have allowed this to be included in the Gospel unless it represented the facts.[4]

The missionary element fundamentally differentiates the N.T. apostleship from the Jewish *shali[a]h* institution. This is true even of the form which it had assumed in the intercourse of Jesus with his disciples and in their sharing in the preparation for the coming Kingdom of God (see p. 37). It is also true of its character ; but

[1] Acts viii, 1 states expressly that the apostles stayed in Jerusalem.
[2] J. Weiss, 1 Cor. *ad loc.*
[3] Cf. I Pet. v, 13 and A. Schlatter, Erläuterungen z. N.T. ; Einl. in d. Bibel 4th ed. (1923), 448 f. Most commentators think Babylon means Rome.
[4] Cf. also Rom. i, 5 ff. ; I Cor. ix, 16.

the situation after Easter led to quite new consequences. The abiding character of the new commission is the result of this new situation, which involves the disciples' experience of the absoluteness of Jesus. The Risen Lord appoints his representatives, no longer for a definite period, but for the whole time between Easter and his return, a period whose length no man knows; [1] that is why there is now only one appointment, and it follows that the apostolate is limited to the first generation and does not become a permanent office in the Church. Otherwise we have a repetition of what happened at the first commission, viz. equipment with power [2] and also the duty of giving a report when the commission is returned to him who gave it. [3] Both these features show that an apostle's business does not depend on his own initiative, but upon obedience to Jesus, as shown in the classical instance of Paul (see p. 62).

Didache xi, 1 ff., does not contradict the limitation of the apostolate in the technical N.T. sense to Paul's generation. [4] This passage only warns the Churches against false prophets, [5] not against false apostles. The word " apostle " seems to be used simply to indicate that the true prophet does not come in his own name, but in the name of Jesus, [6] and also in his spirit, [7] i.e. as a regular member of the Church. [8]

[1] Acts i, 6 f.

[2] Cf. II Cor. xii, 12 ; I Thess. i, 5 ; and the miracles in Acts.

[3] Matt. xxv, 14 ff. par. ; 1 Cor. iv, 4.

[4] W. Seufert (see p. ix) 119 thinks these " apostles " were independent missionaries ; cf. also Harnack, 347 ff. But there is no such thing.

[5] W. Seufert did not see this.   [6] Didache xii, 1.

[7] A prophet is true if he has the ways of the Lord (xi, 8) ; words alone do not prove that he has the Spirit.

[8] Cf. xi, 11. Note that envoys from the Church in Rome to the Church in Corinth are not ἀπόστολοι but ἀπεσταλμένοι (I Clem. lxv, 1).

The Spirit is indispensable for the renewed apostleship, because of the thought of God which produces obedience. In the Spirit, Christians, and especially the apostles, receive assurance of the presence of Jesus and also his power.[1] It is in full accord with the founding of the original apostolate that missionary activity is said to have begun at Pentecost.[2] The Spirit also gives to the apostle the pattern of his life and work, and of what God, or the Christ, works through him [3] as his instrument, although his service is given with full surrender of his own will and not in an ecstatic abandonment to divine power.[4] That is why, as in the case of Jesus, so also in the preaching of the apostles (and evangelists),[5] according to the book of Acts, the central point is the faith of the hearers in Jesus, and not the performance of the preacher or worker of miracles.[6]

It is a complete misunderstanding, not only of the possession of the Spirit, but of the true nature of the apostleship in the early Church, to regard all the miracles in the book of Acts [7] as legends, in some cases even intended to glorify a particular apostle, e.g. Paul in comparison with Peter. In every case the conviction is clear that Jesus himself stands behind the miracle, displaying his power and confirming the authority of his envoys. If " a man's messenger is as the man

---

[1] Cf. W. Grundmann, Der Begriff d. Kraft in d. N.T. Gedankenwelt (1932), 92 ff. Dealing with disciples and apostles, G. is inclined to treat of power as such ; but it must always be conditioned by the person involved.   [2] Acts ii, 14 ff.

[3] Acts x, 26 ; xiv, 15 ; xix, 11, but also iii, 11 ff.

[4] Acts iv, 19 f.   [5] Acts viii, 5 ff., 37 f.

[6] Acts iii, 16 ; v, 14 f. ; xiv, 9, etc.

[7] We are properly only concerned with the miracles of apostles, including Paul and probably Stephen (Acts vi, 3, 8). Otherwise signs and wonders are only associated with Philip (viii, 13) ; but we do not know whether he bore the title of apostle.

himself ", and if the N.T. apostleship is based on this principle, then the absence of miracle would be nothing less than the disproving of the apostolic claim, and the preaching of the Risen Christ would be a piece of human theorising, instead of being the proclamation of an act of God, surpassing all human thought. The signs of an apostle (II Cor. xii, 12) are indispensable, not for the sake of the missionaries themselves, but for the sake of their work, and of Jesus. If any one feels compelled to reject these miracles, he must also explain the miracles of Jesus as legends, or at least try to reduce them to natural terms. That, however, means giving up the apostleship as the central religious institution of the early Church, and leaving it as merely the legal institution of Jesus. But this would not be a true account of the apostleship either in itself[1] or in important features of its development.[2] These considerations do not mean that we can dispense with critical study of the miracles in Acts : on the contrary they make it absolutely necessary.[3]

The whole complex of ideas bound up with the thought of the signs of an apostle goes back to the Semitic office of ambassador (see p. 17). Moses is the type of a religious ambassador, whose divine authority is confirmed by a sign : Exod. iii, 12, includes both the " sending " and the " sign ". There is a parallel to this in the case of Jannes and Jambres, the Egyptian magicians who oppose Moses : they also produce signs ($\sigma\eta\mu\epsilon\hat{\iota}a$: cf. Exod. vii, 11, 22). Cf. also Is. vii, 11 ; Judges vi, 17 ; Matt. xvi, 1 ff. ; John vi, 29 ff.[4]

---

[1] K. Holl (see p. ix) seriously misunderstands the primitive idea of the Church, in not recognising the thoroughly " pneumatic " nature of the apostleship.

[2] Cf. the transmission of the Spirit (Acts viii, 14 ff. ; x, 44 ff. ; xix, 1 ff.).   [3] Cf. Grundmann, op. cit. 98, n. 7.

[4] [See Koehler, Lexicon in V.T. Libros (1948) s.v. 'oth.]

In this connexion it is necessary to guard against limiting to particular circles the powers at work in primitive Christianity.   It is also of the first importance to recognise that the community and not the individual is the sphere in which Jesus is at work as the Risen Lord, and that his apostles can only have his authority as members of it.   We have always to remember their connexion with him and their significance as leaders of the movement in his name.   But as Jesus is exalted over all and his aim is an all-embracing community, their office becomes also universal in its scope.[1]   It is the universality of the commission which finally makes the new authorisation superior to that which was given before the Lord's Resurrection.   He stands behind all the apostles' words and deeds : but since he is ascended, miracles cannot be separated from them ; yet the active subject of their universal evangelism is not found in themselves but in him who sent them.[2]

(b) The Gospel of John confirms the conclusions resulting from our study of the Synoptic Gospels and the book of Acts concerning the renewal and final appointment of the apostolate by the Risen Lord, and concerning its connexion with the possession of the Spirit.   This is all the more important because the word " apostle " only occurs once in John, where it is used in its general sense and not limited to the envoys of Jesus (see p. 26).   " In John the most important section of the Easter narrative directly serves his central idea : he shows how the Risen Lord united the disciples with himself through faith and gave them authority and power for their work." [3]   This applies to Thomas (xx, 24 ff.), but still more to Peter, who

---

[1] Cf. A. Schlatter, Gesch. d. Christus, 534 f.

[2] Matt. x, 18 ff. ;   Luke xii, 11 f.

[3] A Schlatter, Gesch. d. Christus, 532 ;   for the next sentence cf. E. Hirsch, Jesus Christus d. Herr (1926), 39 f.

receives with the apostleship forgiveness for his disloyalty (xxi, 1 ff.).

Here also the writer is concerned with authorisation to represent Jesus, i.e. with obedience and service, not with independent action. Peter is not entrusted with the community as such, but as " my lambs " (xxi, 15) and " my sheep " (xxi, 16 f.) and his work is not described as ruling and directing but as feeding and tending. Here also the one who is commissioned is not only more than a mere instrument; he bears the full burden of a responsibility which can only be borne in perfect union with Jesus (xxi, 15-17 : love). But the parallel with the picture drawn by the other three evangelists goes still further. For John also, possession of the Spirit is indispensable for the discharge of apostolic functions. Accordingly the reception of the Spirit and the giving of the commission are simultaneous (xx, 21 ff.), and no doubt is left that those who are sent have to act as representatives of him who sent them (xx, 21).

A special word is necessary concerning the verbs in John xx, 21, viz. ἀποστέλλειν and πέμπειν (see p. xii). The former on the lips of Jesus refers to the grounding of his authority in the authority of the Father, the latter to God's sharing in his work. Exactly the same usage is found when Jesus commissions his envoys : the work which they have to do is ultimately his work, for he sends them.[1]

Thus for John the thought of authorisation is strictly subordinate to that of the part played by Jesus in their work : he himself is their strength and bears the burden of their office. This explains the fundamental significance of the figure of the Paraclete for the commissioning of the disciples. In him they have

---

[1] ἀποστέλλω is appropriate at Matt. x, 16 ; Luke x, 3, since the envoys represent the earthly Jesus, not the ascended Lord.

the presence of Jesus, sharing in their work, he also being "sent" (xiv, 26; xv, 26),[1] and this is all the more definite because Jesus speaks of his coming not only as the Father's act (xiv, 16, 26) but, in view of the Ascension which places him beside the Father, as his own doing (xv, 26). In him who is the Spirit of truth (xiv, 17) he continues with them as the truth, though he is bodily withdrawn from them (xiv, 5 f; xvi, 7). The Johannine picture of an apostle thus combines the fundamental Christology of the evangelist, which represents the Son as standing and working beside God, with the Jewish view of the fully authorised messenger, and takes precedence of it, but only so far as that is possible without making the apostleship a piece of enthusiastic presumption. John is not inclined that way. On the contrary his interest is in the Son as at work without ceasing from the beginning to the end of all things, and in making him known to his readers. It is possible that the word "apostle" seemed to him unsuitable, because there was a danger of suggesting by its use that the disciple could change himself from slave to master by his own presumptuous strength, forgetting that behind him stood one as his sender who was there before him (xiii, 16).

(c) Nothing certain can be said about the time when the Greek ἀπόστολος came into use as the equivalent of shaliᵃḥ. We can only be sure that the choice of this word was not made by Jesus, otherwise we should have had more evidence for its use. It is very remarkable that a word originally connoting an act or a group of men, without any religious colouring, should come to be applied to an individual man with explicitly religious functions. Perhaps this began at Antioch;

---

[1] Cf. H. Windisch, Die 5 joh. Parakletsprüche, in Festgabe f. A. Jülicher (1927), 132 ff. ; [W. F. Howard, Christianity acc. to St. John (1943), 72-80].

it may be that in the first place the word meant the missionary expedition as such, later denoting those who took part in it ; [1] and finally came to be recognised as the equivalent of shali^aḥ, being a masculine noun. It is even possible that Paul had a share in the process, though it may have been completed before his time ; he is the first man to whom it is applied in the singular (in the Synoptic Gospels it is always in the plural). In any case, however, ἀπόστολος, as the equivalent of shali^aḥ, must never be separated from the corresponding verbs ; its use was only possible on the ground of the relation which these two had to each other long before. This relation was largely determined by the idea of God, and this explains why the same thing is true of the early Christian use of the noun.

A certain difficulty naturally arises from the fact that our sources do not explain the difference between " apostles " (used absolutely) and apostles of the community (Acts xiii, 1 ff.) who certainly preached the Gospel with full authority. The difficulty, however, is not serious if we remember that the formative principle in the early Church is the Spirit, by which Jesus himself is meant, sharing in the apostolic task. It is important that Antioch did not appoint two other members of the group of " prophets and teachers " (Acts xiii, 1) for the mission, but Paul and Barnabas, of whom one certainly had seen the Risen Lord and probably the other also (see p. 28). Further, the act of the community described as ἀφορίζειν and not ἀποστέλλειν, the initiative being ascribed to the long-standing purpose of the Holy Spirit,[2] so that the community only has to give the formal authorisation. It may also be supposed that both men had long possessed

[1] With this may be connected the fact that, apart from Paul's use, the word always occurs in the Plural.

[2] Cf. also Harnack, 348, n. 1.

apostolic authority, but were now to exercise it for the first time. The universal character of the N.T. apostolate appears again here, coupled with the universal claim of the community. The form of the commissioning (fasting, prayer, laying-on of hands) is Jewish (see p. 19). It is significant that Paul never regarded himself as an apostle of the Antioch Christians, but only as the apostle of Jesus Christ (see p. 61).

(d) From what has been said it is certain that the ground of N.T. apostleship as a whole is to be found in the will and commission of the Risen Lord. But it must not be overlooked that this was not at first the only basis of the office.

The account of the replacing of Judas by Matthias shows that another decisive qualification enters in, viz. that of eye-witness. Luke reports expressly that Matthias fulfilled this condition (Acts i, 21 f.). Close contact with Jesus during his earthly life is here the most important point, and this means practically that the Church did not regard the commission of the Risen Lord as something radically new; though definite information is lacking, we shall not go far wrong if we take it that the early Church regarded the new commission as a repetition or continuation of the first. The conclusion follows that the first Christians had not fully understood the fundamental change in the world situation brought about when the Risen Lord made men his representatives; and further, that the story of Jesus as history gave Christian preaching from the beginning its content and its differentia; [1] the apostle of Jesus is always a witness of historical facts, not a teacher of myths : fully conscious indeed that what he proclaims is a contradiction of all human experience.

This connexion of apostleship with personal knowledge of the Jesus of history affects Paul in two ways.

[1] Cf. G. Kittel in Mysterium Christi (1931), 49 ff.

In the first place, the objection to his claim to be reckoned as an apostle along with the Twelve (see p. 61) has obviously a partial justification. Paul did come after the Twelve in that he lacked the fellowship with the historical Jesus with which they were favoured; that, however, was the very reason why he based his apostleship upon ground which both saved him from occupying a secondary position and revealed a fundamental element in the primitive apostolate. The other link connecting Paul with the primitive Church in this connexion is his absolute appropriation of the primitive tradition concerning Jesus (I Cor. xi, 23 ff.; Rom. xv, 1 ff., etc.). His preaching was inseparable from the historical Jesus; and this was the ground of his unity with the original apostles (Acts xv, 12; cf. Gal. ii, 9 and specially I Cor. xv, 11).

3. PAUL THE APOSTLE

Paul is the classical example of a N.T. apostle. He is the only one concerning whose apostleship we have direct information. This is due to his special position in the apostolate and to the wide extent of his activity. Although not one of the original circle, nor among those who had intercourse with the Lord between his resurrection and his ascension, he could say that he had laboured more than all the other apostles in the service of Jesus (I Cor. xv, 10). His sense of commission, based entirely on the experience of being called, reached its highest point in replying to those who contested his right to the title and authority of an apostle. Two features of his self-consciousness stand out in this connexion, viz. the course of his life before he entered on apostolic work, and the peculiarity of his position as apostle in the circle of those who had the authorisation of Jesus.

(a) The outstanding mark of Paul's apostleship is the break in his life with which it began. He himself compared his calling to the coming of light at the Creation (II Cor. iv, 6), indicating that it was something entirely beyond the possibility of human attainment. Paul as a Christian saw behind him the eternal will of God, awaiting only the hour of its fulfilment (Gal. i, 15). The complete change of direction which occurred at his call differentiated him fundamentally from the early disciples of Jesus, who certainly were taken away from home and family, but could never feel that their service of Jesus contradicted their past so sharply as Paul did, whenever he spoke of the beginning of his apostleship (I Cor. xv, 9; Gal. i, 13, 23; Phil. iii, 7 f.). What gives Paul special importance is, that in this connexion he never appears as a "sinner" passing judgement upon himself and his former life; he speaks rather of his Jewish past in exalted terms, because there he was as genuinely obedient to God as he was in the moment of his conversion and afterwards as Christian and apostle.

It is thus clear that Paul's apostolic consciousness is completely determined by his encounter with Jesus on the way to Damascus. This and his immediate surrender [1] differentiate his apostleship from that of the other apostles, who gave themselves fully to Jesus after many hesitations and a long period of education by Jesus. There is no trace of these in the case of Paul; there is only acceptance, as complete as it was sudden, of Jesus, the Messiah whom he had been passionately persecuting. The reason for this is that, while Paul's life from the beginning had been largely determined in thought and action by the idea of God,[2] this now,

---

[1] Gal. i, 16; "immediately".

[2] Paul was the only apostle learned in the Law (Gal. i, 14; Phil. iii, 6).

for the first time assumed absolute supremacy. Herein lies the secret of Paul's self-consciousness as an apostle.

The exact nature of the experience on the way to Damascus is unimportant here ; [1] all we are concerned with is the way in which Paul himself described it. He sees it simply as an act of God, an objective event,[2] not as a vision.[3] The primary cause of what happened is, however, not Christ but God,[4] though it was certainly Christ who met Paul and spoke to him. We can follow Alfred Jeremias [5] in saying that Paul was transformed from an enemy and persecutor of Jesus into his apostle the moment he recognised the voice of Jesus in the *bath qol* (the voice of divine revelation after the cessation of prophecy),[6] and was thereby convinced and cured of his error concerning the Lord. Paul himself gives classical expression to this when he not only calls himself the apostle of Jesus Christ, but adds that he is called through the will of God (I Cor. i, 1 ; II Cor. i, 1 ; Eph. i, 1 ; cf. ver. 5 ; Col. i, 1).[7] It is to be observed that, so far as our sources inform us, Paul is the first to trace the apostolic commission back to God himself; I Pet. i, 2, is dependent upon Pauline ideas.

The dominance of the idea of God in Paul's apostolic consciousness is specially emphasised by the way in

[1] This applies to the question which account of the conversion in Acts is most trustworthy (ix, 1 ff. ; xxii, 5 ff. ; xxvi, 12 ff.). See E. Hirsch in Z.N.W. 28 (1929), 305 ff.

[2] Gal. i, 15 ; Rom. i, 1.

[3] I Cor. ix, 1 ; xv, 8 establish an objective fact ; they do not report a vision.

[4] Gal. i, 15 f. Luke (xxiv, 34 ; Acts xiii, 31) follows Paul (I Cor. xv, 5) in using ὤφθη for the appearances of the Risen Lord.

[5] In a lecture to the 4th Conference on the Jewish question at Nüremberg, Feb. 27-Mar. 1., 1929.

[6] T. Sota, 13, 2.

[7] II Tim. i, 1 echoes this ; but I Tim. i, 1 ; Tit. i, 3 have "God's commandment ".

which he speaks of himself as being separated to the gospel of God from birth. (Rom. i. 1 ; Gal. i, 15) ; in this way he finds himself holding a significant and indispensable place in the Divine plan for the world, indispensable from God's point of view, not from his own (I Cor. iii, 5).[1] So he can only regard the fact of his apostleship as evidence of the grace of God, which has nothing to do with previous qualifications, but brings man to obedient submission under God (I Cor. xv, 10).[2] This links his sense of commission with that of the prophets, especially of Jeremiah and II Isaiah, in a way which can only be understood from Paul's special course of life and is his own doing ; it marks the climax of the sense of commission not only of the apostles but of the early Church as a whole.

The parallels between Paul and Jeremiah have long been observed,[3] but always mainly as concerning outward matters and not from the angle of the apostolic consciousness. Now this is the very point at which Jeremiah is Paul's great prototype.[4] His significance in the history of O.T. prophecy consists in his radical avoidance of any high estimate of man and complete surrender to the commission laid upon him, in full recognition of the desperate position of the prophet, i.e. in the acceptance of the absolute all-importance of the idea of God.[5]

This finds expression in the complete disappearance of the ecstatic element which characterised the older prophets,[6] and even Isaiah,[7] and made its appearance

---

[1] The same idea is expressed at Rom. i, 1 ; I Cor. i, 1 ; Gal. i, 15.

[2] Cf. " immediately " at Gal. i, 16.

[3] Cf. E. Lohmeyer, Grundlagen paul. Theol. (1929), 201.

[4] As suggested by Paul's own ref. in Gal. i, 15 to Jer. i, 5.

[5] See R. Kittel, Gesch. d. Volkes Israel II, 5th and 6th ed. (1925), 336 f.   [6] Elijah as well as Amos and Hosea.

[7] Is. vii, 11 speaks of divine attestation by miracle, like Elijah (I Kings xviii, 21 ff.). [But see J. R. Coates, The Saving History.]

again among Jeremiah's successors,[1] though less as a revival of ancient Israelite prophecy than as a result of the new oriental-hellenistic syncretism and its enthusiastic tendencies. Even where Jeremiah sees signs (i, 11 ff.; iv, 19 ff.) it would be more correct to speak of the vision of faith than of enthusiasm. It is characteristic of him to speak in pictures and parables, which are the result of reasoning and clear insight. "At the beginning prophecy stands completely passive over against its object." So the personality of the prophets " is bound up with the object; when they reflect on this they do it quite objectively, in such a way that they communicate the result of what they have seen ".[2] In Jeremiah the prophetic ego becomes for the first time fully awake, so that the prophet becomes a religious thinker. So pronounced is this, that it is not always possible to avoid conflict with God. In the case of Jeremiah this only occurs when he is resisting God's call and commission; in its full strength it appears first in II Isaiah, the ego coming between God and the prophet in such a way that subsequently " a new medium has to be introduced, e.g. the angel in Zechariah ".[3]

Jeremiah thus represents a higher level even than II Isaiah. This becomes perfectly clear when his calling is seen from this point of view. In the absence of the ecstatic element, the whole emphasis is upon his connexion with God and subordination to his will (xx, 7 ff.; cf. xv, 19 ff.) and therefore all his effort is devoted to the proclamation of God's will, which is not revealed to him from time to time but is continually present.[4] Two results follow. First, the prophetic vocation covers the whole of Jeremiah's life and, since

---

[1] On Ezekiel see R. Kittel *op. cit.* III (1927), 151 ff.
[2] R. Kittel *op. cit.* II, 336.   [3] Ib. 337 and n. 1.
[4] Cf. the attack on the visionaries, xxiii, 25 ff.

the nation is opposed to God, this means that his whole
life bears the stamp of suffering (e.g. xi, 18 ff.; xv, 10,
15; xx, 14 ff., etc.). Secondly, it is the Word alone
which defines the prophet's activity and gives him
strength and authority (xv, 16, etc.). It is this
dependence upon the Word which gives its peculiar
value to the prophecy of Jeremiah. Here office and
life are one under the domination of the idea of God :
God is everything and man is what he is through God,
to bear witness to God as God (i, 9; xv, 19, etc.).

It is difficult, or impossible, to say whether Paul was
knowingly or unknowingly indebted to Jeremiah
in his apostolic consciousness. There certainly is a
connexion between the two, both as regards the element
of suffering in accordance with the will of God [1] and
in exclusive concentration upon the preaching of the
Word ; [2] and closely bound up with these, the avoidance
of enthusiasm as a basis of apostleship. The last of
these appears at II Cor. xii, 1 ff.,[3] where Paul differentiates himself from his opponents, who boast of
their enthusiastic experiences and try to assert their
superiority to him on this ground. The raising of this
question is characteristic of the situation in the Greek
Christian communities, in which enthusiasm played
a great part (I. Cor. xiv, 1 ff.) ; there was a danger of
substituting the ecstatic experience which magnified
the individual for the divine authorisation of the
apostle, and thereby reviving in a new form, viz. the
glorification of those who possessed spiritual gifts, or
falsely claimed them,[4] that worship of man on the

---

[1] II Cor. xi, 16 ff. ; xii, 10 ; Phil. iii, 10 ff. ; Gal. vi, 17 ; but
also II Cor. iv, 6 ff. ; I Thess. iii, 3 f. ; and see E. v. Dobschütz,
Thess, 135.   [2] I Cor. i, 14 ff. ; ii, 1 ff., etc.

[3] Cf. A. Schlatter, Die Theologie d. Apostel, 2nd ed. (1922), 261 f.

[4] Cf. the charisma of " discernings of Spirits " (I Cor. xii, 10)
and Paul's struggle against "those pre-eminent apostles "
(II Cor. xi, 5 ; xii, 11). See p. 67.

ground of his piety which had been discarded by Jesus. It is very important that Paul is able to boast of a high degree of ecstatic experience [1] but guards very carefully against connecting this organically with his apostleship,[2] so as to avoid overshadowing God and what he has done in Christ, and obscuring grace as the only valid principle.[3] The same attitude is seen in Paul's comparatively low estimate of the " signs of an apostle " (II Cor. xii, 12). He only refers to them under compulsion or in order to further his ministry (Rom. xv, 19; I Thess. i, 5), never for his own glorification. Even at II Cor. xii, 12, he is concerned with the justice of his cause, not with his own importance.

The linking of the apostle's consciousness with that of the prophet is no less illuminating with regard to the business entrusted to him. It emphasises absolutely the fact that what he preaches is revelation, and guards against every kind of human corruption. That is why Paul speaks of his apostolic authorisation through Christ when he addresses his converts. The important matter is not himself but his business. Like the prophet, Paul is the servant of his message, i.e. the preaching of the word of the Cross (I Cor. i, 18), which as such is the word of reconciliation (II Cor. v, 19). This explains Paul's passionate attack upon the divisions of the Church at Corinth, on the ground that his name was involved against his will and against the meaning of the Gospel (I Cor. i-iv, esp. iii, 5 ff.) ; and on the other hand, it explains the absence of any tendency towards an *imitatio Christi* either in his own life or in that of Christians who imitate him (I Thess. i, 6),[4] though this very soon appeared in the ancient Church.[5] If Paul

---

[1] II Cor. xii, 1-4 ; I Cor. xiv, 18.
[2] II Cor. xii, 5.   [3] II Cor. xii, 9.
[4] See articles in Kittel on ἀκολουθέω and μιμέομαι.
[5] E.g. Augustine, De Sancta Virginitate, 27 : quid est sequi nisi imitari?

saw the earthly life of Jesus as the pattern of his apostleship,[1] then just because as his apostle he was called
to complete devotion, his apostleship should not be
regarded as merely titular.   What is involved here is
not merely a form of ministry ; it is the obedience of a
slave to his master.[2]

The parallel between the apostles and the prophets
is justified, because they are both bearers of revelation,
the one anticipating its completion and the other ex-
periencing it.   This chronological difference explains
why the old title of prophet could not be applied to the
envoys of Jesus ; the changed situation [3] demanded
a name which referred to the commission given by
Jesus.   On the other hand, it accounts for the way in
which the two are brought together under the aspect
of their historical importance for the origin of the
Church as presented in Eph. ii, 20 ; the considerations
which have been advanced make this not only a
suitable way of speaking in the first Christian generation
but especially appropriate to Paul himself.[4]

It should now also be clear that the N.T. prophets
(I Cor. xii, 28, etc.) in no way correspond to those
of the O.T. and we can understand why, at least when
Paul wrote his greater epistles, Christian prophets are
mentioned with respect, but do not play a specially
prominent part.

(b) Paul's special position in the apostolic circle
cannot be separated from his recovery of the prophetic

[1] Cf. P. Feine, Der Apostel Paulus (1927), 407 ff.

[2] I Cor. iv. 1 f.

[3] Rom. x, 15, referring to Is. lii, 7, expressly makes the Messianic
salvation the subject of apostolic preaching.   Cf. Rom. i, 15 ;
I Cor. i, 17 ; ix, 16 ; xv, 1 f. ; II Cor. xi, 7, etc.

[4] This does not settle the question of the authenticity of Eph. ;
it only points to a time when N.T. apostles and O.T. prophets
were thought of together, as they were when Paul's letters were
written.   See p. 56.

consciousness through the dominant place which he gives to the thought of God. Of course that is not its starting point, which is to be found in the commission corresponding to that of the Jewish *shali*ᵃ*h*, as in the case of the other apostles. One reason for Paul's stronger emphasis on this aspect of his office is found in his opponents' denial of his equality with the other apostles. An instance of this occurs at the beginning of Galatians : his authorisation was being associated with the Church at Antioch (Acts xii, 1 ff.), or with Barnabas, who was said to have introduced him into the early Church (Acts ix, 27) ; so Paul says he is " an apostle not from men neither through a man, but through Jesus Christ " (Gal. i, 1) and goes on to prove the independence of this apostleship (vers. 10 ff.) and the recognition in Jerusalem of his equality with the older apostles (ii, 1 ff.).

Another feature is the vital connexion of the apostolic office, originated in personal experience of Jesus as Messiah, with recognition of the meaning of the Spirit as the Spirit of Jesus,[1] which all who are in Christ possess (I Cor. iii, 16 ; vi, 19, etc.). This accounts for Paul's bold claim to be Christ's representative, calling men to reconciliation with God (II Cor. v. 20), and a fellow-worker with him (II Cor. vi, 1).

Paul's idea of God brings this line of thought to its highest point. Seeing as he does, God's hand at work in the whole of his life, and God's will as the ground of the life, passion and death of Jesus, and of the preaching about him,[2] he even calls himself God's fellow-worker (I Cor. iii, 9),[3] sharing in the divine purpose, of course not in the sense of his own achievement but as God's servant to whom his share of the

[1] Rom. viii, 9, etc.
[2] E.g. I Cor. xv, 3 f. Except at I Thess. iv, 14, Paul always speaks of God raising Jesus (Gal. i, 1, etc.).
[3] Cf. also I Thess. iii, 2.

work has been allotted (I Cor. iii, 8, 11 ff.). This means that to break with him is to break with Christ and to despise the divine work of salvation (Gal. i, 6 ff.; v, 1 ff.). The reason for that is not to be found in himself. Paul only has significance [1] through his commission and the Lord who stands behind it; it is he who has made him all that a man can be through the grace of God.[2] If he is not puffed up on this account, the reason is that because of the Cross he knows himself to be the slave of Jesus, and recognises, along with the grace which he has received, the responsibility resting upon him as an apostle (I Cor. iii, 2 ff.); at the same time because God is in control of the whole of history and Jesus is Lord, the light of victorious joy shines upon all that is involved in being the ambassador of the Crucified; [3] the true apostolic joy which is born of the Resurrection.[4] The idea that God's messenger must suffer and endure poverty finds expression in Plato's Apology, 23b-c. What was a genuine experience in the case of Socrates became for the Cynics almost a pure convention. Paul has the same idea as Socrates though its special form is determined by the nature of his apostolic appointment; it is with him bitter reality, only to be borne because it binds him more closely to his Lord (see II Cor. xii, 10). The old Catholic Church treated Paul's idea of suffering and poverty in the same way as the Cynics in the case of Socrates, but the results in this case were more serious.

[1] Note the " What? " at I Cor. iii, 5 ; the Lord is here of course Jesus, as commissioning and authorising. Cf. also I Cor. i, 13.

[2] Paul's use of " apostleship " and " grace " almost as synonyms is instructive. Cf. p. 68.

[3] The coupling of Paul's suffering as an apostle with that of Jesus is specially clear at Phil. iii, 10.

[4] Cf. II Cor. i, 24 ; vi, 9 f. ; vii, 4.

V. JESUS AS APOSTLE

1. Jesus himself is called " apostle " in the N.T. only at Heb. iii, 1 (see pp. 30 f.). But the question arises whether the Gospel of John does not contain the idea, though not using the word, since it frequently uses the corresponding verb to describe the relation of Jesus to God.[1] This raises the question whether we have here evidence of the influence of oriental myths concerning the redeemer sent from heaven, who is also the First Man. The publication of Mandaean sources [2] has given prominence to the problem; [3] we therefore devote a short chapter to its linguistic aspect.

The Mandaean book of John (chap. 66) uses the following words at the moment of the sending of the redeemer (Manda d' Hayye) to the earth : " Come my son, be my ambassador; come, carry my commission ". This ambassador is then described more fully as " the ambassador of light " (Lidzbarski, Ginza, lviii, 17, 23, etc.) or as " the true ambassador " (lix. 1). In the Manichean Zarathustra fragment, he speaks of himself as being " sent into the world ". The root used in the Mandaean sources for " ambassador " occurs frequently in the Aramaic of the Babylonian Talmud in the simple (not authoritative) sense of " sending ", corresponding to the Greek πέμπειν and

[1] See p. xii and cf. G. P. Wetter, F.R.L. 26(1916), 49.

[2] M. Lidzbarski, Joh. ; Liturg. ; Ginza.

[3] R. Bultmann in Z.N.W. 24 (1925), 100-146 ; W. Bauer on John iii, 17 ; H. H. Schaeder in Reitzenstein u. Schaeder, Studien z. antiken Synkretismus : Aus Iran u. Griechenland (1926), 203 ff., esp. 306 ff. ; H. Odeberg, The 4th Gospel (1929), 117 ff. ; G. P. Wetter (see p. ix).

[4] R. Reitzenstein, Iran. Erlös.-Myst. (1921) ; R. Bultmann op. cit. 106.

not to ἀποστέλλειν.[1] The latter, however, occurs in
the verbal form, in Greek Christian texts such as the
Acts of Thomas.[2] It is used of the sending of Jesus,
e.g. in the Gospel of Peter (56), where the angel at the
tomb says to the women, " he has gone to the place
from which he was sent ".[3] This may only mean the
simple sending, without emphasising authorisation.
Jesus is explicitly called apostle by Justin,[4] the title
having by this time acquired a special significance, as is
shown by I Clem. 65, 1, where the ambassadors of
the church in Rome are not called apostles, but are
said to be " sent ". It might be thought that Justin
is here applying to Jesus the conception of the ambassador which is found in oriental mythology. The
popularity of this title is seen not only in the case of
Mani [5] but also in that of Mohammed [6] and even,
following the example of Apollonius of Tyana, of
Alexander the Great.[7]

In all these cases the divine ambassador is also the
preacher of truth,[8] but above all the medium of
contact between the divine world and the human, in
that he speaks and heals men of their error. This is so
when Justin calls Jesus " apostle ". As God's messenger
he has the task of communicating true knowledge by
what he says ; all his life and work are directed to this
end.[9] The outward parallel with the Mandaean

---

[1] Examples in J. Levy, Wörterbuch IV, 513g.

[2] Examples in R. Bultmann op. cit. 106.

[3] See also Apostolic Constitutions VIII, i, 10.

[4] See p. 31.

[5] G. P. Wetter, op. cit. 15 ff. He has other envoys also (W.
Bauer loc. cit.).

[6] F. Preisigke, Sammelbuch, No. 7240, 5.

[7] Cf. W. Bacher, Nizami's Leben u. Werke u. d. zweite Teil
des Niz. Alexanderbuches (Diss. Leipzig, 1871), 90.

[8] Even Alexander represents the true religion (Bacher op. cit.
90, 94 ff.).

[9] Apol. I, 63, 5. Cf. G. P. Wetter, 28 f.

ambassadors is certainly there, though his aim may
be differently conceived, owing to the nature of his
personality.   Neither in Justin nor in the Mandaean
sources is the emphasis upon the idea of authorisation ;
it is simply on the fact that he comes from a completely
different sphere, known only to himself, concerning
which he only gives hints to his followers.[1] It is
obvious that the choice of the word " apostle " in
Justin and other Christian writings is derived from the
gospel of John.

2. The gospel of John presents a view formally
resembling that which is discussed above, but widely
differing from it in substance.   It is true that Jesus
appears as being sent by the Father (see p. xii), but
this only serves the purpose of exhibiting the true
meaning of his person and work, since it is God himself
who speaks and works in and through him.   This is
shown in three ways.

(a) The " signs " in John show God revealing
himself in Jesus as the one who was promised, and
working in and through him.[2]

(b) Those whom Jesus encounters have their fate
decided by their attitude towards Jesus himself, not
towards the teaching which he brings.[3] That is
only possible if God is present in him, and he literally
represents the Father in his own person.[4]

(c) The death of Jesus, and all his works, are vitally
bound up with his word.   His death and glorification,
i.e. his ascension to share in the glory of the Father and

[1] For fundamental treatment, not specially related to John, see
Wetter, " Ich bin es ", Theol. Stud. Krit. 88 (1915), 224 ff.,
esp. 235.

[2] Cf. John iv, 34 ; v, 36 ; ix, 3 f. ; x, 37, etc.

[3] iii, 18 ; cf. iii, 17 ; xii, 47 and John's general emphasis on
judgement.

[4] viii, 16, 29 ; cf. v, 36 f. ; viii, 18 ; x, 25 ; xii, 49 ; xiv, 10, etc.

thus complete his revelation as the Son, form an indivisible unity.[1]

All this would simply be hanging in the air if the sending of Jesus corresponded to that of oriental Gnosis. Its true analogy is not found in the sending of Manda d'Hayye. It must be remembered that there are two Greek words in the Fourth Gospel for the sending of Jesus, and there can be no doubt as to their relation to each other (see p. xii). It must also be said that the Johannine Christology is not influenced by this conception of Jesus as ambassador, but, *vice versa*, itself gives its own peculiar colour to that conception. Here we see how John's whole way of thinking is linked with the calling of the prophets, and derives its unique quality from the fact that Christ as ambassador is no man, not even Original or First Man, but the Son in whom the Father attests his own presence and himself offers salvation or judgement.

[1] xii, 23 ff. ; from this point of view cf. xviii, 1 ff. with Matt. xxvi, 36 ff.

APPENDIX A

THE expression, "false apostle",[1] is only found in the N.T., where it occurs at II Cor. xi, 13. Paul means by it one who gives himself out as an apostle of Christ without having his authorisation. His shortcoming shows itself in failure to be exclusively devoted to Christ, i.e. to God; self-seeking takes the place of selfless service. The false apostle does not realise that authorisation by Jesus leads to humility and suffering; he acquires an air of superiority (II Cor. xi, 5), a complete contradiction of the true meaning of the word "apostle", which allows of no degrees of comparison. Paul is speaking of his Judaistic opponents, who have no inner right to judge him.

The fact that this expression occurs only once suggests, not only that it is of Christian (perhaps Pauline) coinage, but also indirectly that the same may be true of the word "apostle". The idea of false apostleship is expressed at Rev. ii, 2, though the same word is not used.

---

[1] The compound ψευδαπόστολος is not found outside the N.T. See Pr.-Bauer 1420 *s.v.* ψευδόμαρτυς; A. Debrunner, Griech. Wortbildungslehre (1917), 37; K. Holl, Ges. Aufs. z. K.G. II (1928), 110-114; J. Sickenberger, Rom. & Kor. 4th ed. (1932), 145.

APPENDIX B

THE noun ἀποστολή has a great variety of meanings in secular Greek, corresponding to those of the verb ἀποστέλλειν. Thus (a) Thucydides viii, 9 : a despatch of ships ; (b) any kind of sending forth, including the discharge of a missile, the removal of a person, the entombment of a mummy. Thucydides viii, 8, uses it for an expedition. In all these cases it has an active meaning.

Judaism retains the usual meanings, e.g. Ep. Aristeas 15, but it came to have a more technical sense under the influence of the office of ἀπόστολος, e.g Jul. Ep. 204.[1]

The word occurs twelve times in the LXX,[2] always representing a form of the root *shalaḥ* where there is a Hebrew equivalent, except at Jer. xxxii (xxxix), 36, where the translator has read *dabhar* (word of God) for *debher* (disease) under the influence of his understanding of history [or of his theology]. The word means " gift " at I Kings ix, 16, and elsewhere simply a sending, e.g. Ps. lxxviii (lxxvii), 49.[3] Josephus uses the word for a ceremonial escort at Ant. 20, 50 (cf. Vit. 268).[4]

The N.T. has the word four times, always meaning the office held by an apostle of Jesus ; at Acts i, 25, it is coupled with " ministry ", at Romans i, 5, with " grace ", and stands by itself at I Cor. ix, 2 and Gal. ii, 8. This shows how powerfully the new conception

[1] See Cremer-Kögel ; Preisigke ; Liddell & Scott *s.v.* Cf. S. Krauss, J.Q.R. XVII (1905), 375.

[2] Only partly attested at I Kings iv, 34 ; ix, 16 ; Song iv, 13. III Macc. iv, 4 has ἐξαποστολή.

[3] As Is. xi, 14 Aquila has ἀποστολὴ χειρός.

[4] Refs. in H. St. J. Thackeray, Lexicon to Josephus, 76.

68

of " apostle " affected the meaning of kindred ideas. There may perhaps be an anticipation of this in the Armenian version of the Testament of Naphtali ii, which seems to represent a coupling of ἀποστολήν with shᵉluḥah (Genesis xlix, 21).[1] R. H. Charles, however, omits ἀποστολήν.[2] Rabbinical sources occasionally use the word shᵉliḥuth in reference to the sending forth of messengers (mal'akhim, angels) ;[3] this corresponds to ἀποστολή, but may possibly be derived from it.

[1] F. Schnapp in E. Kautzsch, Apokr. u. Pseud. ad loc.
[2] The Greek Versions of the Testaments of the XII Patriarchs (1908), 145.
[3] Gen. Rabba 50, 1 on xix, 1. See S. Rappaport, Agada u. Exegese bei Flavius Josephus (1930), 105 and J. Levy, Wört. IV s.v.

INDEX OF WORDS AND REFERENCES

(Scripture references are to the English Bible)